T0340297

BEHIND THE MYTH OF EUROPEAN UNION

Despite the rhetoric of 'integration' and a 'single Europe', Europe is marked by sharp social and regional disparities. More acutely than ever, Europe faces the dual problem of how to ensure sustained growth and how to combine it with social equity. 'Cohesion' is the term coined by the European Union for its aim of reducing the social and regional gap in Europe.

This book explores the real prospects for cohesion in Europe. It assesses the difficulties facing Less Favoured Regions in the context of the EU's policies on economic integration and social cohesion, and the wider processes of industrial change in Europe. It argues that current measures which purport to facilitate cohesion will not be adequate. Most of the chapters argue that the EU's measures for promoting growth and productivity are biased towards the interests of the advanced regions and the major corporations. At its core lies a critique of the prevailing neo-liberal growth philosophy which decouples the link between economic efficiency and social equity.

The book is divided into three parts, dealing with:

● the macro-economic environment: assessing the merits and weaknesses of market-led policies
● the social dimension: arguing for an extension and deepening of European social policy
● corporate and regional questions: concluding that the pattern is for an increasing concentration of economic power in the core regions and only partial revitalization in less favoured regions

The book concludes by making a case for putting cohesion measures at the centre of economic policy, rather than making them an adjunct to attempts to make Europe more 'competitive'. In doing so it defends a growth philosophy based on expansionist macro-economic policies, active industrial intervention, protection of worker rights and active supply-side growth measures in the regions. Without such measures the pursuit of cohesion will remain an elusive goal.

Ash Amin is Professor of Economic Geography at the University of Newcastle upon Tyne.

John Tomaney is a lecturer and researcher at the Centre for Urban and Regional Development Studies at the University of Newcastle upon Tyne.

BEHIND THE MYTH OF EUROPEAN UNION

Prospects for cohesion

Edited by Ash Amin and John Tomaney

London and New York

First published 1995
by Routledge
2 Park Square, Milton Park, Abingdon, Oxon, OX14 4RN

Transferred to Digital Printing 2004

Simultaneously published in the USA and Canada
by Routledge
29 West 35th Street, New York, NY 10001

Typeset in Garamond by
J&L Composition Ltd, Filey, North Yorkshire

British Library Cataloguing in Publication Data
A catalogue record for this book is available from the British Library

Library of Congress Cataloguing in Publication Data
A catalogue record for this book has been requested

ISBN 0–415–12552–9 (hbk)
ISBN 0–415–13078–6 (pbk)

CONTENTS

CONTENTS

FIGURES

TABLES

TABLES

THE CONTRIBUTORS

Ash Amin is Professor of Economic Geography at the University of Newcastle. Recently he has edited, with Nigel Thrift, *Globalisation, Institutions and Regional Development in Europe* (Oxford University Press, 1994) and *Post-Fordism* (Blackwell, 1994).

Iain Begg, formerly at the Department of Applied Economics in Cambridge University, is Professor of International Economics at South Bank University. He has published extensively in the field of regional development and cohesion in Europe.

Michael Dunford is Professor of Economic Geography in the School of European Studies at Sussex University. With George Benko he has recently edited *Industrial Change and Regional Development* and, with Grigoris Kafkalas, *Cities and Regions in the New Europe*, published by Belhaven.

Anna Giunta is a researcher in the Department of Economics at the University of Cosenza and at Naples University. She has researched extensively into topics concerning the industrialization process in the less developed regions, focusing on the role of big firms and on development theory.

Neil Hood is Professor of Business Policy in the Department of Marketing at Strathclyde Business School and Director of Strathclyde International Business Unit as well as holding a number of directorships in business. He is author, co-author or editor of eleven books, including *The Scottish Financial Sector* (Edinburgh University Press, 1988) and *Strategies in Global Competition* (Croom Helm, 1988).

Flavia Martinelli is Associate Professor in the Dipartimento di Scienze Ambientali e Territoriali at the Universita di Reggio Calabria in Italy. Her work focuses on regional development and policy, with particular regard to the case of the Mezzogiorno. She has published articles in this field in international as well as Italian journals.

Professor David Mayes is Chief Manager of the Reserve Bank of New Zealand. He was co-ordinator of the ESRC's Single European Market

Research programme until September 1994, a network of research programmes across universities in the UK and elsewhere in Europe. He has published widely on European economics. He has been an editor of the *Economic Journal* since 1976.

Jonathan Michie is a lecturer in economics at the Judge Institute of Management Studies, University of Cambridge, and a fellow and Director of Studies in Economics at Robinson College, Cambridge. He is on the editorial board of the *Cambridge Journal of Economics*, the *International Review of Applied Economics* and *New Economy* and is Director of the Economic and Social Research Council's 'Contracts and Competition' programme. He edited *The Economic Legacy, 1979–92* (Academic Press, 1992) and (with John Grieve Smith) *Unemployment in Europe* (Academic Press, 1994), as well as *Managing the Global Economy* (Oxford University Press, 1995).

Ewen H. Peters is a Partner in the Strategy Group of Scottish Enterprise, responsible for international and economic research. He is also a Visiting Research Fellow with the Strathclyde International Business Unit at the University of Strathclyde.

Harvie Ramsay is Reader in the Department of Human Resource Management at the University of Strathclyde. He has recently published several studies on labour and capital restructuring in post-1992 Europe. He has co-authored *Information Technology and Workplace Democracy* with Martin Beirne (Routledge, 1992) and *People's Capitalism?* with Leslie Baddon and others (Routledge, 1989).

Since leaving the European Commission in April 1992 **Sean Shepley** has worked in the Economics Department of CS First Boston. The department's remit is mostly macro-economic, his own work covering subjects as diverse as the global impact of protectionism, the effects of German unification and the completion of the internal market on the European economies, and the importance of Japanese investment in the UK motor industry.

Paul Teague is Professor of Industrial Relations at the University of Ulster at Jordanstown. He is author or co-author of four books on European integration, including the *European Community* (Kogan Page, 1989) and *Industrial Relations and European Integration* (with John Grahl, Lawrence & Wishart, 1993). Currently he is writing a book on Economic Citizenship in the New Europe with John Grahl.

John Tomaney is a lecturer and researcher at the Centre for Urban and Regional Development Studies, University of Newcastle. He has a particular interest in the impact of European integration on the development prospects of less favoured regions. He is the author or co-author of studies for the European Commission and has recently participated in a cross-EC study of the influence of trade unions on the development of regional policy.

Jonathan Wilmot is in the Economics Department of CS First Boston, and works on macro-economic problems in diverse areas.

Stephen Young is Professor of Marketing and head of the Department of Marketing at the University of Strathclyde. His research and publications are mainly in the fields of international business strategy and industrial policy. He has written or edited eleven books, the latest (with J. Harvill) being *Europe and the Multinationals* (Edward Elgar, 1992).

ACKNOWLEDGEMENTS

This book originates from an international conference held in November 1993 on the topic of Conflict and Cohesion in the Single Market. We wish to thank Tim Frazer, Chris Gentle and Sue Wilkinson for their stalwart support in organizing and contributing to the conference. Our chapters in the volume are based upon research conducted in two projects under the ESRC's Single European Market Programme. Two of our co-researchers, Tim Frazer and David Charles, have prepared a parallel volume based on the results of one of the projects. We wish to thank the ESRC for funding the two projects as well as the conference. Very little of this work could have been achieved without the support of David Mayes, the co-ordinator of the SEM Initiative until autumn 1994, and we warmly acknowledge his help. Our gratitude also goes to the participants of the conference, especially those who agreed to contribute to the volume. Special thanks are due to Sue Robson for lending her wonderful word-processing skills to the project and for helping us deliver the manuscript to the publishers on time, against all the odds. Finally, at Routledge, we would like to thank Alan Jarvis for turning the proposal round so quickly and Sally Close for her patient oversight of the editing process.

A. A.
J. T.

INTRODUCTION

CONFLICT AND COHESION IN THE SINGLE EUROPEAN MARKET

A reflection

David Mayes

Social and economic policies within nation states have a variety of objectives, most of which can only be approached, not attained. Many of these objectives may conflict in the sense that further progress towards one involves less progress towards another, or even divergence from it. The European Union is not immune from these same problems. Indeed, since the EU budget is so small, the policy directorates-general are fairly independent and the ambitions large, the conflicts emerge clearly. This book focuses on one example, the fear that increasing integration is going to lead to a fall in 'cohesion' in the Union. Cohesion has received a variety of definitions but I want to stick to the version Iain Begg and I developed in NIESR (1991), namely that it is the political tolerability of the levels of economic and social disparity that exist and are expected in the EU and of the measures that are in place to deal with them. It is thus both a dynamic and a subjective concept. As time passes, constant or even diminishing disparities may become less tolerable. Widening disparities may be tolerated if major efforts are being made to ease the process and absolute levels are rising.

The main point can be illustrated by a simplified reference to the problems outlined in the White Paper *Growth, Competitiveness and Employment*, produced for the Brussels summit in December 1993. The fear is that with current policies the EU may be improving economic efficiency, *inter alia* through the single market, and increasing the rights of the employed through the Social Action Programme, but decreasing cohesion through increasing unemployment and widening disparities, particularly in some of the least favoured regions of the EU. I have illustrated this in Figure 1, where the bold triangle links the feared outcome in the three dimensions of efficiency, cohesion and rights, labelled E_1, C_1 and R_1 respectively. This is something of a caricature, as 'efficiency' is an intermediate objective in the

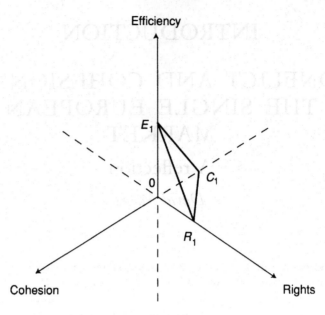

Figure 1 Feared outcome

pursuit of economic growth and higher levels of income per head. (In the same way employee 'rights' are not necessarily an end in themselves but a route towards enhanced social welfare.)[1]

The Maastricht Treaty, on the other hand, is aimed at improvement on all fronts (Figure 2), although of course it does not specify the methods of achieving it. I think it would be fair to say that the UK government does not believe that current EU policies or their likely evolution over the coming few years will be particularly successful in achieving these aims. I have characterized this in Figure 3 as relatively little progress along any of the axes (the set E_3, C_3, R_3). On the contrary, the government is of the opinion that if some of the restrictions on the operation of the labour market can be eased (DoE 1993) it will be possible to improve both efficiency (and hence incomes per head) and employment (reduce unemployment) much more markedly (E_4, C_4, R_4). This should help improve cohesion by improving social welfare. A strong feature of this argument is that some aspects of employee 'rights' may be improved only at the expense of the unemployed or non-employed. I want to stress that these perceptions may not be correct but that it is differences in them which characterize the debate and help explain UK unwillingness to sign the Maastricht agreement on social policy.

Some of the UK's partners feel that if a UK-style policy were applied more generally, although it might improve efficiency rather more than

2

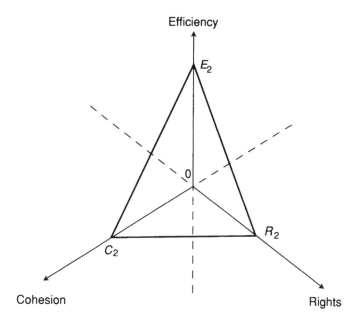

Figure 2 Maastricht aspiration

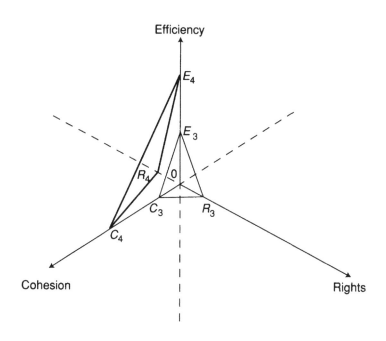

Figure 3 UK proposals and Maastricht results

3

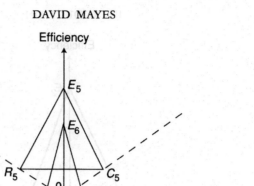

Figure 4 Perception of UK proposals and preferred solution

existing policies, it would decrease both cohesion and rights (Figure 4, E_5, C_5, R_5). A policy mix resulting in a little less efficiency but improvements in both rights and cohesion is therefore greatly to be preferred (E_6, C_6, R_6).

The worry for Europe as a whole is that without some new approach the process of closer integration is going to lead to greater industrial concentration. However, there will not be any substantial movement of capital, through direct investment into the lower-income regions, nor will there be any substantial migration of labour towards the regions of greater employment opportunities. Thus not only will little be done about unemployment but the inherent inequity of the result will lead to pressure to reverse the process of integration, as was revealed in the debate over the ratification of the Maastricht Treaty.

Lindley and Wilson (1991) have drawn out two contrasting views of how this difficulty might be resolved (Gold and Mayes 1993).[2] The first, dubbed the quality scenario, argues that if Europe can concentrate on its areas of strength, namely high-quality skills and knowledge-intensive goods and services, it can continue to have both competitive success and high standards of living because such goods and services tend to have high value added. A second, dubbed the efficiency scenario, argues that effective competition will come from less regulation, greater flexibility and lower costs. Only then can the challenges from Pacific Asia be met. One drawback of this second approach is that there is no means of matching Pacific

Asian labour costs and that a cost-cutting scenario which leads to lower wages is self-defeating in that it ensures that standards of living will fall. The counter-argument, of course, is that employment may rise and unemployment may fall under this scenario, hence providing a rather better distribution of incomes and greater cohesion in the EU.

We do not have the opportunity to resolve this debate here, merely to observe that its existence reflects the great conflict among possible policies at present and the adverse effects upon cohesion that may emerge, not so much from following one scenario rather than another but from failure to agree on a practical way forward. Subsidiarity may appear to offer a solution but in some respects may be merely permitting a more diverse approach to the problem and hence less integration. Subsidiarity works when different instruments in the various member states are a more effective means of achieving a common agreed aim – not, as in the present circumstances, where the aim is not common. (In these circumstances it would make more sense to acknowledge that there was no common policy, but the issue is too central to the ideals of European integration to admit that.)

A problem with the ideals expressed in the White Paper is that the EU has neither the policy instruments nor the institutions to achieve them. In approaching the single market EU policy has been to try to create equality of opportunity to compete. Thus for the less advantaged regions the approach has not been to try to even up incomes per head or social provision directly, as is done in all nation states and federal systems by transfers through the system tax and public expenditure, but to provide the infrastructure and human capital through training necessary for a region to be able to compete. It is up to the various regions to achieve what success they can in the process of competition, given that starting point. We argue in NIESR (1991) and Begg and Mayes (1993) that this process will not be successful and that, to achieve adequate cohesion, traditional methods of transfer would also be required, whether through an unemployment fund, as suggested by MacDougall (1977), or through a 'social fund' whereby transfers are made between social security systems.

However, much can be done even within the existing framework to reduce the inequity of its impact. Franzmeyer *et al.* (1991) in a parallel report to our own show that the regional impact of EU policies, other than structural policies, is if anything anti- rather than pro-cohesive, particularly through the operation of the Common Agricultural Policy. Assuming that the relative importance of the CAP in the budget declines over the years to come, there will be a degree of automatic improvement in cohesion. Second, Padoa-Schioppa (1987) has already shown how budget adjustments can increase equity by ensuring that the net contribution each member state makes to the overall budget is related to its GDP per head. He advocates not exact adherence to a norm but conformity within bands of a few percentage points. Furthermore, he advocates not proportionality but a system whereby the net benefit increases more than proportionately the lower the GDP per head but the net contribution for the richer member states increases less than proportionately. In this way the net benefit is geared towards those most in need and the burden is shouldered widely.

There is, of course, enormous scope for variation in such schemes, but a combination of greater concern for the impact of existing policies on cohesion and a more comprehensive form of budgetary equity than just the rebates for the UK could go a long way to reducing the current conflicts and enhancing the impact on cohesion.

Further progress could be made with new policies. However, these are not likely to be macro-economic, with relaxation of the Maastricht criteria, except in the short run, as that would weaken the credibility of closer integration still further and add an inflation cost. The exception is the proposal to switch from the taxation of labour to the taxation of environmental deterioration. The impact will depend upon the nature of the substitution but it should result in some switch in production towards methods which use fewer scarce natural resources and more labour. This should help achieve environmental objectives and employment objectives simultaneously. However, its potential should not be exaggerated, as competitiveness will still be lower in the medium term compared with countries which do not share the same level of environmental objectives.

More promising are improvements in industrial policy and particularly labour market policies which relate to the quality of human capital. As my colleague Sig Prais and his co-workers at the National Institute have been pointing out for many years (Prais et al. 1990, for example), there is a clear relation between the quality of vocational training and competitiveness at the micro-economic level – a relation which is often apparently much weaker when viewed in macro-economic studies (Prais 1993). Not all parts of the EU can benefit equally in this regard, as countries such as Germany and the Netherlands are often used as international benchmarks as to what can be achieved through vocational education and training. However, the same cannot be said of the UK or of several of the most disadvantaged regions. Hence significant progress which could improve overall competitiveness and cohesion is clearly possible.

However, policy improvements are unlikely to suffice without institutional change. While attention has been focused on EU-level institutions, where there is indeed an argument that more effective regulatory and monitoring bodies may be required (Dehousse et al. 1992), it is at the regional level where there may be the most to learn. Our work on decentralized industrial policies (Begg et al. 1993) has shown that member states with strong regional structures seem to have been relatively successful. Ewen Peters (Chapter 10 in this volume) in his analysis of the IT industry in Scotland indicates a set of steps required in order to maintain the industry's competitive position. Only a few of them are within the power of Scottish Enterprise. Several require action by firms, some require action by the UK government – which it is unlikely to take – while others require changes in the EU's external trade policy.

This leads to his emphasis on partnership, hoping that the other actors can be persuaded to act in a coherent framework. In other member states partnership is institutionalized, whether through social partnership between employers and employee organizations or with local and national government. Northern Ireland is unique in the UK in retaining such a relationship through the Economic Council, but that organization is mainly a forum for discussion. The National Economic Development Council was closed down at the end of 1992. The EU's structural policy in its last and current five-year rounds has encouraged this sort of collaboration in trying to establish Community Support Frameworks.

Stephen Young's Chapter points out that there is more that can be done even now to attract and retain inward investment through 'after care'. Indeed, Ash Amin and John Tomaney's Chapter on inward investment shows that a strategic approach, as followed by Scottish Enterprise and the IDA, *inter alia*, with a focus on particular sectors, has paid off. The problem is not merely to attract investment but to establish 'endogenous growth', expanding the length of the local supply chain, increasing value added, the set of functions within the firm provided in the local plant and moving up market by improving quality.

However, it is also clear as Giunta and Martinelli (Chapter 9) show for the Mezzogiorno and Ash Amin and John Tomaney (Chapter 8) for instances in Portugal, that such a process may not be possible, however appropriate the local institutional structure. While such structures may assist cohesion they do not entail it. However, it is noticeable that in many cases the emphasis still appears to be on attracting the initial investment rather than on upgrading its quality to help the region as a whole. Even so, there may be something to be gained from greater concertation among the various agencies, perhaps with a one-stop shop.[3]

A second reason for recommending appropriate local or regional structures lies in their ability to motivate partners to act in one another's interests as well as their own. This sort of tribalism is well known – indeed, competition policy seeks to avoid some sectional groups gaining an advantage at the expense of others. Nevertheless some groups have a reputation for acting in the common interest. Some of this motivation comes not just from motivation but from democratic legitimacy. Where institutions are imposed from outside, and their main executives and boards are appointed from outside, they may find it more difficult to raise local support.

Of all the countries in Europe, England is probably the most centralized. It may very well be, therefore, that it is the less advantaged regions of England that have most to gain from adopting structures and policies for development that appear to have fared best. The new Committee of the Regions may help to transmit the understanding of what can be achieved across Europe more rapidly. The editors of this volume are to be congratulated in bringing together such a good collection of papers to highlight the problems of conflict and cohesion within the European single market. It is to be hoped that these ideas will be adopted by business, policy-makers and the institutions of government at regional, national and European level.

NOTES

1 I am grateful to Bill Wells in the Employment Department for a helpful insight on this point. The UK approaches the achievement of some aspects of social welfare through the social benefit system. Hence attempts to regulate for their achievement through minimum wages or other costs on employers may be counterproductive in the UK framework, as it can result in lower employment for the group at whom the intended benefits are aimed (because their relative cost to employers has risen). The rights dimension may not therefore be a particularly accurate characterization of the social welfare aim.

2 He elaborates four scenarios; I have picked on only two of them.

3 There is, however, some debate over whether such new arrangements actually add to the complexity rather than resolve it. In a NEDO study in the mid-1980s it was revealed that there were over eighty agencies in the UK's smallest county, Rutland, alone, trying to assist small companies, some set up to provide access to others (often collecting a fee on the way, of course).

REFERENCES

Begg, I. G., and Mayes, D. G. (1993) 'Cohesion in the European Community: a key imperative for the 1990s?' *Regional Science and Urban Economics* 23: 427–48.

Begg, I. G., Lansbury, M., and Mayes, D. G. (1993) 'Decentralised Industrial Policies', paper given at the Regional Studies Association annual conference, University of Nottingham

Dehousse, R., Joerges, C., Majone, G., and Snyder, F. (1992) 'Europe after 1992: new regulatory strategies', European University Institute Working Paper in Law 92/31.

Department of Employment (1993) Green Paper on labour market policy, London: HMSO.

Franzmeyer, F. *The Regional Impact of Community Politics*, European Parliament Research Paper No. 17, Luxembourg: Office for Publications of the European Union.

Gold, M., and Mayes, D. G. (1993) 'Rethinking a social policy for Europe', in R. Simpson and R. Walker (eds) *Europe for Richer or Poorer*, Bath: Child Poverty Action Group.

Lindley, R. M., and Wilson, R. A. (1991) 'SEM Scenarios for the Employment of Women and Men in Great Britain', paper given at the EOC/IER Seminar, University of Warwick.

MacDougall, Sir D. (1977) *Report of the Study Group on the Role of Public Finance in European Integration*, Brussels: Commission of the European Communities.

National Institute of Economic and Social Research (1991) *A New Strategy for Social and Economic Cohesion after 1992*, Research Paper 19, European Parliament, Luxembourg: Office for Publications of the European Communities.

Padoa-Schioppa, T. (1987) *Efficiency, Stability and Equity*, Oxford: Oxford Univeristy Press.

Prais, S. J. (1993) 'Economic Performance and Education: the nature of Britain's deficiencies', Keynes lecture to the British Academy.

Prais, S. J., *et. al.* (1990) *Productivity, Education and Training*, NIESR.

ACKNOWLEDGEMENTS

The author was co-ordinator of the ESRC Single European Market research programme until September 1994. He acknowledges with thanks the ESRC's financial support for this note but the views expressed herein are his own responsibility.

1

THE CHALLENGE OF COHESION

Ash Amin and John Tomaney

The vision of the original architects of the European Union was to create and guide the development of Europe in such a way that economic prosperity and social harmony could be assured simultaneously for the majority of Europe's citizens. Today we have come closer to achieving economic integration, but not sustained growth, nor a reduction in social disparities. Indeed, the contemporary cocktail of economic stagnation, problems of industrial adaptation, mass unemployment, social exclusion and political polarization within the European Union threatens to widen divisions between member states, regions and social groups. More acutely than ever, Europe faces the dual problem of how to ensure sustained growth and how to combine it with social equity. An important manifestation of this problem, recognized by politicians and policy-makers, is the growing gap in social and economic prosperity between the EU's advanced and less favoured regions. It is significant that regional differentials in productivity, unemployment and employment appear to have increased during the last decade, the period in which efforts to integrate the European economy have been most intense.

'Cohesion' is the term coined by the EU to signal its policy aim of reducing the social and regional gap in Europe. In recognition of the possibility that economic integration may not lead to any convergence of living standards, the EU has introduced, since the mid-1980s, a number of measures – from laws and directives to recommendations and statements of principle – to accompany its measures for European economic integration in order to facilitate cohesion. EU social policy and EU regional policy are the two main arenas in which these measures have evolved, with the latter focusing on improving the competitiveness of the EU's less favoured regions and the former aimed principally at upgrading and harmonizing legislation on the rights of employees. In brief, improvements in the employment relation and in the economic potential of the less favoured regions are seen as the main corrective against anti-cohesion tendencies in Europe.

Significantly, the cohesion measures are proposed in parallel to, rather

10

than as a replacement for, the EU's commitment to free-market-led policies for European economic modernization and expansion. The belief is that the cohesion measures will compensate for any negative effects of restructuring which may result from the pursuit of neo-liberal growth policies, enshrined in such initiatives as the Single European Act, the completion of the single European market and economic and monetary union. The cohesion measures are a concession to interventionism within an overall framework of market-led routes to prosperity.

This book explores the real potential for cohesion, through an assessment of the challenges faced by the less favoured regions (both old industrial and 'lagging') and by workers in Europe, associated with the EU's policies on economic integration and on social cohesion as well as wider processes of industrial change in Europe. The book challenges the optimistic outlook of supporters of the single market and of monetary union, and argues that current EU measures purporting to facilitate cohesion will not achieve this goal. It is argued that cohesion will be undermined by the inherent bias of the EU's measures for promoting growth and productivity towards the economic interests of the advanced regions and the major corporations in Europe. At the core of the book lies a critique of the prevailing neo-liberal growth philosophy which rejects the necessity of a link between economic efficiency and social equity.

This book, instead, makes a case for a European project in which cohesion goals lie at the centre of economic regeneration policies rather than being an adjunct of competitiveness priorities. It makes the case for expansionist macro-economic policies, active industrial intervention, protection of worker and welfare rights and supply-side measures in the regions. It suggests that without active support for the weaker regions, without radical institutional change at local, national and European level, and without strong commitment to a growth philosophy based on the extension of social democracy cohesion will remain an elusive goal.

This chapter brings together aspects of the critique of the EU policy orthodoxy on cohesion that is developed within individual chapters. It begins with an illustration of the growing regional disparities in the EU, followed by a summary and critique of the EU's cohesion measures. It highlights the shortcomings of EU regional policy and EU social policy both as antidote against the anti-cohesion effects of the EC's competition and industrial policies and as cohesion measures in their own right. The second part of the chapter broadens the analysis to consider the threat to cohesion posed by deeper transformations within the European political economy and reflects on how EU policy relates to these transformations. It focuses on five connected developments considered to be central in widening the regional and social divide in Europe: the slow-down and crisis of the post-war growth trajectory, the growing significance of 'learning-based' competitiveness, the globalization of corporate networks,

11

growing labour market segmentation and social exclusion, and the transformation of the state under the pressures of globalization and the rise of
neo-liberalism. The final part of the chapter outlines the themes covered
by the book and summarizes the main arguments of the individual
contributions.

SOCIAL AND ECONOMIC COHESION IN EUROPE: THE POLICY FRAMEWORK

Social and economic cohesion have been an aim of the EU since its earliest
days. The Treaty of Rome enjoined the EEC 'to promote throughout the
EU a harmonious development of economic activities, a continuous and
balanced expansion . . . an accelerated raising of the standard of living'
(Article 2). From the outset, the EU has had a particular concern with
spatial disparities and has developed 'structural policies' designed to assist
the weaker regions to adapt to the conditions of an increasingly integrated
economy. The scale of these structural policies has grown with each
enlargement of the EU as the scale and diversity of regional problems
have increased. During the 1980s the renewed effort to complete the
internal market and moves towards monetary union were accompanied
by further expenditure increases – and substantial reform – of the EU's
structural policies. Underpinning these policies has been acknowledgement
that the process of European economic integration poses particularly
severe problems of industrial adaptation for weaker regions. Enhanced
structural policies are deemed necessary to assist the weaker regions to
adapt to new competitive conditions which are the intended consequence
of economic integration.

A second dimension of the EU's concern for social and economic
cohesion resides in its periodic attempts to develop a European social
policy. As with the structural policies, concern with the 'social dimension' has a history at least as old as the EU itself. The Treaty of Rome
first gave expression to this concern when it called on member states 'to
promote improved working conditions and an improved standard of living
for workers' (Article 117). Article 118 of the treaty entrusted the European
Commission with the task of promoting co-operation in matters relating to
employment, working conditions, social security, occupational safety and
health, training and collective bargaining.

This section outlines the main measures which have been developed by
the EU to promote social and economic cohesion and offers a preliminary
assessment of their effectiveness. The area of greatest activity for the EU as
regards cohesion has been in the development of structural policies
designed to tackle spatial disparities. The main emphasis in this section
therefore is on the operation of the EU's structural policies, although we do

briefly outline and assess progress towards what is frequently referred to as 'Social Europe'.

Regional disparities

Typically, the EU measures cohesion as inter-regional differences in labour market conditions and average income per head. This approach is not without its problems. First, such a focus can overlook the extent of intra-regional inequalities. Collier (1994), for instance, has pointed out that *per capita* income requirements for a region can be close to the EU average but can hide quite marked intra-regional differences. A good example are the areas of concentrated disadvantage in Europe's 'prosperous' major cities. Second, there is a fundamental problem in defining and measuring cohesion by reference to 'regional indicators': measures of inter-regional inequality depend on the regional boundaries which are selected (O'Donnell 1993). Despite these caveats, given the centrality of the data to official definitions of cohesion, it makes sense to examine regional disparities in relation to unemployment and *per capita* GDP.

The Commission noted in its fourth report on the social and economic situation of the regions that regional disparities worsened appreciably from the mid-1970s through to the early 1980s (CEC 1991). The most recent regional GDP data (Eurostat 1994a) show a 3 per cent fall in the EU average, mainly as a result of the incorporation of the new German *Länder*, which have a very low *per capita* GDP. GDP figures for 1991, expressed in terms of purchasing power standards, reveal marked differences between member states. Greece, at 49 per cent of the EU average, had the lowest productivity, while Luxembourg had the highest level of productivity, at 131 per cent. Disparities between regions, however, are even more marked. Over 10 per cent of regions recorded figures in excess of 125 per cent of the EU average. However, more than 20 per cent of regions recorded indices below 75 per cent of the EC average, the lowest being the new *Länder* (30 to 35 per cent) and most Greek regions. Spain, Italy, the UK and now, as a consequence of unification, Germany are marked by pronounced inter-regional variations in *per capita* GDP which worsened in the period 1980–91. The general pattern of these disparities is shown in Figure 1.1.

Although unemployment levels in the 1980s were already high by comparison with the 'full employment' years of the 1960s and early 1970s, the labour market situation of the EU has deteriorated markedly during the early 1990s. In April 1993 the unemployment rate in the EU, using the ILO definition, was 10.4 per cent. Unemployment had risen in virtually every region of the EU in the previous twelve months. Regional disparities in employment are wider than those in GDP (Eurostat 1994b). For instance, a number of southern German regions had unemployment rates of less than 4 per cent in 1993, but unemployment rates in some

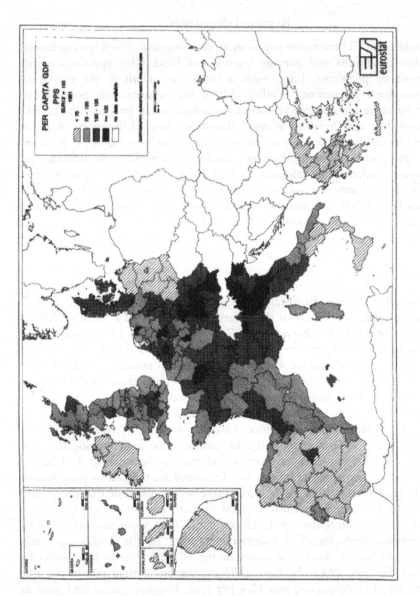

Figure 1.1 GDP *per capita* in the EU (by courtesy of Eurostat)

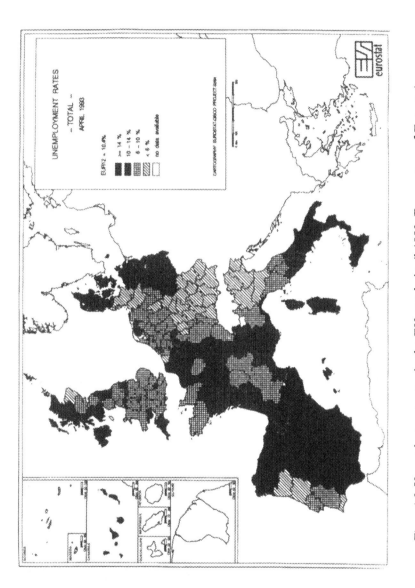

Figure 1.2 Unemployment rates in the EU: total, April 1993 (By courtesy of Eurostat)

Spanish regions exceed 25 per cent. The general pattern of disparity is shown in Figure 1.2.

The economic performance of some regions improved significantly during the 1980s. Among them were such regions as Catalunya, Navarra and Baleares in Spain and Lisboa e Vale do Tejo in Portugal. However, there is no evidence of a trend towards the elimination of disparities. Indeed, disparities within member states such as Spain, Italy and the UK have increased significantly over recent years. Regional inequality remains entrenched in Europe and seems to be growing rather than diminishing. The problem is put into perspective when it is recognized that regional GDP *per capita* disparities in the EU are twice as high as in the US, and unemployment disparities three times higher than in the US (CEC 1991).

EU structural policy

These spatial disparities are supposed to be tackled by the EU's various Structural Funds, which grew in size and importance during the 1980s. The three Structural Funds include the European Social Fund (ESF), the European Regional Development Fund (ERDF) and the European Agricultural Guidance and Guarantee Fund – Guidance Section (EAGGF-GS). The ESF was established under the provisions of the Treaty of Rome, although its scope and resources remained limited. With the rapid increase in unemployment in the 1970s, the resources of the ESF were expanded and its role was defined as that of supporting the vocational training of workers forced out of crisis-hit sectors, particularly agriculture. As such, most ESF expenditures were directed at regions such as the Italian Mezzogiorno. The ERDF was established at the time of the Community's first enlargement in 1974. The accession of the UK and Ireland extended the scale and nature of the regional problem within the EU. In particular the UK brought with it a number of crisis-hit industrial regions. The UK's problems in this regard were particularly acute, but similar problems of concentrated industrial decline emerged in most northern member states during the 1970s, and the problem of 'converting regions in industrial decline' became an important task of the ERDF. During the 1980s the accession of Greece and later Spain and Portugal brought new concern with cohesion, as did intensifying problems in the declining industrial regions. The Structural Funds were reformed in 1979 and 1984 as the Commission sought to increase the available resources and to improve the effectiveness of the funds. A more far-reaching reform of the Structural Funds occurred in 1988. This reform differed from the previous ones in so far as it was one aspect of the renewed impetus to economic integration, represented by the signing of the Single European

Act. This reform, and subsequent developments associated with moves to monetary and political union, are discussed in some detail below.

Cohesion and the single market

The Single European Act was itself partly a response to Europe's low levels of growth in the 1980s. The Single European Act and the accompanying White Paper sought to 'complete' the internal market by the end of 1992 through a series of measures designed to 'free' capital movements and harmonize the standards, policies and taxes of member states. Underpinning this programme was an analysis which held that a major cause of the lack of dynamism of the European economy, relative to that of Japan and the US, was the enduring fragmentation of the European economy into national markets. While the treaties establishing the EU had removed many tariffs and quotas and established a common external tariff, many non-tariff barriers to integrated trade remained. Specifically, the '1992 programme' legislated for the removal of frontier controls between member states, the harmonization of product specifications and service regulations, the removal of local preferences in public procurement and greater controls over state aid, the abolition of exchange controls and the harmonization of VAT rates.

The European Commission's research indicated that the removal of these impediments to the free movement of goods, services, capital and people – referred to as the 'costs of non-Europe' (Cecchini 1988) – would allow more efficient allocation of resources at the European scale, thus stimulating renewed growth. In practice, significant restructuring and rationalization of European business was expected as a result of these measures. It was believed, however, that the weaker regions of the EC would need special assistance to adjust to the new conditions of competition and to ensure that they participated in the new growth opportunities. For instance, the European Commission's own analyses pointed to the degree to which employment in less favoured regions was dependent on industries involved in public procurement and which were expected to experience intense rationalization (CEC 1991). Concern with mitigating the effects of these developments was the major impetus behind the 1989 reform of the Structural Funds.

At the same time the 1989 reform was used as an opportunity to overhaul the way in which the funds operated. The principal effect of the reforms was to achieve greater co-ordination of the hitherto separate funds and to focus their efforts on five clear objectives (see Table 1.1). In particular, the intention was to focus the greatest level of assistance on the 'lagging regions', located mainly on the southern periphery of the EU (Table 1.2).

The 1989 reform was supported by a decision to double in real terms the

Table 1.1 EC Structural Fund objectives

No	Nature of Objective	Funds involved
1	Development of lagging regions	ERDF, ESF, EAGGF-GS
2	Conversion of regions in industrial decline	ERDF, ESF
3	Combating long-term unemployment	ESF
4	Increasing youth employment	ESF
5	(a) Adjustment of agricultural structures (following the reform of agricultural policy)	EAGGF-GS
	(b) Promoting the development of rural areas	ERDF, ESF, EAGGF-ES

Source: CEC, Regulation 2052/88, Tasks of the Structural Funds; OJ L 185, 15 July 1989.

EC's allocation to the three Structural Funds between 1988 and 1993 under the provisions of the so-called Delors I package, which overhauled the finances of the EU. In addition, regions were obliged to undertake what, in effect, was a comprehensive system of regional planning in order to obtain support from the funds. These measures, by assisting improvements in the infrastructure and skills base of regions, were expected to offset any job losses in less favoured regions arising from the harsher competitive environment in Europe generated by the 1992 programme. In this way it was presumed that less favoured regions would become more attractive locations for new investment and entrepreneurship, and would share the increased growth that the single market was expected to generate.

A further increase in funds for EU structural policy was associated with the signing of the Maastricht Treaty. Maastricht reiterated the EU's commitment to economic and social cohesion. A new financial package, known as Delors II, was proposed. A new budget was needed anyway after 1993, but the Commission argued that extra finance would be needed to meet the objectives outlined in the treaty (CEC 1992). These objectives were defined

Table 1.2 Structural Fund budget, 1989–93

Objective	Target	ECU million (1989 prices)	%
1	Lagging regions	38,300	63
2	Regions in industrial decline	7,205	12
3	Long-term unemployment	7,450	12
4	Youth training/employment		
5	(a) Adaption of agricultural structures	3,415	6
	(b) Development of rural areas	2,975	5
	Transitional measures and innovation	1,150	
	Total	60,315	100

Source: CEC, The New Structural Policies of the European Community. European File 7–8/90, Luxembourg, Office for Official Publications of the European Community.

by the Commission as economic and social cohesion, enhancing the competitiveness of European industry (mainly through an enhanced Research and Technological Development policy) and external action (i.e. support for Eastern Europe, North Africa and humanitarian aid).

The proposal for increased financial resources was justified by the Commission on a number of grounds. First the Maastricht Treaty laid down strict 'convergence' criteria in relation to public deficits and debt as well as interest and inflation rates which member states would be compelled to meet before being allowed to progress to full monetary union. It was acknowledged that the task of meeting these criteria might prove particularly burdensome for weaker member states. Second it was recognized that monetary union would prevent weaker member states from adjusting exchange rates as a basis for coping with internal or external economic shocks (see Delors 1989). Thus there was a chance that the European convergence criteria would simultaneously strain public finances and restrict the scope of macro-economic policy choices in the latter states.

The combined effect of these new pressures on less favoured regions, it was argued, warranted an increase in resources to ease the fiscal constraints on weaker member states and regions (CEC 1992). The Maastricht Treaty, therefore, proposed the creation of a Cohesion Fund to support environmental improvements and the development of trans-European networks in the poorest member states. This funding, plus increased funding proposed under the Delors II package, would in the case of Objective 1 regions double funds by 1997. The Commission argued that the previously successful reforms of the Structural Funds illustrated the potential of structural policies. However, as Scott (1994: 79) notes:

> Despite this, the Delors II package quickly ran into trouble. Unsurprisingly, the protaganists in the debate roughly split along geographical lines. The poor countries in the EC's southern periphery, in which the overwhelming share of Objective 1 regions were located, demanded full implementation of the proposals in so far as raising the finance available to the structural policies was concerned, while the rich, northern countries complained of fiscal profligacy on the part of the Commission and insisted that the financial commitment to cohesion should be reduced.

In the event, the package of financial reforms agreed at the Edinburgh summit in 1992 failed to meet the Commission's initial ambitions. The overall level of resource agreed was closer to that proposed in Delors II, but the period for intervention was extended to 1999. In practical terms the Objective 1 regions saw a doubling of funds, while funding for the other structural objectives was lower than that envisaged in Delors II.

19

Limits of EU regional policy

Despite the expansion of the Structural Funds during the 1980s serious weaknesses remain with the EU approach to cohesion and regional development. A major area of concern is that, despite the changes in the operation and the doubling of the size of the Structural Funds, the measures and financial resources involved remain insufficient in relation to the scale and nature of the EU's entrenched regional problems and the threats posed by further integration. In the period 1989–93, during which the single market was completed, total expenditure on Structural Funds was ECU 60.3 billion, equivalent to only 0.24 per cent of the EU's GDP. This figure seems particularly modest when set beside the alleged welfare gains of ECU 216 billion which the Cecchini report predicted would arise from the single market. Indeed, in the 1970s the MacDougall report (1977) on the role of public finance under European integration argued that a federal Europe of reduced disparities would need inter-regional resource transfers of around 20–25 per cent of GDP, while a 'looser' federation would require expenditure of around 5–7 per cent of EU GDP.

A second problem with the EU's approach to cohesion is the faith it places in market forces to stimulate growth and see to its 'trickle down' to the less favoured regions. The clearest expression of the EU approach to cohesion is that given by Delors (1989). Delors rejects the idea that there are inevitable winners or losers in the process of integration. Peripherality, for instance, is no longer seen as a serious problem on the grounds that transport costs are becoming, on average, less important in the location of industrial production. New developments in telecommunications and increased capital mobility are seen to represent an opening up of the locational choices of firms with the implication that this may benefit the less favoured regions. Delors concludes that the most important factor determining the distribution of industrial activity is effective supply-side policies, and for this reason he rejects regional employment and capital subsidies. The former, he argues, give the wrong signal to those responsible for labour competitiveness while the latter encourage inefficient investment. Besides, both measures are seen to contravene the market ethos that underpins the single market. Delors also rejects the case for automatic fiscal transfers between regions. He does not believe the EU should offer guarantees of equal standards of public welfare of the type that justify inter-regional transfers in federal states such as Germany and Australia. Thus he argues for greater policy emphasis on upgrading local entrepreneurship, training efforts, environmental improvements in urban areas and local initiatives which promote innovation.

This approach underpins the policies of the Commission's Regional Policy Directorate (DG XVI). The Fourth Periodic Report on the regions, for example, suggested that the less favoured regions should 'seek to exploit specific regional competitive advantages to serve special-ized product markets' and, in particular, less favoured regions should 'establish niche positions based on the exploitation of local advantages' (CEC 1991: 70–1). Similarly, the Commission is of the opinion that new location factors, including the growing importance of executive 'life style' factors and the viability of advanced telecommunications and information technology, are opening up new possibilities for the decentralization of economic activity away from the European core.

The question is not whether these proposals are good or bad – few would oppose them – but whether they are enough to close the regional gap in Europe. For instance, the assumptions of Delors concerning the decentralizing effects of contemporary technological change are challenge-able. As O'Donnell (1993) notes, while it may be true that distance-related costs are becoming, on average, less important in determining the location of production, it is simplistic to infer that telecommunications and trans-port improvements, because they technically reduce the friction of distance, will cause a dispersal of economic activity and therefore contribute to convergence via regional specialization. This would be to ignore that a powerful countervailing factor will be the dynamic external economies that operate in many sectors as well as the forces of accumulated technological expertise within the most dynamic companies – accumulated technology which is to some extent location-specific in so far as research and technol-ogy ability tends to be clustered in core regions. Thus, rather than decen-tralizing activities to lower-cost regions, large firms in particular might remain firmly rooted in supply-rich regions in order to continue to reap the advantages of existing economies of scale and agglomeration (see Krugman 1991). This observation is particularly important given the centrality of the promotion of scale economies on the single market agenda.

It has to be asked also whether any positive gains resulting from EU regional policy in facilitating cohesion are complemented by EU policy actions designed to enhance European competitiveness. Here the evidence tends to suggest that action in other areas of EU policy is likely to advantage Europe's larger firms and advanced regions. The EU's Research and Technology Development (RTD) Policy, for example, which is aimed at supporting expensive pre-competitive research, is an important part of the effort to improve the competitiveness of European industry. However, the available funds are more easily absorbed by large companies, whose RTD centres are typically located in prosperous regions, with the unin-tended outcome that the EU's RTD policy will militate against the aim of cohesion.

Similarly, the EU's liberal stance under Competition Policy on merger controls within and across borders is likely to encourage market concen-tration at Europe-wide level by facilitating acquisitions and take-overs. This is a development which will strengthen the interests of the largest firms in Europe. Already there is evidence that, in the context of a unified market, multilocational firms have begun to restructure operations, leading to the concentration of research and management tasks in advanced regions, and the rationalization of capacity in the less favoured regions (Amin *et al.* 1992; Tomaney 1994).

The Commission hopes that such outcomes will be compensated for by the overall extra growth that will result from scale economy gains as large companies win new market share. The achievement of scale economies is central to the alleged welfare gains suggested by Commission analyses – some 80 per cent of gains are expected to flow from this source (Cecchini 1989). Yet much research exists to suggest this is a highly optimistic scenario. As Harvey Ramsey points out in his chapter of this volume, studies of mergers in operation suggest few if any real examples of synergy or increased efficiency (see also Geroski, 1989). Moreover, it is by no means certain that 'European' companies will be the prime beneficiaries of the single market. Ramsey's evidence shows that the single European market has attracted investment from Japan and the US almost on the same scale as it has induced internal cross-investment. In addition, since many European companies are already global players, their investment plans are increasingly dictated by a logic of globalization rather than Europeanization. It is not likely, therefore, that increased productive capacity will be created after the first round of rationalizations, in less favoured regions especially, has ended.

The intensification of competition as a consequence of the single market is likely to accentuate the process of cumulative causation through which established centres of innovation and competitive advantage enjoy a virtuous circle of growth, while other regions become locked into trajectories of dependent development, or are denuded of the resources necessary for endogenous growth. In addition, there is no guarantee that improvements in the local skill base or infrastructure base of less favoured regions will automatically benefit local industry – they may benefit inward investors looking for a low-cost location that is well serviced by advanced communication links, or they may pull in cheaper goods from the advanced regions, threatening the survival of local firms and leading to profit repatriation.

Against such a backcloth the emphasis on small firms under EU regional policy is problematic. A battery of research evidence now exists to show that small firm entrepreneurship in the less favoured regions is often of poor quality, characterized by high failure rates and low growth rates, and situated in local market niches unexposed to international competition. Such characteristics are not conducive to the build-up of a critical mass of small firms capable of supporting further entrepreneurship. Moreover, studies of industrial districts – in which small firms collaborate with each other to secure self-sustaining regional economies – suggest that infra-structural improvement, skill upgrading and funding for small firm dev-elopment will be insufficient to achieve self-sustaining growth. Most of the less favoured regions lack the particular institutional, entrepreneurial and social traditions which characterize areas of growth – traditions which are not easily captured by simple policy initiatives such as those proposed by the Commission (Amin and Thrift, 1994). In addition, as already argued, such an approach overlooks the degree to which regional outcomes in the new Europe are being shaped by the interests of strengthened multinational companies.

These problems of regional divergence are likely to be complicated by monetary union. For some commentators, monetary union provides no additional threat to the less favoured regions beyond those raised by the single market programme (CEC 1990a; Holland 1993; O'Donnell 1992). Indeed, the European Commission sees monetary union as contributing to cohesion, arguing that, while partial dismantling of trade barriers will result in economic activity locating closer to the market centre, complete integra-tion will increase the attractiveness of peripheral locations 'where variable costs are lower' (CEC 1990a: 214). Holland argues, 'with the trend to multinational investment and pricing, Maastricht only formalizes the facts' (1993: 33), suggesting that the effectiveness of currency devaluation as a national policy measure has become limited. For other commentators, however, the road to monetary union, as laid down in the Maastricht Treaty, poses a set of threats to the less favoured regions (Begg and Mayes 1993a; Hankel 1994; Hughes *et al.* 1992; Scott 1994). They stress that the require-ments of monetary union go far beyond those of the internal market programme (which does not require close co-ordination of fiscal and other economic policies or the fixed exchange rates demanded under economic and monetary union). It is argued that convergence requirements designed to make monetary union possible will risk aggravating existing disparities by placing further fiscal pressure on the less favoured regions and accentuating the forces of 'cumulative causation' which favour the core regions of the EU (Begg and Mayes 1993a; Doyle 1989).

These fears are partly supported by the recent experience of German monetary union. The introduction of the Deutschmark to the former GDR in 1990, *inter alia*, precipitated a major social and economic collapse. By mid-1993 the new German *Länder* had lost 35 per cent of their jobs and production had fallen by 25 per cent. In the industrial sector nearly 50 per cent of jobs were cut and production was down by 40 per cent (Hankel 1994). For Wilhelm Hankel (1994: 52), former head of the Hessische Landesbank, the lessons of German unification are clear:

When there are real differences in cost and productivity, especially on this scale, the nominal convergences of prices, interests and exchange

23

rates required by monetary union can be achieved only at the cost of social crisis.

There are three dimensions to the threat posed to the less favoured regions by plans for monetary union as laid down by the Maastricht Treaty. First there is the loss of exchange rate autonomy within those less favoured regions which are nation states. Writers such as Holland too easily dismiss the importance of exchange rate adjustment as an instrument of economic policy. Exchange rate adjustment may be an appropriate response to an external shock with a differential impact upon countries participating in a fixed exchange rate regime. Second, although few would advocate devaluation as a general policy, it can be an important short-term policy measure for weaker member states in order to defend the domestic economy against competition from higher productivity member states. Such 'monetary protectionism', as Hankel (1994) describes it, may increase transaction costs on imports and reduce the real income of less productive areas, but it does give weaker economies a breathing space to develop before entering the international economy.

The third dimension of the threat to the less favoured regions comes from the obligation to meet the nominal convergence requirements laid down by Maastricht. The removal of exchange rate autonomy means that fiscal policy will become the main means of securing the regional distribution of income and employment. But here the stringent fiscal discipline which is stipulated in the Maastricht Treaty in the run-up to monetary union poses a severe threat to the very regions which will bear the greatest burden of adjustment in relation to the series of nominal macro-economic variables (inflation and interest rates, public deficit and debt). Clearly the most serious threat is to weak regions in member states with weak fiscal capacity that are running large deficits. For instance, Greece has a deficit of 15 per cent of GDP, while Italy has public debt of 100 per cent of GDP (Begg and Mayes 1993b).

Even among those who see monetary union as posing no additional threat to the less favoured regions there is recognition that structural policies alone are unlikely to be sufficient to establish a trend towards social and economic convergence. Thus O'Donnell (1992) notes that, in existing economic and monetary unions, normal budgetary contributions and expenditures constitute the most significant redistributive mechanism between individuals and regions. Drawing on the theory of fiscal federalism, he argues for a 'new assignment of policy functions' which gives an expanded role to the EU budget, stating that it is necessary for many policy functions to be conducted at the highest level if they are to be effective. Whatever the logical merits of O'Donnell's approach, its political feasibility seems doubtful. The negotiations surrounding the Delors II package revealed only too starkly the reluctance of richer member states to increase expenditure on structural policies, let alone develop a system of automatic fiscal transfers.

Put together, economic and monetary union, EU competitiveness policies and the inadequacies of the structural policies are likely to have little impact in terms of reducing regional disparities in Europe. EU policies will fail to achieve regional cohesion.

The social dimension

Although attempts to add a 'social dimension' to European integration are long-standing, such attempts have proved more politically contested than the development of structural policy, with fewer tangible results as a consequence.

Article 123 of the Treaty of Rome established the European Social Fund (ESF), which remained the EU's main instrument of structural policy until the establishment of the ERDF in 1974. Essentially, ESF expenditure supported the conversion of skills in sectors where employment was declining, such as agriculture. Until the reform of the Structural Funds during the 1980s, its aims remained rather loosely defined. From the 1970s the size of the ESF grew in absolute and relative terms, rising from 5.5 per cent of the EU budget in 1973 to 7.2 per cent in 1989. Employment problems within the EC, of course, worsened considerably during this period, and ESF expenditure remained tiny against the rising tide of unemployment.

Alongside the development of the ESF as a structural policy, the EU has sought to develop its social and employment policies. In particular, from the end of the 1960s, a new concern emerged within the European Commission and among some member states with developing a 'social dimension' to the process of economic integration. The first concrete expression of this new concern was the adoption, by the Council of Ministers, of a resolution on a Social Action Programme (SAP). The SAP set its aims as the 'attainment of full and better employment', the 'improvement of living and working conditions' and 'increased involvement of management and labour in economic and social decision-making' (CEC 1974). The Council stated as its goal the creation of a European Social Union.

However, during the 1970s such concerns tended to be overwhelmed by the forces of recession that swept through Europe. In this context, member states have proved reluctant to give up their control over social and employment policies. Since 1979 the UK Conservative government has been portrayed as the villain of the piece in this regard, but the reality is more complicated. As Lange (1992) argues, the implacable opposition of the Conservative government to extended EU competence in the area of social policy has allowed other member states to engage in 'cheap talk', since they know that UK opposition to a European Social Union protects them, in some cases, from actually having to implement a serious social policy or, in other cases, give up cherished national practice. As a consequence, argues Lange (1992), 'the social dimension is primarily a set of symbolic gestures, general policy commitments, and a few hotly debated, specific EU proposals.

Thus, while the European Commission can point to some success in establishing common standards in areas such as health and safety and gender equality in the workplace, its success has been markedly less in areas such as the regulation of working hours and worker representation within companies. For instance, during the 1970s a series of draft directives and resolutions were prepared, aimed at increased employee participation in company decision-making. They culminated in the production of the draft Vredeling Directive (named after the commissioner responsible). It proposed the introduction of formal consultation and information procedures into large enterprises within the EU (see Chapter 7 of this volume). The inspiration for this approach to employment policy was (and remains) the tradition of co-determination which operates in Germany and some other member states. The Vredeling Directive, however, was fiercely opposed by European employers' organizations (including German employers) and was never implemented.

It was the Commission's promotion of the Single European Act in the mid-1980s which provided a new stimulus to the development of the social dimension. Largely under the influence of the new Commission president, Jacques Delors, the social dimension was given a higher profile in the activities of the EC. Although the original White Paper on the completion of the internal market did not mention social policy, the Commission presented a new action programme to the European Parliament at the beginning of 1985 which, among other things, outlined the social measures designed to accompany the completion of the single market (CEC 1985). According to the Commission the Single European Act would not only contain economic measures but would be accompanied by measures aimed at improving working conditions, facilitating 'social dialogue' and, generally, promoting social and economic cohesion through the reform of the Structural Funds.

In practical terms the social dimension was to be facilitated through a 'Social Charter', which sought to establish a minimum set of standards in the area of labour market regulation (CEC 1990b). The UK government, under Margaret Thatcher, famously failed to sign the Social Charter, seeking to portray it as socialist meddling in the free market. Nothing could have been further from the truth. The Social Charter was simply a statement of principles and aspirations in the area of labour market policy – 'a solemn declaration' and 'a political signal given at the highest level', in its own words – and was not legally binding. It was intended to inform EU and member state social policy in the future, but had no legal authority of its own. Of course, even without the UK's participation, such an approach has allowed plenty of scope for ambiguity and inaction. Member states have shown a marked reluctance to cede powers in the area of welfare and social policy.

The Social Charter made no provision for the development of Europe-wide collective bargaining and did not legally establish the right to strike, as had been the hope of the European Trade Union Congress (ETUC). Instead the Charter, invoking the principle of subsidiarity, left the regula-tion of collective bargaining to the national level. The absence of legal authority meant that an accompanying 'action programme' of measures had to be developed in order to implement the Charter, but each element of the action programme had to be approved separately by the Council of Ministers. The action programme proposed forty-seven measures to be taken by the EC in thirteen areas. Of these only twenty-eight involved the creation of formally binding laws of one kind or another. Of the remaining twenty-eight proposed measures, ten alone related to health and safety (Streeck 1994). The weakness of the action programme and the unlikeli-hood of its more controversial measures being passed prompted IG Metall, the largest German union, to describe the Social Charter and the Action Programme not unfairly as a 'non-binding wish list' (quoted in Silvia 1991: 639).

The version of the Charter finally approved by the Council of Ministers was a diluted version of an earlier draft. The dilution was justified as an attempt to win the approval of the UK government. Although this approach was rebuffed by the Thatcher government, it was the weakened version of the Charter that was finally approved by the Council of Minis-ters, lending support to the argument that other member states welcome British intransigence as a reason for not acting on social policy.

The signing of the Maastricht Treaty represented the next step in the development of European social policy, although the size of the step is frequently overstated. The famous 'Social Chapter', which altered the provisions of the Treaty of Rome, and which the UK Conservative government refused to sign, called for upward harmonization of living and working conditions, improved health and safety at work, the promo-tion of 'social dialogue' between management and labour at the European level and equal pay for men and women. It also extended the EU's competence in a limited way to the areas of education and vocational training.

Britain's opt-out from the Social Chapter means that social policy is dealt with in the treaty itself but in a separate agreement signed by eleven member states. The agreement limits itself largely to following the path laid down by the Social Charter. Although the agreement extends the use of qualified majority voting to areas such as health and safety, a much longer

27

list outlines the areas still requiring unanimous voting – including social security policy, co-determination and so on – effectively guaranteeing national sovereignty over these areas. The agreement on social policy also, for the first time, obliges the Commission to follow a process of consultation with management and labour at the European level when forming social policy. While such an approach has been presented by the European Commission as designed to increase union influence in the creation of a 'Social Europe', as Streeck (1994) notes, in reality it more accurately reflects the desire to secure employer support for the integration project. Given the asymmetries of power between capital and labour, the new formal participation rights simply accord employers the opportunity to obstruct the development of all but the most minimal European social policy measures. While the somewhat increased powers of the European Parliament – including its new power to call for policy proposals from the Commission – and the fact that the Parliament has a socialist majority may ease the profile of EU social policy, it is clear that national obstacles to greater action on social policy at the European level remain all-powerful.

In addition to the problem of weak enforcement of European Social Policy, it has to be recognized that the goal of social cohesion has been less urgent than the goal of raising efficiency and competitiveness. The project of European integration, especially as it was reinvigorated during the 1980s, has been essentially an economic project and one which has strengthened the hands of multinational capital. At each stage of the integration process, concern with developing a European Social Union has been at best secondary rather than central. In addition, to the extent that the single market project has been heavily influenced by a neo-liberal approach there has been a strong emphasis on the removal of 'market distortions' and the reduction of 'burdens' on business, with obvious implications for the creation of a 'Social Europe'. The latter is designed to follow the market, rather than be the basis of competitiveness, resulting in a neo-liberal policy. The autumn 1993 Delors White Paper *Growth, Competitiveness and Employment*, with its strong emphasis on the need to reduce 'non-wage labour costs and to increase labour flexibility' captures the essence of a gradual subordination of EU Social Policy to the requirements of industry instead of defending the intrinsic rights of employees.

This subordination could exacerbate social divisions between rich and poor states and regions. Potentially, there is a fundamental contradiction in plans for monetary union without a concomitant social union. Despite the problems generated by German unification, a key compensation for the new *Länder* was access to the welfare provisions of the federal German state. In Europe there is no prospect of social union in the foreseeable future. Welfare remains resolutely a national phenomenon, and as such the costs of monetary union will be borne by the weaker member states, which, in turn, will not be able to finance the social costs of adjustment. Through

28

this mismatch, the possibility of reducing social disparities will become worse, as a gap grows between the rich nations, able to fund social welfare programmes and support decent employment standards, and the poor nations unable to draw on national or EU resources to raise social standards.

For Hankel the exit of Italy and the UK from the EMS, and *de facto* devaluations of other currencies, vividly highlighted this fundamental contradiction between plans for monetary union and the EU's stated aim of cohesion: 'The member states hit hardest by recession and unemployment needed to protect their job markets, and they preferred to fight for them on a national basis rather than stabilise the EMS exchange rate' (1994: 56). It is this contradiction which will plague efforts to create a 'Social Europe' into the next century. For the present, the dominant agenda appears to be that of endorsing only those aspects of EU social policy which do not conflict with market-based strategies for economic recovery. The weakness of the 'social dimension', in terms of both content and enforceability, will have the effect of separating nations and regions with old economic surpluses and strong social legislation underwriting progressive employment and welfare rights from those which do not have such advantages. The social divide in the EU, thus, is set to grow.

STRUCTURAL CHALLENGES TO COHESION

Policy gaps and policy conflicts within the EC relating to European economic integration are not the only source of difficulties associated with cohesion. This section examines the threats to cohesion arising from deeper changes in the European political economy. It is striking that in the large volume of literature on European integration relatively little attention has been paid to the relationship between EU policies and longer-term processes of change in the European economy. One consequence has been the failure of policy evaluations to consider the appropriateness of EU action in relation to these processes. There are, however, some notable exceptions (Albrechts *et al.* 1989, 1993; Amin and Dietrich 1991; Begg and Mayes 1991; Crouch and Marquand 1990; Dunford and Kafkalas 1992; Grahl and Teague 1990; Holland 1993; Matzner and Streeck 1991 ; Michie and Grieve Smith 1994; Teague and Grahl 1993; Thompson 1993). From the literature emerge a number of structural changes with important implications for the EC's less favoured regions and for cohesion in general.

Slow-down of growth

One major force is the slow-down of growth in the European (and world) economy since the early 1970s, representing a structural crisis in the conditions which produced a unique 'virtuous' spiral of growth in productivity, income, employment and demand for virtually twenty years after the Second World War. This widely recognized crisis of the 'golden age of capitalism' has yet to produce a new growth dynamic, thus the European economy continues to be trapped in a downward spiral characterized by sluggish productivity growth, inflationary pressures, restricted investment, persistent mass unemployment and growing fiscal pressure on the state (Michie and Grieve Smith 1994).

For many Keynesians and heterodox economists, as is reflected in the arguments put forward by Jonathan Michie and Michael Dunford in chapters 3 and 5 of this volume, unless active measures are taken to reflate the economy, no reversal of this state of affairs can be expected. The argument is that current EU economic policy (including the more 'interventionist' 1993 Commission White Paper) fails to recognize this imperative, choosing instead to place blind but misguided faith in the belief that the creation of free and integrated European markets will enhance growth and competitiveness. Added to the considerable re-evaluation that has taken place to show that original Commission forecasts of the efficiency and employment gains from economic and monetary union have been hopelessly exaggerated, this criticism suggests that the problem of slow growth is likely to remain for the foreseeable future.

This problem has obvious negative consequences for the less favoured regions. It is well known that the period of sustained growth from the mid-1950s to the mid-1970s served to reduce the regional gap in Europe, notably in those countries in which an active policy of regional incentives was used to decentralize investment and employment from prosperous to less favoured regions (see Dunford in Chapter 5). This was also a period in which national governments were able to draw upon a healthy balance of payments in order to maintain a steady flow of welfare expenditure and transfer payments towards the less favoured regions. This served not only to underwrite the subsistence of individual communities but also to raise aggregate demand by increasing consumer expenditure. Slow overall growth, in contrast, threatens the less favoured regions by reducing investment opportunities, the availability of financial and other incentives to support reconversion programmes and welfare as well as other transfer payments. In addition, as some observers have argued (Camagni 1992; Peschel 1992; Dunford and Perrons 1994; Begg, Chapter 4 of this volume), economic stagnation tends to refocus investment and employment in the most prosperous regions because their accumulated advantages (external economies of agglomeration, market size and access, availability of finance, technology, skills, know-how, better-quality infrastructure and communications) overshadow the cost savings (especially labour) offered by less favoured regions, as firms seek to survive in difficult circumstances. Stagnation, thus, represents the exact opposite of cohesion in spatial terms, by recentralizing growth in the core regions and drying up opportunities in the less favoured regions.

An emerging learning economy

A second major force of change in Europe, of which the first can be seen as a symptom, is the crisis of the mass production–mass consumption paradigm which underpinned national economic growth in the post-war period, leading to the rise of patterns of organization which make up an as yet uncertain new paradigm for growth. While terms such as Fordism, Fourth Kondratiev, Industrial or Mass Society are used confidently to describe the passing age, epithets such as post- or neo-Fordism, Flexible Specialization, Fifth Kondratiev, Information Economy, are used more tentatively to argue over the characteristics of a new model of industrial organizations (Amin 1994).

Some of the characteristics of an emerging industrial paradigm, however, are clearly discernible. It is acknowledged that a key condition of competitive advantage in the post-mass production or 'learning' economy will be the capacity to generate or control knowledge, information and innovation (technical and social) and harness it to encourage use (Lundvall 1992; Porter 1990). This is an imperative arising from the need to constantly innovate and secure quality in a market context of increasing volatility of demand, rapid product obsolescence and greater consumer discernment and desire for quality as well as value for money. In such a context, competitive advantage will accrue to those who can develop and retain a capacity to renew products, raise productivity through technological and organizational upgrading, and reduce the friction of distance and time through the use of advanced communications systems and informatics. It is self-evident, therefore, that firms, nations and regions which possess such capacity will emerge as the growth centres or beneficiaries of the transition.

The potential regional geography of this development is complex. In some senses, the development of informatics and advanced transport systems potentially liberates the remote areas of the EU from the tyranny of distance by bringing them closer to the markets of Europe, thus allowing development of their productive forces as transport and communications disadvantages are eliminated. Indeed, the principle of infrastructural upgrading as a key condition of regional development is firmly enshrined in current EC regional policy as well as in technology initiatives which are orientated towards the less favoured regions, with their increasing emphasis on developing advanced telecommunications networks (Grimes 1992). Clearly, without adequate transport and communications facilities the less favoured regions cannot be expected to gain a foothold in the emerging industrial paradigm, and to that extent EU policy is not misguided.

31

However, it is also the case that the advantages of such upgrading are double-edged, in the sense that it also allows, as it has done historically, more competitive firms from prosperous regions to increase market share in the less favoured regions, or to decentralize functions whilst retaining control and strategic management within headquarters regions (Camagni 1992).

The 'learning' nexus, which combines knowledge, information and innovation, involves much more than developing the appropriate technical and physical infrastructure for growth. It seems almost certain that the increased salience of this nexus as a factor in competitiveness will work to the advantage of the advanced metropolitan areas and flexibly specialized industrial districts which make up the arc of prosperity that spans the centre of Europe from south-east England to northern Italy. In this arc, 'islands of innovation' (FAST/Monitor 1992) are distinguished by their monopoly over the ideas, expertise, know-how and information circuits which drive the global industrial networks they represent. Their unique strength derives from the density and interdependence of institutions which compose the 'learning economy' (high-tech firms, research centres, technical colleges, service centres, universities, training centres, techno-poles, industrial information and knowledge networks, etc.). These are the centres of agglomeration which will serve as the 'brains trust' for developing new competitive advantages within Europe (Amin and Thrift 1992; Castells and Hall 1994; Storper 1994).

These new competitiveness factors are not the ready properties of Europe's less favoured regions, given their dependence on traditional industries (especially Objective 2 regions) or the absence of the institutional density, diversity and interdependence characteristic of learning-based competition (especially Objective 1 regions). A market-led approach to European integration will compound these deficiencies as skills and other resources are drawn to the prosperous regions, leaving an insurmountable gap in development potential between the 'islands of innovation' and the European economic periphery.

Commission policy (especially regional and technology policy) is not blind to the danger, but, like the innovation-based policy initiatives pursued in the majority of member states, it tends to interpret the brief too narrowly, focusing on solutions for the less favoured regions based on creating high-technology industries and research capacity rather than developing the 'learning' and 'adaptation' potential of existing industrial clusters. However, it is difficult for 'disembodied' technopoles in less favoured regions to develop the strategic capacity that characterizes the primary centres of innovation, and which makes them genuine growth poles (Castells and Hall 1994). This problem is echoed in Chapter 10 by Ewen Peters in this volume, which discusses the problems faced by Scotland as a secondary pole in the world electronics filiere. In addition, current EU policy thinking on innovation-based growth is too firm-centric and too technocratic, seeking as it does to foster high-tech entrepreneurship. It fails to acknowledge that an important aspect of 'learning regions' is that they are agglomerations of collective knowledge, innovation and information capacity: an aspect which goes well beyond technical forms of learning within individual firms. For the present, the reach of EU policy measures falls short of facilitating a more even regional distribution of 'learning' capacity in the new industrial paradigm.

Globalization

The literature on the geography of the 'learning economy' confirms that it is in the central nodes, the 'brains trusts' of the industrial networks which compose it, that we see high levels of regionalization of economic networks, as a consequence of their ability to encourage agglomeration and local interdependence (Storper 1994; Cooke and Morgan 1993). But, parallel to this geography of localization which privileges only the few, has been the longer-term trend towards the organization of enterprises, financial institutions, communications networks and consumption norms on a transnational scale. This is not the place to go into the details of this much discussed process of globalization, other than to note that it represents, simultaneously, the integration of markets on a continental or global scale, and their increasing domination by major transnational corporations and financial institutions (Dunning 1993). In the EU, as a result of much intensified foreign direct investment, mergers, take-overs and joint ventures across national boundaries since the mid-1980s (see Ramsay, Chapter 7 below), globalization represents the long-term replacement of an economic space of independent trading regions and nations by a single Europe-wide corporate economy. The growing density of transnational corporate networks, and the resultant increase in cross-national market concentration levels in Europe (Amin and Dietrich 1991), imply that regional fortunes are becoming tied into, and shaped by, powerful corporate interests organized on a transregional basis (Dicken et al. 1994). The regions of Europe are becoming part of a transnational production system.

The critical question for the less favoured regions is whether globalization represents the centralization or decentralization of development opportunities. There is a sense in the business literature that transnational corporations are no longer the stereotype of old, that is, large, centrally controlled, vertically integrated organizations practising a rigidly uneven distribution of responsibilities between affiliates. Instead, it is claimed, volatile markets, new technologies and the rigidities of vertical integration have forced corporations to slim operations down, make affiliates more autonomous and multi-functional, and rely much more on subcontracting, joint ventures and alliances. The implication for regions of this shift towards decentralized patterns of organization is that it promises greater scope for local autonomy and local linkage formation.

As far as the less favoured regions are concerned, however, the available evidence does not reveal any significant upgrading in the status and development potential of inward investment (see Chapters 8, 9 and 10, by Amin and Tomaney, Giunta and Martinelli, and Peters, in this volume). Traditionally important cost factors such as low wages, unorganized labour and the availability of incentives continue to remain the most important location factors in such regions (Nam *et al.* 1991). Whatever evidence there is to be found of plant upgrading in the less favoured regions, it appears to be the outcome of changes introduced to existing plants in the course of time (Amin and Tomaney, Chapter 8 in this volume; Young *et al.* 1994 and in this volume), rather than the effect of any decision to locate a new type of branch plant. Thus the less favoured regions continue to house investments with relatively poor local economic development potential, with globalization representing disembodied investment, external domination of local markets, and disconnection between the indigenous and the influential 'non-indigenous' corporate sector. If globalization is encouraging more region-centred networks of production, this is likely to be happening in resource-rich regions (e.g. the islands of innovation and metropolitan areas of Europe mentioned earlier) which are able to secure and support the complex requirements of the new type of business unit (skills, R&D, management ability, advanced services, supply chains, etc.). Such an outcome will not be to the advantage of less favoured regions.

As we have already seen, the central thrust of EU policies has been to strengthen the role of large firms in ways designed to improve the competitiveness of 'European' industry. As one observer puts it somewhat starkly, the EU represents 'a union of multinational business interests', constituting a new power bloc in which 'the new sovereign will be the multinational managers, their administrative capital will be Brussels and their flag of convenience that of the EEC' (Hilyard 1993: 43). If the 'multinational managers' run their European operations from the most advanced regions, the less favoured regions will find themselves competing only for global investment that promises little in terms of growth opportunities, since it will be placed in such regions for cost-reducing purposes ('social dumping'), rather than 'performance'-enhancing opportunities.

Social fragmentation and social exclusion

One of the starkest consequences of the slow-down of post-war growth and the breakdown of the political consensus which surrounded it has been growing social fragmentation, to the point of threatening social cohesion.

One manifestion is the problem of long-term mass unemployment, which now confronts all European states, rich or poor. This development is partly the outcome of global stagnation, but is also the result of the labour-displacing effects of new technology. In addition, among those who have been marginalized from active work, there have developed sharp divisions between casual and seasonal workers, those surviving in the informal economy through a variety of activities and those who are forced into poverty and degradation (Mingione 1991). The Victorian nightmare of a large and highly differentiated 'displaced' section of society has returned to haunt the whole of Europe. In countries facing major fiscal or budgetary constraints on welfare expenditure, or in those countries like Britain governed by parties committed to market individualism, this displacement risks becoming a form of permanent social exclusion: exclusion from the mainstream in all senses – economic, social, political and cultural.

The world of work, too, is becoming increasingly fragmented. The shift away from mass production and giant industrial complexes has seen the rise of subcontracting, task devolvement and disengagement by firms from non-essential tasks. The net result has been the growth of dual labour markets, in which relatively stable, well paid and 'socially protected' employees receiving pension coverage and other welfare entitlements coexist with others engaged in poorly-paid, temporary or part-time 'un-protected' work. The distinction is drawn between high-wage/high-skill economies underpinned by investment, innovation and state support (e.g. Germany, northern Italy) and low-wage/low-skill economies like Portugal, Greece and Britain, based on price competitiveness and limited or reduced state intervention (Leborgne and Lipietz 1990; Nolan 1994). Importantly, however, moves towards 'lean production' and the like mean many of those remaining in employment are experiencing an intensification of work and growing insecurity (Tomaney 1994a).

The fragmentation of labour markets and social exclusion are two phenomena which are developing a permanence that risks becoming seen as a 'structural inevitability' by the policy community. There is a danger that Europe could turn its back on problems of labour exploitation, low wages, lack of work, poverty and social marginalization on the grounds that these are 'natural' problems of the post-full employment society. Such an out-come will severely impair any prospect of achieving social cohesion, and will create a politically volatile division between the prosperous or secure sections of the EU and the less prosperous or marginalized groups con-centrated in the less favoured regions or in the major cities of Europe (Minc 1992). The EU recognizes the threat, and much of the 1993 White Paper *Growth, Competitiveness and Employment* expresses concern over this scenario. Yet a key theme, as noted earlier, remains the need to reduce non-wage labour costs, while the Maastricht Treaty poses the threat of harsh fiscal pressures on hard-pressed welfare states.

European Community policy on the problem of labour market fragmentation is a mixture of misconception and frustrated endeavour. At the level of rhetoric, the 1993 White Paper firmly commits the EU to the goal of full employment. In practice, however, the EC's integration policies, rooted in free-market economics, and supported by the White Paper, continue to remain a *source* of unemployment, and also a tacit endorsement of the dual labour markets generated by firms in their search for greater flexibility. As we noted earlier, the development of the 'Social Dimension' has rarely got past the intergovernmental structures of the EU, while the proposals in the White Paper for Keynesian-style investment in infrastructure have yet to materialize. Commenting on the Maastricht resolutions on social policy, Streeck (1994: 172) argues:

> Maastricht extended 'subsidiarity' to management and labour without enabling the weaker group, labour, to make a stronger one, management, bargain in good faith. Subsidiarity of this kind amounts to little else than the provision of a veto right to those whose interest is in non-decisions, and whose preferred policy is to protect the free market from political negotiation; rather than self-governance, all it suggests is voluntarism of the stronger.

A similar tension is echoed in the EC's stance on social exclusion. Here too there is overt recognition of the undesirability of exclusion both on intrinsic grounds and as a threat to social stability. However, national governments have jealously guarded their sovereignty over welfare policy. Though there is support elsewhere in the EU (e.g. in the European Parliament) for some form of 'fiscal federalism' which would serve to create a revenue base, allowing automatic revenue transfers to those most in need, the Council of Ministers steadfastly opposes such proposals, for fear of losing control over national welfare programmes.

The problem of social fragmentation and social exclusion, thus, though recognized as a problem, continues to remain a major threat to the cohesion of the EU.

Hollowing out, neo-liberalism and the nation state

A final 'structural' change likely to affect cohesion in Europe relates to the reach of the nation state. Hitherto the nation state and its institutions have exerted the main public policy influence on outcomes in less favoured regions and disadvantaged communities, through the use of active regional policies, income redistribution schemes and welfare programmes. In the field of international political economy the view is emerging that the role of the nation state as the principal instrument of national cohesion is under threat. It is argued that structural transformations in the world political economy such as the globalization of production, finance and markets, the rise of transnational 'plural authority' structures (including transnational corporations, the UN, the G7, the EU, etc.), and the growth of regionalist movements are challenging the traditional authority and reach of the nation state (Jessop 1994; Sally 1994; Harvie 1994; Hirst 1994). This process of 'hollowing out' of the nation state is said to represent, in essence, two transformations: first, reduced significance of the nation state as the principal or sole governance authority; second, reorientation of state priorities in the direction of securing global competitiveness.

As regards the first transformation, the argument is that globalization and regionalism are forcing the nation state simultaneously to concede power upwards to supra-national institutions (the EU is an obvious example) and downwards to local institutions with detailed knowledge of the strengths and weaknesses of individual regions. Thus there is pressure for certain functions dealing with issues articulated on a transnational scale (e.g. security, migration, competition, financial markets, industrial organization) to be transferred to the appropriate international organizations, or executed on an intergovernmental basis. Similarly there is pressure for other functions, notably the provision of supply-side support for entrepreneurship (e.g. infrastructural improvements, labour market adjustments, support for inward investors, technical and financial assistance to firms) to be devolved to local organizations with better on-the-ground knowledge (Swyngedouw 1992; Begg and Mayes 1993a; Young and Hood, Chapter 11 of this volume).

The second transformation concerns a reorientation of nation-state policy priorities. Globalization is said to have weakened the ability of national governments to rely on traditional measures such as trade and exchange controls, monetary or credit policies, and national industrial policy, in order to protect the national economy. At the same time, globalization appears to have made it an imperative for nation states to develop economic policies orientated towards securing global competitiveness, at the expense of growth models orientated towards the domestic economy (Reich 1991). For one observer (Jessop 1994) the national Keynesian welfare state is being replaced by a 'Schumpeterian workfare state' driven by the rules of global competition. Jessop argues that the breakdown of national growth strategies centred on the mass production–mass consumption norm has led to a reduced national commitment to Keynesian strategies orientated towards boosting output and productivity in domestic industry and maintaining high levels of domestic demand. This challenge to Keynesianism is said to involve, on the one hand, the slackening of industrial and regional policies designed to maximize output and retain full employment, and, on the other hand, the erosion of the welfare state, income redistribution policies and controls on trade and exchange rates as a means of sustaining the domestic market.

Faced with these apparently ineluctable. tendencies, contemporary economic policies are seen to be increasingly reduced to supply-side measures alone, as nation states reject the possibility of a virtuous circle of growth based on the 'national economy' as an integrated system of production and consumption. The new state form is said to represent a number of changes in the direction of economic policy. First, in the new global economy, the commitment to regulate trade in favour of domestic industry is eschewed, as is the commitment to underpin demand via welfare expenditure, income redistribution and so on. Instead, domestic economic policy is seen as shifting increasingly towards supporting internationally competitive entrepreneurship and innovation. Second, the state is compelled to divert resources by indirect measures to boost the competitiveness of private industry, through such schemes as training programmes, innovation and technology transfer support, help for small firms, and infrastructural improvements (ranging from the supply of land and premises to the upgrading of transport and communications networks). Third, however, economic globalization is said to turn state policy much more towards initiatives designed explicitly to make the supply side of the domestic economy more attractive to inward investment, and to force macro-economic policy (especially monetary policy) to be attentive to externally influenced interest rates, monetary fluctuations and national indebtedness. In other words, domestic policy becomes more and more driven by external events. Finally, welfare policies are said to become less concerned with the needs of the unemployed and the economically marginal groups in society (since national consumption is no longer part of the 'growth equation') and more concentrated on reproducing the economically most active groups.

This 'hollowing out' thesis is not uncontested, with critics arguing that the tendencies described above are more a characterization of deliberate choices made by governments committed to the market principles of neo-liberalism than the outcome of an inevitable institutional logic (Amin and Tomaney 1995; Peck and Tickell 1994). Drawing on the example of successful economies underpinned by active state intervention, such as Germany, Sweden and Japan, the critics argue that in at least three areas national policy action remains crucial for securing regional and national economic success. This includes intervention in the area of corporate and strategic industrial governance (Lazonick 1993; Porter 1990), constructing national systems of innovation and learning (Lundvall 1992; Mjøset 1993) and the pursuit of policies to build high-quality labour markets (Peck 1994; Teague, Chapter 6 of this volume). All three are areas of active national state investment and involvement (see Amin and Tomaney 1995 for further details).

Whatever the correct explanation, the belief that economic policy can amount to little more than supply-side intervention has growing resonance in Europe for an increasing number of governments either consciously dedicated to market economics or forced by budgetary or fiscal constraints to cut back and re-focus expenditure programmes. In addition, and importantly, the scenario appears to be gaining strength in EU intergovernmental negotiations, and is already reflected in current EU integration policies (e.g. Delors 1989). As already discussed, the EC's competitiveness policies are orientated towards larger corporate interests, while its macro-economic 'convergence' criteria place considerable pressure on national fiscal and monetary autonomy. Similarly, the Commission's 'Europe of regions' agenda, designed to strengthen the links between EU institutions and regional institutions as a counterbalance to national regulation, is a perfect illustration of the 'hollowing out' scenario of synergy between supranational and regional governance.

The question to be raised is how well 'hollowing out', neo-liberalism or a 'Europe of regions' will work in terms of securing European cohesion. The idea of a permanent weakening of the nation state's ability to operate a successful macro-economic or industrial policy has stark implications for the less favoured regions. Most obviously, the logic implies a reduction in the level of direct state support for industry in the less favoured regions, as the commitment to regional incentives is reduced, as the state disengages from or restructures industry under its ownership, as it deregulates public utilities and services, and as it ceases to direct public procurement contracts to firms located in the less favoured regions. Such disengagement would eliminate what has hitherto been an important mainstay of economic activity and employment in the less favoured regions.

Meanwhile, policies based on tight monetary control, fiscal stringency, the removal of controls on corporate behaviour (for instance, through liberal competition laws) and reduced subsidies to industry would erode many of the instruments that have served to provide a 'protective' framework for less competitive firms in the less favoured regions to develop and grow. Such policies would expose the less favoured regions to market forces working in favour of the most powerful or most competitive firms in the national and international economy and to the detriment of weaker forms of entrepreneurship. In addition, a reduction in welfare expenditure in the name of relieving the burden on business would particularly threaten the less favoured regions in which low-income and marginalized groups are disproportionately concentrated. Paradoxically, such cut-backs would also serve to threaten the knowledge and skill formation processes which are central to innovation-orientated, supply-side policies for growth. It would impede the less favoured regions from developing key factors for successful local economic development.

The danger of an approach which focuses state priorities only on sections of the economy and of society capable of gaining a foothold in the global economy is that it will serve merely to strengthen the economies of the most competitive cities and regions, leaving it to the market to deal with – or exacerbate – the problems of the less favoured regions.

In terms of institution building, as well, a solution based on a partnership between Europe and the regions that sidesteps the nation state is not likely to work in favour of the less favoured regions. In many senses, regionalism is most vociferously espoused by the strongest regions in Europe. The banner of a 'Europe of regions' is vigorously waved in cases such as the 'Four Motors for Europe' project, which has created a co-operation network between four of Europe's economically strongest regions (Baden-Württemburg, Rhône-Alpes, Lombardia and Catalonia). The less favoured regions, in contrast, will struggle to develop the institutional capacity that can empower them with real representational power and voice (Amin and Thrift 1995; Bianchi 1992). It is precisely the absence of adequate structures of representation and political power within the less favoured regions that has necessitated historical reliance upon the nation state for resources, development opportunities and representation. While institutional empowerment within such regions, of course, cannot be judged as anything other than desirable, it has to be acknowledged that the process will require time and a measure of insulation from forces working to the advantage of the more prosperous regions.

For the moment there is no European super-state waiting in the wings to take up the guardianship of Europe's less favoured regions. Commission policies on cohesion expect the regions themselves to develop institutional capacity, while broader EU efforts to facilitate collaboration between regions and to establish a Committee of the Regions remain at best, as Marks (1992) has indicated, a weak link in a chain of decision-making and resource allocation within an EU commanded by the Council of Ministers (i.e. by negotiations between nation states). Thus, from the perspective of the less favoured regions, there is a risk that a 'Europe of regions' agenda will place them in an institutional vacuum as they struggle to develop a 'voice' without support from the wider polity.

In summary, the five structural and institutional transformations which have been discussed in this section are developments which do not bode well for regional or social cohesion in the EU. Contemporary EC policies offer little in the way of dampening or reversing the anti-cohesion effects of these developments.

PERSPECTIVES ON COHESION

The contributions in this book offer a critical perspective on the implications of contemporary processes and policies of European integration for social and regional cohesion. They argue for an alternative, more interventionist, framework to neo-liberalism as a basis for achieving cohesion.

The book is divided into four parts. The first part examines the macro-economic policy environment of cohesion. It debates the merits and weaknesses of the market-led route to economic expansion and regional development in Europe. In Chapter 2 Sean Shepley and Jonathan Wilmot defend the market perspective on convergence and cohesion in Europe, basing their argument in particular on the role of migration, labour flexibility and trade specialization in facilitating a division of roles between core regions and the less favoured regions. The three chapters which follow, in contrast, argue that such a perspective, already embraced by European economic integration policies, will threaten cohesion by encouraging unemployment, social exclusion, unstable growth and the spatial concentration of economic activity. In Chapter 3 Jonathan Michie develops a systematic critique of the neo-liberal vision of European integration, associating it with rising inequality and mass unemployment. He argues that in the absence of a comprehensive policy package in support of sustained growth and full employment there remains little scope for cohesion.

Chapters 4 and 5, respectively by Iain Begg and Michael Dunford, focus on the regional implications of EU policies. Ian Begg, in contrast to Shepley and Wilmot, suggests that market failure is to be expected from EMU, hence it is unrealistic to expect a narrowing of regional disparities without greater public intervention in the form of automatic redistribution of income to the less favoured regions and without close Europe-wide monitoring of the structural problems facing individual regions. In similar vein, Michael Dunford argues that high levels of macro-economic growth during the 1960s, underpinned by Keynesian expansionist policies, resulted in convergence between the regions, while contemporary low levels of growth, underpinned by market-driven and deflationary policies, have fuelled divergence. He argues the case for a package of reforms, including the pursuit of reflationary policies, European fiscal federalism, policies to decentralize investment and new supply-side interventions within the less favoured regions, as essentials for regional convergence in Europe.

The second part of the book focuses on the social dimension of cohesion. In contrast to the pure market option, which calls for wage controls and labour market flexibility, it argues the case for an extension and deepening of European social policy. It defends active intervention in the labour market and an enhanced role for the trade unions in economic governance as a basis for facilitating industrial reconversion towards competitiveness based on skills and high value-added sectors. Though it accepts that major regional differences in labour markets and workplace conditions will continue to exist owing to inherited industrial traditions, it maintains that social cohesion will not be attained in the absence of Europe-wide practices defending the right to work, the right of social inclusion and the right of worker participation in economic decision-making.

In Chapter 6 Paul Teague develops a critique of the fashionable contemporary argument that industrial relations and labour markets are becoming, or should become, more regionalized in a 'Europe of regions'. He argues that the nation state will, and should, continue to play a central role in regulating labour markets, since regionalization is both unrealistic and undesirable, owing to its fragmenting effects on labour. He makes a case for inter-regional equity of opportunity in labour markets based on national negotiations, and for Europe-wide resolutions based on co-operative intergovernmentalism in the EU. In Chapter 7 Harvie Ramsay explores the threat to social cohesion represented by the growing power of transnational corporations in Europe. He argues that rules related to the single European market are strengthening the hand of such corporations at the expense of workers and labour organizations by increasing unemployment, 'social dumping', labour market flexibility and trade union weakness. In order to redress the balance in favour of employees, Ramsay proposes the pursuit of a strengthened European Social Policy with greater vigour and comprehensiveness (notably Social Charter clauses on the right to join a union, to bargain collectively and to strike), together with trade union reforms which facilitate transnational worker networks.

The third part of the book explores the question of regional cohesion by focusing on the changing relationship between large firms and less favoured regions in the new Europe. It asks whether contemporary patterns of corporate restructuring in response to the single European market are favouring the development prospects of Europe's less favoured regions. It concludes that the dominant pattern appears to be concentration of economic activity and economic power in the core regions, and either only partial revitalization of the less favoured regions or their insertion into wider global corporate networks on unfavourable terms. In Chapter 8 Ash Amin and John Tomaney examine whether the development potential of inward investment in selected European less favoured regions is increasing as an outcome of processes of corporate restructuring and plant-level upgrading associated with the single market. They conclude that on the rare occasions when upgrading has occurred it appears to have been a result of gradual changes within established branch investments, supported by innovative forms of intervention from regional development agencies, rather than of any change in the quality of new inward investment within the less favoured regions.

Chapters 9 and 10, respectively by Anna Giunta and Flavia Martinelli, and Ewen Peters, explore the implications of corporate restructuring by focusing on two case study regions. Chapter 9 by Anna Giunta and Flavia Martinelli tells the story of widespread capacity rationalization in the context of corporate responses to globalization or to the single market as well as the tale of little improvement in the regional development capacity of plants which have survived. The authors argue the case for a strengthened regional policy, but one which is capable of negotiating local guarantees (e.g. local supply networks, investment in R&D or training) from inward investors in exchange of financial incentives. Ewen Peters examines the prospects for Scotland associated with reorganization and rationalization in the global electronics industry. He argues that the latter represents a narrowing of opportunities for intermediate regions such as Scotland (notwithstanding their proactive development agencies), since they find themselves trapped between high value-added locations such as California and low-cost locations such as South East Asia.

Stephen Young and Neil Hood focus in Chapter 11 on policy changes which are deemed necessary to maximize the impact of inward investment on host regional economies as companies reposition themselves in the single market. They emphasize the merits of developing agencies which can target investors and offer 'after-care' support as a basis for strengthening the local ties of inward investors. They also stress the significance of including a regional dimension in EU merger, acquisition and joint venture policy as a basis for avoiding outcomes with negative consequences in less favoured regions.

The final part of the book articulates the basic framework of an anti-neo-liberal approach to cohesion. Building on reforms suggested in individual chapters, the editors argue in Chapter 12 that without substantial changes at both European and national level in the direction of managed interventionism working explicitly in favour of weaker regions and weaker sections of society there remains little scope for cohesion. The chapter resurrects the principle of the managed economy as a solution to be applied at a European level, but also cautions against an approach that fails to encourage local solutions or to take account of the enduring importance of the nation state. It makes a case for a return to Keynesian expansionist principles but goes further to stress the role of decentralized industrial policies, measures to tackle the growing power of transnational companies, policies to extend social democracy and strategies which place regional concerns at the heart of national and European economic policy directives. It argues that tackling the cohesion question should be seen as a means of promoting growth rather than as an adjunct to it. It concludes, however, that the key challenge posed by an alternative agenda for cohesion is to create a Europe that is driven by democratic politics at the level of Europe, the nation state and the region, instead of allowing the market and its institutions to shape questions of economic efficiency and social equity in Europe.

REFERENCES

Albrechts, L., Hardy, S., Hart, M., and Katos, A. (1993) *An Enlarged Europe: Regions in Competition*, London: Jessica Kingsley.

Albrechts, L., Moulaert, F., Roberts, P., and Swyngedouw, E. (eds) (1989) *Regional Policy at the Crossroads*, London: Jessica Kingsley.

Amin, A. (ed.) (1994) *Post-Fordism: a Reader*, Oxford: Blackwell.

Amin, A., and Dietrich, M. (1991) 'From hierarchy to "hierarchy": the dynamics of contemporary corporate restructuring in Europe', in A. Amin and M. Dietrich (eds) *Towards a New Europe?* Aldershot: Elgar.

Amin, A., and Thrift, N. (1992) 'Neo-Marshallian nodes in global networks', *International Journal of Urban and Regional Research* 16, 4: 571–87.

Amin, A., and Thrift, N. (1994) 'Living in the global', in, A. Amin and N. Thrift (eds), *Globalization, Institutions and Regional Development in Europe*, Oxford: Oxford University Press.

Amin, A., and Thrift, N. (1995) 'Institutional issues for the European regions: from markets and plans to socio-economics and powers of association', *Economy and Society*, 24, 1: 41–66.

Amin, A., and Tomaney, J. (1995) 'The regional dilemma in a neo-liberal Europe', *European Urban and Regional Studies*, forthcoming.

Amin, A., Charles, D., and Howells, J. (1992) 'Corporate restructuring and cohesion in the new Europe', *Regional Studies* 26, 4: 319–31.

Begg, I., and Mayes, D. (1991) *A New Strategy for Social and Economic Cohesion after 1992*, Luxembourg: Office of Official Publications of the European Community.

Begg, I., and Mayes, D. (1993a) 'Cohesion, convergence and economic and monetary union', *Regional Studies*, 27, 2: 149–65.

Begg, I., and Mayes, D. (1993b) 'The Case for Decentralised Industrial Policy', mimeo, Department of Applied Economics, University of Cambridge.

Bianchi, P. (1992) 'Industrial strategy and structural policies', in K. Cowling and R. Sugden (eds) *Current Issues in Industrial Economic Strategy*, Manchester: Manchester University Press.

Camagni, R. (1992) 'Development scenarios and policy guidelines for the lagging regions in the 1990s', *Regional Studies* 26, 4: 361–74.

Castells, M., and Hall, P. (1994) *Technopoles of the World*, London: Routledge.

Cecchini, P. (1988) *The European Challenge, 1992*, Aldershot: Wildwood House.

Collier, J. (1994) 'Regional disparities, the single market and European monetary union', in J. Michie and J. Grieve Smith (eds) *Unemployment in Europe*, London: Academic Press.

Commission of the European Communities (1974) 'The Social Action Programme', *Bulletin of the European Communities* 10: 370–80.

Commission of the European Communities (1985) *Completing the Internal Market: White Paper from the Commission to the European Parliament*, Luxembourg: Commission of the European Communities.

Commission of the European Communities (1990a) 'One market, one money', *European Economy* 44, Brussels: Commission of the European Communities.

Commission of the European Communities (1990b) *Charter of Fundamental Social Rights for Workers* (the Social Charter). Brussels: Commission of the European Communities.

Commission of the European Communities (1991) *The Regions in the 1990s* (the Fourth Periodic Report on the social and economic situation and development of the regions of the Community), Luxembourg: Commission of the European Communities.

Commission of the European Communities (1992) *From the Single Act to Maastricht and Beyond: the Means to Match our Ambitions.* COM(92) 2001. Brussels: Commission of the European Communities.

Cooke, P., and Morgan, K. (1993) 'The network paradigm: new departures in corporate and regional development', *Environment and Planning D: Society and Space* 11: 543–64.

Crouch, C., and Marquand, D. (eds) (1990) *The Politics of 1992: Beyond the Single European Market*, Oxford: Blackwell.

Delors, J. (1989) 'Regional implications of economic and monetary integration', in Committee for the Study of Economic and Monetary Union, *Report on Economic and Monetary Union in the European Community*, Brussels: Commission of the European Communities.

Dicken, P., Forsgren, M., and Malmberg, A. (1994) 'The local embeddedness of transnational corporations', in A. Amin and N. Thrift (eds) *Globalisation, Institutions and Regional Development in Europe*, Oxford: Oxford University Press,

Doyle, M. F. (1989) 'Regional policy and European economic integration', in Committee for the Study of Economic and Monetary Union, *Report on Economic and Monetary Union in the European Community*, Brussels: Commission of the European Communities.

Dunford, M., and Kafkalas, G. (eds) (1992) *Cities, Regions and the New Europe*, London: Belhaven.

Dunford, M., and Perrons, D. (1994) 'Regional inequality, regimes of accumulation and economic development in contemporary Europe', *Transactions of the Institute of British Geographers* 19: 163–82.

Dunning, J. (1993) *The Globalization of Business*, London: Routledge.

Eurostat (1994a) *Rapid Reports Regions 94/1* (*Per capita* GDP in the Regions of the Community in 1991), Luxembourg: Eurostat.

Eurostat (1994b) *Rapid Reports Regions 94/2* (Unemployment in the Regions of the Community in 1993), Luxembourg: Eurostat.

FAST/Monitor (1992) *Archipelago Europe: Islands of Innovation*, Science, Technology and Economic Cohesion 18 (FOP 242), Brussels: Commission of the European Union.

Geroski, P. (1989) 'The choice between diversity and scale', in Centre for Business Strategy *1992: Myths and Realities*, London: London Business School.

Grahl, J., and Teague, P. (1990) *1992: The Big Market*, London: Lawrence & Wishart.

Grimes, S. (1992) 'Exploiting information and communication technologies for rural development', *Journal of Rural Studies* 8, 3: 269–78.

Hankel, W. (1994) 'Maastricht's EMU is too much, too soon', in Philip Morris Institute, *Is European Monetary Union Dead?* Paper No. 3, Brussels: Philip Morris Institute.

Harvie, C. (1994) *The Rise of Regional Europe*, London: Routledge.

Hilyard, N. (1993) 'Maastricht: the protectionism of free trade', *Ecologist* 23, 2: 45–51.

Hirst, P. (1994) *Associative Democracy*, Cambridge: Polity.

Holland, S. (1993) *The European Imperative: Economic and Social Cohesion in the 1990s*, Nottingham: Spokesman.

Hughes Hallett, A., and Scott, D. (1992) *Monetary Union and the Regions* (Final Report to the Confederation of Scottish Local Authorities), Edinburgh: CoSLA.

Jessop, B. (1994) 'Post-Fordism and the state', in A. Amin (ed.) *Post-Fordism: Reader*, Oxford: Blackwell.

Krugman, P. (1991) *Geography and Trade*, Cambridge, Mass.: MIT Press.

Lange, P. (1992) 'The politics of the social dimension', in A. Sbragia (ed.) *Euro-politics: Institutions and Policymaking in the 'New' European Community*, Washington, D.C.: Brookings Institution.

Lazonick, W. (1993) 'Industry clusters versus global webs: organizational capabilities in the American economy', *Structural Change and Economic Dynamics* 4: 1–24.

Leborgne, D., and Lipietz, A. (1990) 'How to avoid a two-tier Europe', *Labour and Society* 15, 2: 177–99.

Lundvall, B-A. (ed.) (1992) *National Systems of Innovation*, London: Pinter.

MacDougall, D. (1977) *Report of the Study Group on the Role of Public Finance in European Integration General Report*, Brussels: Commission of the European Communities.

Marks, G. (1992) 'Structural policy in the European Community', in A. Sbragia (ed.) *Euro-Politics: Institutions and Policymaking in the 'New' European Community*, Washington, D.C.: Brookings Institution.

Matzner, E., and Streeck, W. (1991) 'Towards a socio-economics of employment in a post-Keynesian society', in E. Matzner and W. Streeck (eds) *Beyond Keynesianism*, Aldershot: Elgar.

Michie, J., and Grieve Smith, J. (eds) (1994) *Unemployment in Europe*, London: Academic Press.

Minc, A. (1992) *The Great European Illusion: Business in the Wider Community*, Oxford: Blackwell.

Mingione, E. (1991) *Fragmented Societies: a Sociology of Economic Life beyond the Market Paradigm*, Oxford: Blackwell.

Mjøset, L. (1993) *The Irish Economy in a Comparative Institutional Perspective*, Report No. 93, Dublin: NESC.

Nam, C. W., Russ, H., and Herb, G. (1991) *The Effect of 1992 and Associated Legislation on the Less Favoured Regions of the Community*, Report to the European Parliament. Munich: Institut für Wirtschaftsforschung.

Nolan, P. (1994) 'Labour market institutions, industrial restructuring and unemployment in Europe', in J. Michie and J. Grieve Smith (eds) *Unemployment in Europe*, London: Academic Press.

O'Donnell, R. (1992) 'Policy requirements for regional balance in economic and monetary union', in: A. Hannequart (ed.) *Economic and Social Cohesion in Europe*, London: Routledge.

O'Donnell, R. (1993) *Ireland and Europe: Challenges for a New Century*, ESRI Policy Research Services Paper No. 17, Dublin: Economic and Social Research Institute.

Peck, J. (1994) 'Regulating labour: the social regulation and reproduction of local labour markets', in A. Amin and N. Thrift (eds) *Globalisation, Institutions and Regional Development in Europe*, Oxford: Oxford University Press.

Peck, J., and Tickell, A. (1994) 'Searching for a new institutional fix: the *after* Fordist crisis and the global–local disorder', in A. Amin (ed). *Post-Fordism: a Reader*, Oxford: Blackwell.

Peschel, K. (1992) 'European integration and regional development in northern Europe', *Regional Studies* 26, 4: 387–97.

Porter, M. (1990) *The Competitive Advantage of Nations*, London: Macmillan.

Reich, R. (1991) The Work of Nations, New York: Random House.

Sally, R. (1994) 'Multinational enterprises, political economy and institutional theory: domestic embeddedness in the context of internationalisation', *Review of International Political Economy* 1, 1: 161–92.

Scott, A. (1994) 'Financing the Community: the Delors II package', in J. Lodge (ed.) *The European Community and the Challenge of the Future*, second edition, London: Frances Pinter.

Silvia, S. (1991) 'The Social Charter of the European Community: a defeat for European labour', *Industrial and Labour Relations Review* 44, 4: 626–43.

Springer, B. (1992) *The Social Dimension of 1992: Europe faces a New EC*, New York: Praeger.

Storper, M. (1994) 'Territorial economies in a global economy: what possibilities for middle-income countries and their regions?' *Review of International Political Economy*, forthcoming.

Streeck, W. (1994) 'European social policy after Maastricht: the "social Dialogue" and "Subsidiarity"', *Economic and Industrial Democracy* 15: 151–77.

Swyngedouw, E. (1992) 'The Mammon quest. "Glocalisation", interspatial competition and the monetary order: the construction of new scales', in M. Dunford and G. Kafkalas (eds) *Cities and Regions in the New Europe*, London: Belhaven.

Teague, P., and Grahl, J. (1993) *Industrial Relations and European Integration*, London: Lawrence & Wishart.

Thompson, G. (1993) *The Economic Emergence of a New Europe? The Political Economy of Co-operation and Competition in the 1990s*, Cheltenham: Edward Elgar.

Tomaney, J. (1994a) 'A new paradigm of work and technology?' in A. Amin (ed) *Post-Fordism: a Reader*, Oxford: Blackwell.

Tomaney, J. (1994b) 'Regional and industrial aspects of unemployment in Europe', in J. Michie and J. Grieve Smith (eds) *Unemployment in Europe*, London: Academic Press.

Young, S., Hood, N., and Peters, E. (1994) 'Multinational enterprises and regional economic development', *Regional Studies* 28, 7: 657–77.

Part I

MACRO-ECONOMIC CHANGE

2

CORE VS. PERIPHERY

Sean Shepley and Jonathan Wilmot

CORE AND PERIPHERIES

At the heart of the great European debate lies the issue of convergence between the rich core and the poorer periphery, or rather peripheries, for there are now several.

Discussion tends to focus on macro-economic variables and national economic performance, as in the convergence criteria attached to the Maastricht Treaty. We look instead at the micro-economic side of economic adjustment, particularly those factors that determine the location of industries, population and jobs.

Our inspiration has been recent work by professor Paul Krugman of MIT (1991). He refines some old but usually forgotten ideas about why firms and workers find it advantageous to cluster together, and how this results in densely populated industrial cores surrounded by relatively poor, sparsely populated, rural peripheries. The arguments matter in themselves but also have implications for the ERM, EMU, the Maastricht Treaty debate, and how location will affect business profitability in the 1990s. Four themes stand out: Germany's privileged position at the heart of the new European market; the case for more imports and fewer immigrants from the EC's poorer neighbours; the case for more flexible labour markets and exchange rates in the run up to EMU; and the case for promoting greater economic specialization by region.

Migration or capital flows

Economic development proceeds in one or both of two contrasting ways:

1 By capital accumulation and technological catch-up in poorer regions, often spurred by a flow of capital, technology and management skills from richer areas, producing a flow of goods and services back the other way.
2 Via labour migration from poorer regions to an existing concentration of

51

capital, an industrial core, which lives partly by exporting finished products to the periphery.

If the first effect dominates, we have convergence; if the second, polarization. If both are of similar importance, then *per capita* incomes in the two areas converge, but the absolute importance of the core increases. However, polarization may be more efficient than convergence if industry is more productive when concentrated and total GDP is higher than if population and industry are evenly dispersed. Cities and industrial cores exploit these efficiencies through a swarming process where capital attracts labour, which increases market size, which attracts new capital, etc. By contrast, rapid catch-up by the US and Germany with Britain after 1870 and by Japan and Europe with the US after 1945 illustrate how convergence can occur over long periods through new industries and new cores.

Both forms of adjustment occur continuously, but their relative importance varies. Adjustment among US regions relies quite heavily on migration away from declining regions. When old industries die, labour moves in search of new expanding industries elsewhere (promoting convergence in the negative sense that total output falls in the declining region but *per capita* output rises as people emigrate). If the new industries happen to locate in the poorer regions, convergence occurs in a more positive sense too. But low-cost labour is seldom the key reason behind new industry location within the US.[1] Indeed, US output and population remain remarkably concentrated in the north-east industrial belt, with convergence mostly based on the formation of new cores around specific new industries, for example in California and the oil states.

In Europe capital movements have dominated in recent decades. In particular, Spain and the UK provided a powerful model of convergence in the 1980s based on capital inflows and rapid productivity growth. This followed structural improvements in both economies. Spain's caused by the move to democracy and subsequent entry to the EC, the UK's by the pro-business climate of the Thatcher years. This model of European convergence – relatively low wages, supply-side liberalization and financial discipline combining to attract new capital and technology – was an attractive one, partly helping to explain the euphoria in 1991 about the hard ERM and EMU. It is now clear that the 1990s will be more complex. To illustrate, we use some simple models of industrial location to analyse three overlapping 'shocks':

1 German unification and the opening of Eastern Europe, which we describe as the arrival of a vital new eastern 'periphery' to compete with the old south-western/Anglo-Saxon periphery within the existing EC.
2 The spread of new technologies and working methods.
3 The completion of the single market, which we model as primarily a

52

reduction in 'trading' costs (everything from the abolition of customs documents, through actual transport costs, to mutual acceptance of standards).

The single market and technological change

Will the single market promote convergence by helping poorer regions attract investment and develop special industrial skills? This effect already seems to work in some areas (Wales in electronics, for example) but is not the only possible result. Simple models of location show that a cut in trading costs can have the opposite effect, encouraging concentration, if the benefits from the scale economies of production in the core outweigh the advantages of lower wage costs in the periphery. It is changes in the relationship between scale economies and trading costs that are crucial to location. The single market or new infrastructure links affect location by reducing trading costs; new technology by altering scale economies.

Steel is an interesting example: refined 'mini-mill' technology promotes greater decentralization whilst, simultaneously, thin strip casting is encouraging the growth in size of established plants in the centre of the EC. Low-cost labour from the new regions (Korea, Brazil and especially Eastern Europe) is another factor. The net effect of these different forces is likely to be: (1) another (big) fall in the industry's employment in the EC, (2) the virtual elimination of medium-sized companies and plants, and (3) a surprising trend for a low-wage country like Spain to lose market share to core regions like North Rhine-Westphalia.

Steel (Figure 2.1) shows how poor regions can lose from structural change. Precise dynamics vary by industry, so predicting overall winners

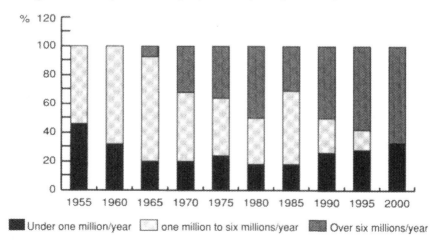

Figure 2.1 Market share, by crude steel production volume of the firm

and losers is difficult. However, US industry is about twice as localized as industry in Europe, so greater European regional specialization is to be expected. Though specialization is more efficient, the transition will be painful: some regions could be (big) net losers, all the more so as new industries, once established, maintain their initial location for decades. This period of accelerated structural change suggests the need for either activist regional policies (which have a very poor record within countries precisely because they work against the industrial logic of location) or increased labour market flexibility, or somewhat greater exchange rate flexibility, or a combination of all three.

Europe of the regions

As Krugman (1991: 70) puts it, the economic benefits of locating close together arise

> from the standard Marshallian Trinity of labour market pooling, supply of intermediate goods and knowledge spillovers. All three of these probably typically arise at the level of the single city or small cluster of cities, an area small enough to make it possible for people to change jobs without changing houses, for hard-to-transport goods and services to be delivered, and for regular personal contact to take place.

Such benefits can and sometimes do flow across national borders. Someone living in Maastricht (the Netherlands) could work in Belgium, France or Germany without moving home, provided only that they speak the appropriate language. North America's car industry is located either side of the Canada–US border (and if it moves is most likely to become concentrated either side of the Mexico–US border).

Governments can restrict the free movement of labour, goods, services and capital, even if indirectly via national policies on regulations or taxes. Remove 'national' policies and, analytically speaking, nations become irrelevant. So completion of the single market should make us think harder about the competitiveness of European cities or regions, rather than countries.

It soon becomes clearer that the real core *v* periphery conflict is the age-old one between town and (heavily subsidized) country, and that Europe's rich 'regional cores' by no means coincide with the 'core' countries thought to be candidates for a Narrow Monetary Union. France, Italy and the UK are deeply split personalities: part core, part periphery. On a regional view, the true core includes most of West Germany, Benelux, Austria and Switzerland, (north) east France, northern Italy, parts of southern England, the Midlands and Denmark. Catalonia and Madrid may also qualify. These regions compete and trade heavily with each other, and indeed the world. The economic interests of cities like Milan, Frankfurt,

Paris and London have far more in common with each other than any of them has with, say, Cornwall, Limousin or the Mezzogiorno. They might form a rather stable monetary union of their own, were it practicable. But since it is not, one could argue (as Karl Otto Pöhl now does) that the only clearly feasible monetary union would cover Germany, Benelux, Austria and Switzerland.

The opening of the east

'The Iron Curtain is the most artificial trade barrier of them all.'[2] Before 1989 no capital, goods, services or labour were able to move through the Iron Curtain: there was no integration at all. (Not unlike Spain and Portugal before the democratic revolutions of the early 1970s.) The opening since 1989, however, has been lopsided. East Germany is completely open, aided by large amounts of public finance, whereas farther to the east and south we find that, *de facto*, people are free to migrate while trade and capital mobility is limited.

Political and credit risks impede capital flows, but without secure access to EC markets there will be neither the domestic savings nor the foreign inflows needed for East Europe to develop, especially since their competitive sectors (steel, textiles and agriculture) are precisely those in which the EC restricts imports. Meanwhile the combination of Germany's liberal asylum laws and very long land borders positively invites an unwelcome and disruptive level of immigration.

The current situation is not sustainable. Ultimately the EC must choose between imports and immigrants, meaning a growing conflict of interest between the German people and (French) agricultural interests.[3] And whether inside or outside the EC budget there will be less German money for the old EC periphery, and more for the new Eastern one.

For the first time in its history Germany is not surrounded by hostile empires but finds itself at the very heart of a vast market, the eastern portion of which has immense growth potential on a twenty to thirty year view. Germany and its immediate environs have thus become an even more attractive location for both firms and workers than before. Compared with the 1980s, it seems inevitable that a larger fraction of Europe's total investment and consumer durable spending will take place in, or very close to, Germany. The last two and a half years have seen only the beginning, not the end, of that process.

The inflexible labour market and rigid cost structures of German industry are beginning to yield to the pressure of unemployment and recession. As they do we think it will become clearer that real interest rates need to remain high compared with most of the rest of Europe for some time to come, posing further problems for the ERM.

At your service

Services are the big employers in modern economies and deserve special mention. They divide into two types. Non-tradable services must locate close to where people live or work (hairdressers, estate agents, restaurants and supermarkets, for example). Service industries like advertising, design, software, broadcasting, publishing, entertainment, law, education, banking, insurance, as well as R&D in general, are much more tradable and potentially footloose.

In these services, labour pooling and knowledge spill-overs through personal contact are important. For that reason they are heavily concentrated in and around leading cities, or universities – in Milan fashion, furniture and car design; in London financial services, for example. New technology may reduce, but will not eliminate, the need to be physically close to other specialists in your field and to good (global) transport links. Even with the arrival of cheap video work stations in every office and many homes, cities will probably not become depopulated in favour of the countryside, nor will a high percentage of jobs move from core to periphery.[4]

But might they move from one part of the core to another? The single market will encourage greater concentration in some sectors, but in others (for example, advertising, publishing, law) differences in language and culture narrow the scope for specialization. For a sector like insurance different national regulations will remain obstacles for some time. (Note that a single currency would greatly facilitate concentration in sectors like this.) And for financial services more generally, the opening of East Europe may give German-speaking cities close to the region (Frankfurt, Berlin, Zurich, Vienna) a special opportunity to increase market share, threatening London's dominance. Whether they take it or not remains to be seen.

Europe unbound

The long-term goal of an 'ever closer union between the peoples of Europe' remains valid, indeed indispensable. But we need an improved blueprint for integration. It must reflect the reality of structural changes that breed high (frictional) unemployment, slow growth and widening budget deficits. It should be able to command popular support long after today's political leaders are gone. And it must respond to pan-European problems, not merely those confined to the EC's boundaries.

If the current emigration from Eastern Europe were to continue, it could become a vicious circle. One of the powerful conclusions from the locational economics is that enlightened self-interest towards the Central European countries is by far the EC's best policy.[5] Above all, that means allowing those countries to trade, and most urgently to sell us more food, steel, textiles and other basic products. But it also means more infrastructure spending to link Eastern and Western Europe, and to encourage private investment in the east. Almost inevitably that will reduce funding available for subsidies and transfers to the existing periphery. Both the transfers and the (food) imports issues are politically explosive, but they cannot be ducked.

But what of the EC's internal problems? The response can be summed up in one word: flexibility. It is needed for exchange rates, labour market policies, and in the future approach to integration.

Currency options

The ERM is not working as originally intended. Indeed, without more flexible (real) exchange rates over the next three to five years there is little chance of beginning EMU by 1999, and there are potentially grave threats to the single market.

The private spending and fiscal effects of German unification mean that Germany needs high real interest rates, both in absolute terms and relative to most of the rest of Europe. Moreover, our locational story suggests that this might still be true even if fiscal policy were much tighter. But, because the Bundesbank still has much more credibility than any other central bank in Europe, countries with lower inflation than Germany cannot reduce their interest rates below German levels.

The result is that real interest rates in those countries rise steadily, even in recession, setting up a time-inconsistent policy which attracts speculators to short their currencies. Resisting with higher rates simply puts real rates on an explosive upward path and weakens the economy still further, attracting more speculation.[6] If all countries resist devaluation the basic mechanism becomes extremely deflationary. One way out would be to move immediately to a single currency for Europe. That would solve the problem of the Bundesbank's excess credibility but would not alter the need for high real rates in Germany. And the system could work very badly without (much) greater labour mobility and more flexible wage and house prices. In practice, as in the US, much of the adjustment would still take place via migration, and calls for protectionism might easily become irresistible.

However, the most important argument against jumping to a single currency is political: public opinion in Germany would almost certainly not accept it, even if it only meant linking up with Benelux and France. Other EC members would do their best to veto the idea. The realistic option is to allow more flexible exchange rates in the run-up to monetary union, meaning more frequent realignments, wider target bands, a reversion to free floating, or some mixture of all three.

More frequent realignments would initially at least mean Deutschmark revaluation. This would work by redistributing inflation within Europe (a smaller share for Germany, a bigger share for the devaluers), permitting real interest rates to fall outside Germany and to decline on average for Europe as a whole. But, to work properly, this mechanism would have to include a decent revaluation of the Deutschmark against the French franc despite the fact that France has better 'fundamentals' at the moment. Otherwise French real interest rates would tend to go on rising at a time when the real rate of return in industry was falling, slowly but surely undermining the French economy and making eventual monetary union with Germany less feasible.

For all European currencies to float freely would be inefficient. Moreover the discipline of ERM membership has been especially important in countries with strong unions. Countries like Italy, Spain, Norway, Sweden and Finland may need that discipline to continue, albeit in somewhat less rigid form. One interesting option might be to allow a wider (perhaps as wide as 10 per cent) fluctuation band for the French franc against the Deutschmark until 1997, keeping the current central rate. Other ERM currencies would then be free to choose whether they pegged against the franc or the mark. Another possibility would be to combine wider bands with a 'concentric circles' system in which there were fluctuation bands of different widths.

Europe's new economic geography argues partly for a revaluation of Germany's real exchange rate,[7] partly for a more flexible exchange rate regime going forward. The macro-reason for flexibility is that the real interest rate needed to control inflation in Germany is deflationary for Europe as a whole (and will probably remain so even during a German recession), which implies permitting Deutschmark overvaluation now, followed by real depreciation later. The micro-reason is that real exchange rate changes of unpredictable size and direction will be needed to cope with the impact of accelerated structural change over the next few years. Such changes would be much easier to accomplish if nominal exchange rates are not totally inflexible. Moreover, less rigid exchange rates would be preferable to less rigid targets for budget deficits, central bank independence and labour market reform, etc.

Competing regions

Unsuitable exchange rate regimes can be disastrous, but a more flexible one is no panacea. Key policy changes for the peripheral regions are to introduce labour market flexibility – despite the fact that parts of the Social Chapter threaten to make their task impossible by over-harmonizing labour market conditions – and to shift their regional policies to a different focus: the development of centres of excellence to promote regional growth. For example, in Denmark an industry has developed around the core of research expertise in insulin, to the extent that Japanese firms are attracted to invest there.

Although the strength of the core continually pulls firms towards it, the combination of these policies acts as the best magnet that the lagging regions can construct. By following this path, the scope for policy-makers to influence regional economic fortunes is much greater than simply through handing out subsidies to allcomers, which fails to encourage the specialization process so important to regional growth.

With the collapse of communism, Europe's economic geography has changed radically, and Europe's politicians need to adapt. In particular, they should:

1 Allow more exchange rate flexibility in the run-up to monetary union but simultaneously insist on policies to make labour markets more flexible.
2 Allow more imports (especially food, steel and textiles) but fewer immigrants from Eastern Europe, the CIS, Turkey and the Maghreb, which would also help revive the old Baltic and Mediterranean trade routes.
3 Phase out the CAP and certain other subsidies to enable more spending on education and infrastructure links with the poorer areas of Europe, west or east.

Realpolitik

Of course, what should and what does happen are often very different things. But when the gap gets too wide financial markets and business interests have an unsentimental way of forcing the issue, especially in the absence of capital controls.[8] Protectionist pressures within Europe will certainly increase but may well focus on low-wage competitors from outside Europe. One can easily imagine, for example, the EC taking a tougher line on textile imports from China and Hong Kong, from where immigration is no threat, while permitting more textile imports from Estonia and Poland. That is the logic of regional trading blocs.

Ironically, events in 1992[9] made widening the concept of Europe seem more urgent, but EMU less so. Good reason, therefore, for firms and equity investors to recall the strategic importance of location in the new Europe. And that despite its reputation for high costs, social unrest and inflexible labour markets, the most attractive place to invest in the 1990s is likely to be in and around Germany: in Europe's old core and its new eastern periphery.

CONVERGENCE

Economic geography

Europe's regional core runs from London and south-east England through the heartlands of the European economy in the Paris basin, Benelux, southern Germany, Austria, the Swiss Mittelland centred around Zurich, south-eastern France, northern Italy and into Catalonia and Madrid in Spain. Around this wealthy core, levels of GDP per head drop sharply both to the south – in the Iberian peninsula – and especially to the east, in the Central European countries. In Scandinavia GDP per head is as high as in the core but the domestic market is small.

This concentration of wealth within Europe is vital for the definition of firms' strategies and their location decisions, as any firm wanting to serve the whole of the core has to develop its production facilities with a view to achieving access to this market.[10] Firms outside the region do not necessarily deny themselves access, but transport costs are generally higher and, because the level of infrastructure, in general, and transport links in particular, are worse, it is harder for firms to adopt modern forms of production.[11] Reductions in trading costs – the physical costs of transport plus the costs of regulation, quotas and tariffs – might seem to be of great benefit to these regions, but this is not necessarily the case, as we demonstrate below.

The uneven regional distribution of wealth within countries is the result of individual firms' location decisions, showing that it is the region rather than the country that is the crucial geographical area in determining economic location. Specific regions become centres of economic activity for particular industries.

Financial services locate in London, machine tools and precision engineering in southern Germany, research-intensive firms cluster around technology nodes developed in Rhône-Alpes and, led by the fashion and design centre, clothing, textiles and ceramics are centred in northern Italy. The economic power base within Europe used to be seen as the four big developed member states of the EC: Germany, France, the UK and Italy. Around them small countries often with lower standards of living and smaller industrial structures complemented the needs of the member of the big four to whose market they were nearest. The internal market has forced us to realize that it is the region and the city, not the state, that is crucial. Whether it be the centre of Swiss industry around Zurich and Basle that spreads up to Mulhouse and into Alsace, Baden-Württemberg and Bavaria or whether it be the centre of economic activity that runs from Antwerp and Rotterdam to Essen, Dortmund and Cologne, these concentrations of economic activity do not respect national boundaries.

At the same time, the EC's periphery can no longer be thought of as the

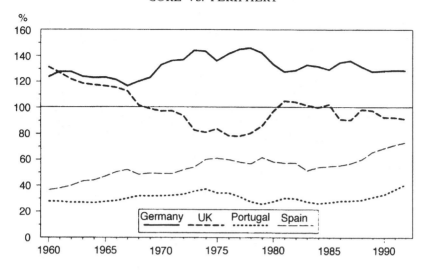

Figure 2.2 GDP *per capita*, current market prices, EU 12 = 100

Mediterranean countries and Ireland: it encompasses western France, large parts of England, northern Germany and Denmark. But it is the opening of Eastern Europe that is the most striking change. The core is surrounded by developing regions, each with different characteristics in wages, education, training and infrastructure. A key element of the battle for the location of production will be the division of economic activity among the regions of the European periphery. But even more crucial will be the determination of the core *v.* peripheries struggle in Europe.

Adjustment

The struggle is between two modes of adjustment: flows of capital to lagging regions, or flows of labour to existing cores. Convergence of output per head can occur through either mechanism or through a combination of the two. However, the fortunes of individual firms, regions and even governments will vary greatly with the way in which convergence occurs. This is why we need to analyse closely the way in which European adjustment will occur. We know that regional centres of industrial production, once established, become very hard to shift: the north-east dominated 80 per cent of US manufacturing production for nearly a century. With the exceptions of the UK and Spain, the rich European countries too have remained relatively rich and the poor countries relatively poor (Figure 2.2).

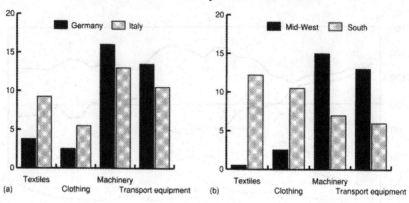

Figure 2.3 Shares of manufacturing employment in (a) Europe, (b) the US

Localization

But there are major differences in the way in which the US and European economies operate. Regional specialization in Europe is not as pronounced as in the US. We take the Mid-West and the south for the US and Germany and Italy for Europe as being a relatively similar pair of 'regions' (Figure 2.3).

The absence of regional data for Europe makes the point harder to demonstrate but concentration of industrial employment is far more advanced in US states. For example, the Mid-West has virtually no textile industry left at all, whereas in Europe Germany's textile industry has nearly half the share of manufacturing employment of its Italian counterpart. The distribution of production in the automotive sector (Figure 2.4) tells a similar story: the legacy of national restrictions – not only trade barriers and different national standards, but also the lagged effects of the infra-structure of dealer distribution networks and rivals' agreements on *de facto* market division – has left production divided between four member states, each having market shares greater than 12 per cent of the total.[12] Again, we have to use country data for Europe, thus distorting our regional argument.

Despite the vastly greater distances required to transport goods in the US, the failure to remove barriers to trade in Europe, government subsidies included, has stifled industrial specialization. To determine the causes of these different industrial structures, we need to look in more detail at the regional economies within the US and European single markets.

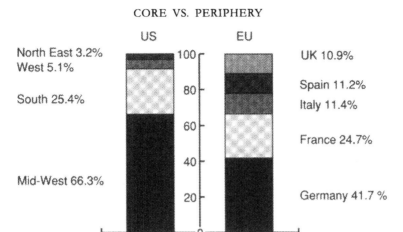

Figure 2.4 Distribution of motor vehicle production, US and EU

The US single market

In the US convergence between states is far more advanced. There is no persistent divergence in unemployment rates away from the national average and *per capita* income is not subject to vast swings in response to the pattern of employment growth but instead is very similar across the country.[13] The individual states do not grow at the same rate. On the contrary, because regional specialization is greater, industry-specific shocks have a much larger regional impact than in Europe. The following charts shows the adjustment process in four states that have suffered during the period since the 1960s: Massachusetts and Connecticut as part of the readjustment in New England, Indiana and Illinois in the Rust Belt (Figure 2.5).

Per capita new capital expenditure has been greater than the national average in these states for most of the period, which is how convergence occurs. Although the rate of convergence – the difference between regional and national new capital expenditure per person – varies considerably across the states, reflecting different regional industrial specializations and their associated capital intensities, the basic adjustment process affects each region in the same way. Figure 2.6 summarizes this process by looking at the effect of a negative shock to regional employment, one example of which would be the closing down of a local defence contractor in response to falling government orders.

Regional adjustment in the US does not involve large movements in wages; instead, migration bears the brunt of the change. Unemployment increases initially and then over a five-to-ten year period, reverts back to the national average as the unemployed migrate to a region with better

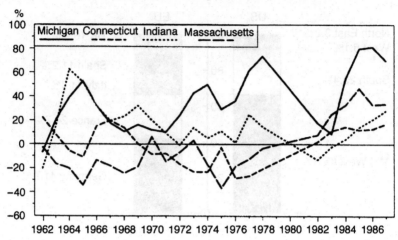

Figure 2.5 Cumulative new capital expenditure per person in the US, relative to the national average

employment prospects. The long-term result is that employment in the region does not recover to its previous level – wages have not shifted relative to the national pattern and, more important, the local market has shrunk. Market incentives for new firms to relocate to the region are limited to the differences in land, congestion and pollution costs that

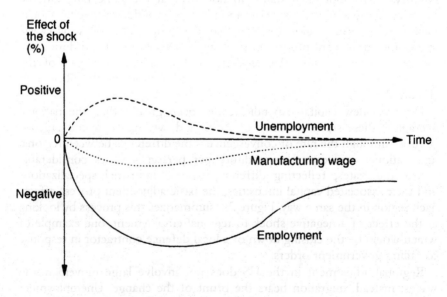

Figure 2.6 Effect of a negative employment shock
Source: Katz and Blanchard (1992) I, p. 8.

64

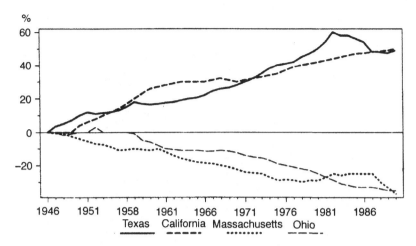

Figure 2.7 Cumulative employment growth in the US relative to the national
average, 1946–90
Source: Katz and Blanchard (1992) I, p. 36.

different levels of economic activity encourage. Although these elements
cannot be ignored, the pattern of industrial activity in the US and Europe
informs us that they are often less important than the agglomeration effects
that encourage firms to locate close together. As a consequence of this type
of adjustment, long-term employment growth can diverge across member
states for decades (Figure 2.7).

Some states have persistently experienced employment growth above the
national trend – the Sun Belt and the oil states – whilst others have grown
more slowly – New England and the Rust Belt.[14] In part, the growth of
California reflects the development of a new core – a burst of new innovations allowed the region to create its own industrial specialization and attract
economic activity. This shows that the blunt message of production centres
being inviolable and the location of economic activity never changing is too
extreme. However, a vast number of conditions, including new technologies,
good local infrastructure and an acceptable labour skills pool have to exist
for this major structural shift of economic location to occur. Once
established, the new core develops its own momentum.

Real convergence?

The US model is one where regional adjustment occurs and migration plays
a pivotal role in bringing it about. In Europe, we know that a spreading of
economic activity has not occurred. Furthermore, regional adjustment in
Europe has not followed the US model, as Figure 2.8 indicates. Although
most of the UK should be treated as peripheral, the fact that part of it is in

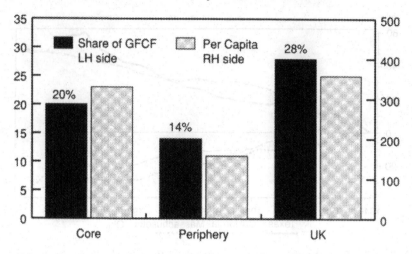

Figure 2.8 Intra-EU direct investment, 1986–90. GFCF: gross-fixed capital formation

the core, combined with the length of US firms' investment there, makes separate treatment more illuminating. Similarly, parts of France, Germany and Benelux should not be counted in the core but we are unable to disaggregate the data to show their true regional nature.[15]

Both as a share of gross fixed capital formation, and in *per capita* terms, direct investment in the periphery is less significant than in the core: the impetus to convergence has been weak (Figure 2.8).[16] Capital flows to lagging regions in Europe have simply been too small to bring about convergence of capital per head, even during the late 1980s, when the conditions for such flows were most propitious. The lack of adjustment has been despite large differences in nominal wages, partly because productivity levels in core and periphery have tended to weaken the incentive to relocate (Figure 2.9).

The fact that nominal wages differ so greatly is itself a major difference from the US – not only does the US adjustment model work, it does not require large changes in wages to bring about convergence. The fact that capital spreading has failed to lead the European adjustment process is a major headache for European policy-makers. All their efforts have been to boost infrastructure in the periphery, supported by financial incentives to private investment. Although from the motor industry alone we can cite individual cases such as Volkswagen's take-over of SEAT, Toyota's and Nissan's new plants in the Midlands and north of England and Suzuki's investment in Portugal, the evolution of critical economic mass in peripheral regions has not advanced.

The sources of the failure of economic activity to spread to the periphery

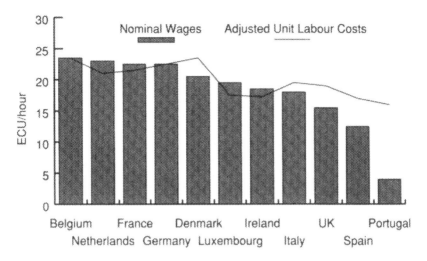

Figure 2.9 European labour costs

are not readily susceptible to public policy influence – at various times the European authorities have targeted direct investment, transport links, training initiatives and general technology levels, but the simple fact of the matter is that the inertia in economic location tends to outweigh other factors most of the time, and there is no reason to expect European policy-makers to have more success in the future than they have had in the past in encouraging economic activity to disperse.

Migration in Europe

In the light of these difficulties, it would appear that the authorities would be better advised to target the lack of adjustment. Here, the source of the problem is quite clear: there is simply not enough migration[17] between the European core and the periphery.

Only Ireland and Portugal have any sizeable share of their populations living in other member states, although there are also large Italian communities in southern France, Germany and London (Figure 2.10). Migration does occur in Europe, but it is largely restricted to flows within countries.

We have a clear view of the adjustment problems in Europe: the internal market will increase industrial and thereby regional specialization. Because economic regions do not respect national boundaries, a simple continuation of existing migratory flows within countries will see a worsening of the relative positions of core and periphery. If that happens there will be enormous social unease in some member states, leading to greater political pressure at a European level to resolve the adjustment problems of the peripheral countries.

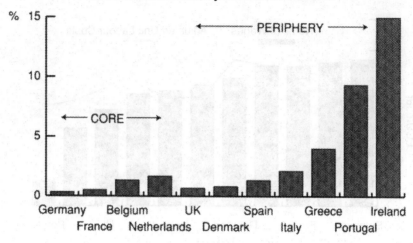

Figure 2.10 EU nationals in another member state as a share of total domestic population, 1993

But these migratory problems pale into insignificance when they are compared with those that are already threatening social stability in Germany.

Imports or immigrants?

Because there are many special factors affecting its case, we need to be cautious in interpreting the evidence from Germany. Nevertheless, in many ways, Germany can be thought of as a microcosm of the core *v* periphery debate. There is one highly developed region and another which is extremely undeveloped. The infrastructure stock in the former East Germany is far smaller than in the west. As in the wider Europe, workers in East Germany are concerned that recovery in their region will not take place, with clear implications for their employment prospects.

The initial burst of migration was spurred by immense relief at the end of communist control as well as by the overriding fear that the Soviet Union would simply not permit unification to occur with the same arbitrary division of population as happened when Berlin was divided. As a result, government policy remains heavily orientated to stemming the tide of migrants. Despite this, the underlying economic factors still encourage migration from east to west, though clearly at a slower rate than prior to unification (Figure 2.11).

The cumulated net balance of migration from East to West Germany in 1991 was just under 1.4 million people. Adding the half a million East German residents who work in West Germany boosts the overall total to

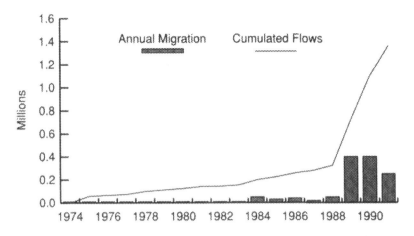

Figure 2.11 Migration from East to West Germany, 1974–90

virtually 2 million people, or 3.1 per cent of West Germany's January 1989 population and 6.8 per cent of its total employment. The results of a survey reported in *Wochenbericht* (30 January 1992) that 62 per cent of all East Germans are willing to migrate in the medium term confirm the strong potential for persisting migratory flows.

Germany is a magnet not only for East Germans seeking work in their own country but for the whole of Eastern Europe. Figure 2.12 shows the trend in migration from a group of Central and Eastern European countries.[18] The cumulative inflow of migrants from these countries doubled between 1987 and 1990. There are 3.5 million migrants: 5 per cent of West Germany's January 1989 population and a startling 13 per cent of the total employed.

Germany acts as a magnet for East Europeans, whether of German origin or from other ethnic groups, because of its prosperity and its cultural ties. In terms of the distance they have to travel, and in terms of fellow nationals abroad, Germany is their natural choice. French immigration contrasts strongly both in the overall trend – the total number of immigrants in France actually fell between 1982 and 1990 – and in the nationality of the immigrants: migrants from the Maghreb account for 16 per cent of the total. Further, the French authorities estimate that illegal migration doubles the number of Algerians in France to about 1.1 million. High unemployment and a young population serve as massive potential for these flows to increase.

In economic terms the adjustment process needs these migratory flows if it is to work. The relative strength of the core increases as a result of the inflows of migrants and the core–periphery relationship between European

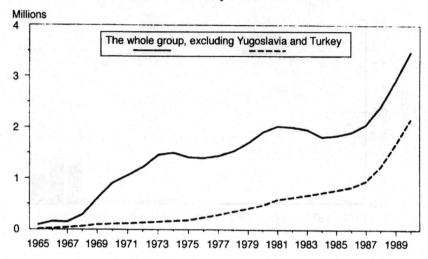

Figure 2.12 Migration from Central and Eastern Europe, 1965–89 (cumulated balance)

regions is perpetuated. The initial effect of the internal market programme will tend to be for the core to receive migrants from the south-western periphery as well: because the Mediterranean countries' industrial structure is less efficient, with more small and medium-size firms producing goods of lesser value-added than in the core and because the larger incumbents in the core can be expected to exercise some dominance, the impact of greater competition will be to depress employment prospects in the periphery.

However, the socio-political problem of migration from Eastern Europe is far more pressing: current migratory flows into Germany are unsustainable. The fiscal pressure caused by unification means that there are precious few resources to ease their integration into German society. The problems are exacerbated by one EC member state taking virtually all the migratory flow. However, the implications of East European migration extend far beyond Germany. For the south-western periphery, one scenario would have seen emigration from Eastern Europe combined with capital accumulation in their own economies. The main alternative is that they lose labour, subsidies and influence within Europe as resources are switched to the east to staunch the tide of immigrants. In political terms, the switch of resources is rapidly becoming impossible to deny – Figure 2.13 shows how the immigration of German migrants stabilized after the initial burst, whereas the monthly flows of asylum seekers increased by a factor of four.

One aspect of the rapid increase in East European migration that should not be ignored is the readjustment that will be forced on some of the EC's

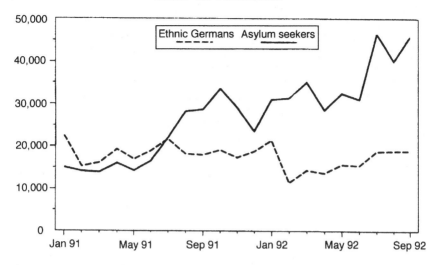

Figure 2.13 Germany's East European immigrants: monthly inflow, January 1991 to September 1992

most vociferous lobbyists: the steel and textile industries and the agricultural producers. By succeeding in having quotas imposed on Eastern Europe, they have helped to depress economic conditions there, thus boosting the emigratory pressures. This underlines that for policy-makers in the core there is a clear-cut choice in Eastern Europe's adjustment: imports or immigrants.

Intuition

In determining firms' location we look at the interaction of demand, economies of scale and transport costs. We can think of the internal market programme as reducing trading costs, which, at first glance, seems to favour location in the regions on the periphery: their low labour costs appear more easily accessible with lower transport costs. In fact, the seemingly commonsense notion that lower trading costs will benefit the low-cost region located away from the major markets can be shown to be simplistic. The impact of reducing trading costs is twofold:

1 They make production in the periphery more attractive.
2 They make concentrating production in one location more profitable than dividing it between two.

The different adjustment processes in different industries have important regional implications, which we explore in Boxes 2.1–2.

71

Box 2.1 Location decisions

We take a world where there are two regions, which we call Germany and France, and two goods: food and manufactures (see Appendix 2.1). Production of food accounts for 60 per cent of the world's labour force, with 30 per cent located in each region. The fixed costs of a manufacturing plant and the cost of transporting a unit of goods are the same in both regions. There are no transport costs attached to serving consumers in the same region as the plant. Demand for the product in each region is directly proportional to the population. In the chart we show the cost functions for a producer considering setting up who wants to serve the world market on the basis of three different assumptions about the location of manufacturing production.

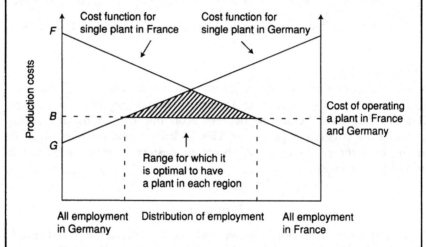

Initially, let all manufacturing production be concentrated in Germany. Because food production is equally divided, this means that the German market is just over twice as large as the French economy. The firm has three choices of where to locate its plant: in Germany, in France or to set up a plant in both regions.

Once these initial conditions are established, a new entrant minimizes cost by setting up one plant in Germany: after entry, manufacturing production will remain concentrated there. If it produces in Germany, the firm faces a total cost of G (equal to the fixed cost of setting up a single plant plus the transport costs of serving the agricultural workers in France), which is less than the cost of producing solely in

France, F, and the cost of having one plant in each region, B. In fact the position is symmetrical: if employment is first concentrated in France, a new entrant also minimizes costs by producing in France. The same is equally true if all existing manufacturers have plants in both countries: the population is evenly divided between the two regions and a new entrant minimizes costs by adopting the same strategy. The area shaded in the diagram shows the employment distribution where it is optimal for a new entrant to operate two plants.

In effect the individual firm's decision is completely determined by the decision of its competitors. There are three possible equilibria; the choice between them depends on other firms' decisions. What is striking is that all these equilibria are stable: new entrants will not seek to destabilize the *status quo* because it is not in their interest so to do. The practical resonances of this model are clear: industry's geographical structure is determined by historical factors – the location decisions of other firms – and, once established, it is very stable and tends to be reinforced by migration: there is inertia in the location of industry

SECTORAL ADJUSTMENT

In the boxes our simple model shows how production decisions depend on changes in the relationship between fixed and trading costs. Lower trading costs produce greater competition and more effective pressure on firms to adopt the most efficient location structure of production. However, the same fall in trading costs produces opposing location reactions in different industries, depending on their capital intensity and the initial relationship between trading and capital costs. Looking more closely at industry in detail, we can tell whether it is capital or labour flows that predominate in bringing about adjustment. We concentrate on three sectors: steel, textiles and agriculture. Not only are they the sectors of greatest East European competitiveness, they also cover the diversity of behaviour predicted in the model (Table 2.1).

'Lower trading costs' shock

Lower trade barriers do not, therefore, result in pure polarizaton or pure convergence. However, in each sector there will be greater concentration of production. Both the Common Agricultural Policy and the Multi-fibre Agreement artificially raise production levels in Europe by nullifying the

Box 2.2 Core *u* periphery

We can now apply the model in Box 2.1 to Europe. To highlight more of the complexity of the decisions, we have two goods in our model of the European economy. The production technologies inherent in the two goods are different: in industry A, fixed costs are far less significant than in industry B. For the sake of simplicity, the fall in aggregate transport costs that we model is identical for the two industries.

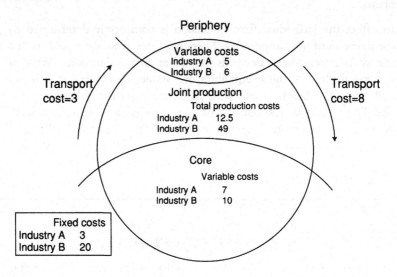

The circle represents the European economy. The effective market for each region is delineated by the arcs on the circle. Technology is the same across all regions: fixed costs are equal in the core and on the periphery. Transport costs are shown as an aggregate of serving the whole market rather than per unit, explaining why the cost is greater from the periphery to the core than for the reverse trip. In the centre of the circle we see the total cost of producing the goods in both regions: as before, there are no transport costs for this option. To demonstrate how we work out total costs for each option, we calculate *industry A's total cost of production in the core* by adding fixed costs, 3, to variable costs, 7, to transport costs, 3. This breakdown is given for all the other options in appendix 2.1. The charts below show the results of reducing transport costs for the intermediate case – cut by half – and for the low case – equal to zero.

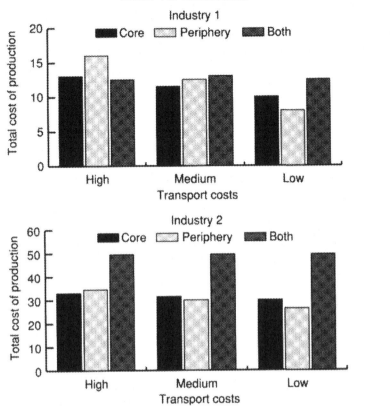

In industry A, production is initially split between both regions. Reducing transport costs by half leads to production shifting to the core. Reducing them further sees production move to the periphery. In industry B, on the other hand, production is initially in the core but moves to the periphery as soon as transport costs fall. The relative size of the two industries effectively tells us whether or not migration dominates capital or flows as the means of adjustment.

forces of competition. In textiles the protectionism has been given extra support (under Article 115 of the Rome Treaty) by the curb applied to intra-EC trade when a national industry is harmed by imports from third countries entering through another EC member state. In steel, European governments are being forced to stop subsidizing their domestic producers and allowing restructuring to take place. However, international restrictions such as 'voluntary' export restraints and anti-dumping are still commonplace.

The removal of the protectionist barrier will tend to cause production to revert to its competitive location. In textiles, advantage generally lies with low nominal wage-cost regions. Traditionally, only the Mediterranean countries have had access to the EC market. However, the association agreements that improve East European countries' access by eliminating tariffs over six years (the phasing out of quotas has yet to be agreed) will change this comparative advantage. Indeed, as the MFA is phased out the bloc of Far Eastern low-wage producers will take more production out of Europe. In agriculture, as support prices move towards the world price, crop production will concentrate in the highest-yielding regions, with clear effects for the location of agro-commodity producers.[19] Perhaps the best example is sugar beet, which cannot be transported more than about 50 km after harvesting to the next production stage. At the moment the CAP so distorts price incentives that sugar beet is grown as far south as Naples, when the area of greatest comparative advantage in Europe lies in regions north of the river Marne, particularly northern France, Belgium and the Netherlands. Sugar producers will be forced to relocate to these high-yielding regions once the trade barriers of the CAP are removed.

However, industrial relocation will not completely erase the impact of the industrial trade barriers. Industrial centres develop an economic infrastructure – suppliers, retailers, training schools and transport links are just a few examples.

This infrastructure does not disappear as rapidly as the industry which spearheaded it. The result is that the general prosperity of a region does not immediately decline to where it would have been had the trade barriers not been imposed.

In individual industries, too, the effects of trade barriers can persist, but only if a protected region's industry develops a new source of competitive advantage whilst it is protected. In textiles, for instance, two factors may allow some European production to be maintained. First, superior European design will continue to attract clothing producers. Second, the responsiveness revolution, which permits firms to satisfy the consumer's demand for greater variety and encourages shorter production cycles, makes pure economies of scale less important in some market segments. The effect is to encourage production close to the final market, reducing the incentive to move production outside Europe. However, in cotton textiles, T-shirts and other sectors where fashion shifts are relatively unimportant production will continue to locate in low-cost centres. Where new inventions make basic technologies obsolete, the second of our shocks, these changes are more powerful still.

'Technology' shock

The Schumpeterian cycle that runs from invention clusters through economic boom to sclerosis, recession and restructuring has reached its new innovatory phase. New technologies not only make incumbent firms more vulnerable to sources of new competition – changing industrial structure within the industry – they also make 'incumbent regions' more vulnerable to new entrants.[20] The reason why the current changes are viewed by all regions as so important is that, once an industry's structure and its new location are decided, our analysis shows it will be broadly stable for decades. To fail to attract industry now will be devastating for the long-term growth prospects of individual regions.

The best example in our three sectors is the development of thin slab casting in steel. It allows small operators, the mini-mills, to compete with the large 'integrated' plants in the key market for flat rolled steel. Although the new technology does not yet provide the very high quality required at the top end of the market, it does make the integrated plants far more vulnerable: the cost savings from the new technology are estimated at US $50–$70 a tonne at a current selling price of US $300 a tonne.

The mini-mills use a more flexible production process, are less capital-intensive, are not unionized and have lower operating costs. The effects are clear: unemployment among the integrated producers and enforced labour flexibility in unionized plants. US Steel's decision to consider building its own mini-mill is indicative of the pressure on the integrated firms. At the same time, however, a separate new technological development – thin strip casting – allows greater economies of scale from the blast furnaces. The result will be fewer, larger, integrated plants.

In this environment of fundamental change, only a clear understanding of the production process can indicate where firms will locate. The integrated plants with their large blast furnaces will remain in the centre of the core, maximizing market coverage and ensuring best access to the inland waterways used to transport both the iron ore and the finished product. The mini-mills, on the other hand, require high-quality scrap metal for their electric arc furnaces, cheap electricity and relative proximity to their final users. We should therefore expect a large number of the EC's peripheral blast furnaces to close, whilst new mini-mills – the first ones were built in Brescia, encouraged by the availability of subsidized electricity – are located close to centres of demand.

'Eastern Europe' shock

The changes in Eastern Europe make the whole relocation process harder to analyse. Not only do they alter the production location possibilities available to firms, because failure to develop creates immediate immigratory pressures on Germany; there is a new element in the bargaining game between capital and labour. Where firms understand the nature of the competition between regions and their labour forces, they can use the option of moving to the periphery as a threat against their unions, provided they can convince them that the prospect of losing jobs to another region is genuine.[21] If labour in the core adopts flexible working practices or accepts lower real wages, moving to the periphery is unnecessary.

In agro-commodities East European producers are likely to be most effective competing in labour-intensive products, for example fruit and vegetables, mushrooms and fish. Upgrading their capital stock to deal with the high standards of processing and packaging demanded by Western consumers would be too expensive – for example, it is estimated that to upgrade the Polish sugar industry to Western standards would cost US $1.5 billion – unless their yields become outstandingly better than those available closer to the final product market. In textiles, although the East Europeans pay lower wages than the Mediterranean periphery, margins will always be compressed by pressure from Far Eastern rivals. Although the negotiations on removing quotas are based on the notion that the East European quotas should be phased out twice as fast as the general MFA quotas, the pressures to upgrade will be the same as those faced by Mediterranean producers. In steel the periphery vs. periphery struggle has already begun. Eastern Europe has a trade surplus greater than 3 million tonnes with the EC – growing despite quota controls – whilst Spain was forced to close four of its six blast furnaces in 1992, and proposed to swap the existing blast furnace at Sestac for a mini-mill. The pressure can only intensify: time is not on the side of the policy-makers.

These are the direct consequences of the three shocks that we identified: the basic pressures of economic development and the driving forces behind industrial location combine to impose severe strains on Europe's economic, political and social systems. The long-term gains from a more efficient production structure could be enormous: faster growth and a greater share of world markets. However, they are shrouded by the short-term dislocations that have first to be overcome and have not yet been properly addressed. One of the reasons why the EC is suffering so many schisms at the moment is the pressure from this regional restructuring. It would have been difficult enough to make the demands of the Anglo-Saxon south-western periphery consistent with the reality of industrial location in a single market. The opening up of Eastern Europe has complicated the trade-offs between the various economic actors by several orders of magnitude.

Investors need to be aware of the risks that are faced by firms currently in the wrong location. The migratory pressures are so strong that the artificial trade barriers with Eastern Europe must be removed far more

Table 2.1 Summary of responses in three sectors

Shock	Steel	Textiles	Agro-commodities
Lower trading costs	Lower state subsidies in the EC	MFA. Article 115	CAP reform
Effect	Rationalization Fewer producers	Less production in Europe. Worst hit: Mediterranean region	Move towards comparative advantage in agriculture
Responsiveness revolution; new technology	Thin slab casting Thin strip casting Greater demand for quality	Greater demand for variety	Greater demand for variety and ease of cooking
Effect	More mini-mills Larger integrated plants	Shorter production runs: more flexibility in production	More R&D spending: more innovation
Eastern Europe	New low-cost suppliers and raw material sources	New low-wage production in Europe	New competition in market segments with high labour intensity
Effect	Eastern Europe may be a peripheral location for blast furnaces – bad for existing peripheral producers	Improves Eastern Europe's position relative to the Far East Worsens position of existing EC producers	More East European production in sectors such as fruit and vegetables, fish, mushrooms
Overall effect	Fewer, larger blast furnaces More mini-mills Fewer producers	Some displacement of existing EC producers; the extent depends on Eastern Europe's success in upgrading	Considerable relocation activity in response to the newly important comparative advantage in agriculture

rapidly than is currently planned. In the new Europe location of production will be as important as product mix, both for firms and for governments.

APPENDIX 2.1

The model: effects of reducing transport costs for the core vs. periphery model

	Fixed	Variable	Transport	Total

Industry 1
High transport costs: Production in industry 1 is in both regions: in industry 2 production is in the core.

	Fixed	Variable	Transport	Total
Core	3	7	3	13
Periphery	3	5	8	16
Both	6	6·5	0	12·5

Industry 2

	Fixed	Variable	Transport	Total
Core	20	10	3	33
Periphery	20	6	8	34
Both	40	8·9	0	38·9

Medium cost: transport costs are halved. Production in industry 1 is now in the core, having initially been in both regions; in industry 2 production shifts from the core to the periphery.

Industry 1

	Fixed	Variable	Transport	Total
Core	3	7	1·5	11·5
Periphery	3	5	4	12·5
Both	6	6·5	0	12·5

Industry 2

	Fixed	Variable	Transport	Total
Core	20	10	1·5	31·5
Periphery	20	6	4	30
Both	40	8·9	0	48·9

Low cost: finally we see transport costs equal to zero. In this extreme case the periphery's advantage in terms of lower labour (variable) costs becomes crucial.

Industry 1

	Fixed	Variable	Transport	Total
Core	3	7	0	10
Periphery	3	5	0	8
Both	6	6·5	0	12·5

Industry 2

	Fixed	Variable	Transport	Total
Core	20	10	0	30
Periphery	20	6	0	26
Both	40	8·9	0	48·9

NOTES

1 Radically lower costs explain the shift of much of the world's PC and sports shoe manufacture to Asia but not why Taiwan became the dominant location.
2 Neal Soss, chief economist, First Boston Corporation, in Soss and Wilmot (1988).
3 The real problem is the monstrous form that European farm subsidies take, not the principle of subsidizing small, inefficient farms because of their environmental or cultural value.

4 Cities may become more stretched out, however, as more people move out to 'exurbia' and 'edge cities'.

5 The same applies to the Maghreb and Turkey, even though the pressure of emigration from these areas is less intense than from Eastern Europe.

6 An over- or undervalued currency makes little difference: countries with an overvalued currency simply hit the deflationary path sooner.

7 Which should ideally have been allowed to happen immediately after unification.

8 There may be a growing constituency in favour of reregulation but EC-wide capital controls are most unlikely.

9 The breakdown of the ERM and, underlying it, the discarding of the assumption that inflation in particular and economies in general would converge.

10 Of course, this is not a necessary strategy for all firms. It may be profitable for small and medium-size enterprises to serve a local market or possibly a niche in a sub-set of the wider European market.

11 That this is only a characterization is demonstrated by Ireland attracting highly competitive companies in industries such as pharmaceuticals and electronic engineering as well as financial services and data processing which aim to serve the EC market by air freight or which can be traded electronically.

12 The Herfindahl index is 0·507 for the US and 0·272 for Europe; US production is nearly twice as concentrated in geograpical terms as European production.

13 Of course, in the US this fact is explained by the system of centralized social security and automatic stabilizers in the federal budget. In the EC all transfer systems are *ad hoc*, such as the CAP, rather than purposely created. There can be no presumption that income *per capita* in the EC will tend to converge without these systems.

14 This trend reflects both the increasing share of services in value added and also the regional shift from a single pole to a multi-polar equilibrium. For more detail see below.

15 The core is defined in 'national' terms as Germany, Benelux and France. The UK is shown separately, leaving the rest of the EC as the periphery.

16 Aggregation hides some of the truth. If we were to look at Spain alone we would find that direct investment *per capita* is much higher.

17 On migration also see CS First Boston Economics (1991, 1992a).

18 Figure 2.12 covers Yugoslavia and Turkey, which have historically been major 'exporters' of migrants to Germany, Poland, Romania, the former Soviet Union and Czechoslovakia. The other Central and Eastern European countries have not as yet been heavily involved in the migration flows.

19 For a more detailed analysis of the implications of these changes see Bertrand Facon's (1992) paper on the food industry.

20 In precisely the same way as occurs in models of firm strategy, it is the level of entry barriers that determines the scope for new entrants to compete. In this case the entry barriers can be thought of in terms of the infrastructure costs necessary to allow 'footloose' production to move to the 'new region'.

21 These themes are developed in CS First Boston Economics (1992b).

REFERENCES

CS First Boston Economics (1991) *Soviet Emigraton: the Impact on Germany*, London: CS First Boston.

CS First Boston Economics (1992a) *Ireland Transformed*, London: CS First Boston.

CS First Boston Economics (1992b) *The New Regions*, London: CS First Boston.
Facon, Bernard (1992) *Food*, London: CS First Boston.
Katz, L., and Blanchard, O. (1992) *Brookings Papers on Economic Activity* I, Washington, D.C.: Brookings Institution.
Krugman, Paul (1991) *Geography and Trade*, Cambridge, Mass.: MIT Press.
Soss, Neal, and Wilmot, Jonathan (1988) *Economic Geography in the 1990s*, London: CS First Boston.

ACKNOWLEDGEMENTS

We are grateful to CS First Boston (UK), London, for permission to reprint paper No. 4 of the same title in the CS First Boston Economics series 'Towards the Twenty-first Century'.

3

UNEMPLOYMENT IN EUROPE

Jonathan Michie

The worldwide growth of unemployment is 'the issue of the 1990s' and represents a 'dangerous potential for human strife' according to the 1993 UN *Human Development Report*. In Europe unemployment is considered to be the 'most pressing problem' by two-thirds of EC citizens.[1]

The first year of the EC's single market, 1993, saw a third year of slow growth in the EC, bringing the worst recession for two decades, with 18 million people unemployed. The German economy stopped growing in mid-1992 and by March 1993 industrial output was 10 per cent below the March 1992 figure. Britain saw negative growth rates for 1991 and 1992 from which it was only weakly recovering in 1993. Ironically this made Britain the only major EC country not in recession in 1993 – thanks to the interest rate cuts and devaluation which followed sterling's departure from the Exchange Rate Mechanism in September 1992, despite the horrors which our political leaders claimed would result.

Overall, employment in the EC fell by about three-quarters of a percentage point in 1992 – the first time since 1983 that the number of people in employment actually decreased – and a similar reduction was expected to take place again in 1993. In absolute figures this meant that in 1993 2 million fewer people than in 1991 would be employed in the twelve member states. At 11 per cent, unemployment had returned to the peak of 1985 – the gains made during the second half of the 1980s were lost again in the first three years of the 1990s. This left less than 60 per cent of the EC's population of working age actually in work in 1993, compared with more than 70 per cent in the US and Japan. There is therefore a pool of hidden unemployment which has to be absorbed before numbers on the dole will fall substantially.

Account thus needs to be taken of the 'non-employed': those who have no job but are not registered as unemployed. The OECD prescription for unemployment, of cuts in the level and duration of unemployment benefits, risks simply pushing the unemployed off the official jobless count and into economic inactivity. The alternative, of subsidizing their employment, in either the private or the public sector, makes more sense than leaving the long-term unemployed to decay.

The rise in unemployment in Europe is due neither to 'over-generous' benefits nor to labour market 'rigidities', but rather to the relation between macro-economic policy, balance of payments constraints and deindustrialization. The idea of pursuing active macro-economic and industrial policies has given way to adherence to monetarism, privatization and labour market deregulation. Yet the resulting growth in low pay, poverty and unemployment have, ironically, placed an increasing burden on the public purse. At the same time, productive efficiency is harmed by the resulting instability in the labour market – particularly in the increasingly low-paid sectors – and the loss of incentives for producers to upgrade their production systems. A vicious circle of low-wage, low-productivity, low-investment activity is generated, leading to loss of competitiveness and growing unemployment, with the increasing burdens on the Exchequer provoking yet further moves down the recessionary spiral.

The second half of the 1980s was taken by the supporters of deregulation as proof of its economic benefits. Economic growth was relatively rapid, with some fall in unemployment, although it remained high. But at the end of the 1980s the revival came to an end with global recession and a return to mass unemployment, the early 1990s having witnessed recession and unemployment comparable to those of the 1930s. Indeed, talk of the need for a 'New Deal' has re-entered the economic policy vocabulary. In April 1993 Japan's government introduced an £82 billion set of economy-boosting measures, including a £53 billion public works programme, while in the US Clinton was elected in 1992 on an explicitly interventionist economic platform. In the twelve countries of the EC (the 'EC 12'), on the other hand, policy is still stuck on the policy path laid down by the Maastricht Treaty[2] – drawn up in the late 1980s era of economic growth, falling unemployment and concern about rising inflation. Any suggestion that these should give way to fiscal and monetary policies for combating unemployment immediately raises the spectre of high inflation in the minds of policy-makers.

This threat receives support in the economics literature from the idea that there is a unique 'Non-accelerating Inflation Rate of Unemployment' (the 'NAIRU'), in other words, the assertion that there is one particular level of equilibrium unemployment at which inflation stabilizes. This NAIRU framework is unhelpful, since it rests on the implicit assumption of unchanged and unspecified policies and practices. The relationship between unemployment and changes in earnings variously measured is plotted for Britain in the 1980s in Michie and Wilkinson (1992) and the results could not be more at variance with the notion of a predictable relationship between the two variables. The historical evidence for any credible relationship between the level of joblessness and the rate of inflation is thus fragile at best.

This NAIRU theory is a version of Milton Friedman's 'Natural Rate of Unemployment' developed by the economists Richard Layard and Stephen Nickell. They argue that as unemployment falls the 'bargaining wage' demanded by workers rises whilst the 'feasible wage' which employers can afford to pay does not rise with output. This failure of the wage which employers can afford to pay to rise as output rises is based on one or both of two seriously flawed arguments. First, it is supposed that as firms increase their level of output productivity fails to rise and may fall. But in fact the opposite is usually the case: in economic expansions output per head generally rises (it increased 20 per cent between 1984 and 1990). This increase in productivity is explained by the fact that old, less efficient plant is scrapped in recessions, capital is operated at a higher level of utilization as demand increases and firms invest in more modern equipment with renewed prosperity. The more reasonable assumption that productivity and hence the 'feasible wage' increase with output destroys one of the bases of the NAIRU law. If increased capacity utilization and, over the longer term, increased and more technologically advanced capacity allows a growth of the feasible wage then there may be no unique 'equilibrium' point (NAIRU) with only that one level of unemployment associated with non-accelerating inflation. Thus even if the bargaining and feasible wages happened to coincide at a given level of unemployment, if unemployment falls with the feasible wage increasing (owing to increased productivity) more than the increase in the bargaining wage, then such a model would actually predict that the reduction in unemployment would result in inflation falling rather than rising.

The second string to the NAIRU bow is the argument that firms have to cut prices to sell more. By enabling firms to lower prices, cuts in wages and other employment costs allow them to sell more and increase employment. But this argument is also fatally flawed. The size of the market of a firm (and hence the employment it can offer) is determined by its price *and* by the price of its competitors. If the workers employed by that firm accept a lower wage so that the firm can retain its monopoly profits at a lower price it will be able to increase its output and its market share but only at the expense of other firms and the employment they offer. But of course if all firms lower their wages there will be no change in relative prices and no increase in demand. In fact if that happens the chances are that demand will decline, because a general fall in wages relative to prices will have reduced the purchasing power of wage income.

The rise of unemployment in Europe can thus be more usefully analysed by ignoring such economic orthodoxy and referring instead to the relationship between macro-economic policy, balance of payments constraints and deindustrialization. European unemployment has been accompanied by a relatively rapid decline in manufacturing employment in the EC 12, and in this process Britain has shown the way. The share of employment in manufacturing fell in the decade 1976–86 from 22·8 per cent to 19·1 per cent in the US, from 25·5 per cent to 24·7 per cent in Japan and from 28·9 per cent to 24·4 per cent in the EC 12. This relative decline represented an absolute fall for Europe, of almost 5·5 million jobs. Of the EC 12, only Portugal and Greece avoided a fall in manufacturing employment, with the UK experiencing the most extreme cut (of 16 per cent, representing more than 2 million jobs).

There has been considerable debate over the causes of such 'deindustrialization' (e.g. Singh 1987; Rowthorn and Wells 1987). A shift in employment from manufacturing to other sectors could simply be the result of a shift in consumption patterns away from manufactured goods towards services and/or differential productivity growth between the industrial and service sectors. However, two important points are clear: first, the decline in manufacturing employment in the EC 12 – and in particular in the UK – has not been caused by shifts in consumption patterns, nor by other sectors' requirements for labour. The loss of manufacturing jobs has been accompanied by an increasing deficit in manufacturing trade and by a rise in unemployment. And in the UK most dramatically, manufacturing has not experienced rapidly rising output as a result of productivity growth but, on the contrary, a stagnant trend in output, with the productivity growth hence translating not into output growth but instead into falling employment.

And second, as stressed by Ajit Singh in his original development of the concept of deindustrialization, an economy's distribution of output (and employment) between sectors can lead to balance of payments constraints, and hence can impact not just on relative shares of output and employment but also on absolute levels. It is this danger of a balance of payments constraint on economic recovery and the achievement of full employment which should be of concern to the EC 12 in the 1990s.

Exchange rate mechanisms and the balance of payments have had two major implications for unemployment in Europe. The Exchange Rate Mechanism has imposed requirements for monetary and interest rate policy, and domestic fiscal policy. These requirements have been biased towards requiring deflationary interest rate rises of countries whose currency is under pressure, rather than reflationary policies in economies with strong currencies. Given the level of domestic demand so determined, the balance of trade indicates the degree to which this is translated into domestic production and employment.

It might be thought that trade imbalances within the EC could not have deflationary implications for the Community as a whole because deficits in some countries would be more or less offset by surpluses in others so that any deflationary implications of deficits would be balanced by expansionary implications for the surplus economies. The effects are not, however, quite so symmetrical. The key surplus economy has been Germany. Since the Second World War the German production system, stimulated as it has been by good labour and social welfare standards, extensive training and strong centralized collective bargaining, has generated competitiveness and hence the ability to export. The tight monetary policy, pursued by the Bundesbank has sterilized the potentially reflationary impact of the resultant trade surplus by restricting domestic demand, translating growth into export surpluses (Robinson 1966).

As for the deficit countries such as the UK, for any level of domestic demand, the more that is met by net imports the lower are domestic output and employment. Thus, for example, the rise in consumer demand between 1978–81 and 1989–92 was met by net imports, resulting in a move from current account surplus (of 2·5 per cent of GDP) to deficit (of 3·8 per cent of GDP) – a swing of 6·3 per cent of GDP in real terms and an equivalent export of jobs. The increase in consumer expenditure represented a growing share (from 59·9 per cent to 65·9 per cent) of a GDP whose growth lagged behind. Indeed, although there was a rise in gross investment (from 16·5 per cent to 18·7 per cent of GDP), manufacturing investment actually fell as a share of GDP (from 3·0 per cent to 2·7 per cent). The latest available figures show that even in 1992, at the depths of the longest recession since the 1930s, UK net imports were still equivalent to 1·7 per cent of GDP, with a lower share of GDP devoted to investment (at 15·1 per cent) than in Italy (20·3 per cent), France (20·7 per cent), West Germany (21·2 per cent) or Japan (30·9 per cent).[3]

GOVERNMENT POLICY AND LOW PAY

The switch in macro-economic policy towards the belief that direct government intervention is counterproductive and that the economy can be effectively regulated only by monetary means has as its micro-economic corollary the assertion that joblessness results from impediments to the working of the invisible hand in the labour market. As a result, the policy response to the growth of unemployment resulting from restrictive monetary policy and balance of payments constraints has been labour market deregulation. A consequence of such liberalization is that inequality has increased in most EC countries over the 1980s, but it was in the UK that inequality was most deliberately pursued through the government's labour market policies.

Post-1979 British governments have attributed much of the blame for unemployment to 'market rigidities'. In particular, Ministers have argued that 'artificial' constraints on the labour market have prevented wages falling to adjust to changed conditions, and that for many groups wages are being held above their true market level, thereby 'pricing' workers from jobs. To cure these supposed rigidities a large number of measures have been implemented, designed to reduce wages and then enable the 'market to work more freely'. Employment rights such as unfair dismissal protection and maternity provisions have been watered down and their coverage reduced; public services have been contracted-out to private firms, often at wages and conditions much poorer than in the public sector itself; other government services have been privatized, removing the low-paid from the coverage of collectively negotiated agreements; wage protecting conventions such as the fair wage resolution and Schedule 11 have been abolished; and the Wages Councils, introduced to set legally binding minimum wages in low-wage sectors, first had their scope and powers drastically reduced in 1986 and were abolished in 1993. Concurrently the rolling programme of trade union legislation has seriously impeded trade union organization and the ability to gain bargaining rights – to the particular disadvantage of low-pay sectors.

While earnings for some sections of the population rose fairly rapidly in Britain during the 1980s, this fact masks a huge increase in inequality, with the pay of the higher-paid growing more rapidly than that of the lower-paid. This is reflected in the more rapid increase in non-manual earnings and in the tendency for the increase in pay to be higher at successively higher points of the earnings distribution. Thus at the lowest decile for manual males the increase in real pay from 1979 to 1992 was only 4 per cent whilst at the highest decile for non-manual workers it was 53 per cent; for females the increases were 10 per cent and 61 per cent respectively. However, when considering the relative performance of female earnings, account should be taken of the increase in part-time work from 40 per cent to 46 per cent of female workers, and the fact that hourly pay for part-time work is on average less – and has increased at a slower pace – than hourly pay for full-time work.

This change in the structure of earnings can be explained by three main factors. First, the decline in employment in manufacturing and in other non-service sectors has concentrated mainly in the middle range of the earnings distribution. Second, the increase in employment was concentrated in sectors such as banking, insurance, finance and business, where earnings are relatively high, and in hotel, catering and other such services, where earnings tend to be low. The disappearance of jobs from the middle of the earnings distribution and the increase at each end would explain at least part of the widening of the earnings distribution. The third factor explaining the changed distribution of earnings is the tendency for the earnings of the higher-paid to grow rapidly and those of the low-paid to increase relatively slowly since 1979. This is indicated by the fact that earnings in manufacturing grew by five percentage points more than in services. But the main differences in the rates of increase in earnings between different industrial sectors were within the service sector itself, with earnings in the highly paid banking, insurance and finance sector growing two and a half times more than those in the low-paid distribution and hotel and catering sectors. Moreover, it is in the low-paid service sectors that the growth in part-time female employment has been located.[4]

UK governments have added to the regressive effects of its labour market policies on the distribution of income by its tax and social security policies. The elimination of higher tax brackets, the switch to indirect taxation and increases in National Insurance contributions have favoured the rich. Meanwhile, the least well-off have been hit by the elimination of the earnings-related elements, and dependants' benefits, from unemployment and sickness pay; by the break in the link between social security and earnings, and even, in some cases, between social security and inflation;[5] and by the restrictions on eligibility for out-of-work benefits, and the coercion of the unemployed into accepting poorly paid jobs by the redefinition and the more rigorous enforcement of 'availability for work' rules.

As a consequence, in 1989 social security benefits were a smaller proportion of GDP than in 1979, despite an increase in the number of pensioners of around 1 million, a similar increase in those without work and claiming benefit and an increase in the recipients of Family Credit of some 250,000. Redistribution has therefore been from the poor to the rich and within the different categories of the poor.

The overall effect of the increase in unemployment, differential rates of pay increase, the growth of part-time work and the government's tax and welfare policy is that between 1979 and 1991 the share of household income of the bottom half fell from 33 per cent to 27 per cent, and by even more – from 32 per cent to 25 per cent – after deducting housing costs.

The objective of labour market deregulation – rooted as it is in the notion that social security and labour standards, imposed by trade unions and government, seriously impede the effective working of the labour market – is to generate a higher level of employment by securing equilibrium between supply and demand. However, the evidence is that the labour market is in unstable equilibrium, held in balance only by high levels of unemployment, and that low pay is a major cause of labour market instability. For example, almost 40 per cent of the vacancies notified to the Department of Employment Job Centres are in the low-paid distribution, hotel and catering and repairs, although this sector accounts for only 20 per cent of total employment. As a percentage of employment, notified vacancies in distribution, hotels, catering and repairs were 23 per cent in 1988, the peak of the boom, declining to 14 per cent in the first half of 1991. Comparable figures for all other industries and services are 10 per cent and 7 per cent respectively. This suggests that, except, possibly, in periods of exceptionally high unemployment, in the low-pay segments of the labour market there is a substantially greater degree of unsatisfied demand for labour, meaning that, compared with other sectors, wages are too low. Recession brings supply more into line with demand by destroying alternative job opportunities. Thus, rather than low pay being an answer to unemployment, high levels of joblessness are a condition for many people accepting low-paid jobs, which they soon quit when job prospects improve.

Low pay and the resultant labour force instability also prove to be major obstacles to effective training and personnel policy. When unemployment is high the pressure on management is relaxed and when the labour market tightens firms are reluctant to train because labour turnover is high and potential recruits are reluctant to take training seriously because of the poor job prospects. Entry to low-paying trades is often a last resort and quitting is at the first opportunity. Consequently, investment in training shows a poor return to both employer and employees.

These problems became increasingly pressing in the low-paying sectors of British industry in the late 1980s as the labour market tightened with economic recovery, as the declining birth rate threatened the supply of cheap labour and as employers faced the implications of Equal Value legislation. This situation led to a spate of new company policies and collective agreements designed to improve the relative position of low-paid and part-time workers, to extend fringe benefits to part-timers, to introduce job evaluation and to train, motivate and involve workers at the lower end of the job hierarchy more effectively.[6]

But these necessary reforms were confined to the leading firms and sectors where unions were well organized. The vast majority of under-valued workers were not included. Moreover, with the growth of unemployment the threat of the 'demographic' time bomb has receded and with it the pressure on firms to improve their personnel policies so as to increase pay and to improve productivity and quality of service. In fact quite the opposite has happened. Major employers, such as the Burton Group of retailers, have taken advantage of high levels of unemployment to casualize jobs, cut pay and worsen conditions of work (IDS 1993). Elsewhere there has been widespread use of new legal powers and other legally more dubious devices to intensify the exploitation and intimidation of an increasingly vulnerable work force. Reporting on the increasing level of enquiries about employment problems the National Association of Citizens' Advice Bureaux concluded that 'Numbers of employees are faced with impossible choices – accepting a severe deterioration in their working conditions; or losing their jobs. With unemployment standing at over 3 million, the implications of this dilemma are obvious' (1993: 49). Thus the aim of social security legislation has increasingly been to sharpen 'work incentives', on the assumption that the unemployed are made reluctant to take up available paid work by the receipt of benefits and by the poverty and unemployment traps. Simultaneously, paid work at the lower end of the labour market has been made more and more unattractive, both to the unemployed and to those in employment, by the dilution of social and employment protection and the consequent decline in job quality. It is a matter of fine judgement whether the net effect of this policy of making the receipt of out-of-work income less and less attractive, while at the same time reducing the range of decent jobs available within employment, has been to induce greater labour market participation among the unemployed. But there can be little doubt of the degenerative effect of employment practices and intensified exploitation on economic efficiency.

LABOUR UNDERVALUATION AND WORKER EFFICIENCY

Orthodox economists argue that low pay reflects low levels of productivity. When, as is the more usual case, low pay and poor working conditions result from the undervaluation of labour due to the imbalance of power in the labour market, the direction of causation runs in precisely the opposite direction. Such circumstances are not conducive to worker co-operation, and workers may use the power they derive from their ability to withhold labour and from the additional skill and information they acquire from work experience by, for example, keeping effort within prescribed limits, working closely to the 'rules' so as to resist any flexible use of their time and by keeping managers uninformed of improvements in technology and working methods learned on the job. The consequence of all this is an adjustment of work effort and co-operation (which may require more ingenuity and effort than the work itself) to match employers' perception of workers' worth as represented by the pay and conditions on offer. But in these cases the direction of causation runs from low pay to low effort rather than the reverse.

Another way in which the undervaluation of labour leads to its dissipation can be accounted for by the relationship between low pay and poor working conditions on the one hand and skill and training on the other. The orthodox explanation is that low pay is the result of lack of training and skill and that an increase in pay will further discourage employers from providing training. But a closer examination reveals again a quite different direction of causation. First, low-paying employers are the least likely to train. Inefficient low payers require undervalued labour to subsidize poor management or keep obsolete equipment in production and cannot afford to train except in the narrowest sense. The interests of predatory low payers are in exploiting human capital rather than in creating it.

Second, skill is to an important degree a social category, and jobs with poor terms and conditions of employment are unlikely to be afforded high status whatever their skill level. Moreover, status as well as the content of jobs will determine the willingness of individuals to acquire the necessary entry qualifications by undertaking education and training. The identification of particular jobs with socially deprived groups lowers their skill status and the training routes by which they are acquired. One of the effects of the process of deindustrialization in the UK and elsewhere has been a decline in levels of pay and conditions of work in the industries directly affected, as well as in those industries into which the redundant workers have been crowded.

Deindustrialization creates conditions for social deskilling in four closely related ways which add to the spiral of decline. First, rapid increases in unemployment weaken workers' resistance to employers' offensives against the terms and conditions of employment and traditional forms of control of skilled work. Second, a common response by firms to their declining fortunes is to cut back on training. The cut-back may take the form of a reduction of in-house training and/or a decline in support for external provision by training agencies so that the local infrastructure for skill generation is weakened. This, and the migration from the trade of workers in a position to do so, create a skill shortage. The response, in the face of the decline in formal training, is thirdly the substitution of on-the-job instruction with a focus on a narrow range of specific skills to meet the firm's immediate needs, often accompanied by the exclusion of worker representatives from the training design and implementation processes. Consequently the skill content of jobs is diluted and this interacts with the deterioration in the terms and conditions of employment and the increasing pessimism about the prospects of the industry to discourage new entrants from traditional areas of recruitment.

And, fourth, any subsequent relaxation of hiring standards to meet the labour shortage serves to reinforce further the social downgrading of the job, the dissipation of skills, the loss of competitiveness and industrial decline.

The response by government to the twin problems of increasing unemployment and a growing skill shortage has been to institute new training schemes. Whatever the original intention, or indeed the quality of much of the training, these schemes tend to acquire a reputation for disguising unemployment, for creating new forms of cheap labour and for failing to provide adequate training. The general effect is therefore a downgrading in labour market terms of the participants and the job areas at which the schemes are targeted. Individuals then become increasingly unwilling to take part in training programmes because they think them a waste of time and effort, and individuals who have so trained tend to quit the resultant job at the earliest opportunity.

A related problem is that by targeting training at the unemployed to get them into jobs with low-paying firms in need of undervalued labour to keep obsolete equipment in operation and outdated product lines profitable is a waste of training resources. Such firms need skills which are specific to outdated technology and are therefore effectively obsolete. The cumulative effect of low pay and poor working conditions and of policy responses by employers and the state is therefore to weaken the skill base (in both technical and social terms), discourage individuals from undertaking training and misallocating training resources. In these circumstances, lack of demand for training rather than paucity of supply explains skill shortages and reinforces deindustrializing processes.

COSTS OF INEQUALITY

Inequality and poverty also have detrimental effects on the balance of payments constraint, with a transfer of resources to the better-off, who import more (see Borooah 1988); on the government's own fiscal deficit (the Public Sector Borrowing Requirement, or PSBR); and on the real economy as consumer spending is depressed and the pressure on firms to upgrade their production processes is weakened.

On the PSBR, rising inequality and poverty mean that the costs of social security, benefits and income support grow. A growing share of the income of the working poor is met not by their employers but by the taxpayer. This not only increases both the spread and the grip of the poverty trap (whereby any increase in pay by employers is matched by an equivalent loss of benefit from government), it also increases the burden on public expenditure. And if total government spending is constrained – for example, by the Maastricht 3 per cent formula – the burden has to be met by public spending cuts imposed elsewhere, cuts which may well exacerbate unemployment. An alternative response is to cut *per capita* income to the poor, as was done in Britain in the 1980s and as is being considered by the EC.[7] A further possibility which is increasingly being touted is a direct subsidy to employers to provide jobs for the out-of-work.

This increasing use by private capital of low-paid workers, requiring public funds to raise their income to a living wage, is in essence a return to the 'Speenhamland system' adopted under the Poor Law in Britain in the eighteenth and nineteenth centuries.[8] The Poor Law was thus no longer something to fall back on but became the general framework of the rural labourer's life. 'The distinction between worker and pauper vanished' (Hobsbawm and Rudé 1969: 47). There are also parallels with the currently fashionable 'basic income' schemes. Indeed, the following description sounds uncannily like advocacy of the present 'basic income' ideas:

> No measure was ever more universally popular. Parents were free of the care of their children, and children were no more dependent on their parents; employers could reduce wages at will and labourers were safe from hunger whether they were busy or slack; humanitarians

93

applauded the measure as an act of mercy even though not of justice and the selfish gladly consoled themselves with the thought that though it was merciful at least it was not liberal; even the ratepayers were slow to realise what would happen to the rates under a system which proclaimed the 'right to live' whether a man earned a living wage or not.

(Polanyi 1945: 85)

It is therefore perhaps particularly important to remember that:

It was at bottom an attempt to maintain the ancient ideal of a stable though unequal society . . . setting its face against the only thing which could have at least provided some defence against the fall in wages, the combination of the workers.

(Hobsbawm and Rudé 1969: 48, 50)

Given the likelihood of the EC seeking to tackle unemployment by cutting employment taxes on firms – and in particular by subsidizing low-paid sectors[9] – it is worth quoting at length on the implications for the production system of the Speenhamland system:

The traditional social order degenerated into a universal pauperism of demoralised men who could not fall below the relief scale whatever they did, who could not rise above it, who had not even the nominal guarantee of a living income, since the 'scale' could be – and with the increasing expense of rates was – reduced to as little as the village rich thought fit for a labourer. Agrarian capitalism degenerated into a general lunacy, in which farmers were encouraged to pay as little as they could (since wages would be supplemented by the parish) and used the mass of pauper labour as an excuse for not raising their productivity; while their most rational calculations would be, how to get the maximum subsidy for their wage-bill from the rest of the ratepayers. Labourers, conversely, were encouraged to do as little work as they possibly could, since nothing would get them more than the official minimum of subsistence.

Nobody can measure the dehumanisation or, in economic terms, the fall in productivity which resulted.

(Hobsbawm and Rudé 1969: 50–1)

SUBSIDIZING JOBS – THE SOLUTION OR A DIVERSION?

The key to a return to full employment is, then, to shift the emphasis of policy, to concentrate on employment creation rather than unemployment treatment. The current orthodoxy among policy-makers is that further deregulation is still the way to more jobs and that there is no macro-economic policy route to higher employment (although the orthodox economists never make it clear why; they just build the assumption into their models). The recommended cures which follow seem to be either to get the low-skilled to accept low-paid jobs or to train them so they can compete more effectively for the high-paid ones. It is not obvious how such an increase in the supply of people willing and/or able to take jobs can affect the overall level of employment unless there is an increase in demand for goods and services and hence an increase in the number of jobs available. Although it may be argued that either higher skills or lower pay will increase the competitiveness of Europe and increase the number of jobs there, no such increase in competitiveness is likely to do more than reshuffle world employment unless there is an easing of macro-economic policy.

The high level of overall unemployment at the European level can be explained by the deflationary bias in the macro-economic policy of Germany. Even so, there can be little doubt that there is no easy route to full employment in the UK through demand management alone, whatever happens at the European level, because the UK economy is balance of payments constrained. The historically progressive deindustrialization of the UK economy exacerbated by the Thatcherite experiment means that even with a prolonged recession and unprecedented unemployment the current account of the balance of payment remains stubbornly in deficit. This growth of the current account deficit has important deflationary consequences and also indicates the extent to which full employment of the industrial capacity of Britain is progressively lower than that level necessary to employ the work force fully. It should be further noted that the erosion of the industrial base has gone furthest in the capital goods sector, so that the re-equipping of industry to remove the balance of payments constraint has serious implications for the balance of payments.

The policy-makers are reassured that the balance of payments does not matter by the argument that international capital markets' willingness to lend Britain money – so that the capital account surplus offsets the current account deficit – is a measure of confidence in the British economy. This ignores completely the importance of short-term speculative gains in triggering international capital flows, the destabilizing affects of these movements and the consequences for interest rates of being obliged to attract hot money to offset current account deficits. In 1979 world trade stood at US$1,500 billion and foreign exchange trading at US$17,500 billion. By 1992 trade had tripled to US$4,700 billion, yet foreign exchange trading had increased almost fifteenfold, to US$252,000 billion.

Thus in 1978–81 commercial bank interest rates, adjusted for producer prices, averaged 1·9 per cent but in 1989–92 they averaged 7·3 per cent. This almost fourfold increase in real interest rates has serious implications for industrial costs and investment and consequently has made – and continues to make – its own contribution to the erosion of the industrial base and the lowering of the sustainable level of employment.

The explanation given by the British policy-makers for the country's lack of competitiveness and high unemployment is the inflexibility of the labour market. To remedy the problem they have followed the US down the route of reducing labour and social standards. But in neither country has this reversed economic decline; rather, both countries have become increasingly uncompetitive, generating larger and larger balance of payment deficits. Both countries have a growing proportion of their population in primary poverty and have larger and larger budget deficits as the costs to society of deindustrialization and unemployment mount. The consequence has been an interrelated downward spiral of social and labour market standards and a growth in the number of casualized, part-time and low-paid jobs with bad working conditions.

The increasing number of takers for these jobs can be explained by the increase in poverty, a decline in the ability of labour to defend employment conditions against the combined efforts of employers and the government to reduce them, the pressure on families to throw more of their members on the labour market in an attempt to maintain customary living standards and an increasing tendency to subsidize employment by various means, including the topping up of low wages by social security. These effects have combined both to increase the number of jobs and to reduce meaningful employment. Despite this and the warnings from other economic indicators, the ability of the US and UK to increase the job count has, in the minds of many commentators, made the labour market and social security policies of those countries a model for effective full employment strategies elsewhere. Various measures are being proposed for increasing labour market flexibility in Europe to increase employment.

The European Commission is considering two different but related policy programmes for reducing indirect employment costs as a way of gaining international competitiveness and reducing unemployment. First is the idea of a general reduction in the employment taxes and other charges which fall on employers for each worker employed. The argument is that such indirect costs (that is, additional to the direct wage costs) are higher on average in the EC than in the US or Japan, and that a reduction would allow a concomitant reduction in prices, boosting international competitiveness, world market share, output and employment. However, a number of questions are begged by this hoped-for virtuous circle. First, would the entire reduction in employment costs feed directly through into lower output prices, or might some go in higher profit margins, or, by reducing market pressure on the firms to pursue international competitiveness through productivity gains and quality improvements, might these tax reductions be accompanied by lower gains in productivity than might otherwise have occurred, resulting in no net gain in unit costs? Second, from where would the lost tax revenue be recouped? There are, of course, arguments against increasing income tax, VAT or any of the other possible candidates. And if the lost revenue were not to be made good, then what would the implications be for the government budget deficits, which are already greater than allowed by Maastricht's convergence criteria? If the fall in employer taxes were to be matched by government spending cuts, then the harm which such cuts might do, not least to the functioning of the production system and hence to international productivity and world market share, would also need to be considered. Indeed, in the present economic and political climate, where there is pressure to reduce government deficits yet resistance to increasing income tax, it may be that raising money to pay for public services from insurance-type charges, such as employers' National Insurance contributions in Britain, will have to play a greater rather than a reduced role. That these and other questions should be researched in more detail is suggested by the fact that one of the few EC countries with employer charges already down to the US and Japanese levels is the UK, and there is little sign there of the correlation with market share and employment success on which the Commission's policy is predicated.

The second policy programme for reducing indirect employment costs being considered by the European Commission is to reduce them particularly on low-paid (or, as such employment is usually described when proposals of this nature are being advocated, low-skilled) employment. The idea is to encourage the sort of employment creation witnessed in the US in the 1980s, through a combination of expanding the sectors of the economy in which such labour is employed and encouraging the further substitution of labour for capital in such sectors. Again, however, there are other possible consequences which need to be investigated, first to have a clearer picture of what the likely impact of such a policy would be and, second, to consider whether there are any additional or alternative measures which would allow the employment gain without the associated loss of productivity pain. Specifically, the idea that labour–capital substitution follows changes in relative prices does not, at that general level, enjoy any empirical (or indeed theoretical) support. More generally, the idea of differential cuts in indirect employment costs is a type of labour subsidy towards that type of labour, and as such there are various associated dangers. First, there may be a disincentive to upgrade the production system if it would involve the associated labour losing its subsidy. Second, there is the risk that the economy is diverted towards the low-skill, low-investment sectors which are subsidized.

FULL EMPLOYMENT IN THE FUTURE

Throughout the 1950s and 1960s almost all countries enjoyed full employment, meaning that anyone who wanted a job was generally able to find one. In the capitalist countries there was of course always some registered unemployment as people changed jobs, but the long-term involuntary unemployment of the inter-war period had gone. All this came to an end in the early 1970s. And the 1990s threaten to be the worst decade yet for mass unemployment. So full employment is certainly possible, but it will not return automatically. A return to full employment will require a fundamental change in government policy across the world. Governments cannot be held responsible for everything; but what they can be held responsible for is government policy.

However, there are various arguments to suggest that full employment may not even be a desirable objective. First, it has been argued that unemployment may be necessary to make those in employment work harder. But this ignores completely the rapid economic and social progress made during the twenty-five years 1948–73, when there was full employment, when economic growth was actually faster than it has been since and when the response to wide job opportunities was progressive work-force upgrading. Compare that with the cost of the enforced idleness and the enormous loss of prospects for those entering the labour market since the mid-1970s.

Second, not everyone wants a full-time job. But everyone should be given that opportunity: the choice will be made real only if individuals are not forced into employment by poverty and if they are not discriminated against on the grounds of their sex, their age, their educational creditation, their disabilities or the number of hours they prefer to work.

Third, there are environmental constraints. This means that we should think about the type of economic growth we want, not just the amount. But there is no reason to suppose that environmentally friendly economic progress is less labour-intensive than a more environmentally unfriendly path. Nor that the physical environment will in any way be served by a progressive deterioration of the social environment.

There is a separate argument that full employment is no longer possible, however desirable, because new technology is displacing workers at a faster pace than the growth in demand can re-employ them. This is simply wrong. There is no evidence at all of a sea change in output per head. In fact the rate of increase of labour productivity has slowed in the past two decades. Moreover, even a casual glance at the world today would indicate that public and private needs place few constraints on employment, whatever the improvement in technology. There may be problems with the willingness or ability of present forms of political, social and economic organization to meet even the basic requirements of the majority of the world's population but that does not disguise the want.

The industrial world is in the grip of an unemployment crisis of historic proportions which bears a striking resemblance to its 1930s predecessor. In the 1920s the world economy was highly volatile, with unprecedented stock market and currency speculation. Organized labour was on the retreat and wage-cutting and labour market deregulation were the order of the day, especially in the US and the UK. The consequent underconsumptionist tendencies were exacerbated by the collapse of commodity prices in the early 1920s, which benefited industrial profits but ruined agriculture. This unstable economic base collapsed in 1929 when the world financial system was completely disrupted by the Wall Street crash and industry was undermined by the Great Depression, against which national governments proved individually and collectively powerless. Economic orthodoxy, then as now, held trade unions, state labour market regulation and social welfare payments responsible for unemployment and preached against state intervention to counter joblessness and for balanced budgets. When translated into policies these notions, by deepening the recession and multiplying social deprivation, had the opposite of the predicted effect, and the consequent widening of the credibility gap led to weak and vacillating governments. In Britain the Labour Government split over policies which cut pay, reduced unemployment benefit and introduced means-testing, policies which were insisted on by international bankers and finally implemented by the National government led by Ramsey MacDonald. In Germany 6 million unemployed, widespread poverty and cuts in unemployment pay paved the way to fascism and ultimately to the Second World War.

The lessons learned from this debacle, at the level of economic theory and public policy, laid the groundwork of the post-war prosperity. National governments committed themselves to full employment and a welfare state policy which included health, social security, education and housing. In the labour market collective bargaining was encouraged, minimum employment rights were guaranteed and industrial training was strengthened. At the international level agreements on finance and trade were concluded which were designed to encourage international commerce but which were targeted at currency speculation and the problems of chronic surplus countries. These were reinforced at the national level by controls on international capital movements. Contingency plans were laid for the stabilization of commodity prices but made little headway after the end of the Korean War crisis when the collapse of raw material prices turned the terms of trade in the favour of industrial countries. The purpose of these policies was to create a framework of rules for encouraging the creativity of free enterprise whilst prohibiting the strong predatory and exploitative tendencies in capitalism.

This national and international collectivist effort created the promise that from some small proportion of the world's working class poverty would at last be lifted. The promise was most fully realized in those countries of northern Europe which most completely adopted the co-operative state model; no more so than in Sweden, where the Social Democratic Party embraced the 'wage solidarity' with 'active labour market' policies formulated by the trade unions so that labour effectively managed capitalism. At the international level the growth in the market of industrial countries helped create new opportunities for economic development. The real failure of the post-war period was at the international level. It can be explained by the dominant economic power of the US and that country's continued adherence to the notion that capitalism operates at its best when completely unrestricted. This philosophy came to pervade the workings of the international agencies (the IMF, World Bank and GATT) and subverted their role as agents working for world economic stability. The cost to the US itself was great. Its own unrestricted capital moved the production base of the US economy offshore and came increasingly to be dominated by short-term speculation on the stock market rather than by long-term industrial investment. This and the fact that deteriorating industrial relations and labour market conditions in the US made it incapable of meeting the quality competition from abroad undermined US competitiveness, so that it joined the UK as a newly deindustrializing economy.

The combination of, first, the lack of any effective stabilizing international institutions and, second, the progressive decline in the economic power of the US played a major part in recreating the sort of international finance and trade volatility last seen in the inter-war years. This undermined the ability of governments to exercise control and destroyed the credibility of the policies which had formed the basis of post-war economic prosperity. The return to the pre-Keynesian orthodoxy in macro-economic management completed the circle. Restrictive monetary policies, intensified competition for a share of markets which were growing more slowly than production capacity and unrestricted currency speculation interacted to recreate world recession.

Unemployment today is therefore not due to the working of mystical economic laws regulating wages. There is no substance in the claim that if the worst-off in society accept a cut in their living standards, long-term prospects will be magically restored; the opposite is more likely to be the case. Nor is unemployment the result of there being too little work needing doing to employ fully all those who seek employment. Private need and public squalor are both on the increase. The physical environment needs to be improved; more work should go into education, health and public services generally; housing and other infrastructure work would in almost all countries be welcome. The problem is not a shortage of things that need doing. It is a shortage of political will to do them.

Yet business leaders are constantly pressing for cuts in taxes, for lower wages and for reduced social security contributions to be matched by cuts in government expenditure. The argument is that if the rewards to capital are increased, then enterprise will be stimulated. But after a decade or more of 'putting capital first' in most of the member states, and certainly in Britain, where is the evidence of the renaissance? Britain's balance of payments is firmly in the red, investment was lower between 1979 and 1992 than in the previous thirteen years, manufacturing investment is substantially lower, and the largest firms are increasingly creaming off the benefits of policy largesse and investing abroad. The only obvious signs of dynamism are the remarkable stock market gains and increases in distributed profits. But these have been at the expense of enterprise. The predatory pressure of stock market players has forced firms to sacrifice long-term growth for quick profits.

Governments are under continual pressure from business, from the banks and from international bodies such as the IMF and World Bank to stick to financial orthodoxy and to cut back on public employment and public intervention in the economy. Such pressure needs, therefore, to be met by greater pressure for progressive economic policies which put people before profit. In practical policy terms such pressure needs to focus on achieving a more equitable distribution of income; on forcing government to expand public employment; on improving the welfare state and pursuing genuine environmental programmes, as well as on taking measures to force up the level of industrial investment and upgrading the production infra-structure; and thereby creating the conditions for sustainable economic growth.

A massive shift of income and wealth towards the rich took place on a global scale as well as domestically in Britain throughout the 1980s and has continued into the 1990s. Reversing it by increasing employment, cutting unearned speculative gains in the interests of benefiting creative enterprise instead and reducing the differential between the highest and lowest paid would relieve pressure on public finances as people were raised out of state dependence and as the cost of administering the tax/benefit system fell. Increased purchasing power from the developing countries, and from the mass of consumers in Britain and Europe, would allow demand to grow alongside supply. It is also in this context that the need for training should be seen, training for jobs which were actually being created in the real economy and which would be sustained beyond the life of the associated training programme. Just as economic development can suffer from skill shortages, so training can suffer from lack of genuine job opportunities.

Job opportunities have to be created to suit people's needs and prefer-ences. Where today people such as security guards are having to work eighty hours a week to make up their take-home pay of £100, that level of pay (and more) should be available for a forty-hour week. And even at that new rate of pay – in other words, double the present level on an hourly basis – creating the additional jobs would not be expensive from the point of view of society as a whole, since the cost of unemployment pay and so on would be saved and extra tax would be paid. But while job-sharing in this context can be a vital part of progress, where it is achieved as a genuine right which workers can choose to exercise, it is important at the same time to guard against the all too common regressive use of such measures as employer-imposed tactics, often as a way of deliberately undermining employment rights.

It should also be recognized that many people may want to work who are prevented from doing so by the lack of adequate child-care facilities. Providing child care would thus increase the number of people seeking work, but that should not be seen as an obstacle to the achievement of full employment. First, the disguised unemployment of having someone forced to stay at home to look after children is hardly an achievement, and, second, the creation and development of a national child-care system – for after-school care as well as for pre-school-age provision – would itself be a labour-intensive activity.

It is important, then, not to allow the progressive right to 'job-share', or work flexible hours, to spread the illusion that there is only a given lump of work which therefore has to be spread around. The truth is that there are huge numbers of jobs which need doing that are simply not being done. Nevertheless, as part of a strategy for full employment, a reduction in working hours would help bring unemployment down further and more quickly. Historically the length of the working week has tended to remain more or less static for several decades, with a large reduction then being achieved, setting a new norm. The time for a major reduction is surely here again. This is not an abstract demand; the past few years have seen major campaigns by workers to win a reduction in the length of the working week, but employers have resisted stubbornly.

The lessons of history have to be relearned. Just as today's economic orthodoxy, political commentators and ruling elites have all resorted to repeating the free-market dogmas of the 1920s, so we need to remember the lessons learned at such enormous cost from the resulting Great Depression and the rise of fascism. At the international level those lessons included the need for really effective international agreements – not to 'set free' capital but rather to stabilize trade flows and restrict speculative activity. At the national level there was not only a commitment in principle to full employment and a welfare state, there was also a recognition of the need for generally applicable, effective labour market and social conditions, including meaningful employment rights.

COMMUNITY POLICIES FOR JOBS

With Delors warning that even a return to growth in 1994 might not prevent the continued rise in unemployment to 20 million or more, the EC's December 1993 biannual summit was billed as the one to tackle unemployment. Indeed, Delors warned that the Community's unemployment total could be heading for 30 million by the late 1990s if the policies he presented in his White Paper to the heads of government are not adopted:

> People who have jobs are being selfish – not only wage-earners, but their trade unions and employers. That must change if we are not to see 30 million unemployed by the end of the century . . .

> Solidarity between people who have jobs and those who have not should be at the basis of society . . . We need a political and social dialogue between those with jobs and those without to discuss the gains from productivity.[10]

Similar sentiments have been articulated by the EC's social affairs commissioner, Padraig Flynn, who has described the White Paper as a plan for creating 20 million jobs by the end of the decade.[11]

The summit at which this White Paper was launched was followed by US President Clinton's world jobs summit in 1994. But will these summits do more than rearrange the deckchairs? And in these days of globalized markets and footloose capital is a proactive policy agenda from governments possible?

The European Commission president, Jacques Delors, has warned against the ultimate horror – of an English-style Europe:

> What I see is a European construction drifting towards a free-trade zone, that is to say, an English-style Europe which I reject and which is against the spirit of the founding fathers of the Treaty of Rome . . .

> If we do nothing, this drift will lead in fifteen years to a break-up [of the EC] . . . I reject a Europe that would be just a market, a free-trade zone, without a soul, without a conscience, without a political will, without a social dimension.[12]

President Mitterrand of France has called for a doubling of the EC's spending on infrastructure and growth projects, as has Jacques Delors, who has proposed in particular a widening of the programme to include investment in labour-intensive sectors such as housing, as well as subsidizing borrowing for small and medium-size enterprises. Even these rather modest proposals have been scorned by the German and British governments.

Indeed, less than half the £5·6 billion already earmarked for recovery projects by the European Investment Bank had been committed by the end of October 1993, with Commission officials blaming the low take-up on the lack of commercially viable investment projects – hardly surprising in a recession – and because companies were failing to provide the matching finance required from the private sector.

The jobs initiative debated at the Community's Copenhagen summit in June 1993 involved radical changes in the EC's tax and social security systems. The Commission wants member states to reduce employers' National Insurance contributions, shifting the tax burden on to others. The rationale for such policies is that non-wage costs such as firms' social security payments add rather more in the EC states on average than they do in Japan or the US. Yet such non-wage costs are already down to Japanese and US levels in Britain, so there is clearly no automatic link between them and low unemployment. Indeed, employment in manufacturing – which should be particularly sensitive to factors affecting competitiveness – is lower in Britain as a percentage of the population in work than it is in Germany or France, despite the far higher indirect employment costs in those countries.

An additional policy idea from the Commission has been to introduce such reductions in employer taxes on unskilled labour in particular. On the general idea of an employment subsidy, expanded public employment would be a more effective method of tackling unemployment, particularly where there are either inflation or balance of payments constraints. The specific idea of a differential subsidy for unskilled work – generally defined in these contexts as low-paid work, which raises a rather separate issue of why skills such as cooking or cleaning tend not to be recognized as skills – risks reducing firms' incentive to improve productivity and upgrade production techniques.

Indeed, investment in research and development is already lower in the EC than in Japan or North America. In 1987 the EC went into deficit on international trade in high-tech goods – a deficit which has been deepening since. Yet while both Japan and the US announced public measures in 1993 to boost spending on R&D, the EC remained preoccupied with Maastricht.

As for Maastricht itself, despite its ratification, no member state other than Luxembourg met its convergence criteria in 1993 – and even Luxembourg failed the inflation test. It is vital that these convergence critiera should give way to policies for recovery. Quite apart from the short-term damage which adherence to the convergence criteria would cause, the longer-term aim of monetary union is ill conceived without major political and economic changes not envisaged in the Delors report or the Maastricht Treaty. Thus, for example, the MacDougall report suggested that an EC budget equivalent to 7 per cent of GDP would be necessary just to tackle 40 per cent of existing inequalities, yet the budget at present is set at 1·27 per cent and the more ambitious proposal rejected at the 1992 Edinburgh summit was for this to rise to only 1·38 per cent. And the treaty's specific provisions, such as the requirement for an independent central bank, with the overriding objective of achieving price stability, would risk locking the EC into recession.

Behind the present talk of jobs packages, therefore, lies the longer-term agenda of economic and monetary union. What has been amply demonstrated in the academic and policy literatures is that, measured against the criteria for being an 'optimum currency area', even the present fifteen member states (never mind a Community with additional members) fall some way short, and this shortfall will have to be made up – if the process of integration is to proceed, and to do so without straining cohesion to breaking point – by active industrial and regional policies to ensure continual (not just one-off) economic adjustment to so-called 'shocks' and, more generally, to different levels and growth rates of output and productivity.[13]

With talk today of the possibility of a 'two-speed Europe' – with Germany and the Benelux countries (with or without France) moving more rapidly to monetary union – it is worth recalling that the ill-fated gold standard did not collapse in one go in the 1930s: some countries attempted to maintain the fixed exchange rate system, thus heralding a two (or multi)-tier system. The ones who stuck with the system grew more slowly, those that left first grew fastest. Hence the 'speed' with which countries move towards fixed exchange rate systems should not be confused with the speed at which their economies will grow. In a two-speed Europe the 'slow' lane may be preferable.

Of course, one of the stock responses to any call for growth is to refer to the expansionary policies of the Mitterrand government in 1981, and the subsequent U-turn of 1983. The orthodox interpretation of this experience is that the Keynesian policies were discovered to be unsustainable because of balance of payments and exchange rate constraints and hence had to be abandoned. This is simply false: these difficulties were not something that had to be learned from the 1981–3 experience in France but were perfectly well understood and stated quite explicitly by, among others, the French Socialist Party before it took office. The problems which any government pursuing such expansionary policies would encounter were documented in advance, as were the additional policies which would be necessary to see the expansion through – including the use of trade policies to ensure that imports grew only in line with exports. The point is that no attempt was in fact made actually to introduce these additional, necessary policies. The government chose instead the beggar-my-neighbour route of 'competitive disinflation'.

While co-ordination is preferable (as Kalecki pointed out in 1932), there are nevertheless viable programmes for raising employment in a single country. Indeed, the only way of building support for an EC-level expansion may be through the contagious impact of a successful expansion of employment in one country first.

The 'co-operative' route – of completing the internal market and pursuing economic and monetary union – has tended to increase industrial concentration and exacerbate regional disparities, and an active industrial policy is needed instead to ensure the development of industrial activity outside the European core. To consider the form such an interventionist strategy to bolster industrial performance might take, it is necessary to draw a distinction between the notion of a developmental state, organized and concerned to promote economic and industrial development, on the one hand, and a regulatory state on the other, concentrating instead on competition policy. A broadly conceived industrial strategy (as opposed to just a 'policy') is needed to offset the forces of cumulative causation which will otherwise increase disparities and exacerbate the underutilization of resources in backward regions in particular.

A range of exchange rate issues also need further analysis, including that of how to overcome the 'fault lines' of the Exchange Rate Mechanism. Problems due to currency speculation could be tackled by taxing foreign exchange market transactions, simply reducing the profitability of such activity. Speculators might move 'offshore', but in that case their transactions could be exempted from legal status so that unpaid debts would not be backed by the force of law.

In the short term, changes in the conduct of monetary and fiscal policies are needed so that they support rather than impede growth, and structural policies need strengthening to boost development and job creation in those regions which are most in need. Longer-term policies are then also needed for boosting investment – and developing mechanisms for funding public investment – as well as for developing specific job creation measures.

Current levels of unemployment are a reflection of the political priorities attached to different objectives of economic policy. The low demand created by monetarist and restrictive economic policies has eroded the capacity to produce: plant capacity, management structures, sales organization, skilled and experienced labour, and the number of firms have all settled down at a level consisted with 9–10 per cent unemployment. Higher demand is therefore needed, but will have to be sustained if capacity is to be rebuilt. This is unlikely with an independent European central bank dedicated to achieving price stability. The emphasis has to be shifted towards restoring full employment. If it involves a short-term increase in government debt, then that – in the words of ex-Chancellor Norman Lamont – would be a price well worth paying.

CONCLUSIONS

Even the IMF believes that labour market policies 'have been unsuccessful in addressing persistently high unemployment, especially in Europe'. Much of the criticism from the IMF's spring 1993 *World Economic Outlook* is reserved for the EC countries. Despite cuts in short-term German interest rates, monetary conditions are held to be tight, exacerbated by 'substantial interest rate differentials relative to Germany, associated with recent exchange rate turbulence'; the weakness of the German economy is said to justify further cuts in interest rates; and economic recovery is predicted for Britain only because of the lower interest rates consequent upon sterling's departure from the Exchange Rate Mechanism.

And the OECD's 1993 annual report on labour market trends stresses the importance of long-term commitments in the workplace and active labour market management. Even the *Financial Times* had to acknowledge the irony of the OECD – usually associated with a more pro-market approach than the European Commission – emphasizing long-term human resource development at a time when the EC is considering further deregulation.[14]

Unemployment in the EC can in large part, then, be attributed to restrictive macro-economic policies, and its distribution as between member states by a failure to develop balance of payment adjustment mechanisms which do not throw the burden of adjustment on to the deficit counties. Persistent unemployment is creating increased pressure for the abandonment of minimum social security levels, labour market standards and employment rights, orchestrated by free-marketeer theorists who mystify real-world processes by reference to immutable economic laws which load the responsibility for economic stagnation on to its principal victims. But the fatal flaw in the argument that the way to economic and social progress is by immiserizing an increasing proportion of the population is to be found in the UK and US, where the experiments in competitive economic and social degradation have been taken furthest. There the Speenhamland trap has already been sprung, with its downward spiral of social welfare and labour market standards and economic performance and its upward spiral of Exchequer costs – processes which interrelate to produce social, political and competitive degeneration.

With its escalating internal problems there is every danger that the EC will follow Britain in a drift towards poverty, low wages and poor employment conditions for a large and growing section of its work force. The economic, social and political dangers in this cannot be overemphasized, and their avoidance depends on the ability of the countries of Europe to come together to produce expansionary policies which have at their core full employment and high and equitable social welfare and labour standards. In economic terms a strong welfare state is essential for a healthy, well educated and well trained work force; high wage and employment standards are essential for inducing the most effective use of such a work force; and full employment is the guarantee that no part of the work force is diverted into non-productivity. To achieve this collectively the European states require two essential safeguards regulating their relationships. First, measures are needed to deal with countries with persistent balance of payments surpluses, so as to prevent deficit countries adopting deflationary policies, thereby beggaring themselves and their neighbours. Second, centrally enforced common labour and social standards are required to prevent companies and nation states competitively devaluing their workers.

107

NOTES

1 Gallup poll published by the European Commission, reported in the *Guardian* of 19 October 1993.
2 See Michie (1993) for an analysis of the dangers which implementation of the Maastricht Treaty's provisions could pose to social and economical welfare.
3 Datastream and WEFA, reported in the *Financial Times*, 26 April 1993. The figures for France and Italy are the latest available, referring to 1991.
4 The impact of labour market policy on relative earnings, including the unequal growth of earnings as between different sectors of the economy, is analysed in greater detail in Deakin *et al.* (1992).
5 See Rowthorn (1992) for an analysis of government spending and taxation in the Thatcher era.
6 Firms involved include Tesco, Sainsbury and Safeway in retailing, Coats Viyella and Courtauld's in textiles and clothing and a range of leading firms in hotels, catering and leisure.
7 See, for example, the report in the *Financial Times*, 13 May 1993.
8 During the depressed years of the mid-1790s the rulers of the countryside, following the example of Berkshire magistrates meeting at Speenhamland, decided to subsidize low wages out of local rates where the labourers' family income fell below subsistence. See Hobsbawm and Rudé (1969) for a description and discussion of the system, on which this section draws.
9 A May 1993 EC document on tackling unemployment proposed reducing employers' social security contributions for unskilled workers (see the *Guardian*, 14 May 1993). The dangers associated with such arrangements whereby private-sector wages are subsidized from the public purse are also relevant in considering the relative merits of government employment creation policies of, on the one hand, expanding public-sector employment and, on the other, subsidizing employment in the private sector, as discussed by Andrew Glyn and Bob Rowthorn (1994), who find in any case that subsidizing private-sector employment is less desirable in terms of balance of payments and inflation constraints.
10 Jacques Delors, quoted in the *Guardian*, 14 October 1993.
11 Padraig Flynn, quoted in the *Guardian*, 20 October 1993.
12 Jacques Delors, speaking on Luxembourg radio, 17 October. His remarks were published by the Commission on 18 October, as reported in the *Guardian*, of 19 October 1993.
13 Similar concern about the North American Free Trade Agreement is reported to have played a part in the greatest parliamentary defeat in world history, suffered by the Canadian government in October 1993 (whose representation fell from 169 seats to two).
14 See the report in the *Financial Times* of 21 July 1993. The OECD's annual report on labour market trends was published on 20 July 1993.

REFERENCES

Blaug, M. (1963) 'The myth of the Old Poor Law and the making of the New', *Journal of Economic History* XXIII: 151–84.
Borooah, Vani (1988), 'Income distribution, consumption patterns and economic outcomes in the United Kingdom', *Contributions to Political Economy* 7: 49–63.
Deakin, Simon, Michie, Jonathan, and Wilkinson, Frank (1992) *Inflation, Employment, Wage-bargaining and the Law,* London: Institute of Employment Rights.

Glyn, A., and Rowthorn, R. (1994) 'European employment policies', in J. Michie and J. Grieve Smith (eds) *Unemployment in Europe*, London: Academic Press.

Hobsbawm, E. J., and Rudé, George (1969) *Captain Swing*, London: Lawrence & Wishart. (Page references are from the 1993 reprint, London: Pimlico.)

Incomes Data Services (1993) *Report 639*, London: Incomes Data Services Ltd.

Kalecki, Michal (1932) 'Is a capitalist overcoming of the crisis possible?' and 'On the paper plan', in J. Osiatynski (ed.) *Collected Works of Michal Kalecki*, London: Oxford University Press.

Kitson, Michael, and Michie, Jonathan (1994) 'Depression and recovery: lessons from the inter-war period', in J. Michie and J. Grieve Smith (eds) *Unemployment in Europe*, London: Academic Press.

McCombie, John, and Thirlwall, Tony (1992) 'The re-emergence of the balance of payments constraint', in J. Michie (ed.) *The Economic Legacy: 1979–1992*, London: Academic Press.

Michie, Jonathan (1993) *Maastricht – Implications for Public Services*, Manchester: NALGO (now UNISON).

Michie, Jonathan, and Grieve Smith, J. (1994) *Unemployment in Europe*, London: Academic Press.

Michie, Jonathan, and Wilkinson, Frank (1992) 'Inflation policy and the restructuring of labour markets', in J. Michie (ed.) *The Economic Legacy: 1979–1992*, London: Academic Press.

Michie, Jonathan, and Wilkinson, Frank (1993) *Unemployment and Workers' Rights*, London: Institute of Employment Rights.

Michie, Jonathan, and Wilkinson, Frank (1994) 'The growth of unemployment in the 1980s', in J. Michie and J. Grieve Smith (eds) *Unemployment in Europe*, London: Academic Press.

Michie, Jonathan, and Wilkinson, Frank (1995) 'Wages, government policy and unemployment', *Review of Political Economy* 7 (2).

National Association of Citizens' Advice Bureaux (1993) *Job Insecurity*, London: NACAB.

Polanyi, K. (1945) *Origins of our Time*, London: Farrar & Reinhart.

Robinson, Joan (1966) 'The New Mercantilism: An Inaugural Lecture', Cambridge: Cambridge University Press; reprinted in *Collected Economic Papers* 4, Oxford: Blackwell, 1973.

Rowthorn, Bob (1992) 'Government spending and taxation in the Thatcher era', in J. Michie (ed.) *The Economic Legacy: 1979–1992*, London: Academic Press.

Rowthorn, Bob, and Wells, John (1987) *Deindustrialisation and Foreign Trade*, Cambridge: Cambridge University Press.

Singh, Ajit (1987) 'De-industrialisation', in John Eatwell, Murray Milgate and Peter Newman (eds) *The New Palgrave Dictionary of Economics*, London: Macmillan.

ACKNOWLEDGEMENTS

This chapter reports work done with Frank Wilkinson (Michie and Wilkinson 1992, 1993, 1994, 1995; Deakin *et al.* 1992) and by the various authors of Michie and Grieve Smith (1994).

4

THREATS TO COHESION

Iain Begg

The European Union has been through a difficult time in the last three years. The delay in ratifying the Treaty on European Union, the wrangle over the budget at the Edinburgh summit and the severity of the recession have progressively undermined the optimism of Maastricht. The preoccupation at the subsequent Copenhagen and Brussels European Councils with the rise in unemployment and the threats to Europe's international competitiveness reinforced this malaise. A common thread can, however, be discerned in many of the concerns about further integration in Europe. This is the recognition that monetary union, on its own, cannot be relied upon to deliver both improved economic performance and an equitable distribution of income and wealth.

The various worries about EMU coalesce in the debate on 'cohesion'. Cohesion, however, is a slippery concept, making it hard to determine the weight it deserves in the priorities for economic integration. In part this is because much of the economic theory which underpins economic integration assumes distributional issues to be of secondary importance. Thus, although cohesion is associated both in the Single European Act and in the Treaty on European Union with disparities between regions (Article 130a), there is no objective way of ascertaining how narrow disparities need to be for cohesion to be assured. It is also confused by emphasis on the further concept of 'convergence' as a condition of economic and monetary union (EMU), in which nominal criteria relating to monetary variables are apt to be confused with real convergence, which concerns comparative welfare.

Since Maastricht the economic debate has centred on the feasibility of these nominal convergence criteria laid down in the treaty being attained. Yet it is clear from, first, Article 2 of the treaty itself and, second, the strength of feeling in the debate at the Edinburgh European Council in December 1992 on the budget that the distribution of the costs and benefits of EMU is a critical part of the political economy of European integration. Although nominal convergence is necessary for the successful technical implementation of monetary union, it does not assure convergence in real living standards, employment opportunities or social

110

standards, which are the sort of consideration that ultimately concern electors.

This chapter examines the various threats to cohesion in the EU, and considers the options open to policy-makers to forestall those threats or to address the consequences of unbalanced development of the EU economy. The next section explores the concept of cohesion and considers in more depth how it can be advanced. This is followed by a review of the different factors that can be expected to influence cohesion in the rest of this decade. Policy options are then explored in the concluding section.

COHESION AS AN OBJECTIVE

The definition of cohesion needs careful thought, particularly the question of whether it is synonymous with real convergence. Faster growth may be associated with a widening of disparities, even though all parties benefit. As an illustration, Bradley et al. (1992) demonstrate that on plausible assumptions about reforms of the CAP, the effects of EMU and the changes in the Structural Funds, Ireland will marginally increase its GDP growth, but will see its *per capita* income slip relative to the EU average.[1] Equally, slower aggregate growth in the EU may well be linked with greater efforts at redistribution which, while assuring real convergence, will impair the efficiency of resource allocation.

In practice, as has been suggested in Begg and Mayes (1991), cohesion is about politically and socially tolerable divergences – which must be expected to evolve through time – rather than target levels of supposedly objective variables. It may be tolerable, if undesirable, today that income per head in the ten least favoured regions is only a third of that of the ten most favoured regions, but if such a gap were to persist it might threaten the survival of the economic union. The difficulty with this approach is that it does not provide an unambiguous means of monitoring progress or determining when a 'state of cohesion' exists. Nevertheless the pork barrel is part of the politics of European integration, and we neglect the political dimension at our peril.

There is no simple and unequivocal way of comparing regional circumstances. Supposedly objective measures such as GDP per head or unemployment rates are the indicators most commonly used. But they are open to criticism because of inconsistencies of definition or because they fail to capture less tangible elements of 'social welfare' such as social conditions or the state of the environment. Nevertheless, practical considerations mean that relativities in income or unemployment are central to policy targeting and also serve as reasonable proxies for more complex social problems.

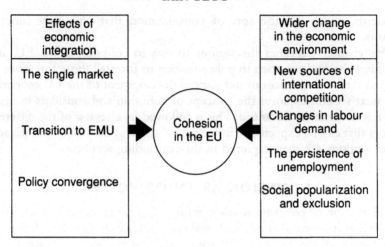

Figure 4.1 Threats to cohesion

INFLUENCES ON COHESION

Although the debate on cohesion has tended, so far, to be associated directly with the various strands of economic integration in the EU, a variety of other influences on it are worthy of mention. These are summarized in Figure 4.1. Many of the more fundamental influences derive from wider changes in the economic environment which are shaping labour demand and the organizational structures of employers. These changes give rise to threats to cohesion which the EU would need to contend with irrespective of the path chosen for economic integration. Recognizing these multiple influences is essential in order to formulate an appropriate policy response. It is also worth noting that the various tiers of government can have an effect on distributive issues, implying that cohesion is not merely a challenge to 'Brussels' but requires a co-ordinated approach involving other tiers of government.

Effects of economic integration

The eventual impact of economic integration on any individual region will be influenced by a wide range of factors. The standard neo-classical analysis[2] predicts (as Barro and Sala-i-Martin 1992 demonstrate) that convergence in GDP *per capita* will occur. This is because diminishing returns to capital set in as an economy develops, so that lower-income economies have higher returns to capital. This attracts capital and thus has an equilibrating effect. The process of convergence is accelerated if there is strong interregional labour mobility and rapid diffusion of technology

112

between regions. This analysis depends critically on the familiar restrictive assumptions of the model, such as perfectly competitive markets and homogeneity of factors of production, for its prediction that specialization according to comparative advantage will occur, making gains in welfare possible.

Recent theorizing on models of 'endogenous growth' and the impact of trade[3] has led to some reappraisal of the welfare effects of integration, suggesting that the outcome may not be easy to predict, because the dynamic consequences of existing disparities in, for example, human capital endowments or technology are uncertain. Moreover the reality of the EU is that, in spite of the single market programme, there will still be significant market segmentation and barriers inhibiting genuine free trade will persist.

The patchy evidence on the likely impact of completion of the internal market on the less favoured regions as a group is that, at best, they will keep pace with the EU economy, rather than converging in terms of income per head (for example, CEGOS-IDET 1989; Nam and Reuter 1991; IRES-RIDER 1990; Commission of the European Communities 1991; GREMI 1991; Begg 1992; Quévit 1992). Some regions will inevitably do better, but there are also signs that several, notably among the least favoured, will have a struggle. As the EU economy becomes progressively more integrated the relative competitiveness of regions will come under scrutiny. Location decisions by companies will reflect assessments (and perceptions of these) of regional attributes. Viewed in this way, it is the absolute rather than the comparative advantage of regions that will determine whether or not a region is well placed to gain from market integration. To shed light on the influences on regional competitiveness, one approach is to extend the analysis by Porter (1990) of factors affecting competitive advantage to the level of the region. An alternative outlook is that adopted by IFO (1990), which measures a region's competitiveness by looking at national, regional and company-specific factors.

Figure 4.2 attempts to synthesize the various approaches by bringing together four categories of factors which feed into regional competitiveness. These are:

1 *Sectoral and macro-economic variables*, which determine how the region's export base is likely to be affected (Mayes 1991). This will depend on variables which have a direct effect on operating costs, such as relative unit labour costs, as well as indirect effects stemming from the path the economy takes. Macro-economic conditions may suit some regions better than others. Camagni (1992), as an illustration, argues that in an integrated economy the weaker region has to contend with too high an exchange rate. This makes it more difficult to compete in high-tech

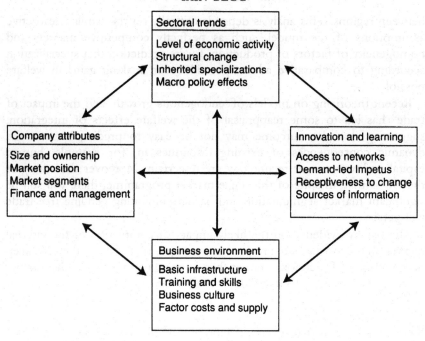

Figure 4.2 Determinants of regional industrial performance

sectors, pushing it back towards low-productivity activities with poor growth prospects.

2 *The regional business environment*, which includes the quality and costs of the assorted factors of production (labour, property, etc.), various characteristics of the region's location and endowments (peripherality, transport and communications infrastructure) and the effects of local administrative and fiscal arrangements. It is likely, for instance, that low-wage regions will face upward pressure on wage costs in a more open market, while the reverse applies in high-wage areas. In addition the competitive position of regions will be affected by less tangible factors such as the local business culture, the character of local and regional institutions or the industrial relations climate.

3 *Attributes of industrial and commercial companies* in the region, such as their organization, success in external markets, size structure or financial strength. Few dominant large companies are located in less favoured regions, and it is often the case that the leading exporters are subsidiaries or branches of externally owned multinationals, engendering vulnerability to decisions to relocate. An example is Ireland, where branches of foreign-owned multinationals are judged to be the most competitive in the industries most affected by the single market (Bradley *et al.* 1992).

114

Amin *et al.* (1992) argue that corporate restructuring will generally work against the less favoured regions, where there tend to be fewer opportunities for attaining economies of scale and not many large 'anchor' companies to act as the core of networks.

4 *The ability to innovate and to learn.* This fourth category is perhaps the most difficult aspect of competitiveness to pin down, yet in many ways it is the most critial. In the business world of the 1990s it is widely believed that the ability of companies to learn, to adapt and to react quickly will be the key to success.[4] It is important, too, to recognize that, in an age of rapidly evolving technologies, diffusion of new technologies and mastery of their use is a problem as much of organization and management as of invention or basic scientific discovery. Networking is increasingly being recognized as an important factor affecting innovation, and the very uneven distribution of research activity in the EU (Hingel 1992) is considered a problem for cohesion.

The transition to monetary union

Although there may be some casualties, supporters of economic integration argue that it will, ultimately, increase the prosperity of most regions. However, keeping in mind Keynes's well known dictum about the long run, what happens during the process of transition cannot be ignored. The main threats to cohesion in this context come from the need for both structural and macro-economic adjustments necessary to enable member states of the EU to participate in EMU. This was articulated in the 1989 Delors report on monetary union: 'If sufficient consideration were not given to regional imbalances, the economic union would be faced with grave economic and political risks.' The nominal convergence criteria, in many ways, exemplify the political dimension of cohesion. In principle, they are consistent with sound macro-economic policy and, assuming some flexibility in their application, could be considered sensible whether or not monetary union is on the agenda. For the majority of the member states they represent attainable targets, even if the current recession-coloured viewpoint has engendered some doubts.

However, the costs of adjustment will be far from negligible for those member states with the least propitious indicators, and the spatial incidence of any reductions in public expenditure deemed necessary to curb excessive deficits is also likely to be inimical to cohesion. Thus, in Italy, net fiscal transfers account for over a fifth of the income of the Mezzogiorno. For member states with inadequate infrastructure, substantial public investment will be needed to underpin competitiveness at a time when the EMU criteria call for cuts in public spending. This could lead to an invidious choice between investment and social spending, damaging cohesion.

Submitting to these fiscal and monetary disciplines is justified if the eventual gains are sufficiently great to offset the short-term costs. Lower transaction costs, a more efficient capital market, lower interest rates, increased credibility for fiscal policy and the prospect of more rapid growth for the EU economy leading to strong markets for a region's output are all reasons for accepting these short-run costs. However, it has to be recognized that the gains from EMU will not accrue equally to all regions, and, unless the danger of a cumulation of disadvantage is recognized and acted upon, cohesion could be seriously threatened. Even countries such as Ireland, which appear quite well placed in relation to the criteria, may find difficulty in continuing to adhere to the criteria as pressures for growth and lower unemployment mount. A double jeopardy in this regard is that emigration – one of the main mechanisms by which very high unemployment is attenuated – is inclined to fall as job opportunities diminish in host countries and regions. This could mean that a greater share of the aggregate burden of dealing with the social consequences of the transition to EMU could fall on the less favoured regions and member states.

Policy convergence

Although the nominal convergence criteria will, in principle, threaten cohesion only in the run-up to EMU, the policy stance adopted by the EU beyond stage 3 of EMU must also be considered. The emphasis given to price stability in the mission of the European central bank, and the constraints on discretionary fiscal policy, may prove beneficial in the long run, but by removing options from lower tiers of government they may prove divisive in the short run.

While it would be foolhardy to hazard a guess about the future development of the EU macro-economy, the need for large-scale transfers from the 'old' to the 'new' *Länder* in Germany following monetary union illustrates the potential problem.

The EU's need to boost competitiveness

In assessing threats to cohesion it is important not to overlook the extra-EU dimension, especially the pressure of international competition and the fear that operating costs in the EU have become too high. The discussions at the Copenhagen summit and the Delors paper *Entering the Twenty-first Century: Prospects for the European Economy* indicate the worries being felt. The paper highlights two basic weaknesses of the EU economy: it has failed to create sufficient jobs and its competitive position has deteriorated. This has called into question the scale and means of financing social protection and has prompted demands for a recasting of the welfare system.

The international dimension is also important because in an increasingly globalized production system more companies can opt to relocate or to shift their sourcing to lower-cost parts of the world. If the EU is too far out of line because of high social costs it will simply lose activity. The interplay between social protection and competitiveness is, however, a complex one. Work in progress at the OECD (1994) is looking at ways of boosting employment and growth while enhancing competitiveness, and has identified social charges as an area of reform.

From the perspective of cohesion, this raises a number of issues. First, cuts in welfare budgets which reduce the living standards of beneficiaries of welfare support, however reasonable, would cause resentment. Second, upheavals can be caused when attempts (however well conceived they may be) are made to reform tax structures. Third, there is a risk of competitive lowering of social provision, which has drawbacks similar to competitive devaluation and may ultimately prove futile. As an illustration, consider the disquiet surrounding the 1993 closure of the Hoover factory in Dijon, although there have so far been few signs that social dumping is widespread.

Persistent unemployment

According to the Commission of the European Communities (1993), 'Unemployment is now the major economic and social challenge facing the Community in the 1990s.' The number out of work is heading towards 20 million, with some social groups (such as youths) and some of the worst affected regions subject to particularly high rates. Although much of the recent rise is cyclical, it is widely accepted that there is a substantial and apparently intractable structural component to unemployment in the EU. Even at the peak of the last economic cycle, unemployment in Europe did not fall below 8·3 per cent, and for most of the last decade it has remained obstinately in double figures.

A comparison between the EU and the US in rates of unemployment is striking, as can be seen in Figure 4.3. This shows unemployment by region in the EU and by state in the US at a comparable point in the economic cycle, when both were moving into recession but before unemployment had increased significantly. The range in the US is from 2 per cent to 8 per cent, whereas in the EU it is 2 per cent to 26 per cent. Relativities in the EU partly reflect the timing of the economic cycle in different member states, notably the low rates in most parts of West Germany, but are mainly due to regional differences. Italy, for example, has regions with less than 5 per cent (Emilia-Romagna and Lombardy) and over 20 per cent (Sicily and Campania). Apart from the narrower range in the US, the chart also shows that, unlike the US, the EU has a long 'tail' of regions with very high rates of unemployment. This suggests that there is greater scope for migration in the US as a means of reducing regional disparities.

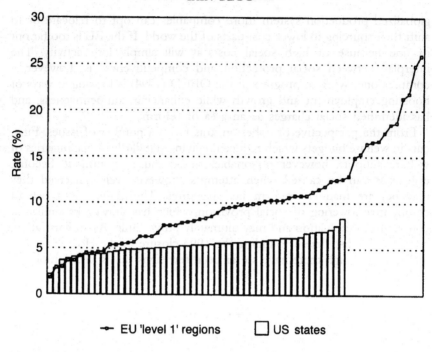

Figure 4.3 Unemployment rates in EU regions (1992) and the US (1990)

In his introduction to the 1993 *Employment in Europe* report (CEC 1993) European Commissioner Padraig Flynn warns against simplistic solutions such as protectionism or reductions in wage costs. Equally, it has become clear that macro-economic expansion at plausible rates, on its own, is unlikely to achieve enough employment growth to deal with the problem. It is, however, important for cohesion to acknowledge that some possible solutions to unemployment, while reducing the aggregate of unemployment, could widen disparities between localities or between different social groups. A key reason for highlighting unemployment as a factor in cohesion is its impact on social structures *within* regions, particularly where a high rate of unemployment imposes a heavy burden on those in work to support welfare payments. This leads to resentment both from those affected by unemployment and from those who are taxed to pay for welfare benefits. A further problem is the concentration of unemployment among the least skilled. Drèze and Malinvaud (1993) attribute this partly to the 'wedge' between the private and social cost of, particularly, unskilled labour and argue (as part of a package to restore growth) that this obstacle to employment creation needs to be addressed.

Labour market trends are especially significant in the dynamics of cohesion. Data reported in CEC (1991) demonstrate that most of the

118

Objective 1 regions (i.e. the regions 'lagging' behind in their economic development – the southern and western periphery of the EU) have above-average natural rates of population growth. These mean that they would need to create employment at a markedly higher rate than elsewhere in order to absorb labour market entrants or to make inroads into high rates of long-term unemployment.

Social exclusion

There can be little doubt that economic integration will cause social change. The spatial reallocations of resources that will be induced by economic change must be expected to affect different social groups unevenly. In particular, if the intensification of competition that is one of the main objectives of integration causes a labour shake-out, the bulk of the resulting job losses will be among the least qualified employees. This could create problems for the most vulnerable social groups – ethnic minority immigrants or displaced agricultural populations migrating to large, congested cities, for example – and may also lead to concentrations of social problems in specific localities. In France, as an illustration, the Délégation Interministériel à la Ville (DIV) has identified over 400 disadvantaged precincts in urban areas, many in cities which are otherwise prosperous.

According to DIV, residents in these areas face multiple handicaps in trying to secure better opportunities. In addition, crime, drug dependence, declining standards of health and other consequences of social deprivation tend to accumulate in such areas. Social cohesion calls for recognition of the effects of economic and political change in fomenting social problems and for action to alleviate them. Improving social provision can, in addition, be regarded as a political objective aimed at consolidating the sense of belonging to the EU. If residents of less favoured regions or of disadvantaged communities in favoured regions perceive the gap in social provision between them and more favoured areas to be either excessive or not narrowing sufficiently, social cohesion will be difficult to achieve. In particular, if the EU is unable to address poverty in whatever form it manifests itself (low rural incomes, inactive or discriminated-against inner-city or suburban populations), it will struggle in vain to attain social cohesion and shall see an upsurge of social exclusion.

The protracted economic slow-down in the EU has exacerbated an already growing problem of social exclusion. In many large cities, especially, concentrations of disadvantaged groups are increasing, causing social polarization and putting pressure on the capacity to respond of public agencies. These pressures can be self-reinforcing, because as problems mount the capacity to respond diminishes, leading to the sort of vicious cycle seen in so many US cities.

Apart from the budgetary pressures arising from the nominal convergence criteria, social policy is hampered by concern about the incidence of social charges and its effect on competitiveness. At the same time, social exclusion highlights a new and more insidious threat to cohesion because it is symptomatic of a decline in solidarity. Taxpayers may be prepared to pay to support the disadvantaged in domestic society but draw the line at 'foreigners'. To be credible, any policy response to deal with social exclusion has to command the support of the community at large in a way that the EU has so far failed to do.

THE POLICY RESPONSE

Cohesion is an issue that the EU cannot afford to treat as secondary to the overriding aim of achieving EMU. As the European economy becomes progressively more integrated the distribution of costs and benefits will become an increasingly visible political matter. Regions or social groups which feel that they do not share sufficiently in the gains from integration will be tempted to opt out, putting the whole process at risk. Policy responses, consequently, have to be fashioned so as to ensure that the benefits are achieved while providing scope for the less competitive to participate effectively.

The weight of evidence suggests that 'market failure' is endemic to the process of regional economic development and it is quite unrealistic to expect a significant narrowing of regional disparities either within member states or across the EC without public-sector intervention of one kind or another. Moreover, adjustment, either through factor migration or relative price changes, tends to be painfully slow and falls a long way short of correcting regional income per head and unemployment disparities (Begg 1989).

Starting from the presumption that the EU will continue to be faced with severe problems of structural adaptation and persistent spatial disparities, a number of questions must be addressed with regard to public policy. A central question is whether policy should be primarily concerned with tackling the underlying causes of perceived problems or with ameliorating some of the more intractable symptoms of those problems. A second policy question concerns the appropriate tier of government at which policy may best be formulated and in particular whether there is any justification for policy intervention at a European level to complement and support policies designed at a national or regional level.

Reductions in regional disparities are bound to play a key role in cohesion. In this context, what is needed is a policy framework that enables less competitive regions to react. Difficult decisions are needed about how much reliance to place on market forces and the appropriate scale of direct intervention. Even where the need for intervention is accepted, there is a choice to make between correcting the underlying problem –

which takes time – and providing immediate support. The priority, however, should be to provide scope for improving the economic performance of less favoured regions, rather than compensation for disadvantages. This implies attempts to secure equality of *opportunity* rather than equality of outcome. Given that the single market is concerned with the creation of a level playing field, improving the competitive ability of the players is an appropriate counterpart.

Advancing cohesion is a long-run objective rather than something that can be achieved rapidly. It follows that there are neither quick and easy solutions nor realistic alternatives to long-term policy initiatives. On the whole this is recognized in regional policy, with the emphasis on investment (i.e. future welfare) rather than transfers to increase consumption (i.e. current welfare). Latterly, as Amin *et al.* (1992) note, the dominant approach to regional policy is what they call 'growth from below' – the promotion of indigenous industry. The essence of this is to improve the ability of the less favoured regions to compete and to raise their productivity levels closer to those in the favoured regions.

Despite the considerable increases to come over the life of the new Financial Perspective, the Structural Funds will still amount to less than $0 \cdot 5$ per cent of Community GDP by 1999. In comparison, public spending in the member states accounts for between 40 per cent and 60 per cent of GDP, and consequently has a major impact in forestalling wider disparities, as was shown in the MacDougall report (1977). This comes not so much from explicit regional policy as from the interplay of tax and expenditure systems: less prosperous regions pay less tax and tend to receive more expenditure because of higher demands for social welfare spending. In addition, grants from central governments to lower tiers of government or interregional transfers such as the German system of *Länderfinanzausgleich* also have equalizing properties. Smeeding *et al.* (1993) show that non-cash social expenditure (on health or education) also has a significant equalizing effect.

Because the available resources have to be thinly spread, EU policies as at present constituted cannot realistically be expected to play a major role in promoting real convergence. This is likely to be an especially acute problem in regions which are not eligible for the most intensive support from EU sources but which are, nevertheless, adversely affected by restructuring. For such regions, member state and regional government initiatives are inevitably going to be the mainstay of policy, yet where such policies involve direct support for firms they can fall foul of the rules on the use of 'state aids' in Articles 92 and 93 of the treaty (Lehner and Meiklejohn 1991). The dilemma to be resolved is how to retain the spur of fair competition while ensuring that cohesion objectives are not overlooked. This calls for effort by policy-makers to find what one official in DG XVI of the Commission

121

of the European Communities has called 'the sparks which will ignite regional development'.

Although efforts to advance cohesion are bound to rely predominantly on member state initiatives, it can be argued that the EU tier has two vital roles to play. First, by acting as a 'referee' it can ensure that policies adopted within member states do not have unreasonable spill-over effects on other regions. Second, where the scale of structural problems attributable to economic integration requires intervention beyond the means of the member state or region, it should be incumbent on the EU tier to assist. In this context it is also pertinent to ask whether, as in most nation states, it would be desirable for the EU to have some automatic system for redistribution of income, as advocated in the MacDougall report. Although political considerations make it highly unlikely that a system akin to that in Germany could be introduced in the foreseeable future, such a mechanism will have to be reconsidered if the EU does become an EMU. The difficult trade-off that needs to be negotiated in any such mechanism is between providing necessary support and engendering an ultimately counterproductive culture of dependence.

A frequently expressed view is that overall EU growth is the key to cohesion. For some, the implication is that the focus of policy should be on overall growth, with cohesion accorded only a secondary priority. Even if the logic of this argument is accepted unreservedly, however, the uncomfortable fact remains that cohesion has political as well as economic dimensions that have to be addressed. Threats to cohesion consequently have to be treated as direct threats to the process of economic integration.

NOTES

1 The reason is that higher growth reduces net emigration, which in turn cuts the measured increase in GDP per head.
2 For a summary of the development of this model see Jacquemin and Sapir (1989).
3 For a survey see Baldwin (1992).
4 Such issues are highlighted in Best (1990), Scott Morton (1991) and Shimada (1991).

REFERENCES

Amin, A., Charles, D. R., and Howells, J. (1992) 'Corporate restructuring and cohesion in the new Europe' *Regional Studies* 26: 319–31.
Baldwin, R. E. (1992) 'Are economists' traditional trade policy views still valid?' *Journal of Economic Literature* XXX: 804–29.
Barro, R., and Sala-i-Martin, X. (1992) 'Convergence', *Journal of Political Economy* 100: 223–51.
Begg, I. G. (1989), 'The regional dimension of the "1992" proposals', *Regional Studies* 23 (4): 368–76.

Begg, I. G., and Mayes, D. G., with Shipman, A., and Levitt, M. (1991) *A New Strategy for Social and Economic Cohesion after 1992*, Luxembourg: Office for Official Publications of the European Community.

Begg, I. (1992) 'The spatial impact of completion of the EC internal market for financial services', *Regional Studies* 26: 333–47.

Best, M. (1990) *The New Competition*, Cambridge: Polity Press.

Bradley, J., Fitzgerald, J., Kearney, I., Boyle, G., Breen, R., Shortall, S., Durkan, J., Reynolds-Feighan, A., and O'Malley, E. (1992) 'The role of the Structural Funds: analysis of consequences for Ireland in the context of 1992', Policy Research Paper No. 13, Dublin: ESRI.

Camagni, R. P. (1992) 'Development scenarios and policy guidelines for the lagging regions in the 1990s', *Regional Studies* 26: 361–74.

CEGOS-IDET (1989) 'Les Conséquences régionales de l'ouverture des marchés publiques', report to the Regional Policy Directorate of the Commission of the European Communities.

Commission of the European Communities (1991) *Employment in Europe 1991*, COM (91) 248 final, Luxembourg: Office for Official Publications of the European Community.

Commission of the European Communities (1993) *Employment in Europe 1993*, COM (93) 314, Luxembourg: Office for Official Publications of the European Community.

Drèze, J. H., and Malinvaud, E. (1993) 'Growth and employment: the scope for an European initiative', *European Economy Reports and Studies* 1: 77–106.

GREMI (1991) 'Development Prospects of the Community's lagging Regions and the Socio-economic Consequences of the Completion of the Internal Market: an approach in terms of local *milieux* and innovation networks', report to the Regional Policy Directorate of the Commission of the European Communities.

Hingel, A. J. (1992) 'Science, technology and Community cohesion: research results and RTD policy recommendations', Monitor-FAST Programme Prospective Dossier No. 1, Brussels: Commission of the European Communities.

IFO-Institut für Wirstchaftsforshung (1990) 'An Empirical Assessment of Factors shaping Regional Competitiveness in Problem Regions', report to the Commission of the European Communities.

Jacquemin, A., and Sapir, A. (eds) (1989) *The European Internal Market: Trade and Competition*, Oxford: Oxford University Press.

Lehner, S., and Meiklejohn, R. (1991) 'Fair competition in the internal market: Community state aids policy', *European Economy* 48: 7–114.

MacDougall, D. A. (1977) 'Report of the Study Group on the Role of Public Finance in European Integration', Brussels: Commission of the European Communities.

Mayes, D. G. (ed.) (1991) *The European Challenge*, Hemel Hempstead: Harvester-Wheatsheaf.

Nam, C. W., and Reuter, J., with Gälli, A. (1991) *The Effect of 1992 and Associated Legislation on the Less Favoured Regions of the Community*. Luxembourg: Office for Official Publications of the European Community.

Organization for Economic Co-operation and Development (1994) *The OECD Jobs Study: Facts, Analysis, Strategies*, Paris: OECD.

Porter, M. (1990) *The Competitive Advantage of Nations*, London: Macmillan.

Quévit, M. (1992) 'The regional impact of the single market: a comparative analysis of traditional industrial regions and lagging regions', *Regional Studies* 26: 349–60.

Quévit, M., Houard, J., Bodson, S., and Dangoisse, A. (1991) *Impact régional 1992: les régions de tradition industrielle*, Brussels: De Boeck University.

Scott Morton, M. S. (1991) *The Corporation of the 1990s: Information Technology and Organizational Transformation*, Oxford: Oxford University Press.

Shimada, H. (1991) ' "Humanware" technology and industrial relations', in OECD, *Technology and Productivity: the Challenge for Economic Policy*, Paris: OECD.

Smeeding, T. M., Saunders, P., Coder, J., Jenkins, S., Fritzell, J., Hagenaars, A. J. M., Hauser, R., and Wolfson, M. (1993) 'Poverty, inequality, and family living standards impacts across seven nations: the effects of non-cash subsidies for health, education and housing', *Review of Income and Wealth* 39: 229–56.

5

COHESION, GROWTH AND INEQUALITY IN THE EUROPEAN UNION

Michael Dunford

The last twenty years have been difficult ones for most of the economies of the European Union and of other advanced capitalist countries. Among the symptoms of these difficulties three trends warrant particular attention. First, average rates of economic growth and of productivity growth have slowed down. The slow growth of productivity is particularly remarkable, as it coincides with developments in information and communications technologies that amount to a technological revolution and that seem to offer the possibility of dramatic increases in the productive potential of human societies. Clearly, advanced societies have so far failed to realize this potential, as the US economist Solow (1987) indicated when he made the remark that 'I can see the computer age everywhere but in the productivity statistics.'[1] Second, slow growth has coincided with increases in unemployment. With the arrival of the trough of each successive economic cycle the level of unemployment increased. In the 1993 recession 18 million people in the EU were unemployed. As unemployment increased the size of the inactive population expanded as 'discouraged workers' dropped out of the work force altogether. As a consequence in 1993 less than 60 per cent of the EU's population of working age was in work. Of those in work many had had to accept part-time, insecure or casual employment. Third, social and spatial inequality has increased. Job loss and growing unemployment, along with the fact that the large majority of women who have entered employment came from households with at least one other income earner, have led to an increase in the share of households and of the population dependent on state welfare benefits. At the same time the increasing dispersion or polarization of employment structures and earnings has led to an increase in gross wage differentials and social divisions between those with secure and well paid jobs and those who suffer from economic insecurity and low pay. The divide is particularly marked in the case of male wage earners. In Britain, for example, the wages of the top 10 per cent of male wage-earners increased from 1·67 times the median wage in 1979 to twice the median in 1993, while the wages of the poorest-paid 10 per cent declined from 68·5 to 58·2 per cent of the median (Gregg and Machin 1994).

In the 1950s, 1960s and early 1970s the situation was very different. In what is increasingly seen as an economic 'golden age' growth rates were double those of recent decades, there was near full employment and social and spatial inequalities declined. In that era, in other words, dynamic growth went hand in hand with economic convergence and increasing economic and social cohesion.

These dramatic contrasts in the economic performance of advanced economies and the fact that in the past increases in cohesion were associated with more rapid growth are clearly key issues in any debate about the future of Europe. The aim of this chapter is to present some elements of an explanation of these phenomena and to spell out some of their implications for debates about the character of a new European order. What I shall argue is that in the golden age rapid growth, full employment and declining inequality interacted with and reinforced one another in a virtuous circle of growth and development. Accordingly spatial and social convergence and cohesion were functional to the reproduction and growth of Europe's mixed economies. Conversely I shall argue that in the more recent period a vicious spiral has predominated owing to the tendency for slow growth, mass unemployment and greater social and spatial inequality to reinforce one another.

An important cause of the perverse interaction of inequality, employment and growth in recent decades is the dominance of new market-orientated rules of the game which contrast sharply with the rules that underpinned the 'golden age' model of growth. At the root of the latter were a series of attempts to regulate the contradictions of market-led development and market rationality which, as Polanyi argued in *The Great Transformation*, was one of the major causes of the economic disorder and political conflict of the first half of the twentieth century.[2] Regulation of market-led development is itself, however, a source of new contradictions, as the widespread criticisms of the post-war social order showed. In the 1970s it was argued that the social and institutional structures of the mixed economies of Europe were an obstacle to modernization. At that stage there were, however, two courses of action. One was to adapt the prevailing structures, modes and principles of market regulation to the new circumstances. The other was to strip them away through deregulation and a looser rein on the destructive potential of the market. The choice of the second course of action can be explained in part by the fact that there were many who gained from it. The neo-liberal agenda also allowed change to be imposed through the operation of impersonal market forces. In this way governments could disclaim responsibility for what happened. Admittedly the short-term costs of market-led adjustment were great but there was no need to secure a consensus over the redeployment of resources. What this choice over-looked, however, wat the fact that the post-war order was itself a response to the self-destroying character of unregulated markets and the fact that in many situations markets fail. In market societies there are a wide range of costs that individuals would choose not to pay but which are functional to the medium-term reproduction of a socio-economic system. A social optimum is not the sum of a set of individual optima: there are, in other words, fallacies of composition in the argument that what is best for society is what is best for each of the individuals who make it up. As a result market-led models of development lead to a whole series of dysfunction-alities and contradictions. At present awareness of these longer-term costs of market-led development is increasing and there is growing interest in alternatives. In this chapter I shall therefore set out a number of ideas about the shape that a new regulatory order might assume. First, however, I shall outline the character of the 'golden age' model of development and the implications of the market-dominated rules of the game which came to prevail in much of the EU in the 1980s.

THE MODEL OF DEVELOPMENT IN THE *TRENTE GLORIEUSES*

In the thirty years that followed the Second World War growth rates were double those of recent decades, there was near full employment and inequalities declined. The successes of this era stemmed in part from the fact that there was a set of regular dynamic relationships between growth, employment, income distribution and social demand. First, trends in the structure and organization of the spheres of production and value creation laid the foundations for rapid productivity and output growth. Included were the implementation of Taylorist methods of work organization and the exploitation of scale economies. Second, national mechanisms of wage determination and value transfer resulted in a division of value added between employers and the work force, between the working and depen-dent population and between the capitalist and non-capitalist sectors that led to a regular growth of real income. Third, the steady growth of real income in conjunction with credit creation led to the regular expansion of social demand, which validated the expansion of production capacities and ensured near-full employment.

At the root of growth was the expansion of domestic demand and of the incomes on which demand depended, while growth itself reinforced the expansion of demand, completing a virtuous circle of development ten-dencies. Growth was also reinforced, however, by the integration of less developed countries and regions with areas that were more advanced. On the one hand the expansion of markets in less developed areas fuelled the process of economic growth. On the other the existence of near-full employment in more developed areas and the integration of the supplies of human and material resources in less developed areas implied a high level of resource mobilization which itself reinforced growth. Full employment of formerly underused human resources in developed and less developed areas was therefore functional to growth in a double sense: it helped expand markets and it mobilized resources to reduce supply bottlenecks.

The successes of these years were somewhat unexpected. At the end of the Second World War there was a fear that the difficulties of the 1930s might recur. The years after the war were, however, years of fundamental reform in which new social compromises saw the integration of the wage-earning class into the project of the Keynesian welfare state: a state that advanced the interests of industrial capital with an offer of modernization, social reform, individual consumption, equal opportunities, and steady economic advance (see Hirsch and Roth 1986: 74–7). This project was at the root of a major transformation of the advanced industrial economies. Indeed, the economies that resulted were economies that could not be characterized simply as capitalist market economies. To varying degrees the advanced industrial countries were mixed economies with a combination of public and private ownership. In these societies the public sector and the planned, non-market provision of goods and services played a major though varying role. All witnessed a partial decommodification of the wage relation and of many social reproduction activities with the development of a welfare state granting nearly everyone the possibility to consume, even in cases of temporary or indefinite incapacity to earn money from work owing to illness, unemployment or retirement. Governments assumed a major role in economic management, state planning systems were developed, and the market itself was extensively regulated.

At an international level the overwhelming dominance of the US economy and the dependence of most countries on US goods led to the establishment of the dollar as international credit money. (At the end of the war the US accounted for three-quarters of the world's invested capital and two-thirds of its industrial capacity, giving it 'a near-monopoly on [the] all-important factor for sustaining life' (Smith, cited in Horowitz 1967: 74)). At first, however, the US did not insist on the immediate liberalization of trade, payments and capital flows. As the country with the largest trade surplus the US sought to overcome the dollar shortage in Europe (and Asia) through the provision of multilateral aid to advanced countries to finance reconstruction, industrial modernization and the reinstatement of markets and to allow advanced countries to purchase US goods. Included, of course, was the US $13 billion of Marshall Aid for Europe. (The great danger for the West after the Second World War was that Europe and Japan would not be able to afford the imports needed for recovery, would run out of gold and dollars and would be obliged to deflate.) As the dominant economic power the US also accepted limitations on US access to overseas markets and allowed its partners to protect their economies to allow domestic industries to recover.

Aid and protectionism were, in short, preferred to the imposition of free trade and a liberal monetary order. Over the course of time this path proved to be one of enlightened self-interest. At the root of these decisions were, however, other, more immediate, concerns. One was the fear of US economic isolation. Another was a desire to contain communism. The extension of the Soviet sphere of influence and the strength of communist and socialist parties in a number of Western countries thus played a key role in the reconstruction of the advanced market economies.

As a whole these developments were the consequence of compromises between different social and political forces, particularly in Europe and the US (Lipietz 1993). The result was the development of mixed economies and to a lesser extent of an international order in which the commodity exchange relation and the wage relation, which are constitutive of capitalist market economies, were regulated and transformed through the development of a complex set of social institutions and rules of conduct. In theories of regulation these complexes of social institutions are called modes of regulation. Modes of regulation are codifications of social relations that (1) give a contingent material expression to social divisions, conflicts and contradictions and (2) allow strategic conduct that expresses contradictions but mediates, normalizes and regulates them. In so far as a mode of regulation can normalize conflicts and tensions – or transform underlying antagonistic social relations – relatively stable models of development prevail. If, however, the fundamental social relations are left intact and new rigidities and conflicts escape the normalizing effects of the mode of regulation, instabilities and crisis tendencies reappear on the surface of society, as happened at the end of the golden age.

THE CRISIS OF THE 'GOLDEN AGE' MODEL

The Keynesian welfare state project was remarkably successful. After the Second World War there were almost thirty years of stable and sustained growth – what the French call the *Trente Glorieuses*. In the late 1960s and early 1970s, however, the (Fordist) model of development that underpinned the 'golden age' model broke down, and in the mid-1970s the Keynesian project was abandoned. The new dominant ideology was that of private ownership and the market.

The causes of the breakdown of the 'golden age' model were twofold. First there was a supply-side crisis. The main manifestation of this supply-side crisis was a productivity slowdown whose roots in turn lay in the exhaustion of the potential of the prevailing Taylorist productive order, in inequalities which placed limits on diffusion of the model of mass consumption and in the inability of the mode of national regulation to contain social conflicts. Second, there was a demand-side crisis whose roots lay in a remarkable globalization of economic life (see Lipietz 1993).

A supply-side crisis and the exhaustion of consumption norms

In the second half of the 1960s the rate of productivity growth declined and the capital–output ratio increased. Investment and capital intensification in the investment goods sector slowed down, though the effects of this slow-down were offset in part by an acceleration in the development of the export sector. At the same time real wages increased and workers' struggles against Taylorist modes of work organization grew in importance. Together these factors resulted in a decline in the rate of profit and a crisis of valorization.

The change in the rate of profit varied from one sector to another. Investment was channelled into sectors whose growth potential seemed greater. As a result the situation of excess capacity and over-investment was exacerbated in a wave of expansion that preceded the oil crisis. Moreover the response of firms to the fall in profitability was to increase prices. As prices increased so did wages. As a result an inflationary spiral was set in motion.

At the same time there were a number of changes in market conditions. In spite of the fact that there were social strata and countries that had not been integrated into mass-consumption norms owing to their lack of purchasing power, markets were saturated. The economic slow-down also coincided with much greater uncertainty and financial instability and marked and rapid changes in the volume and composition of demand. These new market conditions created severe difficulties for large (rigid) Fordist firms, which could not adapt quickly to a rapidly changing economic environment.

Globalization and a demand-side crisis

At the root of these new market conditions and in particular of the great uncertainty about interest rates, exchange rates and growth prospects was not just a supply-side crisis and the exhaustion of the consumption norms of the golden age. In the 1970s demand-side difficulties of a macro-economic kind were added to the supply-side crisis owing to the globalization of production and finance and the international interpenetration of industry, finance, commerce and other services. A number of interrelated mechanisms were at work (see Lipietz 1993). As wages increased, and the rate of profit fell, domestic investment declined and investment in low-wage countries increased. Increasingly the export sector was the propulsive sector. With this internationalization of production and markets the connection between the wages paid and the demand for goods and services was weakened. At the same time new meanings were given to profit: profit was not just the return on the shareholders' capital but also the investment required for the survival of the firm. An emphasis on the second interpretation meant that all wage demands and all attempts to maintain the purchasing power of the wage could be presented as a threat to jobs and to the survival of the firm the employees worked for. Accordingly after 1977–80 wages in most countries were seen largely as a determinant of competitiveness and not as a determinant of the level of final demand for domestic firms. In these conditions the struggle against trade unions intensified, there was a movement of investment to areas where the power of employers was greater and wages were lower, and unemployment increased.

At the start of the phase of slower growth job loss resulted not in a major drop in aggregate demand but in an increase in the costs of the welfare state that provided the unemployed with alternative incomes. As a result a 1930s-style collapse was avoided. (To pay for these transfers, however, government borrowing and taxes increased.) In 1976–9 the situation changed: national Keynesianism was abandoned and monetarism was embraced. Credit was restricted, 'inefficient' industries were bankrupted and welfare provision was diluted. (To a significant extent this course of action was self-defeating, as the growth of unemployment and poverty raised the direct and indirect costs of the residual welfare state.)

With the switch to monetarism, the growth of wages slowed down, unemployment increased and domestic demand stagnated. Domestic demand is, however, a part of international demand, and so austerity in one country slows down the growth of global demand. What was more, the use of this deflationary method of gaining competitive advantage led other countries, whose relative competitiveness deteriorated, to react in similar ways, reinforcing the deflationary spiral. What prevailed, in effect, was a free-trade model of adjustment. First, in order to reduce its balance of payments deficit, each country whose imports exceeded its exports sought larger wage reductions than its rivals to reduce imports and increase exports. (At the same time there was also a sharp increase in competition for mobile capital invesment.) As this competitive struggle intensified, deflation and the stagnation of international demand and growth intensified. Second, in order to improve its capital account each country introduced yet higher interest rates to attract international deposits. As the cost of credit increased, the required rate of return on investment increased, marginal investment projects were dropped and the recessionary spiral was given a further twist.

STRUCTURAL CHANGE AND THE EVOLUTION OF THE CRISIS

As a result of the crisis of the 'golden age' model there were a series of profound changes in the structure and development of advanced European countries. Major changes occurred in the productive order, the relations between different fractions of capital, the composition of output and employment, the resource endowments of different places and the geography of economic activities as cities, regions and countries that adapted successfully to the new conditions of production and exchange increased their competitiveness and gained market share at the expense of places that adapted less successfully.

At the centre of the transformation of the productive order, as Durand has shown (Boyer and Durand 1993), was an attempt to increase the ease and speed of reaction of firms to changes in their external environment. First, in the face of the saturation of markets and the absence of new products capable of renewing the consumption norm, strategies were developed to accelerate obsolescence and to stimulate shifts in fashion in order to speed up replacement. Second, attempts were made to increase the variety and/or to improve the quality, price and performance of normalized products to gain market share at the expense of rivals. These two strategies require more production flexibility, which was achieved in a variety of ways: integration of research and development and product manufacture; integration of marketing, design, manufacture and management; integration of activities in 'extended firms'; reliance on greater organizational productivity and automation to improve the responsiveness of manufacture and assembly to variations in the volume of demand without adversely affecting the commitment of workers; and an increase in the skills, learning abilities, functional flexibility and involvement of the work force in the struggle for improved productivity and quality. What resulted was a new productive order centred on the mass production of quality goods at low cost and the widespread use of information technology.

At the same time there were changes in the character of the wage relation and the industrial relations systems. Often there was an erosion of collective agreements, a squeeze on real wages, more individualized negotiation of wage agreements and career progress and increases in the intensity of work.[3]

As far as location is concerned two aspects of this reorganization of the productive order are important. First, the quest for greater co-ordination/ integration of the system of production as a whole and the creation of networks of relations within firms and between them and their markets and suppliers confers advantages on, and enables firms to secure gains from, locations well positioned on major infrastructures: as Veltz (1991) argues, 'one can therefore imagine very closely integrated but geographically spread

132

out systems of production distributed along major transport axes provided that the latter remain efficient'. Second, the increase in the relative importance of upstream (marketing, design of products and plant and operational management) and downstream (distribution and sales) stages in the production of goods and services relative to the central phase of manufacture and the increase in the relative importance in manufacture of maintenance relative to direct production entail a shift in the composition of employment towards high-skill and high-productivity jobs. As a result the distribution of executives and of individuals with technical skills has become a major location factor. These emphases on the economies of networks, integration and the distribution of infrastructures and on the role of centres of skilled workers give a considerable advantage to large cities and metropolitan regions.

These developments in the structure and geography of the productive system are of critical importance for two reasons. First, the productive system is central to the creation of wealth. Second, the development of the productive sector is the most important determinant of the competitiveness and trade success of firms, cities, regions and countries. In market societies, however, commercial, logistic and financial actors also play an indispensable role: commercial and logistic activities play a crucial role as intermediaries between producers and between the owners of resources and the consumers of the goods and services made with them, while financial institutions perform a critical function as providers of credit.

Commercial and financial activities are in the last instance dependent on the capacity of the productive sector to create wealth. In the period since the mid-1970s, however, their scale, influence, scope and relative significance have increased. At first it was the difficulties of accumulation and the uncertainty and instability of markets that led, as in most phases of economic crisis, to an increase in the attractiveness of financial and commercial capital, of other fluid ways of holding wealth and of other *rentier* and speculative incomes. In the 1970s transnational US financial institutions used the savings they had centralized to finance industrial development in peripheral and semi-peripheral countries, although at the end of the decade the countries that did borrow found themselves squeezed between stagnation of demand and an increase in interest rates (see Lipietz 1993). Throughout much of the 1980s high interest rates were a major stimulus to the diversion of investment from productive to financial activities as the quest for financial gain led to dramatic speculative movements of money capital into and out of property and land, stocks and shares, and debt and currencies.

The significance of the growth of commercial, financial and speculative activities lies in the fact that activities of this kind do not create wealth. Instead their remuneration depends on their capacity to secure a part of the wealth created elsewhere. As Palloix (1993) argues, such redistributions of created wealth occur wherever intermediaries can control and levy charges for access to markets. A crucial way in which wealth is at present redistributed is in his view through the sale of what he calls pseudo-services: services which must be purchased to gain access to markets but which create no new value and whose remuneration implies a compression of the margins of the producers of the goods and services in question. Commercial and financial gains are made, however, not just through the appropriation of wealth from the productive sector but also from other spheres of life. Gains are made from the exploitation of the domestic economy, the informal economy, drug dealing, corruption, crime, long-distance trade in agricultural surpluses and the scramble for the spoils of the fragile economies bequeathed by the collapse of communism in East Central Europe.

Palloix (1993) goes as far as the suggestion that this increase in the relative importance of pseudo-productive financial and commercial capital, which he dates from the early 1970s, is so marked as to warrant the claim that there has been a historical reversal of the relationship between productive and pseudo-productive capital. Whereas in the industrial era commercial gain was subordinated to productive gain, in recent years productive interests have been subordinated to commercial and financial interests. Palloix (1993) identifies three aspects of this shift. First, pseudo-productive capital has used its control over the access of productive capital to markets to shift decisively the distribution of value added in its favour. Second, the squeeze it has applied to the productive sector has increased competition, squeezed wages and prompted a strong drive for productivity growth. As productivity growth occurs without output growth, the consequence is the exclusion of a large and growing section of the population from the world of paid work and from the world of commodities. Finally, through its dominant role in the restructuring of metropolitan economies and systems of cities, pseudo-productive capital has created new hierarchical orderings of geographical space which raise its status and profile at the expense of the productive sector.

THE RULES OF THE GAME

With these structural changes there were significant modifications of the map of economic development, employment and exclusion, owing to the differential success of cities, regions and countries in their adaptation to them. Areas that were well endowed with the critical resources and assets required by modern productive activities and that successfully adapted to the new principles of production and exchange were less adversely affected by deindustrialization. Areas that won were, however, not just areas of productive strength but also areas specialized in the services and speculative activities that gained from the redistribution of wealth and income.

An analysis of the strategies of successful companies and places is clearly suggestive of strategies for 'development'. At present, however, it is questionable whether everyone can win. First, in areas that win there are social groups that lose, so that even in successful regions problems of development remain. Second, there are many situations in which one region wins at the expense of another, and there is some doubt as to whether all regions can win at one and the same time. The cause of this situation lies in the fact that in many cases the competitive struggle is a zero-sum game in which any improvement in the relative position of one area or enterprise is achieved at the expense of others.

Micro-economic approaches in which the inhabitants of cities, regions and countries seek to upgrade their skills and their infrastructures and attract investment will enhance their position and increase their chances of employment provided that improvement occurs faster than elsewhere. A generalization of strategies of this kind will raise skills everywhere, but as long as not everyone can win the consequence will be an increase in the skills of the losers. The implication is therefore that if a general solution is desired attention must also be paid to the character of the rules of the game and to the question as to whether and how it is possible to create a new positive-sum game in which everyone can win.

The dominance of zero-sum situations differentiates the last twenty years from the golden age. In that earlier period interregional transfers, investment decentralization and migration helped solve regional balance of payments problems and contributed to disinflation and national full-employment growth (see Dunford and Perrons 1994). On a European scale the early phases of national economic integration were associated with the interaction of two complementary virtuous circles: a circle of disinflation and moderate growth in the more advanced economies of northern Europe and a circle of very fast growth and rampant inflation in the less developed economies of southern Europe (see Aglietta 1982). At the end of the Fordist golden age, however, the autonomy of national economies declined, national mechanisms of macroeconomic stabilization and productive modernization were weakened, the post-1945 order disintegrated and more emphasis was placed on liberal market integration. The earlier virtuous circles of growth gave way to vicious circles (see Aglietta 1982).

At the heart of the change in the rules of the game was the internationalization of capital. To aid the internationalization of capital attempts have been made to remove barriers to the mobility of goods, of capital and in some cases of labour. To justify these changes, claims are made about the gains that will accrue from free trade, from deregulation and from greater reliance on market mechanisms. At an international level free trade is presented as a source of gains in welfare. In Europe the development of a single market defined as 'an area without frontiers in which the free circulation of goods, services, persons and capital is ensured' was expected to add 6 per cent to EU GDP, and it was claimed that 'recent developments in trade theory and past experience with the removal of intra-EC tariff barriers indicate that redistributive effects in the wake of freer trade need not be excessive' (Cecchini *et al.* 1988).

The dominance of these ideas is in part a reflection of the dominance of neo-classical and neo-liberal economic ideologies. According to neo-classical views of trade a single market offers regions opportunities to specialize according to their comparative advantage and offers successful and competitive firms opportunities to expand their markets and increase output to the minimum efficient scale of production. (The presumptions are that the trade creation associated with the removal of tariff and non-tariff barriers within the single market is not offset by trade diversion associated with the establishment of higher external trade barriers and that there are substantial untapped scale economies.) Trade creation and economies of scale for firms in a larger market will bring welfare gains to all through lower prices and wider consumer choice.[4] Greater European integration will thus create overall welfare improvements, while free trade will lead to an equilibrium in which the prices of all goods and of all the factors of production, or of all costs, incomes and productivities, will be equalized.

Alongside neo-classical models of trade lie neo-classical models of regional growth and development. Neo-classical regional growth models differ from trade models in two ways. First, interregional capital and labour mobility is anticipated. Second, the existence of a single currency rules out adjustment through changes in exchange rates. Adjustment occurs instead through the migration of wage earners from areas with low wages to more prosperous areas, and through the movement of capital in the opposite direction until incomes are equalized. If therefore unemployment in an area increases owing to a change in economic circumstances, wages will fall, attracting inward investment, and wage earners will emigrate, equalizing rates of unemployment and wages.

Among orthodox economists there is some debate about the validity of these neo-classical models. In the case of regional growth models, for example, the neo-classical position is criticized by economists who think that regional differences will remain, owing to differences in the mobility of labour, regional differences in the technological content of investment and the extent of technology transfer and the reproduction of differential resource endowments owing to variations in public infrastructural investment (see Cunéo and Hatem 1993).

As Cunéo and Hatem (1993: 124) point out, there has been a significant increase in trade between members of the EU, especially in the 1960s and 1970s: in 1990 intra-EU trade accounted for 14 per cent of EU GDP, compared with 12·2 per cent in 1980 and 6·4 per cent in 1960. In the 1980s the internationalization of capital accelerated sharply. The number of inter-firm agreements, mergers and alliances grew rapidly. And there was a sharp increase in direct foreign investment in other EU countries: in 1980–90 it increased sixfold, from US$15 billion per year to US$88 billion, while total investment increased 2·2 times. French estimates suggest that in 1988 30 per cent of the manufacturing output of EU countries was produced by subsidiaries of foreign firms, of which half were European. In the 1960s and 1970s US companies invested in Europe owing to fear of protection and the search for access to markets. In the second half of the 1980s Japanese companies followed suit. Also in the 1980s European firms reorganized their operations on a European scale to exploit the differential resource endowments of Europe's regions, to enter new markets and to reach a minimum efficient scale of operation.[5] In consequence capital mobility increased quite dramatically, and a Europe for capital is well on its way to completion: restrictions on the movement of capital have been eliminated, taxes on capital have been reduced to the lowest levels that prevailed in the EU and competition for investment has increased. Whether this mobility of capital equalizes differences in development is, however, more questionable, for two reasons. First, much of the investment that occurred involved acquisitions. Second, there is some doubt as to whether a significant transfer of technological know-how and research and development activities to less developed areas has occurred and as to how far the interregional division of labour has changed. As Amin and Tomaney argue in Chapter 8, it is possible to identify 'performance plants' which could contribute to the development of less developed areas but their decentralization and their integration into less developed economies will depend upon the development of specific public policy initiatives.

This increase in the mobility of capital between EC countries has not been accompanied by a corresponding increase in the mobility of labour. Orthodox economists would argue that in these circumstances wide differences in unemployment and wage costs could persist. Cunéo and Hatem (1993: 124) add that the existence of national governments that spend very different amounts of money per inhabitant on public services and infrastructures could also limit convergence.

There are, in short, major disagreements about the empirical relevance of the assumptions of neo-classical models. What is much less common is any attempt to challenge the principles that underlie neo-classical models. In particular almost all regional economists assume that the resources released as a result of the substitution of cheaper imports for locally produced goods and services will find alternative employment in activities with a higher relative productivity and in which the country has a comparative advantage. All areas should therefore gain from market integration, and market mechanisms should result in full employment as the existence of unemployed resources will mean that the opportunity cost of producing the imported good domestically is zero, except in so far as production could occur only if materials and capital goods were imported.

The sequence of economic changes which lead to a reallocation of factors of production and the creation of net gains is, however, far from automatic, and in practice the existence, size and distribution of gains depend on the specific character of the adjustment mechanisms. In a neo-classical world, of course, what exist are hypothetical vectors of non-negative prices and interest rates which, if established, would result in full employment, while movement from one to another simply involves changes in relative prices and a reallocation of factors of production from one activity/region to another. What the neo-classical view overlooks, however, is (1) the deflationary impact of the trade deficit that results from the loss of protection for weaker economies and the substitution of imports for domestic production, (2) the difficulties and the duration of shifts in specialization, especially in economies that are not highly diversified, (3) the risk that adjustment will fall on installed capacity, output and employment instead of on prices and (4) the cumulative nature of many growth processes, especially in situations where increasing returns prevail.

At the root of these criticisms is the question of the validity of neo-classical concepts of market adjustment and the unsatisfactory character of the settlement between Keynesian and neo-classical economists. According to this settlement the distinctiveness and significance of Keynes's work can be reduced to two propositions (Leijonhufvud 1969: 299). The first proposition is that Keynes's model is a special case derived as a result of the imposition of certain restrictions – of which the most important is the downward rigidity of wages – on the neo-classical model. The second is that this special case is important, as its assumptions about wage rigidity correspond more closely with the actual real-world situation than do those of orthodox theories of general equilibrium. As Leijonhufvud (1969: 299) pointed out, however, the idea that an era in which there was a drastic fall in wages could be modelled as one of wage rigidity is paradoxical. In his words:

> [the fact] . . . that a model with wage rigidity as its main distinguishing feature should become widely acceptable as crystallizing the experience of the unprecedented wage deflation of the Great Depression is one of the more curious aspects of the development of Keynesianism, comparable in this regard to the orthodox view that 'money is unimportant' – a conclusion presumably prompted by the worst banking debacle in US history. The emphasis on the 'rigidity of wages, which one finds in the 'new economics', reveals the judgement that wages did not fall enough in the early 1930s. Keynes, in contrast, judged that they declined too much by far . . . to Keynes, wage rigidity was a policy recommendation and not a behavioural assumption.

In recent decades the classical view has re-emerged: markets will lead to the full employment of resources and if full employment does not occur the reasons why lie in the existence of monopolies, minimum wage legislation or other institutional constraints which prevent the adjustment of prices. The policy recommendation is a removal of restrictions and in particular reductions in real wage rates. As Leijonhufvud (1969: 299) points out, however, Keynes was a fierce opponent of the idea that depressions were due to the existence of obstacles to price adjustment, while wage rigidity, which orthodox economists see as the cause of unemployment, was for Keynes a policy required to combat unemployment.

The fact that wage rigidity was espoused as a policy recommendation is indicative of the fact that Keynes's critique of classical and neo-classical conceptions of economic dynamics was much more profound than the settlement between orthodox economists suggests. Indeed, what Keynes argued was that the initial response to a decline in demand was not a price adjustment but a quantity adjustment. Keynes did not deny the existence of a hypothetical vector of non-negative prices and interest rates which, if established, would result in full resource utilization. What concerned Keynes were the difficulties of reaching the market-clearing vector in economies in which (1) all the information needed to ensure the perfect co-ordination of all the current and future activities of all traders does not exist and is not provided free of charge by an all-knowing Walrasian auctioneer, and (2) money is the medium of exchange. If a resource is made unemployed by a change in demand traders do not have perfect information about the new market-clearing price. The seller will set a reservation price in the light of past experience and a knowledge of the current price of comparable services and search for the highest bidder, adapting the reservation price as the search unfolds. Adjustment is not, therefore, instantaneous, and in this state of disequilibrium trading occurs while the resource itself remains unemployed.

To this argument it is necessary to add another. In this state of disequilibrium the loss of income from the services of the unemployed resource will impose a constraint on the owner's effective demand for other goods and services. This constraint on money expenditure and on effective demand provides the rationale of the multiplier analysis of competitive markets. What is more, this constraint is, as Marx and Keynes demonstrated, a defining characteristic of a money economy. As Clower (1969) has pointed out, in a money economy it is essential to draw a clear distinction between activities that are often conflated. First it is essential to draw a distinction between offers to exchange money for goods (purchase offers) and offers to sell goods for money (sale offers). Second, it is important to draw a related distinction between planned transactions (what an economic agent intends to do) and realized transactions (what an economic agent actually does). According to Say's law no economic agent plans to spend money on the purchase of goods or services without at the same time planning to earn the money to pay for them, whether from profit receipts or the proceeds of the sale of other commodities. If resources are unemployed, however, realized current receipts will fall short of planned receipts. In these circumstances actual consumption expenditure as expressed in effective market offers to purchase goods and services will fall short of desired consumption expenditure. As Keynes showed, therefore, current income constrains current expenditure: an individual who is forced by a lack of buyers to sell less of a factor than he or she wishes to sell is also forced by a lack of money income to spend less than he or she wants to spend. To make sense of the way a decentralized money economy functions, the Walrasian *tâtonnement* process which lies at the heart of neoclassical conceptions of price adjustment should at the very least be redefined to ensure that *no purchase order is accepted unless the purchaser already has sufficient income to pay for the transaction as a result of the completion of a previous sale order.* (This analysis abstracts from the fact that an economic agent may be able to borrow money.)

The implications of this conception of market adjustment are profound. In orthodox general equilibrium theory it is assumed that the sum of excess demands – the difference between the quantity demanded and the quantity supplied of each good and service – is zero. A consequence of this proposition – which is called Walras's law – is that the existence of excess supply of any factors of production necessarily implies the simultaneous existence of excess demand for other goods and services and will lead to movements in the structure of relative prices that will cause the economic system to converge on equilibrium. If, however, allowance is made for the mediation of money in all exchanges, it is clear that Walras's law is valid only in situations on full employment. If full employment does not prevail there will be excess supply of some factors of production, yet this situation of excess supply will not correspond to an effective excess demand for other goods and services. Wherever goods can be exchanged for money and money for goods but goods cannot be exchanged directly for other goods, realized current income is, in short, an independent constraint on effective demand. Excess supply in the labour market – involuntary unemployment – diminishes effective excess demand elsewhere. As Clower shows, with unemployed resources there is an excess supply of factors of production and there is a notional excess demand for goods but adjustment will not occur, as the effective excess demand for goods is zero, owing to the fact that the demand for goods is constrained by the lack of money income that stems from unemployment.

What this account of market adjustment shows is that unregulated market economies do not tend towards full employment and that involuntary unemployment is a result not of market imperfections but of the mediating role of money and the costs and time involved in the acquisition of information. As soon as this point is understood, it is possible to understand why the neo-liberal agenda, whether in the shape of the single market or in the form of structural adjustment programmes, has had such devastating deflationary consequences.

CONCLUSION

At present the economies of EU countries are suffering from a vicious circle of slow growth, mass unemployment and greater social and spatial inequality. An important cause of the perverse interaction of inequality, employment and growth in recent decades is the dominance of neo-liberal market-orientated rules of the game which contrast sharply with the rules that underpinned the 'golden age' model of growth. With the crisis of the 'golden age' model, competition increased. Cities, regions and countries sought to reduce costs to gain market share at the expense of other areas, with devastating consequences for the overall level of demand. A self-defeating competitive struggle for inward investment set one area against another. Companies which had preferred oligopolistic collusion in the golden age engaged in aggressive competitive struggles in order to increase their market share at the expense of others. Competition often had dramatic consequences: actual unit costs often exceeded anticipated unit costs, owing to the lower than expected volume of sales, while the competitive pressure on prices made it difficult to set margins at the levels required to recover the cost of past investment and of R&D and to finance future investment. Governments acted as if competition were an end in itself. At the same time restrictive policies were adopted to contain inflation and reduce budget deficits. As a consequence the rate of growth slowed down. The idea that inflation and public-sector deficits were in part a result of slow growth does not seem to have crossed the minds of the neo-liberal establishment. Yet deficits are in part a consequence of mass unemployment, which stems in part from slow growth, while inflation results in part from dynamic shortages of supply that result from insufficient rates of industrial accumulation (see Bruno 1993).

An escape from the current cul-de-sac requires a significant and sustained change of direction which itself would involve a number of elements. First an attempt should be made to co-ordinate growth at a European level and to establish an investment-led Europe-wide development plan to create (public-sector?) European champions in strategic sectors, to develop modern public transport and telecommunications infrastructures and to invest in energy conservation (Bruno 1993; Tylecote 1994). An important aim of such a plan would be the creation of a credible climate of expectations of long-term expansion. Confidence about the sustainability of expansion is an essential condition for higher rates of investment, on which sustained development depends. Another aim would be to schedule growth and

141

income formation to cope with the distortions that stem from the different time paths of stock and flow variables. When investment growth accelerates incomes are paid to factors of production before the installation of additional production capacity is completed and before the production of more consumer goods starts: if disposable income and demand increase ahead of production capacity a supply–demand gap will emerge and will lead to price increases and increased imports, which could threaten growth. In these circumstances there is a case for a deferral of the expenditure of money incomes until new production capacity is in place. A third aim is to overcome the financial obstacles to growth through programmes of public expenditure financed out of taxes on land, property speculation and pollution, direct intervention in the financial system to generate extra lending to firms at low interest rates, and legal requirements upon financial institutions to purchase bonds issued by nationalized industries to finance capital investment programmes (see Hutton 1992).

Any consequent renewal of growth could also increase the productive potential of weaker economies and of the underclass which has at present little to contribute either as producers or as consumers and in this way increase demand for the goods and services of the stronger economies and groups. What would be required, however, would be the development of an alternative non-contractionist mode of integration,[6] which itself presupposes two steps. The first is the creation of a set of fiscal and adjustment mechanisms to ensure that competitive deflation is not the only response to external shocks and the inevitable disequilibria that accompany the integration process. The possibilities include the creation of a framework that ensures that regional economies which choose to grow faster than average are not penalized, co-ordinated expansion and the creation of a single federal political authority with responsibility for fiscal policy and the capacity to transfer resources to weaker areas. The second is a real convergence of Europe's regional economies, which itself requires above-average growth in less developed areas and the decentralization of productive investment from the centre, effected either via regional policies[7] or via an increase in the value of strong currencies.

While a renewal of growth is important as a means of reintegrating those sections of the population who have been excluded and marginalized, growth cannot be discussed independently of its content. Clearly, in advanced countries environmental constraints place limits on the scope for growth-led solutions of the Fordist kind. In future far more attention will have to be paid to the sustainability of growth in the light of the finiteness of the earth and its resources. In this context questions of equity which suggest that the populations of advanced countries have already laid claim to far more than their share of the earth's resources assume increased importance. The scope for growth is also limited, however, because of the interaction of two other economic factors. First, the new information and communications technologies have not yet led to the creation of new products and new needs of sufficient value to relaunch the virtuous spiral of mass consumption and mass production. Second, the rate of growth of productivity in the productive sector has increased very sharply. In these conditions full employment with full-time work is probably not possible. As Lipietz (1993: 145) has argued, there are two ways of dealing with this situation. The first is the development of 'a third sector of community work schemes which would be self-managed, contractually bound to end users and part of the logic of local development founded on partnership'. The second is the creation of more cohesive societies in which work is shared, everyone has more free time and extra-economic activities expand.

At present structural change is leading to the creation of societies in which growth is slow and which are divided socially and regionally. The stance of the neo-liberal state reinforces these trends and tendencies. The consequent decline in cohesion has, however, gone hand in hand with a deterioration in overall economic performance. A rediscovery of generalized prosperity requires recognition of the reciprocal dependence of cohesion, economic performance and welfare and the development of institutions and mechanisms of regulation that in current circumstances can establish a new set of complementarities between them. To cope with the globalization of economic life and the increase in economic interdependence there is a need to develop political structures above the national level and to foster closer co-operation and integration. And to escape from the economic and social cul-de-sac there is a need to recognize the self-destroying character of unregulated markets. In market societies there are a wide range of costs that individuals would choose not to pay but which are functional to the medium-term reproduction of a socio-economic system. Recognition of this situation would suggest that a solution to the crisis of the social democratic compromise lies not in an attempt to throw the reforms of the post-war era into reverse gear but an adaptation and deepening of the structures, modes and principles of market regulation to the new circumstances.

NOTES

1 Aggregate data on productivity suggests that in manufacturing the productivity pay-off of the new information and communications technologies has been limited and very slow to appear, while in the service sector productivity seems to have declined. There are a number of explanations of these phenomena. The decline in service sector productivity is due in part to the expansion of low-productivity services, while in some of those areas in which computers and telecommunications do add significantly to human abilities the productivity gains associated with automation were offset by increases in the amount of data to analyse, store and disseminate. According to a 1990 OECD report cited by Sweeney (1994) the problem is that 'the social environment has not been

sufficiently adaptive to, and supportive of, a rapid diffusion of these technologies. In particular the reluctance of firms to change their work organisation, labour relations, decision-making structures and management styles means that the spread of information technologies is currently slower than it could be, or is not achieving the full potential productivity gains . . . The full exploitation of the new technologies implies a shift away from the Taylorist model of production typical of the previous phase of industrialisation.'

2 As Hobsbawm (1994) argues, it was the enforced transformation of capitalist societies through the sweeping reforms after the Second World War that led to their unprecedented post-war economic success and 'it is one of the ironies of this strange century that the most lasting results of the October revolution, whose object was the global overthrow of capitalism, was to save its antagonist both in war and peace . . . by providing it with the incentive – fear – to reform itself after the Second World War, and by establishing the popularity of economic planning, furnishing it with some of the procedures for its reform'.

3 There are some important academic and political disputes as to the significance and meaning of recent changes in the organization of work and the wage relation. Some argue that these changes amount to the emergence of a new productive order, an increase in the autonomy of the work force and the humanization of work. Others see them as a refinement of the principles of Taylorism/Fordism and as a reinforcement of the control of capital over production (Boyer and Durand 1993).

4 Wider choice results from the availability alongside locally produced goods and services of imports and the increased possibilities of marketing specialized regional products in distant markets. If there are, however, substantial untapped economies of scale and if local producers disappear the consequence will be a reinforcement of the widely observed tendency for consumption norms to be standardized and made uniform.

5 These flows of investment also reflected the differential strengths of currencies, with flows out of countries whose currencies appreciated and into countries whose currencies depreciated. Two monetary factors encouraged the outward flows: first, the increased command over resources that stemmed from appreciation stimulates the acquisition of overseas assets; second, the negative impact of appreciation on the competitiveness of export industries is a stimulus to the substitution of overseas for domestic production. At the same time, however, exchange rate instability added considerably to the risk of such investments.

6 After the Second World War Keynes argued that a system of international exchanges and payments should satisfy two principles. The first is the principle of the symmetry of adjustment, which means that the burden of adjustment should fall not just on debtor countries but also on creditor countries, which are more able to support it. The second is the principle that a system should have an expansionist rather than a contractionist bias. This point was made very forcefully when he said that 'no responsible person today contemplated the use of the old weapons, deflation enforced by dear money, resulting in unemployment as a means of restoring international equlibrium' (cited in Williams et al. 1992: 226). Keynes's statement about the irresponsibility of the acolytes of neo-liberalism is equally valid today.

7 Three sets of measures are involved. First, direct national and EC-level action is required to redistribute resources, regionalize public investment and public expenditure and develop public-sector-led counter-cores. Second, controls over competition between places to attract investments through the offer of increasingly large subsidies is required, as is the development of new means of leverage

– such as targets for investment in different areas and planning agreements with
all major European firms and inward investors – over investment location.
Third, where public financial resources are advanced the advance should
assume the form of equity capital in part to avoid the losses that stem from
subsequent decisions to disinvest.

REFERENCES

Aglietta, M. (1982) 'World capitalism in the eighties', *New Left Review* 136: 1–41.
Boyer, R., and Durand, J.-P. (1993) *L'après-Fordisme*, Paris: Syros.
Bruno, S. (1993) 'Boosting European Growth: strategies for integration and
strategies for competition', paper presented at the conference on 'The
European periphery: facing the new century' held in Santiago de Compostella,
Spain, 30 September–2 October.
Cecchini, P., Catinat, M., and Jacquemin, A. P. (1988) *1992: The European challenge:
the benefits of a single market*, the Cecchini report, Aldershot: Wildwood House.
Clower, R. W. (1969a) 'Foundations of monetary theory', in R. W. Clower (ed.)
Monetary Theory, Harmondsworth: Penguin, pp. 202–11 (first published in 1967).
Clower, R. W. (1969b) 'The Keynesian counter-revolution: a theoretical appraisal',
in R. W. Clower (ed.) *Monetary Theory*, Harmondsworth: Penguin, pp. 270–97
(first published in 1965).
Cunéo, P., and Hatem, F. (1993) 'UEM et localisation des activités en Europe',
Economie et Statistique 262–3: 123–34.
Dunford, M., and Perrons, D. (1994) 'Regional inequality, regimes of accumulation
and economic development in contemporary Europe', *Transactions of the Institute
of British Geographers*, New Series, 19 2: 163–82.
Gregg, P., and Machin, S. (1994) 'Is the UK rise in inequality different?', in R.
Barrell (ed.) *The UK Labour Market: Comparative Aspects and Institutional Develop-
ment*, Cambridge: Cambridge University Press, pp. 93–125.
Hirsch, J., and Roth, R. (1986) *Das neue Gesicht des Kapitalismus. Vom Fordismus zum
Post-Fordismus*, Hamburg: VSA Verlag.
Hobsbawm, E. (1994) *The Age of Extremes, 1914–91: the Short Twentieth Century*,
London: Weidenfeld & Nicolson.
Horowitz, D. (1967) *From Yalta to Vietnam: American Foreign Policy in the Cold War*,
Harmonsworth: Penguin.
Hutton, W. (1992) 'It may sound like intervention, but it spells recovery', *Guardian*,
Wednesday 2 September 1992, p. 10.
Leijonhufvud, A. (1969) 'Keynes and the Keynesians: a suggested interpretation',
in R. W. Clower (ed.) *Monetary Theory*, Harmondsworth: Penguin, pp. 298–310
(first published in 1967).
Lipietz, A. (1993) *Towards a new Economic Order: post-Fordism, Ecology and Democracy*,
Cambridge: Polity Press.
Palloix, C. (1993) *Les marchands et l'industrie. Un essai sur les rapports entre la société et
l'économie*, Amiens: ERSI.
Polanyi, K. (1944) *The Great Transformation: the Political and Economic Origins of our
Time*, Boston, Mass.: Beacon Press.
Solow, R. (1987) Review of S. S. Cohen and J. Zysman, *Manufacturing Matters: the
Myth of the post-Industrial Economy*, New York Times, 12 July, p. 36.
Sweeney, G. (1994) 'Learning Efficiency, Technical Change and Economic
Progress', Dublin: SICA Innovation Consultants.
Tylecote, A. (1994) *Riding the Long Wave*, London: Employment Policy Institute.
Veltz, P. (1991) 'New models of production organisation and trends in spatial

145

development', in G. Benko and M. Dunford (eds) (1991) *Industrial Change and Regional Development*, London: Belhaven.

Williams, J., Williams, K., and Haslam, C. (1992) ' "Leap before you look": the implications of EMU for the future of the EC', in A. Amin and M. Dietrich (eds) *Towards a new Europe*, Aldershot: Edward Elgar, pp. 212–33.

Part II

SOCIAL COHESION

Part II

SOCIAL COHESION

6

EUROPE OF THE REGIONS AND THE FUTURE OF NATIONAL SYSTEMS OF INDUSTRIAL RELATIONS

Paul Teague

In recent years the idea of a 'Europe of the regions' has become a popular theme in debates about the future of European integration. Although frequently invoked, the concept or term continues to elude precise definition. But in broad terms it is taken to mean a new distribution of tasks between different levels of government – regional, national and supranational – in the European Union. Parallel to this development have been observations that the regional level is becoming an increasingly important new strategic site for industrial relations activity (Piore 1993). In particular, it has been argued that regional forms of industrial relations may allow new trust relations to be established between employers and employees in the absence of formal rules (Lorenz 1993). This is a departure from the 'traditional' industrial relations approach which suggests that an employment relationship should be governed by a range of institutional arrangements. Put together, these separate arguments or insights suggest a recasting of labour market governance in Europe in a way that will see the demise of national systems of industrial relations.

The purpose of this chapter is to assess the plausibility of this thesis of a regionalization of industrial relations in Europe. The first part examines the key influences that are encouraging assessments that economic and political life in Europe is on the verge of regionalization. Three important influences – political, monetary and productive – are identified and outlined in some detail. Then the chapter evaluates the feasibility and desirability of regional labour market systems in Europe. It is argued that on both counts the scenario is deficient. Instead of ushering in a benign new model of labour market organization, a programme of regionalization would cause enormous institutional fragmentation and disorder. As a result, labour market performance in the new Europe would be further distorted.

The conclusion suggests that it is perhaps more realistic to assume that a clash between a competitive and a co-operative form of intergovernment-alism is dominating the European integration process. Under both options the member states would remain at the centre of the EU's decision-making. But competitive intergovernmentalism emphasizes competition between existing national rules. In contrast, co-operative intergovernmentalism is about the member states recognizing that the integration process gener-ates spill-overs and interdependences which require collaborative action at the extra-national level. Whichever scenario wins will have considerable implications for the future 'social model' of Europe.

POLITICAL INFLUENCES

In recent years, several European countries have pursued programmes of administrative decentralization which have resulted in sub-national tiers of government acquiring considerable new powers (Keating 1993). These initiatives have corresponded with, or perhaps have been a response to, the atrophy of political and social bonds that have made nation states in Europe cohesive for more than a century and the hypertrophy of regional and ethnic identities. Virtually every member state now contains some type of regionalist, and even separatist, movement. For many of these move-ments a constitutionally stronger EU represents an ideal way to disconnect themselves further from a national political formation with which they have little empathy. Thus for some time the slogan of the Scottish Nationalist Party has been 'A new Scotland in a new Europe'. The Lega Lombarda in Italy, the separatist group in Corsica and the Basque 'nationalist' movement in Spain, among others, have similar rallying calls. Other political parties which are not regionalist in character none the less support administrative decentralization largely on the basis that it leads to more efficient and accountable forms of government.

In the context of the EU these rather desperate political forces have come together to demand a 'Europe of the regions' (Scott *et al.* 1994). A central part of this project is to recast the EU along integrative federalist principles. Instead of being a tidy constitutional package, integrative fed-eralism is a mixed breed, containing elements of two different intellectual traditions. One is Roman Catholic social teaching on subsidiarity. In Britain the debate about subsidiarity has concentrated on whether the concept promotes decentralized decision-making. But in most other parts of Europe the term is not seen in such a narrow and administrative way. Instead it is regarded as a guiding principle for the social and political organization of society, particularly with regard to creating a balance between the interests of individuals and those of society as a whole. Or, perhaps more precisely, between liberty and authority (Adonis and Jones 1991).

According to Catholic social theory, such a trade-off can be secured by a society having a transparent combination of obligations and rights (Van Kersbergen and Kerbeck 1994). The main obligation constraining individual behaviour is the non-infringement of property rights. But a range of secondary obligations should also exist encouraging individuals, among other things, to play an active role in society. Counterbalancing obligations should be a body of political and social rights. Thus individuals should have the right to free speech and complete freedom of association. In addition, they should enjoy a range of social rights, protecting them from poverty and allowing them civilized standards of health and education.

Catholic thinking on subsidiarity also focuses on the institutional provision of rights. Whereas the social democratic tradition suggests that the state should be the main provider and guarantor of rights, the Catholic perspective is that the central authorities should not have such a direct role (Hanley 1994). Instead, social protection should arise mainly from the activities of lower tiers of government as well as associations in civil society. Social intervention by the state is regarded as a policy of last resort – a lifeboat operation to rescue local social safety nets. The American bishops put it like this: 'Governments should not replace or destroy smaller communities and individual initiative. Rather it should help them to contribute more effectively to social well-being and supplement their activity when the demands of justice exceed their capacities' (cited in Scheltex 1991: 39). Thus, from this perspective of subsidiarity, social protection should be the outcome of rich and dense interactions within civil society, involving the family, community, voluntary organizations and the Church, whilst the state operates as the social exoskeleton to this process.

The other pillar of the integrative federalist project is that part of the fiscal federalist literature which emphasizes the capturing of economies of scale, positive externalities and so on (CEPR 1993). Capturing economies of scale normally relates to the administrative functions of government. In the fiscal federalism literature there is a clear preference for decentralized policy-making, especially in large political units. At the same time, it is recognized that it is inefficient for certain functions to be implemented at the local level. In other words, centralization allows specialization and less fragmentation. For the most part, it is the realizing of positive externalities or spill-overs that justifies the assignment of policy functions to a higher tier of government. Within the EU context, the argument is that the number of negative spill-overs between the member states may be reduced if the EU centre were to have a stronger role in policy formation. Thus, for instance, it may be more beneficial and efficient if public investment in transport systems or public policies for the environment were co-ordinated by Brussels rather than by each European capital. Perhaps the most sophisticated and thorough articulation of this view was the MacDougall report (1977).

A mixture of Catholic thinking on subsidiarity and fiscal federalist principles is the substance of integrative federalism (Moravesik 1993). To introduce such a system inside the EU would involve reorganizing the present political structures to create a new institutional balance between the EU centre, national governments and regional administrations. Such a reordering would produce a new hierarchy of norms and a sharper delineation of competences between the different tiers of governments inside the EU. As a result of these changes, the contestable character of the EU's politcal structure would be reduced. Instead of relations between the member states being embittered by disputes about whether or not the EU should have a presence in a certain policy area, a new legitimacy would be attached to EU-level interventions (Teague forthcoming). Moreover the weak institutional connections between the member states and the EU centre, which in the past has reduced the impact of so many EU policies, would be replaced by new, more robust and stable support structures. All in all, integrative fiscal federalism is about copper-fastening the political ties between the different levels of government in a way that allows the EU to operate as a more effective political and economic entity.

Thus the 'Europe of the regions' project is about weakening national-level economic and political institutions and increasing the scope of local-level and EU-wide policy actions. Political reorganization along the above lines would have important implications for industrial relations arrangements. Under integrative federalism, individual member states would not be totally free to determine their own system of labour market governance. Rather they would have to comply with certain employment policy interventions decided upon at the EU level, particularly with regard to the objectives of the proposed actions. Thus integrative federalism could lead to a strengthening of EU social policy. At the same time, the new-found freedom of the EU more easily to set down social policy objectives and even obligations would not automatically be a licence to introduce heavy harmonizing measures. On the contrary, if the subsidiarity principle were adhered to, then an EU social policy based on 'Continental uniformity' would be eschewed. An integrative federalist employment policy is more or less about ensuring that each member state establishes a minimum level of social protection, with any of them free to implement more advanced measures. In addition, it is about the EU centre having the capacity to support (as opposed to override) the regimes of social protection and labour market regulation of lower tiers of government, particularly if they appear to be fragmenting.

An integrative federalist EU would also give considerable momentum to the already existing trend of local and regional governments expanding their repertoire of policy interventions. With new-found powers and competences these local municipalities and similar institutions would sooner or later get involved in labour market matters by promoting

152

training schemes, active labour market policies, better relations between unions and employers, and so on. Thus integrative federalism would create the political foundations or the institutional conditions for the regionalization of certain industrial relations practices. With policies being pulled upwards and pushed downwards under such a political system, the notion of *national* systems of industrial relations would be punctured. But the state's involvement in labour market affairs would not completely wither away. Too many policies for the labour market which are organized at the national level could not be easily transferred either to local institutions or to the EU centre. A good example would be social security systems. Thus the nation state would maintain a presence in industrial relations under integrative federalism.

However popular the political slogan among regionalists (and federalists) across the EU, it is unlikely that the 'Europe of regions' programme could win the assent of the European Council. National sovereignty is still a powerful norm in defining the outlook and behaviour of politicians and government elites in the member states. As a result, it is doubtful whether they would agree to a programme that would drastically modify their influence on political and economic life. Thus the political front door appears firmly closed to a recasting of the EU along integrative federalist lines. But one calculation is that an economic back door may exist for integrative federalism owing to pressures that may arise in the wake of monetary union in Europe and moves toward productive decentralization. These influences may be worth examining in some detail.

MONETARY INFLUENCES

At the heart of the Maastricht Treaty is a plan to establish monetary union in Europe. If this actually happens the monetary policy of the member states will be passed from the national level to an independent European central bank. A single currency will be established and the control of inflation as well as interest rate policy will be the responsibility of the new bank. In addition, member states will no longer be able to adjust their exchange rates unilaterally either to offset differential inflation rates between EU countries or to deal with country-specific shocks.

Establishing European monetary union would almost certainly impinge on wage-setting institutions and behaviour, with implications for the content of EU social policy. But the way this impact is felt and by how much is a matter of some dispute. One view is that EMU would remove any exchange rate illusion that may exist in the European economy (Spencer 1992). As a result, Spanish workers, for example, may demand Danish rates of pay even though their productivity levels are much lower. However, as trade unions' 'orbits of coercive comparison' continue to be national in character such pressures are unlikely to emerge at least in the short and medium run (Teague and Grahl 1993). Thus little weight should be given to this perspective.

An alternative, more subtle, view is that EMU would encourage fragmented and decentralized wage bargaining behaviour (Eichengreen and Frieden 1993). In co-ordinated labour market systems such as Germany the central bank deters trade unions from pursuing pay claims that would have a damaging impact on competitiveness (Streeck 1994). Essentially, the central bank signals that it would appreciate the currency to offset the impact of high real wage increases. Trade unions regard this threat as credible and as a result constrain collective bargaining demands. With the powers of national central banks being effectively emasculated under European monetary union, this institutional sanction against unruly wage behaviour is removed. Accentuating this problem is the fact that EMU changes the economic context in which wage bargaining takes place. In a co-ordinated bargaining situation pay levels and increases are heavily influenced by prevailing economic conditions – unemployment and inflation rates, the balance of payments, and so on. But monetary union downgrades these national reference points, since the main macroeconomic indicators will be European inflation rates and unemployment rates. Thus, by removing certain institutional constraints and eroding the economic and social parameters of co-ordinated wage bargaining, EMU may have a disruptive impact on the positive features of European industrial relations (Henley and Tsaksolotos 1994).

To compensate for the loss or weakening of wage co-ordination mechanisms at the national level, the EU could attempt to establish similar arrangements at the European centre. Institutionally this would mean the European trade unions and employer bodies having a much bigger say in wage formation. It would probably operate along the lines of the European social partners alongside EU authorities determining norms for pay rises after examining European-level economic data. Then the trade unions and employers would use their institutional channels to diffuse these norms to lower negotiating tiers in the hope that they would be taken on board.

Whether such a European system of collective bargaining could be established is open to question. Certainly, major changes would have to be made in the present social policy framework of the EU. The European social partners would have to be given more authority and resources, and appropriate formulae would have to be established for the setting of credible European wage norms. Invariably, such a system would entail some centralization of wage determination. But again, a big doubt exists about whether national trade unions and employers, as well as member governments, would be prepared to transfer authority upwards with regard to wage formation, even under monetary union conditions. However, queries about such an arrangement go beyond its institutional feasibility. Setting Europe-wide wage norms would be paramount to creating a form of transnational corporatism. Yet problems of scale and of heterogeneity may themselves make EU-level corporatism impossible. Sweden, one of the largest countries to have adopted corporatist procedures, has a work force of some 5 million people with a single language and a common culture. In the EU of twelve member states there are some 120 million employees in the most divergent economic circumstances, divided by language and by cultural, ideological, national and regional traditions. In this situation it would be very difficult for the EU to establish pay norms that would be credible at the ground level (Teague and Grahl 1993).

At the same time, Europe-wide unco-ordinated and decentralized pay negotiations could lead to sup-optimal labour market outcomes. Under decentralized bargaining, trade unions are less aware of the impact of wage claims on the price level and as a result will be less likely to have moderate wage aspirations. Similarly, if employers do not co-ordinate their wage offers, and pursue only their individual self-interest, each will continually seek to leapfrog over others in an effort to recruit and retain efficient workers. Layard (1990) gives a concrete example as to why unco-ordinated pay deals may have a distorting impact. He argues that some industrial sectors have inherently greater productivity growth than others, which is mainly due to technological factors and not to the efforts of workers. Thus he points out that between 1979 and 1986 productivity growth in UK manufacturing varied hugely between industries -- doubling in man-made fibres while remaining constant in brewing. If pay had been based on productivity, wages in man-made fibres would have doubled relative to those in brewing. But in fact the wage increase was identical in both industries (70 per cent). In other words, competition for labour always produces a going rate, and where high productivity growth enterprises grant large pay increases other industries end up paying the same in order to retain labour.

Thus, while the centralization of wage formation may not be feasible at the EU level some degree of pay co-ordination is nevertheless desirable. To resolve this conundrum, the idea of regional labour market systems or regional industrial relations systems is gaining currency (Sabel 1992). The functions of such a system would be more or less the same as present national arrangements. Thus one dimension would be the absorption function, whereby the wage system is structured so that it helps to promote low unemployment. The regions are potentially a more appropriate level for the unemployment/real wage trade off. Employers ought to have a strong interest in preventing their competition for labour spilling over into higher wages. Unions should also have incentives to restrain wages regionally in order to provide alternative employment opportunities in the case of lay-offs. A second function of a regional industrial relations system would be to assist the drive to improve economic performance. A key part of this task is the development of extra-firm institutions such as training and active labour market strategies to assist skill formation by enterprises, and so on. A third element would be the promotion of equity within the employment system so as reduce potential distortion effects in the labour market. With norms of fairness it is more likely that opportunistic behaviour which reduces the ability of regional industrial relations systems to deliver wage restraint and collective productive goods would be marginalized (Solow 1990).

PRODUCTION INFLUENCES

The assessment that European monetary union will trigger in its wake a regionalization of labour market structures reinforces a popular theme in economic geography and wider political economy discussions that production is becoming more spatial in character. According to this literature, the 1950s and 1960s were the era of the big corporation. Firms grew bigger to capture internal economies of scale in an effort to service mass, relatively homogeneous, product markets. But economic changes are making this system of mass production, sometimes called Fordism, increasingly obsolete. For one thing, whereas economic life under Fordism was characterized by reasonably high levels of stability, the market place is now turbulent and volatile. On the demand side, there is increasing instability as the modern consumer continually seeks new products and product variety. On the supply side, firms face intensified commercial pressures as a result of the globalization of economic life. To succeed in this rather uncertain environment firms must be flexible and adaptable. But the Fordist internal economies of scale model, which is predicated on inflexible and rigid production techniques, is inappropriate to these more volatile conditions (Sengenberger 1992).

In recent years there has been a significant shift towards production decentralization to make enterprises more symmetrical with the new patterns of consumption. Thus the emphasis has been on firms becoming smaller, with the capacity to move in and out of market niches with relative ease. To realize this objective, new technologies are used to allow production to take place in small batches. Widespread production decentralization has led to the sharper delineation or creation of regional economic systems. This is because the competitive ability of firms has become increasingly dependent upon the spatial infrastructure of the market in which they operate. Put differently, productive decentralization has in some instances given rise to external economies of scale (Romer 1994). In such cases a range of dynamic commercial effects emerge which are external to individual firms but internal to the economic system. Examples of these regional economic systems vary a good deal: Emilia Romagna in Italy and Baden-Württtenburg in Germany are given as examples of regional manufacturing complexes, whereas Paris (advertising), London (finance) and Madrid (fashion) are regarded as examples of the geographical concentration of service sector activity.

Just why these regional economic systems emerge and ensure that the collective commercial effort is greater than the sum of the individual parts is not at all clear. But there appears to be a number of factors at play (Saglio 1992). All the successful regional economies have dense connections between individual firms and strong linkages between external non-market institutions and these commercial networks. One benefit that arises from these dense commercial relationships is a low transaction cost environment. Information is more fully available and better processed, thereby making enterprises more sensitive to market developments. As a result, firms are in a better position to do business. Another advantage from commercial collaboration is the creation of a high level of trust between firms. With the suspension, or at least a reduction, of a self-interest calculation, opportunistic behaviour is reduced, allowing firms to pursue commercial strategies that they would not otherwise pursue. For example, the moral hazard problem of firms not undertaking certain types of investment because they cannot internalize all the benefits is to some extent eased. Thus regional production systems that capture external economies of scale generate a range of dynamic gains that improve commercial performance.

Perhaps it is unrealistic to believe that all regions can realize external economies of scale or that all the benefits associated with such an arrangement will arise simultaneously. Nevertheless, regions that can produce such effects will gain a considerable competitive advantage. A theme that emerges constantly in the academic literature on this topic is that industrial relations practices and institutions play a key role in the formation of dynamic regional economic systems. Locke (1990) describes how Italian trade unions and employers in the textile industry have broken away from national sector agreements and are establishing geographically defined collective agreements so that working conditions and practices are more closely tied to local circumstances. Moreover, in this new bargaining arena, trade unions focus on a wider range of issues than simply pay. As much importance is given to training, the organization of working hours, and so on, which allows for more encompassing collective agreements.

Sabel (1991) pushes the point even further by arguing that industrial relations in successful regional economic systems depart from and even eschew the formalized and hierarchical forms of collective bargaining that have emerged in industrialized countries during this century. In particular, he suggests that employee relations in such districts are based on informal deals and agreements in principle rather than elaborate and detailed rules or codes. As a result of this implicit social compromise a common understanding is produced that employers will not pursue exploitative practices in return for employees agreeing to the flexible deployment of labour and machinery. The trust relations that sustain this social compromise are seen

157

as arising from the *social embeddedness* of firms. By social embeddedness Sabel appears to mean the situation where the boundaries between the firm and the wider civil society or community become blurred. Thus communities that have dense harmonious interactions between citizens or share a common view based on the same ethnic or cultural heritage will generate co-operative social relations that influence the relationship between employers and employees inside the firms. In other words, the implicit social compromise inside the firm has its origins in the formation of social trust outside the firm.

The significance of Sabel's arguments is far-reaching, as they depart from the traditional way the academy has approached industrial relations matters. Industrial relations have no widely accepted theoretical roots, but the text that is widely regarded as the pioneering work in the area is John Dunlop's *Industrial Relations Systems*, published in 1958. The two main arguments of this book are that the relationship between employers and workers needed to be governed by an institutional web of rules and laws and that the state has an important role in the formation and operation of such a system. Sabel directly challenges these two assumptions by suggesting that the strategic site of much industrial relations decision-making has moved from the national to the regional level and that the substance of the bargain between employers and employees has changed. No longer are industrial relations about how different (national) systems manage conflict between capital and labour; instead they are about how such systems connect the world of work with society in a way that establishes trust relations between the two parties. Thus, for Sabel and others, the regionalization of economic life is transforming the political and social foundations of industrial societies.

The potentially crushing impact of monetary union on national economic management, the growth of regional production complexes and the political calls for a Europe of the regions are the chief factors encouraging assessments that the traditional structure and conduct of industrial relations are under threat. At first glance, the idea of regionalized employment systems is attractive: decentralized political and economic structures more sensitive to local conditions; an EU committed to promoting decentralized labour market practices and production structures tied to wider social and community influences. But, on closer examination, a number of significant shortcomings can be found in this model of regional labour market systems. In particular, questions can be raised about the feasibility and even the desirability of the model.

TOWARDS REGIONAL LABOUR MARKET SYSTEMS IN EUROPE?

One problem is that it is not at all clear how regional forms of economic and labour market adjustment could be realized in the New Europe. Some clues to answering this puzzle may be gained from an assessment of the US economy, which has operated a single market for more than a century. In the US there appears to be a well developed pattern of regional adjustment to adverse economic shocks based on migration and not movements in wages (Katz and Blanchard 1992). Thus when an adverse economic shock occurs virtually immediately people seem to respond to bad economic times by moving to more prosperous parts of the country. In the longer term, after a period of about ten years, the migration process allows the unemployment rate to move back towards the national average. However, employment does not recover to its initial level, indicating that the regional economy has shrunk and that the stock of jobs has fallen. At the same time, a negative employment shock has a negligible downward impact on wages, and in the long term the regional wage level more or less coincides with the average national wage level. All this suggests a high level of convergence in terms of income between the various states of the US.

Whether the European economy could adopt a spatial adjustment process based on migratory flows is doubtful, at least in the short term. Figure 2.10 on p. 68 shows the number of EC nationals residing in a member state other than the one of their birth. It clearly shows how little labour mobility exists inside the EU. Only Ireland and Portugal seem to have a sizeable share of their populations living in other member states. Ironically, labour migration between European countries was higher in the early 1950s, before the creation of the Common Market in 1958. Of course, there is labour mobility in Europe but it tends to be confined within member states. Thus root-and-branch changes would be required before the EU could imitate the regional pattern of adjustment found in the US. At present the European Commission is pursuing a number of programmes aimed at removing the obstacles to the free movement of people inside the EU. One initiative is to get the member states to recognize each other's qualifications and diplomas in similar occupational categories to improve the labour market matching process across countries. Another measure is to bring the member states' social security systems closer together so that there can be for the first time portability of pensions inside the EU. If successful, such schemes will undoubtedly make it easier to move from one part of the EU to another. But they are unlikely to trigger a big wave of Europe-wide migration. A range of formidable cultural and linguistic influences will continue to stand in the way of an open, fluid European labour market

Marsden (1992) suggests that current developments are indicating a

Figure 6.1 Map of the European labour market post-1992

European labour market 'map' along the lines of Figure 6.1. At the higher end of the occupational structure, he suggests, there is increasing cross-border mobility. Much of this increased movement is the result of a greater number of companies operating in more than one member state. To improve company efficiency and to satisfy the demands of young skilled workers many enterprises are developing Europe-wide internal labour markets. In the 1950s, there was a huge traffic in unskilled workers across European countries in response to the demands of the Fordist production trajectory. After the demise of the golden age of economic growth this form of labour mobility declined rapidly. However, there continues to be some movement of unqualified labour inside the EU, particularly in the service areas of the economy. But the vast majority of workers continue to operate within nationally delineated labour market systems, which can vary a great deal from country to country. For example, some member states, most notably Germany, have occupational labour market structures which emphasize the merits of the economy-wide certification of training so to encourage transferability of skills between enterprises. Other member states promote firm-specific training which encourages workers to stay with one employer and develop their career through internal labour markets. These distinctive national systems are unlikely to wither away, even if monetary union is established in Europe. As a result, regional patterns of employment adjustment based on migration are unlikely to emerge across the member states in the foreseeable future.

TOWARDS REGIONAL WAGE ADJUSTMENT?

Another way regional labour markets could arise in the New Europe is by encouraging spatial forms of wage adjustment. It is neo-classical economics that most directly makes the connection between regional pay and employment by arguing that unemployment can be kept low if the wage level is flexible downwards. But virtual consensus has now emerged in economics that the wage level should be regarded as relatively sticky and that it is a fairly blunt and ineffective way to secure labour market adaptation at the regional level. Certainly this appears to be the case in Europe, where nominal wages are fairly rigid and much less responsive to price changes than in North America, as Table 6.1 shows. In North America only 14–18 per cent of a price increase is passed through to nominal wages, but in Germany the transmission is 75 per cent, in Italy 60 per cent and in the UK 50 per cent. Given this situation, it seems overoptimistic to assume that Europe would be able to contain the pressures due to monetary union by creating flexible regional wage systems (Eichengreen 1992)

One alternative possibility would be to encourage regional collective bargaining structures so that pay-setting could move in line with economic conditions that may emerge in the aftermath of European monetary union and the on-going changes in production. To a large extent this view has been encouraged by the fragmentation of corporatist or centralized bargaining in Europe and the concomitant growth in decentralized pay arrangements (Calmfors 1993). But there are few signs of any wideranging reconstituting of the wage bargain or any other industrial relations function at the regional level. Table 6.2 outlines the structure of pay bargaining in the EU. The table shows that the general trend is for a certain amount of wage bargaining to take place at the sector or national

Table 6.1 Summary measures of wage flexibility

	Elasticity of nominal wage regarding	
Country	Unemployment rate	Prices
Belgium	−0·25	0·25
Denmark	−0·10	0·25
France	−0·29	0·50
Germany	−0·11	0·75
Italy	−0·39	0·60
Netherlands	−0·27	0·50
Spain	−0·20	0·25
UK	−0·15	0·33
US	−0·61	0·14
Canada	−0·51	0·18
Japan	−1·87	0·66

Table 6.2 Institutional framework of collective bargaining in the EU

Country/Level	Content of negotiations
Germany	
No multi-sectoral bargaining	Sectoral bargaining covering job
Sectoral bargaining at regional (*Land*) level (every three years)	classifications (grading scale), wages, working conditions, duration and
Agreements concluded for two years in certain sectors	content of employment contracts
Wage increases (annual) on the basis of company agreements	
Italy	
Tripartite national agreements until 1984; sectoral bargaining thereafter	Sectoral agreements (three years) on all employment conditions; length of
Wages fixed nationally, index-linked to cost of living (*contingenza*) pusuant to 1983 protocol	contracts and working conditions for:
Minimum rates fixed at sectoral level (every three years)	• Manual workers (*operai*) • Non-manual workers (*impiegati*) • Executives (*quadri*) (new category)
Wage increases agreed at company level: *superminimi*	Senior managers (*dirigenti*) are covered by a separate grading agreement negotiated nationally outside the sectoral framework.
UK	
No multi-sectoral wage bargaining	Employment contracts, organization of
Minimum rates (or basic wages) negotiated between unions and employers at sectoral level (annually, sometimes biennially)	work, unemployment benefit Shortcomings of job classification system
Real wage increases decided at company or plant level	
Belgium	
Collective agreements concluded at multisectoral level in the National Labour Council	National employment agreements Sectoral bargaining covering wages, working conditions and shorter working
Minimum rates of increase decided at sectoral or regional level	hours
Wage increases agreed at company level	
France	
Minimum rates of increase fixed by (annual) sectoral agreements	At sectoral level: wages, job classification and salary structures, employment
Annual rates of increase (general and/or individual) decided at company level	contracts, working hours

Table 6.2 Continued

Country/Level	*Content of negotiations*

Denmark

Direct state intervention or federal negotiations to fix incremental margins
Minimum rates of increase fixed every four years at sectoral level (provision for review after two years)

At multi-sectoral level: general agreements (e.g. on co-operation) or specific topics (e.g. shift work)
Mainly at sectoral level: working conditions, wages, working hours
Frequent company agreements to supplement sectoral agreements

Ireland

From 1972 to 1982 wages negotiated at multi-sectoral level by the Employers– Workers Conference (permanent body set up by formal agreement between the two sides)
Sectoral bargaining on minimum rates of increase
Company wage increases

General bargaining at multi-sectoral level in the Economic and Social Committee
Usually at sectoral level in the older industries: working conditions, working hours, wages
Company bargaining, particularly in the case of small businesses, to supplement sectoral agreements

Luxembourg

Sectoral or company

Collective bargaining at sectoral or company level on working conditions, job classification and wages

Netherlands

Federal negotiations to fix incremental margins (Economic and Social Committee)
Sectoral agreements on increases in wages

Central agreements (e.g. on wages in 1973 and work sharing in 1982)
Mainly sectoral agreements: working conditions, wages

Spain

Tripartite agreements (economic and social accords)
Minimum incremental rates fixed by sectoral agreements
Actual rates fixed at company level

Sectoral bargaining on working conditions and wages

Portugal

Formal consultation between two sides of industry
Collective sectoral bargaining (annually) on minimum rates of increase
Actual rates fixed at company level

Sectoral bargaining almost exclusively confined to wages

Greece

Sliding wage scale
Sectoral since January 1988
Company level for various forms of disguised increase

Sectoral wage bargaining

level, supplemented by pay negotiations at company level. Thus, despite the move away from centralized wage formation, many member states continue to seek an interface between the macro and the micro aspects of wage determination so that some type of trade-off is possible at the aggregate level between unemployment and inflation, whilst at the same time firms enjoy a degree of freedom to set pay levels in line with commercial conditions (Teague 1994). Perhaps the best term for such a system is 'connective bargaining'

Connective bargaining is not a coherent system of wage formation and thus should not be confused with the model of co-ordinated bargaining put forward by Soskice (1989). One feature of such a system is that it is not embedded in strong institutions or social support structures. As a result, it is prone to breaking down. For instance, trade unions may be fragmented, decentralized or have a low membership rate, which impedes the emergence of strong 'encompassing' labour organizations so crucial to the success of corporatist pay-setting in places like Sweden in the past. Employer organizations may display similar characteristics that reduce their capacity to contain centrifugal influences within labour markets. Alternatively, the industrial relations environment may have a tradition of adversarialism, making it difficult to establish consensus-building industrial relations institutions. Thus some countries have connective bargaining arrangements because they have failed to create co-ordinated or ordered employee relations, at least on a sustainable basis.

Another feature of connective bargaining, which really only follows from the above observation, is that the relationship between the macro and micro aspects of pay-setting is seldom symmetrical and is for ever changing. At one point the emphasis may be on enterprise-level bargaining, whereas in another period national pay deals may grow in importance. Moreover, such trends are seldom similar among countries. For example, Italy and France have recently attempted to rejuvenate sector and national-level bargaining whilst in Belgium and the Netherlands the move has been in the opposite direction, towards decentralized wage agreements. Furthermore, the nature of the connection between the macro and micro levels varies over time and between countries. In some cases, trade unions use the scope for decentralized bargaining to capture pay increases above the minimum rate set at the sector or national level – the problem of wage drift. In other instances the increase occurs through employers securing concessions from trade unions at the local level in the context of a national bargaining framework.

All in all, connective bargaining sets out to capture the situation where governments strive for a symbiotic relationship between the macro and micro aspects of the wage-setting process but fail to create such a relationship. Most member states appear to have this type of wage-setting. Rather than capturing an array of positive externalities from a co-ordinating bargaining regime, most governments in the EU are involved in an on-going process of reforming, reordering and patching up the connections between enterprise-level and more aggregate forms of pay negotiations. Important to the discussion here is that the regional level hardly figures in the connective bargaining framework. In other words, the member states, unable to create sustainable national systems of co-ordinated bargaining, are not turning towards the regional level as a new strategic site for industrial relations activity. Instead, most persist with a second-best frame-work to connect the macro and micro dimensions of pay-setting. This means that the institutional foundations are not in place for regional systems of wage formation and root-and-branch change would have to occur before any such arrangement could take effect.

TRUST OR FLEXIBILITY? THE CURRENT DYNAMICS OF EUROPEAN INDUSTRIAL RELATIONS

The proposition that decentralized or regional forms of production are encouraging the formation of sutainable trust relations between employers and employees can also be challenged. Streeck (1992a) terms this view of industrial relations 'neo-voluntarism', as it downplays the role of formal institutions and rule-making in the resolution of conflict at work and in the generation of consensus between the social partners. The vision is of workers and managers being bound together by informal social norms of reciprocity. Such social processes, which have the effect of suspending self-interested calculations, may exist in certain local communities, particularly in the much researched Emilia Romagna district of northern Italy. But it would be misleading to suggest that the generation of trust relations through informal procedures and mechanisms is the dominant pattern in European industrial relations (Hyman 1994). A more convincing thesis is that most European governments are busy attempting to introduce greater flexibility into their systems of labour market regulation. In other words, the search for labour market flexibility appears to be the overriding industrial relations issue across the EU (Brewster and Hegewisch 1994).

Of course, the pursuit of labour market flexibility can take a variety of forms. In Britain a thoroughgoing deregulation programme has been enacted to curb the role of law in employee relations and to give managers greater freedom of action. Spain is currently following a similar course, particularly with regard to relaxing many of the complex and detailed rules governing the hiring and firing of employees. A more measured approach seems to be favoured elsewhere as governments attempt to mesh flexibility with regulation. For instance, in 1991 Belgium adopted a new regulatory framework for typical employment. On the one hand, the law removed many of the remaining impediments to the greater use of part-time and temporary workers. On the other hand, it codified and made the legal rights of such employees clearer. For instance, the law introduced a range of rules regulating the amount of overtime that a part-time worker can perform, controlling the variation in hours worked by part-timers, and giving such employees priority treatment in respect of full-time positions which become vacant in the company for which they work.

More recently the government in France has launched a similar initiative. As part of a wide-ranging and innovatory package of labour market policies, the French government has introduced a law that aims at balancing the promotion of part-time and temporary work with giving those in such employment a degree of protection. Thus the law reduces employer social security contributions by 30 per cent in respect of part-time workers whose contracts meet certain requirements, including a guaranteed minimum continuous duration of any period of working, the right to priority consideration when a full-time job becomes available and compliance with the principle of equal treatment.

Although these various reform packages are different, all are concerned with the extent to which the European labour market should be governed by legal rules and formal institutions. Those who argue that legal intervention has gone too far and has triggered sclerotic tendencies in the European labour market are not over-concerned with how a symbiosis can be created between the interests of workers and employers. They are more eager to restore managerial prerogative in European industry and allow market forces to work more freely. The agenda of those who seek to mesh flexibility and regulation is to recast and update the European 'social model' (Regini 1993). This camp accepts that some of the key assumptions that have underpinned labour legislation for decades are no longer applicable. As a result, there may be growing incongruity between labour market institutions and newly emerging employment systems at the ground level. Thus regimes of labour market regulation require modification to smooth out this asymmetry. This is a quite different project from the deregulation approach, which simply seeks to roll back the rules governing the employment relationship.

The dominant trend in European industrial relations is this clash between labour market deregulators and modernizers. Those who argue that this type of division is being left behind by social and economic forces that are driving employers and employees towards a new consensus in the absence of formal rules seem to have misinterpreted developments. They have simply exaggerated the significance of certain isolated and local moves toward industrial districts in Europe. Ulman (1992) has observed that it is somewhat naive to expect industrial societies to function without formal mechanisms for dispute resolution. Thus to argue that a new *milieu* of co-operative and self-sustaining employee relations is just around the corner may actually be harmful, as it may encourage downgrading of or move away from the idea that the labour market should be regarded as a social institution requiring formal rules and laws to hold it together. In other words, should the advocates of the 'neo-voluntarist' approach to industrial relations win the day, the result might be labour market fragmentation (Streeck 1992b). And, as the 1993 ILO World Labour report notes, where legal rules governing the labour market have been relaxed, employers have lost little time in exercising their control of the employment relationship.

THE PROBLEM OF NATIONAL SYSTEMS OF PRODUCTION

The US experience suggests that regional employment systems work better when productive activity is also organized on a spatial basis. But in Europe there is much less regional production specialization than in the US (Begg and Mayes 1992). This difference reflects the fact that the US has operated a single market for more than a century whereas Europe is still mainly made up of separate national economies. A consensus has emerged that these separate national economies have caused fragmentation and segmentation of the European market, making industries in the area less efficient and competitive relative to their US counterparts. Indeed, the programme for completing the European single market was sold on the basis that it would encourage more specialization and capture further economies of scale (Emerson 1988).

Thus, at the moment, the strongly national orientation of production structures, or at least of regional production systems housed within the boundaries of existing member states, is not particularly conducive to the creation of regional labour market systems in the EU. Deeper market integration between the member states may trigger greater Europe-wide industrial specialization. But market segmentation may be reduced at the expense of increasing regional income equalities in the EU, which could have a strong bearing on the type of regional employment systems established in Europe. This argument is worth exploring in greater detail. Currently there are considerable regional disparities in income levels and general economic performance inside the EU. European Commission figures indicate that those living in the ten poorest regions have an income level about 45 per cent of the EU average, whereas people residing in the ten richest regions enjoy a standard of living 45 per cent above the average. Obviously the disparity eases when the sample is made less extreme, but nevertheless the gap is still large. Thus, when the top and bottom twenty-five regions are examined, the figures show that the less prosperous areas have an income per head of about 57 per cent of the EU average, while the richer areas are about 35 per cent above the median. All in all, then, the prosperity gap is quite large.

Standard integration theory suggests that any such gap should wither away with the removal of all barriers to trade between the member states

(Buiges *et al.* 1990). A genuinely open internal market, it is assumed, would promote convergence by allowing each member state to specialize in economic activity in which it has a comparative advantage and by encouraging corporate movement to poorer regions to capture cost savings. But this conventional view of income equalization through deeper market integration is being increasingly challenged. Krugman (1991), for instance, argues that, rather than taking advantage of lower factor costs, firms in the New Europe may congregate in richer regions to reap economics of scale and agglomeration. In other words, in the search for industrial specialization firms may abandon the less favoured regions and relocate in the European core. The likely outcome of such a scenario would be an accentuation of the economic divide between the richer and poorer parts of the EU.

Growing economic divergence would have far-reaching implications for the regionalization of employment systems in Europe. On the one hand, the vision of regional labour market structures promoting productivity coalitions between employees and employers, giving rise to industrial relations practices in tune with local production circumstances, and so on, is to some extent plausible for the richer parts of the EU. But such a benign view is not convincing for the poorer regions. On-going research into industrial performance in the peripheral regions of the EU suggests that many of these are trapped in low-skilled and low value-added forms of production. Moreover, the labour market rules that exist tend to reinforce this pattern of commercial activity. Thus, for example, few incentives exist for firms to upgrade the skill levels of employees, and the labour market regulations that do exist on health and safety, equal pay, and so on, are poorly enforced. If the extent of divergence inside the EU were to widen, the prospects of poorer regions moving from labour market arrangements that emphasize the cost route to competitiveness to industrial relations systems that encourage quality-orientated commercial activity would be reduced. The reverse might actually happen, with the less favoured regions intensifying their drive to capture market share by lowering costs. It is this scenario that has fuelled the debate about social dumping.

Implicit in the 'Europe of the regions' thesis is a benign, positive-sum vision of local economies embedded in high-value, high-quality forms of production coexisting co-operatively. But if deeper economic integration triggers greater spatial bifurcation inside the EU, the reality could be different. A negative-sum game may emerge, with certain regions winning at the direct expense of other regions (Bowring 1986). As a result, a head-to-head clash might be caused not only between the richer and poorer regions but among the poorer regions themselves as they vie with one another to catch up with the core. One argument is that such an unseemly scramble for economic progress would be reduced by the EU centre operating a regime of fiscal transfers to compensate areas losing from

168

deeper integration. At the moment the EU has not got the budgetary capacity to effect such transfers. The Structural Funds would have to increase by a factor of about ten before they could become effective as a redistribution mechanism.

Should the EU be recast along 'Europe of the regions' principles, there would certainly be considerable pressure for the expansion of these funds. But a sequencing problem could arise here. Putting the EU centre in a position to be able to operate a fiscal transfer system would obviously be a protracted affair. In the meantime the pursuit of industrial specialization by enterprises at the market level might deprive certain regions of the capacity to grow endogenously (Barro and Sala-i-Martin 1992). As a result, the danger would increase that any EU-level redistribution mechanism established would go largely towards raising income levels in beleaguered regions rather than to improving production performance. In other words, the depressed regions might become reliant on external subsidies rather than on their own internal capacities to secure a better standard of living. This is a problem of dependent development in which some regions of Europe such as southern Italy and Northern Ireland have become trapped. Thus the presence of a fiscal transfer arrangement does not necessarily resolve the 'insider'–'outsider' regional problem that may emerge in the wake of deeper integration. The basic point is that a malign scenario can be developed for the 'Europe of the regions' thesis which is as convincing, if not more so, as the benign model which appears to dominate discussions on the matter. More balanced assessments need to be developed of the merits or otherwise of regionalizing employment structures in Europe.

CONCLUSIONS

All in all, major questions can be raised about the efficacy of the EU adopting a regional model of labour market governance. Doubts must also now exist about the capacity of the EU to move in that direction even if it so wished. For central to the project of breaking up national systems of industrial relations, and economic management more generally, was the plan for creating monetary union in Europe. But the enactment of such a plan appears unlikely after the debacle surrounding the ratification of the Maastricht Treaty. The climate is cold for any bold schemes to bring about systemic change inside the EU. With the demise of Europhoria the political conditions are inhospitable for the 'Europe of the regions' project. It may well be that it is a project whose time has come and gone.

Whilst events appear to have tamed moves towards a federal or regionalist Europe, controversy continues to rage about the political direction of the integration process. In particular, although member governments seem to be once again in control of the EU decision-making structures, there is disagreement over what form this intergovernmentalism should take in the future. On the one hand, the British government champions a model of competitive intergovernmentalism. Under this type of political system the EU centre would encourage competition between existing national rules to improve the efficiency of public policy-making and the delivery of public provision. This view of institutional competition has its roots in the economics of federal systems. The basic idea is quite straightforward: regulatory institutions will vary in the quality of their performance – some will be less efficient than others. To reduce the incidence of inefficiency, competition between these institutions should be encouraged so that the good performers drive out bad ones. Thus, in the EU context, the political scheme should be not to try and add to the powers of the centre but to increase competitive and market measures to maximize efficient government. For the most part, competitive intergovernmentalism is about creating a neo-liberal Europe, hence the appeal of this approach to the Conservative government in Britain.

The alternative vision is for the integration process to be based on co-operative intergovernmentalism. According to this perspective, political and economic integration between separate nation states gives rise to a range of negative externalities and market failures that can be addressed only through collaborative action. An uncontroversial labour market example would be the need for EU-level policies to reduce the potential tension between the key integration objective of free movement of workers with existing national rules that favour domestic workers over those from other member states. Thus at the heart of co-operative intergovernmentalism is the belief that policy co-ordination is required between the member states to ensure that the economic and political interdependences that exist between them do not generate tensions or block the integration process. Thus, from this viewpoint, EU-level policy intervention is legitimate and functionally necessary. The main issue is whether the particular policy is appropriate or suitable to what it sets out to achieve. A majority of the member states appear to favour co-operative intergovernmentalism, or at least some variant of it.

Each scenario has different implications for the conduct of EU social policy. Should competitive intergovernmentalism gain the upper hand, the emphases will be on curtailing EU intervention in the labour market and encouraging the member states to adopt British-type deregulatory employment policies. Removing labour market rigidities and improving flexibility will be the theme phrases. On the other hand, shoud co-operative inter-governmentalism win the day, the EU centre will probably continue to push for pan-European social policies. However, the long-standing controversies and problems associated with EU labour market policies would probably not disappear. They would continue to exist and no doubt be the cause of political battles between the member states. But the important principle of the EU being able to intervene in labour market matters would be conceded.

With regard to the 'regional issue', this is something that will not go away despite the 'Europe of the regions' project being eclipsed (Loughlin 1993). The questions of administrative decentralization, greater powers and rights for specific regional or ethnic groups, and so on, will continue to be important political questions for many of the member states. But crucially these matters will most likely be resolved, or at least addressed, within the confines of existing national boundaries. A Europe-wide remedy for regionalism appears to be off the political agenda. Of course, the links between local municipalities and the EU centre will continue to exist, particularly with regard to the operation of the Structural Funds. But these connections will only complement or augment the key power relation between the regional administrative tier and the national government. A Europe of the member states will be with us for a considerable time to come.

REFERENCES

Adonis, A., and Jones, S. (1991) Subsidiarity and the Community's Constitutional Future, Discussion Paper No. 2, Oxford: Nuffield College, Centre for European Studies.

Barro, R. J., and Sala-i-Martin, X. (1992) 'Convergence', *Journal of Political Economy* 100 (2): 609–41.

Begg, I. G., and Mayes, D. (1992) 'Cohesion as a precondition for monetary union in Europe', in R. Barrel (ed.) *Economic Convergence and Monetary Union in Europe*, London: Sage.

Bowring, J. (1986) *Competition in a dual Economy*, Princeton: Princeton University Press.

Brewster, A., and Hegewisch, A. (ed.) (1994) *Policy and Practice in European Human Resource Management: Evidence and Analysis*, London: Routledge.

Buiges, P., Ilzkovitz, F., and Lebrun, F. J. (1990) 'The Impact of the Internal Market by Industrial Sector: the challenge for the member states', *European Economy/ Social Europe*, special edition.

Calmfors, L. (1993) 'Centralisation of wage bargaining and macro-economic performance – a survey', *OECD Economic Studies* 21 (3): 391–417.

Centre for Economic Policy Research (1993) *Making Sense of Subsidiarity: How Much Centralisation for Europe?* London: CEPR.

Commission of the European Communities (1993) *Growth, Competitiveness and Employment: the Challenges and Ways Forward into the Twenty-first Century*, White Paper, Luxembourg: Office for Official Publications of the European Community.

Crouch, C. (1993) *Industrial Relations and European State Traditions*, Oxford: Clarendon Press.

Eichengreen, B. (1992) *Should the Maastricht Treaty be Saved?* Princeton Studies in International Finance, Princeton: Princeton University Press.

Eichengreen, B., and Frieden, J. (1993) 'The political economy of European

171

monetary unification: an analytical introduction', *Economics and Politics* 5 (3): 4–21.

Emerson, M. (1988) *The Economics of 1992: the EC Commission's assessment of the economic effects of completing the internal market.* Oxford: Oxford University Press.

Hanley, D. (ed.) (1994) *Christian Democracy in Europe: a Comparative Perspective*, London: Pinder Press.

Harrison, B. (1992) 'Industrial districts: old wine in new bottles?' *Regional Studies* 25 (5): 431–43.

Henley, A., and Tsaksolotos, E. (1994) *Corporatism and Labour Market Performance*, London: Edward Elgar.

Hyman, R. (1994) 'Industrial relations in Western Europe: an era of ambiguity', *Industrial Relations* 33 (1): 4–32.

Katz, L., and Blanchard, O. (1992) *Brookings Papers on Economic Activity* I, Washington, D.C.: Brookings Institution.

Keating, M. (1993) 'The Political Economy of Regionalism', London, Ont.: Department of Politics, University of Western Ontario, mimeo.

Krugman, P. (1991) 'Increasing returns and economic geography', *Journal of Political Economy* 99 (3): 83–99.

Layard, R. (1990) *How to end Pay Leapfrogging*, Employment Institute Economic Report No. 5, London: Employment Institute.

Locke, R. (1990) 'The resurgence of the local union: industrial restructuring and industrial relations in Italy', *Politics and Society* 18 (3): 321–44.

Lorenz, E. (1993) 'Flexible production systems and the social construction of trust', *Politics and Society* 21 (3): 407–25.

Loughlin, J. (1993) 'Nation–State–Region in Western Europe', Rotterdam: Department of Public Administration, Erasmus University, mimeo.

MacDougall, D. (1977) *Report of the Study Group on the Role of Public Finance in European Integration* 1 *General Report*, Brussels: Commission of the European Communities.

Marsden, O. (1992) 'European Integration and the Integration of European Labour Markets', Department of Industrial Relations, London School of Economics, mimeo.

Masser, I., Swiden, O., and Wegener, M. (1992) *The Geography of Europe's Futures*, London: Belhaven Press.

Moravesik, A. (1993) 'Preferences and power in the European Community: a liberal intergovernmentalist approach', *Journal of Common Market Studies* 31 (4): 311–37.

Piore, M. (1993) 'Human resource management: a critical assessment', *Review of Employment Topics* 1 (1): 1–12.

Regini, M. (1993) 'Human resource management and industrial relations in European companies', *International Journal of Human Resource Management* 3 (3): 432–59.

Romer, P. (1994) 'The origins of endogenous growth', *Journal of Economic Perspectives* 8 (1): 3–18.

Sabel, C. (1991) 'Decentralised Production Systems and Trust Relations', Cambridge, Mass.: Department of Politics, MIT, mimeo.

Sabel, C. (1992) 'Studied trust: building new forms of co-operation in a volatile economy', in F. Pyke and W. Sengenberger (eds) *Industrial Districts and Local Economic Regeneration*, Geneva: International Labour Organisation.

Saglio, J. (1992) 'Localised industrial systems in France: a particular type of industrial system', in A. Scott and M. Storper (eds) *Pathways to Industrialisation*, London: Routledge.

Scheltex, K. (1991) 'La subsidiarité – principe directeur de la future Europe', *Revue du Marché Commun* 34 (4): 171–89.

Scott, A., Peterson, J., and Millar, D. (1994) 'Subsidiarity: a Europe of the regions *v.* the British constitution?' *Journal of Common Market Studies* 32 (1): 64–82.

Sengenberger, W. (1992) 'Intensified competition, industrial restructuring and industrial relations', *International Labour Review* 131, 34 (2): 262–89.

Solow, R. (1990) *The Labour Market as a Social Institution*, Oxford: Blackwell.

Soskice, D. (1989) 'Wage determination: the changing role of institutions in advanced industrialised economies', *Oxford Review of Economic Policy* 7 (3): 85–103.

Spencer, J. (1992) 'European Monetary Union and the Regions', Belfast: Queen's University, mimeo.

Streeck, W. (1994) 'Pay restraint without incomes policy: institutionalised monetarism and industrial unionism in Germany', in R. Dore and R. Boyer (eds) *The Return to Incomes Policy*, London: Pinder Press.

Streeck, W. (1992a) 'National diversity, regime competition and institutional deadlock: problems in forming a European industrial relations system', *Journal of Public Policy* 12 (2): 279–302.

Streeck, W. (1992b) *Social Institutions and Economic Performance*, London: Sage.

Teague, P. (1994) 'Employment policy in the European Union: between new Keynesianism and deregulation', *Journal of European Public Policy* 1 (3): 1–32.

Teague, P. (forthcoming) *Labour Market Governance in the New Europe*, London: Routledge.

Teague, P., and Grahl, J. (1993) *Industrial Relations and European Integration*, London: Lawrence & Wishart.

Teague, P., and Grahl, J. (1994) 'Economic citizenship in the new Europe', *Political Quarterly* 98 (3): 309–26.

Ulman, L. (1992) 'Why should human resource managers pay high wages', *British Journal of Industrial Relations* 30 (1): 87–94.

Van Kersbergen, K., and Kerbeck, B. (1994) 'The politics of subsidiarity in the European Union', *Journal of Common Market Studies* 32 (2): 227–42.

7

LE DÉFI EUROPÉEN

Multinational restructuring, labour and EU policy

Harvie Ramsay

When Jean-Jacques Servan-Schreiber intoned against the threat of *Le défi americain* (The American Challenge), he struck a theme which has persisted in the composition of industry policy by the Commission of the European Community ever since. That theme orchestrates the need to create European solidarity against the external challenge, later augmented by the Japanese menace, in particular by promoting the creation of effective European champions to counter the invasion.[1] Research and development initiatives (such as ESPRIT, which seeks to exclude non-European players), concessions under Competition Policy to certain European co-operative arrangements, and efforts to promote restructuring in declining industries, can all be seen dancing to this tune.

The most sustained pursuit of this Euro-champions policy may be found in the promotion and justification of the single market initiative, launched in 1985 and reaching official fruition on 31 December 1992 (or perhaps, more accurately, with the ratification of the Maastricht Treaty on 1 November 1993). A number of commentators have identified a near obsession with the putative single market benefits for European citizens of economies of scale, restructuring and enhanced competitive efficiency in the global market place, *provided* these are concentrated in large companies *of European origin.*[2] Moreover, a number of reasons for concern have been voiced by such observers as to the nature and impact of the process set in motion and encouraged by the Commission.

These doubts as to the outcomes of the policy leanings of the 1992 project, as it came to be known, fall under a number of related but distinct headings:

1 The extent to which the encouragement of large, and particularly multi-national, companies will be of benefit to consumers or workers in the EU.
2 The extent to which a Euro-champions policy, discriminating among multinationals to favour those of European origin, is feasible or promises any special benefit.

3 The extent to which restructuring is actually occurring, and in what forms, relative to the Commission's aspirations or expectations.

4 The assessment of less readily quantifiable, non-economic costs from this Commission policy.

5 The ability of the EU to control any negative implications for employees, in particular through the so-called 'social dimension' of the 1992 project.

The inclusion of the last two points signals a central rationale of this chapter. The restructuring of capital entails the rationalization and reorganization of labour also, both as means and as consequence. This is recognized in the analyses of the European Commission itself of costs and benefits from the single market programme (Cecchini 1988; Emerson *et al.* 1988), and tackled through the attempt to promote a 'Social Charter' to help alleviate the impact of the change process. The question remains whether this aspect of Commission policy can manage the repercussions of the corporate response.

THE RESTRUCTURING OF CAPITAL

Idolizing scale

Although it has become standard cliché to pay lip service to the encouragement of small and supposedly flexible producers, the European Commission has persistently (if not always explicitly) seen large scale as a key factor in economic efficiency and competitiveness. This is no doubt reinforced by the visibility of big corporations as national symbols and market leaders, and further by their consequent access to the channels of dialogue, whether through consultation of firms by the Commission or their lobbying activities.

The Commission's analyses, which were presented as economic justifications of the 1992 project,[3] thus do not stress only the freer movement of goods, services and labour across intra-European frontiers and the consequent sharpening of competition as sources of welfare gains. On the contrary, a major role in achieving the target gains for the EC economy is ascribed to the realization of economies of scale through the concentration of effort made possible by the removal of barriers. For these to be achieved, it is recognized that a major restructuring process is required, and this is envisaged as taking three forms:

1 *Internal restructuring*, rationalizing activities within a single company.

2 *External restructuring*, rationalizing activities across companies, usually made possible through mergers or take-overs.

3 *Co-operation*, which replaces the antagonistic or unequal relationship between partners implied in external restructuring with a co-operative pooling of resources through some kind of joint venture.

The first form does not increase scale, and so achieves economies by other means which in the Commission's eyes may still leave the company at a disadvantage in relation to larger non-European competitors. The second has the cost of achieving scale through the sacrifice of some companies, companies which may well be symbols of national pride within member states, to the control of others. If that is the route to be followed, none the less, the Commission's hope and intent are that it should take place between firms across frontiers but within Europe, to create Euro-champions, as discussed in the next section. The third form, co-operation, is thus the preferred model, again provided it transcends national boundaries but combines the strengths of representatives of European capital.

The problems of assuming that greater scale yields economies which are passed on through greater efficiencies have been well rehearsed elsewhere,[4] and it will suffice to summarize them here. There is strong evidence that gigantism does not yield better corporate performance than large-scale operation, so that existing large European companies are not demonstrably disadvantaged in most sectors as compared with any larger overseas competitors. This is reinforced by the observation that the minimum efficient scale of production is attained for most sectors with 5 per cent or less of the European market (Geroski 1989, 1991). Against the arguments for scale must be arrayed the body of research which shows that large, and especially multinational organizations face numerous organizational and strategic dilemmas which are both costly and riddled with pitfalls. Furthermore, the dangers of monopolistic or oligopolistic control to the distribution of welfare benefits are thoroughly recognized in economic orthodoxy and in Commission policy also, as expressed particularly through the efforts of the Competition Directorate (DG III).

The argument concerning efficiencies may be extended specifically to cover the observed effects of mergers or co-operative ventures. Here the evidence is clamorous as to the typicality of failure or at least disappointment relative to expectations of synergy between combined businesses, often leading to subsequent demerger in the current business fashion for a retreat to core activities.[5] The problems are again typically organizational and managerial, areas which economic analyses such as those in the CONE studies either ignore or pronounce optimistically upon without convincing reason. Again, these problems are usually compounded when an international dimension is added.

Euro-champions

The argument for scale *per se* having been questioned, what then of the specific encouragement for European corporate restructuring and enlargement? It is clear that the largest European corporations were instrumental in the genesis of much of the 1992 project, as they were of the ESPRIT

176

programme,[6] and this invites a certain scepticism about the distribution of benefits from completion of the single market. However, the Commission should not be presumed to be merely reflective of business pressures, injecting its[7] own agendas and priorities (such as those embodied in the Social Charter). The rationale and outcomes of this aspect of industry policy thus demand further consideration.

The purpose of restructuring, as conceived by the European Commission, is to make the EU more 'competitive' as a means of enhancing the economic welfare of its citizens. The large European firm is seen as the agency for this, contributing to the prosperity of its workers and of the EU *in toto* by becoming a more effective combatant against non-European capital both within Europe and beyond. Such an idea is widely embraced, even implied in the analysis of such influential tomes as Michael Porter's *The Competitive Advantage of Nations*. But as Samuel Brittan (1990) observes, competitiveness as a concept applies to firms, not to nations or groups of nations. This point must be taken further: it remains to be convincingly demonstrated that the successful expansion of a company overseas benefits the home base; or that the greater competitiveness of a home-based company compared with a foreign *inward investor* (as distinct from a foreign producer whose goods are imported) has a net welfare yield to the people of a country/trading bloc.

Indeed, precisely these issues have been debated in a variety of terms and across the political spectrum of political economy, without any definitive conclusion. The arguments of conventional international trade theory, taken to their logical conclusion and shorn of the 'countrification' of trade relations, could support only the benefits of the most efficient, 'nationless' capital, embracing the assumption of the global firm in advance of its reality in many sectors. The arguments of left-of-centre critics would eerily shadow some of this, seeing multinational corporations as essentially self-serving and profiteering whatever their nationality, and at the cost of whoever must be made to pay, be it consumers, citizens or employees. And trade unions, starting with those in the US in the 1960s, have long feared the export of jobs as a consequence of successful internationalization of domestic companies, whilst regarding foreign investors with a mixture of suspicion and welcome. The confusion of these views does not invite certitude, but it does raise critical doubts about the supposed net benefits of a Euro-champion, Euro-restructuring policy.

In any case, there are also question marks against the feasibility of the EU approach. The wolves of foreign capital are not at the door, after all; they are already inside it. Ford began production in the UK in 1911, following the migration of many other US firms (such as Singer, General Electric or Westinghouse) into Europe from 1870.[8] Firms such as IBM, General Motors, ITT and many others have two or more generations of history in European economies, long predating the Treaty of Rome. Even later

arrivals, such as the Japanese investors of recent times, are already posses-
sively embraced by those countries in Europe that they have selected for
their activities. Discriminating against such companies and in favour of
Europe's 'own' capital is thus extraordinarily difficult, especially with such
thick-fingered gloves as European Commission industry and competition
policy. Arguments as to whether Nissan or Toyota production in the UK
has sufficient local content to quality as 'European' (and so avoid being
counted against EU import quotas) illustrate the dilemmas well.

The same is true in reverse also, with active FDI by companies from
European countries antedating World War I.[9] Indeed, this provokes consideration of another problem for Commission policy: the successful
expansion of European companies is likely to mirror that of their
American and Japanese rivals, in being primarily pursued by acquisition
and greenfield venture outside Europe. Historically the prevalence of
European outward over inward investment pre-World War I even suggests
that the reflection faces the other way, but this nicety need not delay us.
Whilst the era of *Le défi américain* was correctly characterized as one of the
dominance of US investment into Europe, this has ceased to be the reality
for over a decade. By the mid-1980s the stocks of FDI from Europe in the
US matched those in the reverse direction, and in most years since then the
flows have been stronger towards the US from Europe than vice versa. By
1990 UNCTAD estimated that US$280 billion FDI from European com-
panies in the US clearly outweighed US$226 billion from US multinationals
in Europe (UN 1993). Figure 7.1 shows how the largest three European
national players each at times rivalled the FDI flows from Japan and the US
from 1985, with the UK leading the way in several years. However, the
recovery of FDI flows from the US in the early 1990s reflects the upsurge
of American corporate interest in investing in Europe in preparation for the
completion of the single market. Thus the EC, which had attracted 46 per
cent of all world FDI in 1986–90 (this including cross-border investment
within Europe), drew 70 per cent in 1991 and 88 per cent, no less, in 1992
(UN 1993). By 1991 intra-regional investment in the EC considerably
exceeded that which had entered from the US.[10]

Two observations may now be made. First, current European Commission policy has attracted 'the enemy' on almost the scale it has induced the
internal cross-investment that was sought to promote the emergence of
Euro-champions.

Second, many European companies were already multinationals before
the single market programme was launched, and were often major global
players; the development of these and other large EU-based companies is
therefore likely to be dictated increasingly by the logic of globalization
(Grahl and Teague 1990). The FDI flows, usually expressed as taking place
between nations, are therefore more accurately regarded as measures of
corporate activity than country performance. Even those companies that

178

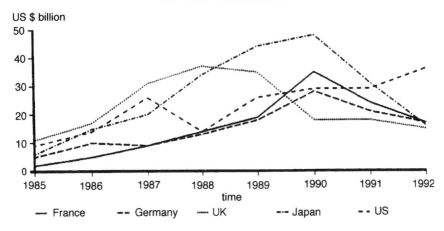

Figure 7.1 Outflows of foreign direct investment from the five main source countries per annum, 1985–92

have hitherto been largely national, or at most European, in scope are likely to see their future in becoming world players – and so in investing abroad. The debate about the costs and benefits of such capital export is thus likely to become more relevant than ever, and as noted already the evidence is by no means in favour of such a shift as a source of net economic welfare benefits for the citizens of the 'home' country or region.

The pattern of restructuring

These points lead us to a closer examination of the actual pattern of restructuring in Europe as compared with the European Commission's aspirations discussed earlier. An increase in intra-EC investment was noted above, but has this been achieved through the kinds of co-operative and mutually beneficial alliance preferred by the Commission? In a critical commentary Kay (1989) argues that data up to 1987 show a pattern of more aggressive merger and acquisition activity within the EC, joint ventures being more likely between European and non-European players. The mutual advantage of such international alliances was more apparent from the standpoint of competitive strategy, giving non-European companies access to Europe, and avoiding co-operation between immediate market rivals (which adversaries will prefer to see as targets for take-over and submission, Kay suggests). Kay's arguments do not allow for the capacity for oligopolistic collaboration within markets shown by capital, nor for the presence of many non-European firms as rivals already, but while these factors may dilute the processes the predicted configuration may still emerge.

In fact subsequent data lend support to Kay in many respects, and also

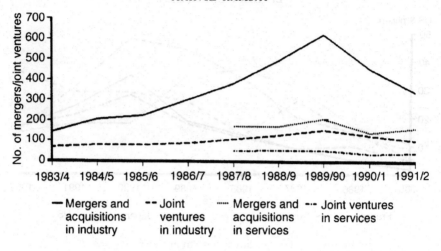

Figure 7.2 EU mergers, acquisitions and joint ventures in industry and services, 1983/4–91/2

invite other commentary here. Data from the Commission itself, while not perfect by any means, provide the most reliable available source. Figure 7.2 presents information up to 1992, the most recent Commission data available at the time of writing. For the latest five-year period, separate data are provided for services as well as industry. These figures demonstrate the sharp rise in restructuring activity in the late 1980s, falling away somewhat as the recession of the early 1990s began to bite. Yet almost all the variation is in merger and acquisition activity: the number of joint ventures remains remarkably stable. The ratio of take-overs to co-operative arrangements thus varies directly with the level of overall merger activity, increasing steadily from 2·2 : 1 in 1983/4 to a peak of 4·0 : 1 in 1989/90, then falling to 3·3 : 1 in 1991/2. Restructuring in the EC in advance of the completion of the internal European market was thus predominantly of the 'external', or non-co-operative, variety.

Next we should examine the data which break restructuring activity down according to whether it takes place within national boundaries, across borders but within the EC, or between EC and non-EC firms. Table 7.1 provides this breakdown for industry, and Table 7.2 for services, for the period from 1983/4.[11] The data show for industry that the number of mergers and acquisitions is fairly steady, and that most of the rise in overall activity in the late 1980s was in both the EC and the international categories, as was the fall in the early 1990s. To some extent the EC data satisfy the Commission's enthusiasm for a relative rise in cross-border restructuring activity, then, even if most of it is non-co-operative; but it also confirms that such activity is part of a general multinationaliza-

180

Table 7.1 Mergers/majority acquisitions in industry, by geographical domain

Year	National	EC	International
1983/4	101 (65)	29 (19)	25 (16)
1984/5	146 (70)	44 (21)	18 (9)
1985/6	145 (64)	52 (23)	30 (13)
1986/7	211 (70)	75 (25)	17 (6)
1987/8	214 (56)	111 (29)	58 (15)
1988/9	233 (47)	197 (40)	66 (13)
1989/90	241 (39)	257 (41)	124 (20)
1990/1	186 (41)	170 (37)	99 (22)
1991/2	175 (51)	119 (35)	49 (14)

Sources: calculated from Kay (1989), CEC (1993).
Note: Figures in parentheses indicate the percentage of all merger and acquisition activity in the indicated domain for that year.

Table 7.2 Mergers/majority acquisitions in services, by geographical domain

Date	National	EC	International
1987/8	107 (61)	34 (19)	34 (19)
1988/9	119 (68)	28 (16)	27 (16)
1989/90	112 (53)	58 (27)	41 (19)
1990/1	94 (67)	28 (20)	19 (13)
1991/2	113 (69)	40 (24)	11 (7)

Source: calculated from CEC (1993).
Note: Figures in parentheses indicate the percentage of all merger and acquisition activity in the indicated domain for that year.

tion of take-over activity, and is consistent with the globalization arguments advanced above. For services, interestingly, the pattern is more steady, activity within national boundaries remaining prevalent, and international activity falling relative to that within the EC.

Finally, from these data, the pattern of co-operative or non-co-operative restructuring at different spatial levels may be considered. Kay's argument for the period from 1983/4 to 1987/8 (Kay 1990) was that the collaboration 'aversion ratio' fell as the domain scope increased, i.e. that joint ventures were a larger proportion of such activities as one moved from national to EC and finally to international corporate links, in line with the strategic competition argument outlined above. Table 7.3 summarizes the calculations for the most recent period, alongside those presented by Kay. For industry the pattern confirms that discovered and explained by Kay. In the service sector the national level shows a very high prevalence of take-overs over joint ventures, while the international ratio is actually a little higher than that at EC level.

There are clear indications, then, that the 1992 project has unleashed, or

Table 7.3 Aversion ratios, by geographical domain

	Industry		Services
Domain	1983/4 to 1987/8*	1988/9 to 1991/2	1988/9† to 1991/2
National	4·5	5·25	7·5
Community	3·3	4·3	2·1
International	1·0	1·8	2·6

Sources:
* From Kay (1990: 15).
† Calculated from CEC (1993).
Note: The 'aversion ratio' is calculated as the number of mergers divided by the number of joint ventures, following Kay.

at least lent impetus to, a massive wave of restructuring in Europe. Most of that restructuring has been 'internal', achieved through efficiency drives within companies, or 'external', through take-overs and mergers which usually involve the reluctant submission of some firms to others; co-operative ventures such as those between GEC and Siemens (ironically, to take the knife to Plessey) or GEC and Alcatel–Alsthom exist, but are not typical. Meanwhile few moves towards the European super-company have yet emerged post-1992: the apparent potential of the alliance in publishing between Reed and Elsevier, or of Kingfisher's take-over of Darty to become the leading European electrical retailer, both during 1993, remain much quoted exceptions to date. Pan-European consolidation has also been slower than expected in most sectors, though in one or two, such as insurance, a series of mergers have moved the industry closer to Commission aspirations.[12]

Globalization

Finally, the point was made earlier that much of the international restructuring being witnessed in recent years, while it may have been partially shaped and accelerated by the 1992 project, remains essentially a matter of globalization by companies, not of the success or failure of regions of the world economy. To the extent that this is true, Commission policy will be ineffectual as a tool for achieving the stated objectives of Cecchini and others.

A cursory examination confirms that international foreign investment has accelerated as rapidly as cross-border EC investment over the last decade, and the logic of corporate strategy dictates that many mergers and alliances involve restructuring to strengthen global reach rather than to create bright new Euro-champions. Such developments are most visible in industries with established global markets, such as electronics, chemicals or motor vehicles. However, they are also spreading to companies in other sectors seeking financial and marketing economies despite the continued localization of many aspects of product/service design and marketing.

The open intent of many multinationals of European origin endorses this reading of developments. Companies like ICI, BAT or Hanson have long pursued a globally spread strategy, but examples can now be found in all sectoral directions. In the food industry, for instance, expansion by acquisition is the route being taken by all the major European players. Unilever made twenty-two acquisitions worth £300 million in 1992 alone and, with Nestlé has led the way for European food companies, but Grand Metropolitan, Allied-Domecq, United Biscuits, BSN and, most aggressively, Cadbury Schweppes have all sought expansion in North America and the Pacific rim as well as in Europe in order to keep pace.

In retail, too, the desire for expansion has been global rather than merely European among the larger players. Marks & Spencer, Dixon's, Benetton, Sainsbury and Ratner's have all sought to move into the North American market, though not without setbacks, and many chains are looking to the Far East also. Ikea and the Body Shop have been particularly successful in their internationalization efforts, the former trading from 100 stores in twenty countries by 1993, while the latter had 1,053 shops in forty-five countries.[13]

In electronic and electrical engineering the same North American and Far East ambitions to go global are evident, with ABB, Babcock International and the GEC–Alsthom joint venture all exploring these routes.[14] Siemens, the German electronics corporation, had 55 per cent of its operations outside Germany by the early 1990s, and has announced the intention of expanding most actively beyond Europe in future.[15] In the vehicle sector, Mercedes-Benz has caused a stir by announcing a decision to shift further commercial vehicle production out of Germany, increasing activities in Latin America, the US and Asia, and establishing its first passenger car production facility outside Germany, in Alabama.[16]

If the multinational corporation has truly arrived as a global actor (Julius 1990), though, the recession of the early 1990s continues to slow its progress. First estimates by KPMG Peat Marwick (*Financial Times*, 24 January 1994) suggested a 15 per cent decline in the global rate of cross-border mergers from 1992 to 1993, with sharp cuts in expenditures by Japanese, French and German companies. US and British companies, however, increased their activities, with acquisitions by British companies doubling in value to consolidate the international power of UK-based corporations.[17] Spending on European cross-border mergers was reckoned to have fallen 40 per cent in 1993, to the lowest level since 1988.[18] In the longer term, however, a further massive acceleration of FDI as world recession lifts in the second half of the 1990s is envisaged,[19] facilitating a continuing restructuring of global corporate activities as both markets and production sites are reassessed on a basis well outside the grasp of a European policy.

THE RESTRUCTURING OF LABOUR

The assessment of European Commission policy under and after the 1992 project has thus far been conducted largely according to economic criteria (if not always within the traditional discourse of economics as a discipline). We now turn our attention, albeit briefly, to some of the social consequences of the developments described above.

The impact on employment

In an earlier commentary (Ramsay 1990) the author observed that the job losses from the restructuring aspects of the 1992 project were far more likely to be achieved or exceeded than the projected longer-term gains. A few examples, many of them from companies whose global expansion was noted in the previous section, suggest that this pessimism has probably been justified.

Thus Unilever, the food and detergents multinational, has announced plans to cut 7,500 jobs by 1997, the lion's share of them in Europe, following a lack of improvement in European margins despite a £300 million reorganization commencing in 1991.[20] Elsewhere in the food sector Rank Hovis McDougall was acquired by the conglomerate Tomkins (after a tug-of-war with Hanson), and within a year twenty-two operations had been closed and the work force cut by 2,860 (11 per cent).[21] Meanwhile Grand Metropolitan announced 3,000 job cuts worldwide and a major reorganization of its food, drinks and retailing activities in September 1993.[22]

In electronics Philips, traditionally regarded as a major player in European business lobbies, has been pursuing an internal restructuring programme which has cut jobs by 68,000 (22 per cent) in five years from 1989. Although Philips has been associated with major product innovations, in consumer electronics especially, the heaviest staffing cuts have been those in R&D (37 per cent) by comparison with 18 per cent in production and 12 per cent in overhead staff. 'Our organization is still characterized by too much tolerance,' was the view of the chief executive of the company.[23] Elsewhere in the sector Olivetti, another blue-chip Euro-company, set out to cut 10,000 jobs in a restructuring exercise in 1992, while similar reshaping has gone on at Siemens/Nixdorf and Bull.

Pilkington's announced plans in 1991 to reorganize in preparation for the single market, creating an integrated flat and safety glass operation across Europe, with its headquarters in Brussels, and cutting 750 jobs in the process.[24] In 1994 the company reported a doubling of profits, but accompanied the news with the announcement of 1,500 job cuts (6 per cent of corporate employment), mostly in Germany and to a lesser extent in the UK.[25] In heavy engineering the much-feted joint venture between GEC and Alsthom has cut its work force by 6,500 to 73,000 over four years to 1994, with a further 3,000 jobs at least expected to go by 1995.[26]

In the car industry a reduction in the number of major producers was assumed inevitable by the late 1980s. The proposed merger of Volvo and Renault led the way, with preparations including the closure of Volvo's Kalmar and Uddevalla plants, much admired for their innovative forms of work organization; the collapse of the merger in 1994 seems unlikely to reverse such moves at Volvo, to judge by the divestment and restructuring plans cast as 'streamlining' in the April 1994 corporate plan.[27] At Renault, Peugeot and Fiat work force reductions have been pursued relentlessly, while the collapse of Leyland-DAF saw heavy job losses amidst industry policy disarray, with the Belgian and Dutch governments supporting survival heavily whilst the UK government refused to take part in the rescue operation. Volkswagen, meanwhile, negotiated a two-year four-day week with 15 per cent wage cuts as an alternative to 30,000 job cuts for 1994–5. Rover, an erstwhile national champion, was taken over by BMW early in 1994 amidst some ruffling of UK pride (though Honda had been expected to acquire the company anyway); this move followed an active period of reorganization and 'Japanization' at Rover plants, but further European rationalization of models, and of power train production, was expected to follow in due course.

These examples, admittedly chosen largely from internationally competitive sectors, none the less suggest that job losses are the order of the day as Euro-restructuring proceeds. However, any assessment of this claim is made difficult by the infeasible taskmaster of *ceteris paribus*: the impossible task of disentangling job losses caused by the recession, or by other forces in global competition, from the specific impact of the completion of the single market. In practice the 1992 project has probably been overwhelmed by the wider economic environmental influences, in the short to medium term at least. None the less there are countless examples of restructuring involving redundancies and few indeed of consequential employment increase. The emphasis appears to be, at best, on damage limitation in this respect. The wider picture confirming this pessimistic reading may be captured by considering unemployment as a whole, especially on the wider definitions which take account of part-time and 'non-employment' not detectable through official figures (see Michie, Chapter 3 above).

The 'social dimension' debate

As the 1992 project got under way the issue of the allowable and desirable consequences for employees was quickly raised. The result was an attempt, led by the Germans, French and Belgians among others, to promote a 'social dimension' of the restructuring process, this in turn resulting in the Social Charter, agreed by all EC members but the UK in 1989, and later the abortive Social Chapter of the Maastricht Treaty in December 1991. While this chapter cannot concern itself with the detail of the proposals,[28] it will consider briefly the implications of the restructuring process and related developments for the social dimension, and vice versa. In particular, it will become apparent that interpretations of multinational corporations' decision-making on investment location are central to the debates.

The European Commission justifies the attempt to extend employee rights and protection embodied in the Social Charter in two main ways. The first evokes the substantive irrationality and immorality of achieving economic 'prosperity' at the expense of the labour utilized to attain this. Thus common minimum standards are proposed, to prevent 'social dumping', whereby those areas with better conditions and legal provision for employees are forced to attenuate them to compete with other areas offering low wages/weak restraints on capital. The implication here is that unfettered flexibility of wages and employment terms is politically and socially unacceptable, though the market and managers might otherwise seek to exploit them.

The second argument is more positive, asserting that the provision of rights and the encouragement of participation will generate consensus and a co-operative outlook among employees, with beneficial consequences for adaptability and acceptance of necessary restructuring. The flexibility invoked is allied more to the functional (multi-skilling and active support for change) notion than the numerical (cheap, disposable labour) variant.

This latter view, cautiously endorsed by the OECD (1994) also, is particularly incomprehensible to the New Right world view championed by the UK government in particular. The latter analysis concentrates instead on the social dumping argument, and derides it as self-defeating. The increased costs incurred by business, the argument runs, will be a burden which will deter investment and handicap European employers in the world market place. The UK government has thus insisted on opting out of as much Euro-legislation on employment matters as it can, arguing that reduced union influence and employment protection have brought jobs from the rest of Europe to the UK. The 'social dimension', on this account, should be restricted to facilitating the free flow of labour across internal European borders.

It is far too early to assess the overall effects of the 1992 project, of the Social Charter or of the UK opt-out on employment rights and labour conditions. Indeed, these various effects will probably never be satisfactorily disentangled from each other, or from the wider effects of recession and global restructuring already noted.

None the less, we can predict with confidence that the exclusion of the

UK from social legislation will strengthen the hand of management *vis-à-vis* labour. Even if the (highly plausible) case is made that the current and planned legislation is relatively anodyne, the symbolism of rights and standards is important to the legitimacy of actions, and is likely to be a real if not powerful constraint on employers. Conversely, the qualification of rules by exception serves the reverse signifying role. In any case, though, no standard basic wage or wider level of labour costs is remotely implied by existing or proposed Euro-legislation. At most, certain levels of training, consultation and information rights, rights for 'non-typical' employees and the like are sought, and the effect on costs is thus likely to be marginal.

Pay, conditions and social dumping

This appears to leave the door wide open to 'social dumping'. A few examples of relocation have already attracted shrill public attention on these grounds, the most notorious being the Hoover case. In January 1993 Hoover announced the closure of its Dijon factory and the transfer of work to its Cambuslang factory, near Glasgow, after concluding a deal for greater flexibility and reduced pay and conditions with its Scottish work force. The subsequent outcry uncovered UK government advertisements seeking to attract German companies to the UK, where they would find a cheap and compliant work force,[29] and outrage was fuelled by celebratory claims from UK government spokespersons citing the move as a vindication of the UK opt-out. In response, European politicians, spearheaded by President Mitterrand and Jacques Delors, president of the European Commission, condemned the move, with Delors reported as saying that the proposed European works councils would prevent such actions.[30] In fact a dispassionate assessment suggests that no existing or planned social legislation, including Euro-consultation, would have been able to exert any significant influence on Hoover's decision (*EIRR* 1993).

It becomes clear, therefore, that the provisions of the Social Charter are not designed to block restructuring. A cynical view is that they are merely intended to soften its impact, and so enhance acceptability, by avoiding the blunt exercise of power brandished by Hoover, acting without prior consultation to prepare the ground. Moreover, it is arguably rational management bargaining strategy to use the comparison of labour costs and conditions to gain concessions, and likewise the heightened belief in the mobility of capital across Europe, even if no move is really being entertained. The pressure applied more recently by Daimler-Benz and Bosch on German workers to make concessions before locating fresh investments in their home country, for instance, seems to fit this strategy well.[31]

Comparative labour costs Moreover, significant differences in labour costs survive between EU member states. In terms of direct costs, employers in Germany and Denmark pay employees on average more than three times as much as employers in Greece, and five times as much as those in Portugal, with the UK in the lower middle range, with approximately two-thirds the Danish level.[32] When indirect costs such as employer pension and national insurance contributions or training levies are added, however, the UK appears markedly cheaper for employers than Italy or France, and almost comparable with Ireland and Spain. The emergence of the UK as a relatively cheap-labour location was very much a feature of the 1980s, with a decline in relative total labour costs from a level comparable to that of Italy in 1981 to one 25 per cent lower in 1990.

Yet over the long term unemployment rates have been fairly comparable among the larger European states, and, even allowing for the vagaries of jobless calculations between states, the figures do not correlate with labour costs. Nor do figures for employment creation, where the UK's record over the period 1970–92 is particularly poor compared with its major competitors.[33] A number of reasons may be adduced for this, some of them relating to labour issues (though not merely costs) and some not.

One extension of the debate about social regulation of employment costs and conditions concerns the degree to which labour markets remain state-regulated and impose restrictions on employers. Multinational corporations, especially from the US, are reported to be building ease of exit or rationalization into their criteria for assessing prospective investment sites.[34] In this respect Spain, Greece, Portugal and Italy are reckoned the least unattractive to investors, while the UK, Ireland and Denmark are least confining where sackings and closures are concerned. In orthodox theory this should further enhance the UK's relative advantage, even over lowest-cost European competitors, and so does not help to explain relative employment patterns. It may be taken to account for the relative success of the UK in attracting FDI, but other explanations for this (such as language and cultural familiarity for US firms, and for Japanese firms stepping on from the US) seem more plausible.

Arguably a more important influence concerns productivity. Differences in wages are found to be fairly well counterbalanced by productivity differences across Europe,[35] thus rendering unit costs of production far more equal than a consideration of costs alone would lead one to expect. The reasons for this thus become a battleground for the competing political visions of the social dimension rehearsed above. The New Right see a lax approach to labour costs as having eroded an advantage gained through investment and technological advance in Germany and the other high-wage countries. In contrast, the supporters of a more interventionist social policy see the higher costs of employment and greater rights of employees in some states as allowing investment in training, providing greater job security, and generating a greater sense of partnership and higher labour motivation. Credence is lent to this view by a report from the consultants Ernst & Young which reported that foreign investors rated the UK's key vulnerable areas as its lack of commitment to Europe, congested road network and 'insufficient emphasis on training workers in the industries of the future'.[36]

Flexing human resources Two other notions which figure prominently in the New Right pantheon are mobility and flexibility. The hope that labour will become competitive across borders is based partly on the idea that migrant labour will become far more prevalent, thus forcing the price of labour down in high-wage areas (see Shepley and Wilmott, Chapter 2 of the present volume). As yet, however, the barriers to movement (language and attitudes especially) remain too high for this to be a significant factor in Europe, and seem likely to remain that way for a considerable time. Migration rates across frontiers within the EU have been well under half those between states in the US, for instance (*Financial Times*, 1993), and only 2 per cent of EU citizens are living in an EU country other than the land of their birth.[37] In any case, the social costs of mobility, not so much between states as between employers, may outweigh any competitive gains. Not only do recent US studies question the New Right catechism that higher minimum wages cost jobs,[38] but they also suggest that more numerically flexible labour results in greater inequality, unacceptable insecurity for employees, and greater unwillingness to provide training by employers.[39]

Labour costs and location This does not end the challenges to the spurious common sense of New Right arguments. The shared assumption in all the above discussions is that labour matters are central to investment decisions by multinational corporations. Yet studies of multinational location suggest that employment costs may not be a key issue for many companies. Indeed, one recent survey of 200 foreign-owned companies found that labour costs were ranked bottom of a list of factors involved in choosing to locate in the UK, being mentioned by only 6 per cent of the firms surveyed.[40] A review of US investors for the European Commission itself reported that market access was their most important motivation, and that job cuts arose from technological and managerial efficiency savings rather than from shifts to low-cost locations (*Financial Times*, 1994). Other important factors include access to financial and other services, which tends to encourage to the most developed and prosperous regions, sometimes depicted as the European 'blue banana'; and the cost of office space and managerial salaries, which notionally at least could draw HQ locations towards the periphery instead (Barnett 1994).

This analysis suggests that management priorities will vary according to the type of business, and the particular function within a given business whose location is under consideration. As noted above, all multinationals will find it useful to play the cost or productivity cards, but whether these are truly of critical importance is a contingent question. The more pan-European the market the greater the possibility of considering one or a few large-scale operations whose location will be shaped by labour and other unit cost factors; the greater the variation in local demand, or in effective access to a market, the greater the need for fragmented and localized provision of the product or service. Meanwhile the importance of skilled and motivated labour will also vary with the product, the link from employee to customer, and the production strategy adopted.

Figure 7.3 offers a simplified model of some likely variations in labour market priorities, particularly as they may be expected to influence location. The implication of this analysis is that wage costs are indeed unlikely to be prevalent in determining the location of much multinational activity. Labour costs are likely to count for most in highly price-competitive markets, particularly for mature products (where product distinction usually counts for less). Skilful, adaptable and co-operative labour will tend to be more important where a distinctive product, or the quality and image of product/service, is the chief asset of the firm. The simple two-way distinction produces four boxes, though a more complex analysis would introduce greater variation (and would need to include other factors than labour also).

Box A might include banks, up-market retail, non-mass-produced elec-

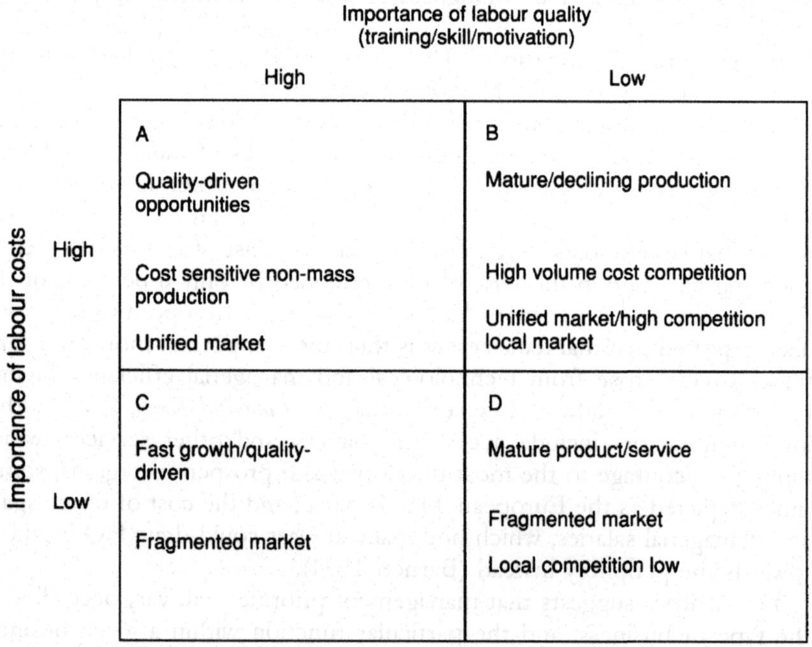

Importance of labour quality
(training/skill/motivation)

	High	Low
High (Importance of labour costs)	A Quality-driven opportunities Cost sensitive non-mass production Unified market	B Mature/declining production High volume cost competition Unified market/high competition local market
Low (Importance of labour costs)	C Fast growth/quality-driven Fragmented market	D Mature product/service Fragmented market Local competition low

Figure 7.3 Labour-related influences on location

190

tronics – or R&D functions in multinationals. Box B embraces white goods and other household consumer durables, cars, electronics assembly or clothing/textiles. Box C might contain specialist financial, architectural or consultancy services, or the headquarter operations of multinationals. Box D would include work such as catering, cleaning, fast food and super-markets, transport and other distribution. (Though in many of these areas wages are low in most locales relative to local wages, it is not the level of wages relative to other areas which determines location, but usually market demand and the requirement of access thereto.) The classic low labour cost location argument thus applies most strongly to box B companies such as Hoover, and should not be simplistically generalized.

Clearly, for trade unions, multinationals' sabre-rattling on wage costs should be set against the viability of transferring operations affecting the product or service concerned, and the nature of local price competition in a fragmented market. The shift of Nestlé jobs *from* Glasgow *to* Dijon, almost simultaneously with the Hoover move the other way, seems to have been a market-driven shift, where labour costs were not so important. The dangers of social dumping are real, but they are made all the greater by retreatism born of lending credence to simplified stereotyping of location decisions such as those offered by the UK government.

Influence

The discussion of how unions may view multinational corporations' pro-clamations on labour costs brings us to the final consideration in this section: the impact of EU policy and restructuring developments in the lead up to and since 1992 on the balance of power between employers and employees.[41] The issues are captured well by a recently reported case where closure was announced by Hasbro International at its MB Ter Apel factory in the Netherlands, threatening 160 jobs. 'Negotiations' with the local works council commenced with the announcement, but a sense of power-lessness there led the employees to plan a flight to lobby management at the company headquarters in Middlesex. To the union the plant was 'a very good factory . . . well equipped and profitable for many years. They do not see any reason why it should close.' Hasbro's president accepted that the factory was profitable, but insisted that closure was necessary to rationalize activities across Europe, including two larger and more modern plants in Ireland and Spain.[42]

This example captures the dilemma of attempts to legislate on worker participation in a way which would restore the balance of power disrupted by unleashing restructuring. The management decision is rational in multi-national corporations' terms, but not to employees from the plant. No amount of advance information, consultation or negotiation can alter this clash of rationalities; nor, in a context where restructuring is the *raison d'être* of EU policy, is it easy to see how any judicial assessment could force management to alter its decision, other than if the procedures of consultation had not been followed.

CONCLUSION

It has been argued above that a number of developments in the activities of multinational corporations, particularly those of European origin, have been seen to have accelerated from the late 1980s, at least partly under the influence of the 1992 project. Even allowing for sectoral and company variations, generalizations are pretty robust: globalization of company activities, rationalization and restructuring of European operations especially, and reorganization of management activities (typically decentralizing personnel and production matters while centralizing financial and investment control) are all characteristic developments. In the process, jobs are likely to be lost, and decision-making thereon at the same time becomes more impersonal, with options replaced by seeming inevitability.

In this context European works councils and any other such provisions will usually prove powerless against decisions which are not an abuse of multinationals' 'rational' commercial management, even where they *are* an abuse of employee security and prosperity. The most they can do is to stand up for rights which will make management cautious in exercising its power, especially where public image may suffer, and seek to negotiate transitional arrangements such as retraining and extended notice. It is only a wider climate of concern about the activities of multinationals which would counsel management caution – and then perhaps only if markets were threatened through image disfigurement.

It would be wrong to close merely on negativism, so let us consider what possible policy shifts might make an impact on the situation we have described, however long the shot.

First, then, for the Commission of the European Union, there would need to be a shift from the prevailing (and confused) Industry Policy preoccupation with Euro-champions and the drift from the regulation of capital restructuring. This would entail giving greater priority to Competition Policy, to Regional Policy, and generally to the priorities of employment creation. In some ways, at least, Delors's White Paper on employment, growth and competitiveness, launched in November 1993, attempts to nudge debate towards such a shift in priorities.

In particular, too, the role and significance of Social Policy would need to be lent far greater weight, and pursued with greater vigour, confidence and comprehensiveness. Again some reassertion of this sort is evident in the determination to push through the European Works Council Directive in the face of employer hostility and the UK opt-out. That opt-out would need to be challenged at the next opportunity (barring an electoral defeat of

192

the Conservative government before then) in 1996, a possibility currently being brandished in Brussels. More significant still would be a return to the principles of the Social Charter, which would revive the importance of wider harmonization on participation rights than just for multinationals, and should greatly increase the requirements for firms to pay for training, and grant other rights far beyond those currently proposed for 'peripheral' workers.

Perhaps the most potent reinvocation of the Social Charter would be to revisit the clauses on which all has been silent – on the right to join a union, to bargain collectively, and to strike. In their campaign against the European Works Council Directive the Multinational Business Forum, a gathering of fifty of the largest (European and non-European) multinational corporations, drew on the findings of Cranfield/Price Waterhouse surveys of information and participation practice (MBF 1993). The correlation with national legislation providing information and consultation rights and actual provision was found to be non-existent; a far stronger correlation was reported with the northerly clime of the countries. However, this correlation may be turned another way: to suggest that management practice actually follows the effectiveness of union organization and collective bargaining. The implications for an effective policy on employee influence in multinationals would then be quite different from that intended by the Forum.

Turning to labour movement responses, one obvious step would be to put far more energy and self-assurance into arguing the case for the above policy shift. To achieve this, far more sustained campaigns against the logic of a Euro-champions policy and against the logic of a 'free' market in labour to drive labour costs down would need to be mounted – including a demonstration of the contradictions of these two logics.

Second, a contingency analysis of corporate strategy, of which one dimension (that of labour costs) was roughly sketched above, suggests a need for unions to engage far more actively in the dissection of multinational behaviour. Such an approach, utilizing existing business information sources augmented by their own intelligence, would allow a far more effective assessment of multinationals' likely manoeuvres and threats.

Beyond this, the main task of trade unions would be to revitalize the idea of transnational networks and combine committees across borders within companies. This is necessary both to collect information and to disperse it to the level at which it can be put to effective use. In this, unions are currently being given some financial support by the European Commission to set up such networks (to the tune of ECU 17 million in each of 1993 and 1994) in the context of preparation for European works councils, though activity remains nascent and piecemeal. The use of modern information systems and networking technology to tap into business databases, and make a digested form of company information accessible to local activists, remains in its infancy, partly through the defensive grip many unions wish to keep on the dissemination of information to their own members. Arguably, though, international trade unionism faces the most favourable conjuncture at any time, buttressed by the melting of internal divisions earlier sustained by the Cold War. The opportunities to educate, to create the conditions for linkages and awareness of issues on at least a European scale, and to prove themselves relevant are there for the grasping.

It would not be difficult to deflate these suggestions as wishful thinking, infeasible, given the real situation in Brussels and in the labour movement. But at least a clear notion of what could be done creates the chance, however faint, that it will be done.

NOTES

1 See Ramsay (1992a, b) for a detailed account of the Commission's Euro-champions policy.
2 See e.g. Geroski (1988, 1989), J. Kay (1989), N. Kay (1989), Neuberger (1989), Ramsay (1990).
3 The *Costs of Non-Europe* (CONE) studies, published in sixteen volumes.
4 See e.g. Ramsay and Haworth (1989), Ramsay (1990, 1992a), Geroski (1989, 1991).
5 Mueller (1980), Cowling (1982), Peacock and Bannock (1991), Wallace *et al.* (1992).
6 The most influential lobbying consortium was the Round Table of European Industrialists, which effectively set the single market ball rolling with a key memorandum in 1983 advocating integration to allow European companies to compete more effectively against non-European companies.
7 Even this shorthand reference to 'the Commission' conceals a variety of different emphases and priorities in policy, e.g. between DG III (competition), DG IV (industrial affairs) and DG V (social affairs). No simple unitary approach may therefore be presumed in such an intensely political setting.
8 Wilkins (1970, 1974) provides the now classic account. See also Church (1986), Dunning (1988).
9 Teichova *et al.* (1986), Hertner and Jones (1986), Jones, (1986), Stopford and Turner (1984).
10 By 1991, while American FDI in Europe had reached around $250 billion, over $300 billion of cross-border but intra-EC investment was recorded (UN 1993: 16, 40, 44).
11 The data presented in these tables record the numbers rather than the value of mergers, and should not be assumed to provide a guide to the scale of investment flows in different directions. They do provide a better indication than value data of the level of activity, however, since the latter may be overwhelmed by one or two huge mergers.
12 See *Financial Times*, 17 September 1993; *Guardian*, 11 June 1994.
13 *Herald*, 17 May 1993; *Guardian*, 23 August 1994.
14 *Financial Times*, 17 May 1994.
15 *Guardian*, 22 November 1991; see also *Financial Times*, 25 May 1994, on similar expansion plans for the Bosch–Siemens joint venture.
16 *Financial Times*, 20 December 1993; 20 January 1994.

17 *Financial Times*, 24 January 1994.
18 Estimate by Translink, reported in *Financial Times*, 24 January 1994.
19 *Financial Times*, 13 June 1994.
20 *Guardian*, 23 February 1994; *International Management*, November 1993.
21 *Financial Times*, 11 January 1994.
22 *Financial Times* & *Guardian*, 28 September 1993.
23 *International Management*, July/August 1994.
24 *Guardian* and *Financial Times*, 9 October 1991.
25 *Guardian*, 10 June 1994.
26 *Guardian*, 19 July 1994.
27 *Eurobusiness*, May 1994.
28 See instead Ramsay (1991, 1994).
29 Incomes Data Services 1993; *Sunday Post*, 9 May 1993.
30 *Observer*, 7 February 1993.
31 See *Financial Times*, 1994, item by Goodhart on 28 February; *Guardian*, 16 December 1993. In a classic strategy employing the perceived mobility of capital investment, Mercedes-Benz gained agreement from its employees to reduce employment at the Ratstatt site by 7,800 in return for agreeing to build a new small car there, having made a show of examining sites in the UK, France and the Czech Republic.
32 Figures cited are for manufacturing, for 1990, when the last EC survey was carried out – from CEC (1993a).
33 *Financial Times*, 1994.
34 *Financial Times*, 15 February 1993; 1994.
35 *Financial Times*, 1994; CEC (1993a). See Oulton (1994) for calculations more favourable to the UK on unit labour costs.
36 Quoted in Barnett (1994).
37 Cited from the EU Green Paper on Social Policy (October 1993) in Suchard (1994).
38 Balls (1994a, b), Hutton (1994).
39 Gregg and Wadsworth (1994); *Financial Times*, 1994; Balls (1994b).
40 The survey was carried out by the Invest in Britain Bureau, as reported in *IRS Employment Trends* 496, September 1991.
41 See Ramsay (1994) for a more detailed assessment of the issues touched upon here.
42 *Guardian*, 26 March 1994, 5 April 1994.

REFERENCES

Balls, E. (1994a) 'US findings defy logic that minimum wage costs jobs', *Guardian*, 2 May 1994.
Balls, E. (1994b) 'Looking beyond the flexibility rhetoric', *Guardian*, 6 June 1994.
Barnett, A. (1994) 'Relocation: the race is on for Europe', *International Management*, June: 34–37.
Brittan, S. (1990) 'Conditions of progress', *Financial Times*, 28 June 1990.
Cecchini, P. (1988) *The European Challenge 1992: the Benefits of a Single Market*, Aldershot: Wildwood House.
Church, R. (1986) 'The effects of American multinationals on the British motor industry, 1911–83', in A. Teichova, M. Lévy-Leboyer and H. Nussbaum (eds) *Multinational Enterprise in Historical Perspective*, Cambridge: Cambridge University Press.
Commission of the European Communities (1993a) *Employment in Europe 1993*,

report by the Directorate General of Employment, Industrial Relations and Social Affairs, Brussels: CEC.

Commission of the European Communities (1993b) *XXIInd Report on Competition Policy, 1992*, Brussels: CEC.

Cowling, K. (1982) *Monopoly Capitalism*, London: Macmillan.

Dunning, J. H. (1988) *Explaining International Production*, London: Unwin Hyman.

Emerson, M., Aujean, M., Catinat, M., Goybet, P., and Jacquemin, A. (1988) *The Economics of 1992: the E.C. Commission's Assessment of the Economic Effects of Completing the Internal Market*, Oxford: Oxford University Press.

European Industrial Relations Review (1993) 'The Hoover affair and social dumping', *EIRR*, March: 14–19.

Financial Times (1993) 'The European single market', survey supplement to *Financial Times*, 19 January 1993.

Financial Times (1994) 'Can Europe compete?', series in *Financial Times*, February/March 1994 (later published as book under same title, 1994).

Geroski, P. A. (1988) 'European industrial policy and industrial policy in Europe', *Oxford Review of Economic Policy* 5 (2): 20–36.

Geroski, P. A. (1989) 'The choice between diversity and scale' in E. Davis, P. A. Geroski, J. A. Kay, A. Manning, C. Smales, S. R. Smith and S. Szymanski, *1992: Myths and Realities*, London: Centre for Business Strategy, London Business School, pp. 34–45.

Geroski, P. A. (1991) '1992 and European industrial structure', in G. Mackenzie and A. J. Venables (eds) *The Economics of the Single European Act*, London: Macmillan, pp. 7–26.

Grahl, J., and Teague, P. (1990) *1992 – The Big Market: the Future of the European Community*, London: Lawrence & Wishart.

Gregg, P., and Wadsworth, J. (1994) 'How to liberate British workers from the country's economic apartheid', *Guardian*, 23 May.

Hertner, P., and Jones, G. (eds) (1986) *Multinationals: Theory and History*, Aldershot: Gower.

Hutton, W. (1994) 'An end to the rule of fish market economics', *Guardian*, 25 July.

Incomes Data Services (1993) 'Social dumping', *IDS Focus Quarterly* 66, April: 4–16.

Jones, G. (ed.) (1986) *British Multinationals: Origins, Management and Performance*, Aldershot: Gower.

Julius, D. (1990) *Global Companies and Public Policy: the Growing Challenge of Foreign Direct Investment*, London: Pinter.

Kay, J. (1989) 'Myths and realities', in E. Davis, P. A. Geroski, J. A. Kay, A. Manning, C. Smales, S. R. Smith and S. Szymanski, *1992: Myths and Realities*, London: Centre for Business Strategy, London Business School, pp. 1–28.

Kay, N. M. (1989) *Corporate Strategies, Technological Change and 1992, Standing Commission on the Scottish Economy*, Working Paper Series, Glasgow: Fraser of Allander Institute.

Kay, N. M. (1990) *Industrial Collaborative Activity and the Completion of the Internal Market*, Glasgow: Department of Economics, University of Strathclyde (mimeo).

Mueller, D. C. (1980) *The Determinants and Effects of Mergers: an International Comparison*, Cambridge, Mass.: Oelgeschlager Gunn & Hain.

Multinational Business Forum (1993) *Thriving on Diversity: Informing and Consulting Employees in Multinational Enterprises*, Brussels: MBF.

Neuberger, H. (1989) *The Economics of 1992*, Brussels: Report for British Labour group of Euro MPs.

Organisation for Economic Co-operation and Development (1994) *Employment Outlook: July 1994*, Paris: OECD.

Oulton, N. (1994) 'Labour productivity and unit labour costs in manufacturing: the UK and its competitors', *National Institute Economic Review* 148, May: 49–60.

Peacock, A., and Bannock, G. (1991) *Corporate Takeovers and the Public Interest*, Aberdeen: Aberdeen University Press/David Hume Institute.

Porter, M. E. (1990) *The Competitive Advantage of Nations*, London: Macmillan.

Ramsay, H. E. (1990) *1992: the Year of the Multinational? Corporate Restructuring and Labour in the Single Market*, Warwick Papers in Industrial Relations 35, Coventry: Industrial Relations Research Unit, University of Warwick.

Ramsay, H. E. (1991) 'The Commission, the multinational, its workers and their charter: a modern tale of industrial democracy?', *Work, Employment and Society*, 5 (4): 541–66.

Ramsay, H. E. (1992a) 'Whose champions? Multinationals, labour and industry policy in the European Community after 1992', *Capital and Class* 48: 17–39.

Ramsay, H. E. (1992b) 'A critical assessment of the 1992 project agenda for industry policy', in K. Cowling and R. Sugden (eds) *Current Issues in Industrial Economic Strategy*, Manchester: Manchester University Press: 210–18.

Ramsay, H. E. (1994) *Euro-unionism and the Great Auction: an Assessment of the Prospects for Organised Post-Maastricht*, Occasional Paper 5, Glasgow: Department of Human Resource Management, University of Strathclyde.

Ramsay, H. E., and Haworth, N. (1989) 'Managing the multinationals: the emerging theory of the multinational enterprise and its implications for labour resistance', in S. Clegg (ed.) *Organization Theory and Class Analysis: New Approaches and New Issues*, Berlin: De Gruyter: 275–97.

Servan-Schreiber, J.-J. (1967) *Le Défi americain*, Paris: Denoel.

Stopford, J. M., and Turner, L. M. (1984) *Britain and the Multinationals*, Chichester: Wiley.

Suchard, D. (1994) 'Staying put', *Eurobusiness*, July/August: 44–6.

Teichova, A., Lévy-Leboyer, M., and Nussbaum, H. (eds) (1986) *Multinational Enterprise in Historical Perspective*, Cambridge: Cambridge University Press.

United Nations Centre on Transnational Corporations (1993) *World Investment Report 1993: Transnational Corporations and Integrated International Production*, New York: United Nations.

Wallace, T., Flecker, J., and Thompson, P. (1992) 'The urge to merge: organisational change in the merger and acquisition process in Europe', *International Journal of Human Resource Management* 3 (2): 285–306.

Wilkins, M. (1970) *The Emergence of Multinational Enterprise: American Business Abroad From the Colonial Era to 1914*, Cambridge, Mass.: Harvard University Press.

Wilkins, M. (1974) *The Maturing of Multinational Enterprise: American Business Abroad from 1914 to 1970*, Cambridge, Mass.: Harvard University Press.

Part III

CORPORATE RESTRUCTURING

8

THE REGIONAL DEVELOPMENT POTENTIAL OF INWARD INVESTMENT IN THE LESS FAVOURED REGIONS OF THE EUROPEAN COMMUNITY

Ash Amin and John Tomaney

INTRODUCTION

After more than a decade of policy emphasis on the potential of small firms and indigenous entrepreneurship for revitalizing the ailing economies of the EU's less favoured regions, attention appears to be shifting back to the role that could be played by large firms and inward investment. In part this shift might be due to the fruits of research in the 1980s which has revealed that small firm entrepreneurship in less favoured regions tends to be fragile and therefore unable to constitute the seedbed for self-sustaining regional economic development. Attention has been drawn to weaknesses such as low small firm growth rates, high failure rates, specialization in low to medium-quality goods and services which are destined usually for saturated local markets, and the absence of a network of firms and institutions able to support individual entrepreneurship (Mason 1991; Curran and Blackburn 1994; *Regional Studies* 1994; Storey 1994).

The policy shift may be due also to a changing perception of the dynamics and benefits of inward investment. There is a view among policy-makers and practitioners that the expanded market opportunities associated with the completion of the single European market will raise the level of inward investment into the EU. There is acceptance however, notably among officials of the EC, that the spread of investment will not be automatic but will continue to be dependent upon the incentives and locational advantages offered by individual member states and regions. Conscious of the growing interregional competition for inward investment, the Regional Directorate of the Commission (DG XVI), for example, is increasingly concerned about the mismatch between the scale of incentives offered to individual companies and the contribution of inward investment to regional value added. This concern is heightened by awareness that the integration of markets across the EU is likely to intensify processes of restructuring among existing multilocational firms within Europe (see Chapter 7 above). Such restructuring may intensify the rationalization or closure of duplicate or excess capacity in different less favoured regions. There is, thus, a desire to ensure that projects attracted by lucrative regional incentives should maximize their economic contribution to the host region.

The question which follows is whether the locational practices of inward investors in the context of less favoured regions are changing, or can be made to change. Recent academic literature on business organization and management tends to suggest that the use of territory by multilocational firms may well be changing. As is well known, the experience of 'branch plant' industrialization in less favoured regions during the 1960s and 1970s is judged to have fallen short of meeting the original expectation that inward investment could act as a 'growth pole'. The argument is that during this period companies used regional policy incentives to locate either capital-intensive or low-wage 'cathedrals in the desert', which offered the host economy little in the way of skill formation, technology transfer, linkage opportunities, transmission of new managerial and entre-preneurial know-how or reinvestment of profits. Terms such as 'branch plant economy', 'dependent development' and 'industrialization without growth' were coined to highlight the incorporation of such regions within the global business logic of firms governed from elsewhere – a logic working against any self-governing and self-sustaining regional economic development logic (Firn 1975; Massey 1984).

Today, however, there is a sense among researchers that the nature of the multilocational firm may be changing. A distinction has been found between the cost or price-sensitive company which dislocates specific tasks to less favoured regions for financial incentives and cheap labour and the 'performance' company that derives its competitive advantage from product excellence and seeks locations which can offer qualified personnel and innovation-rich environments (Schoenberger 1991). 'Performance' companies are those which operate in rapidly changing, specialized and demanding segments of a product market. It is said that the acute pressure on such companies, associated with the volatility and changeability of products and technologies, has favoured the development of organiza-tional structures and strategies based on integrated manufacture, erosion of traditional divisions between managerial, scientific and manual functions, and the establishment of closer and more collaborative ties with suppliers (Porter 1990; Mytelka 1991; United Nations 1993; Best 1990; Clarke and Monkhouse 1994).

This distinction at the corporate level is mirrored at the plant or divisional level. The cost-driven company, specializing in large-volume, medium-technology goods continues to be characterized by task-specific plants displaying different levels of functional complexity in different locations – all closely tied into a framework of centralized and hierarchical governance. In contrast, 'performance' companies, it is said, appear increasingly to be moving over to product-based, rather than task-based, plant structures for the management of worldwide operations, especially in manufacturing. Overseas plants have responsibility for developing, producing and marketing particular products, and, often, on the basis of possessing a continental or world product mandate (Howells and Wood 1993). Such plants are of strategic importance within the corporation, and functionally far more complex than the traditional branch plant. The plants have leading roles for particular products or technologies – a responsibility accompanied by upgrading of capabilities across the spectrum of tasks and duties. 'Performance' plants appear to work on a co-operative basis with each other and with HQ offices, with the former emphasis on domestic 'lead' and overseas 'lag' in terms of the division of research and production expertise gradually disappearing (Cusumano and Elenkov 1994). Finally, with the change in plant status comes devolution of management and decision-making ability, allowing local managers and workforces to respond rapidly and successfully to changing circumstances. The 'performance' plant is part of a 'heterarchical' system of management (Hedlund 1986; Ohmae 1989; Drucker 1990; Dunning 1993) which is quite different from the older, centralized and hierarchical patterns of control within branch plants.

The 'performance' plant, operating in markets for ever changing, innovation-intensive and quality goods, possesses a set of distinctive attributes which make it an attractive opportunity for stimulating endogenous development within less favoured regions. Four attributes in particular justify a re-examination of the role of inward investment as a stimulus to self-sustaining local economic development. First, the 'performance' plant is likely to incorporate a wider range of functions, thus serving to enhance the skill base and entrepreneurial qualities of the host region. Positive effects may range from the growth of local R&D to the transfer of state-of-the-art skills and industrial practices into the local labour market. Second, the possession of decision-making authority serves to create a local management committed to the long-term survival of the plant, as well as to secure the transfer of vital entrepreneurial ability into the labour market of less favoured regions. Third, the 'performance' plant has the potential to stimulate more extensive and qualitatively better local supplier linkages than the traditional branch plant. It requires a wider range of inputs as well as flexible but reliable links with suppliers – conditions which could be secured, at least in part, by physical proximity. Fourth, the strategic position of the 'performance' plant within the corporation turns the threat of closure or rationalization, so typical of older branch plants, to a positive opportunity for further expansion.

What is less evident from this new academic literature stressing the rise of 'heterarchy', 'networking', 'vertical disintegration' and 'performance-based' competition is whether the 'performance' plant has emerged or could emerge in the context of less favoured regions (Dicken *et al.* 1994). Such regions may, for instance, lack the infrastructure to attract quality-seeking inward investment. Nor is it clear whether 'performance' plants are attracted to particular types of region, or, if so, whether 'best practice' may be transferable to other less favoured regions via appropriate policy interventions. Finally, it is not self-evident whether improvements in the status of plants in given less favoured regions, where such improvement is observed, are the result of the rise of the new organizational forms suggested above or the outcome of different reasons. It has been observed that certain plants in less favoured regions gradually acquire and develop research and technical skills, often associated with local problem-solving and adaptation to local markets (Hakansson 1990; Young *et al.* 1993). This distinction between *in situ* upgrading and new 'performance' plants has important policy implications, in suggesting that the difference may lie between an approach based on attracting a certain type of inward invest-ment and one designed to enhance the status of existing plants.

This chapter addresses these questions by examining the quality of projects considered to be 'flagship' investments in a selection of less favoured regions in the EU. It draws upon a study for the Directorate General for Regional Policy of the European Commission completed in March 1993 (Amin *et al.* 1994). The study was stimulated by a desire on the part of the Commission to explore ways in which the offer of EC regional incentives might be calibrated to the 'value added' offered by mobile investment to host regions. It sought to identify the scope for attracting quality-based investment into the less favoured regions and to outline the policy priorities in order to maximize their economic contribution to the region. The study selected four less favoured regions with different inward investment characteristics and different local attributes – Scotland, Ireland, Portugal and Brandenburg in eastern Germany. It also studied the experi-ence of the Rhône-Alpes region in France, an advanced region which has succeeded in attracting high-quality investment without the help of regional incentives. In each region the quality of half a dozen 'flagship' investments was measured, on the basis of data for the following plant-level indicators: functional complexity and decision-making autonomy; innovation potential; training intensity; quality of labour; local content. The study also appraised the influence of regional incentives and the policies and practices of local development agencies on the quality of investment attracted by the regions.

This chapter draws upon material from the case studies in Scotland, Ireland and Portugal. It argues that to date there is little evidence to show that new 'performance' plants are being located in the less favoured regions: 'Flagship' companies with international reputations continue to locate plants of modest quality in these regions. The chapter finds instead that the evidence for gradual, evolutionary upgrading of plants is far more significant, and that such upgrading is related more to the offer of 'softer' forms of support to inward investors than to quality-related conditions attached to the offer of incentives. The next section summarizes the findings of the case studies, while the last section discusses the policy implications of the findings.

FLAGSHIP INWARD INVESTMENT IN THE LESS FAVOURED REGIONS – 'PERFORMANCE' PLANTS?

Table 8.1 summarizes some of the characteristics of companies examined in Ireland, Scotland and Portugal. The majority of plants belong to well known international corporations operating in growing or dynamic markets. The majority of the plants were opened in the course of the 1980s. In all three regions the investments were considered by local agencies to be among the most prestigious attracted into the region.

Strategic functions and decision-making autonomy

Despite the fanfare in Portugal which has surrounded investments such as those by Ford-VW, Delco-Remi and Blaupunkt, these prestige projects exhibit a strong bias towards final assembly and packaging activities, and the absence of top and middle-order management activities. The plants have limited financial autonomy, while the functions of purchasing, product strategy, sales, marketing and investment are controlled by divisional or head offices outside Portugal. In addition, senior executives tend to be expatriates showing little long-term commitment to the Portuguese plants.

In Ireland the tendency – in all four plants visited – appeared to be the opposite, with evidence that the plants were making gains both in the range of functions and in levels of management autonomy, although none of the plants had marketing or sales departments. Each plant, over a period of time, had been awarded either a continental or a world product mandate by its parent company. Although integrated into wider corporate networks, in two cases, the plants contained functions of strategic importance to the corporation as a whole. In the case of one engineering plant – Garrett Ireland (owned by Allied Signal) the original plant had acquired an important foundry which significantly increased the status of the plant in the corporate hierarchy. More generally, there is evidence of the emergence of an Irish management cadre which presses for greater decisional autonomy. Typically the Irish managers are strongly committed to the success of their plant, which often leads to upgrading of the status of the plant over time.

Table 8.1 Characteristics of selected 'flagship' investments (a) in Portugal

Investor	Total investment (ECU million)	Total grant (% of total investment)	Training grants (%)	Local content (national value added)[a]	Size of plant (No. of employees) full capacity	Main product	Major market	Comments
AutoEuropa (Ford VW) est. 1991	2,700·0	40	90	45	5,000	Multi-purpose vehicle (people carrier)	Europe (US)	Greenfield investment. Largest ever FDI project, 95% of units exported. About a third of Portugal's total exports
Delco Remi (GM) est. 1990	56·1	38.6	100	22	550	Electronic ignition	Worldwide	Greenfield site. World market mandate
						ABS braking systems		Located in tax-free zone. Part of global purchasing network
								Division of ACG. Components subsidiary of GM
Blaupunkt (Bosch) est. 1990	25·0	–	0	0	1,500	Car radios	Europe, worldwide	Expansion of existing Grundig site.
Celbi (Stora Group) est. 1967	93·0	–	95	20	740	Paper pulp	Worldwide (Sweden)	Greenfield site

Note: (a) National value added is defined as the total cost of all local imports, including sales and depreciation costs.

Table 8.1 Characteristics of selected 'flagship' investments (b) in Scotland

Investor	Total investment (£ million)	Total grant (%)	Local content (% of supplies)	No. of jobs	Training spend £ million)	R&D (No. employed)	Main markets	Comments
Caledonian Paper (Finland) est. 1989	215	9	70	430	0·45	40	UK, EC US	Capital-intensive Operates in tandem with other European plants
Health Care International[c] (US) est. 1991	180	16	50[b]	800	3·0		EU	Provision of advanced medical care and research
NEC (Japan) est. 1982	174	20	30	830	2% of payroll	0	EU	High capital intensity (£210,000 per job) No R&D
Inmac (US) est. 1987	4	20	35	120		4	EU	World product mandate

Notes: (*b*) Fifty per cent of start-up procurement budget. (*c*) In autumn 1994 the project went into receivership owing to lack of demand.

Table 8.1 Characteristics of selected 'flagship' investments (c) in Ireland

Investor	No. of employees	Products	R&D/technical support	Comments
Rhône-Poulenc est. 1967	60	Semi-solid pharmaceutical products	2–3 Quality control and technical staff	1984 World Product Mandate (WPM) for all semi-solid products (secondary production) and suppositories
Allied Signal (Garrett) est. 1979	345	Foundry and production of automotive turbochargers	9 R&D process development workers	After 1982, WPM or Continental Product Mandate (CPM) for two products. New R&D process development unit. Software development unit (30 employees)
Lotus est. 1982	300	Production of packaged software	20 in Unix development group	1985 CPM for software packages 1986 'Translation' unit move from UK to Dublin.
Yamanouchi est. 1987	150	Production of bulk pharmaceutical intermediaries (primary production)	5–10 technical division	1986 new product added. New pilot plant and facility. Process development unit

In the Scottish case, the profile of top corporate functions and decision-making autonomy differed according to sector. The electronics sector, which has a large presence in Scotland and has been a target sector for development agencies, was characterized by a limited range of corporate functions and constrained management autonomy. Some plants, however, do appear to have continental or world product mandates. On the other hand, investments in the health care and pulp and paper industries appeared to have an extensive range of corporate functions, including control over marketing and sales activities. They were important sites of decision-making in the global management hierarchy.

Innovation capacity

The Portuguese plants visited were characterized by the lack, or the presence of only rudimentary, research capabilities. There is evidence that more recent investment has been characterized by higher levels of R&D in terms of numbers employed, but activity remains heavily biased towards process development (engineers rather than scientists).

In Ireland an internal study by EOLAS, the science and technology agency, suggested that significant increases had occurred in the expenditure of overseas companies on R&D. In addition, Ireland has succeeded in attracting some large-scale research activity. For instance, General Semiconductor relocated a large R&D centre from Arizona to Macroom in County Cork. However, in general the EOLAS survey found that research is process-orientated, although in the companies we visited we found evidence of Irish plants beginning to provide corporate-wide R&D services, especially in IT areas. A case in point was Garrett (Allied Signal), which after extensive negotiations with its parent, won a key computing service activity. Indeed, in one important case, that of Lotus, a pool of relatively low-cost graduate computing skills in Ireland had been ajudged a key location factor for the firm. A further feature in Ireland is the apparent growth in links between overseas firms and Irish universities. There is also evidence that the R&D capability of overseas firms in Ireland is beginning to improve, but the improvement has occurred over a long period and has been supported by a range of 'soft' policy measures and extra finance provided by the Irish Industrial Development Authority (IDA) and EOLAS.

In Scotland the picture on R&D was mixed. In the electronics sector, research evidence, confirmed by the plant visits undertaken for this study, indicates low levels of R&D (in terms of expenditure, numbers employed and type of activity) and tends to confirm the traditional branch-plant character of this sector in Scotland. By contrast, establishments in the medical services and pulp and paper sectors which were visited were found to fund relatively high levels of R&D. These two establishments were also characterized by a greater level of plant autonomy in other strategic areas. In the case of Health Care International a key declared locational attribute was the existence of a pool of (English-speaking) medical graduates and research strengths in Scottish universities. Paradoxically, however, the venture ran into considerable financial difficulty in 1994 owing to its inability to build sufficient demand from the world's rich for its expensive private medical care.

Training intensity

Cross-national differences in training performance are notoriously difficult to measure, and researchers have found it hard to draw meaningful comparisons between regions and investors. Measurement in this survey concentrated on the volume of formal training provided. There were insufficient data available on the quality and effectiveness of training to allow reliable comparisons between regions.

In Portugal the level of training was limited (in terms of both budget and training days) and tended to be on-the-job. Given that training effort was heavily supported by public (often European Social Fund) grants, it seems to be the case that large amounts of public funds are being used as a wage-cost subsidy.

Recent pronouncements on Irish industrial policy (Culliton 1992) have suggested that there is significant room for improvement in the provision of training in Ireland. It is of significance that the Irish authorities do not measure the training performance of overseas plants in the same way as they do R&D performance. However, the plants visited for this study were characterized generally by a high level of training. Particularly important appeared to be initiatives (especially for supervisory grades) related to upgrading towards total quality management systems. The involvement of Regional Technology Colleges in this effort appeared to signal the gradual improvement of the training infrastructure in Ireland.

Although the UK as a whole can be criticized for the failings of its training system, in Scotland there was evidence of a comparatively high level of training at the plants visited, including significant off-the-job training. All plants had relatively large training budgets. The provision of bespoke training packages by Local Enterprise Companies for inward investors was a distinctive feature in Scotland. For instance, Dumbartonshire Local Enterprise Company was providing training in specialist medical skills for the investment by Health Care International. For the authorities in Scotland the provision of such packages is a means of offering additional inducements to firms that might otherwise be drawn away by the higher levels of direct subsidy available in southern Europe.

Overall, the training demands of firms differed significantly between Portugal and the other two regions. In Ireland and Scotland awareness of the link between training and quality of investment has led to reorganization of the training system, although the immediate effects are as yet unclear.

Quality of labour

Attempts to quantify differences in labour quality, similarly, are confounded by the difficulties of cross-plant, let alone cross-regional, comparisons, given the absence of uniform measures. Information provided by firms, therefore, had to be supplemented by more qualitative impressions in the survey, in order for comparisons to be made.

The occupational profile of the Portuguese plants was heavily skewed towards semi-skilled assembly work. Also significant was that top management jobs tended to go to expatriates rather than the indigenous population, despite the large size of the Portuguese managerial labour market.

In Ireland, by contrast, there is evidence that some improvement has occurred in the labour profile of overseas plants over time. As noted earlier, in the case of Lotus, the existence of a pool of graduate software skills was a significant locational factor, and the firm had established a 100-strong software development team. In other plants visited the occupational structure remained skewed towards manual grades but all were characterized by steady improvements in the number of non-manual (notably technical) staff. In contrast to Portugal, a key feature of the plants – and of Ireland more generally – is the presence of Irish managers in key management positions. This appears to be a key factor in explaining the improving quality of overseas investment in Ireland, as Irish managers fight tenaciously for further rounds of investment for their plants.

In Scotland the labour profile differed by sector. In electronics the work force structure was heavily skewed towards semi-skilled manual occupations. By contrast, in the other sectors the labour profile was more diverse, in part accounted for by the different nature of the processes and by the wider range of strategic functions attached to each facility. As in Ireland, a significant feature of the Scottish plants was the presence of Scots as managers in key positions.

In general, and despite examples of best practice in Ireland and Scotland, the occupational profile of the plants visited bore more resemblance to the archetypal branch plant than to the 'performance plant'.

Local content and supplier linkages

The degree of local supply content is perhaps the most significant indicator of the embeddedness of an investment in its host region. A variety of measures of local content were found to be utilized across the regions. One measure is value added (revenues less expenditure), which, of course, gives no direct measure of the extent of local supplier linkages. In other cases total expenditure within a region is used as a proxy for local content, but this can include such items as wage costs, taxes and even interest on loans. The measure gives only a limited indication of the scale of local multipliers. The most accurate indicator of quality is the proportion of expenditure on materials and services within a region, although the majority of firms examined were unable to (or unwilling) to provide this information. When such information was made available, companies were generally reluctant to give specific information on the value distribution of purchases.

In Portugal a significant level of local content was achieved by a pulp manufacturer which used locally grown eucalyptus trees. With this exception, the plants surveyed in Portugal were characterized by few local linkages. In some cases the production process amounted to little more than the assembly and packaging of imported components. Even in the case of the pulp plant, it had originally been agreed to establish a paper plant next to the pulp facility as part of the aid package. However, the company in question had not done so and appeared to have no intention of doing so in the future. The anticipated arrival of AutoEuropa, the biggest investment ever in Portugal, by Ford and VW, has prompted a new concern with local linkages and the setting up of a linkage development initiative. As yet there appears to be little evidence of significant increases in local purchase agreements.

The Irish plants visited for this study generally had low levels of local content. The pharmaceutical plant owned by Rhône-Poulenc imported 80 per cent of its raw materials from a sister plant in Germany, although the pharmaceutical plant owned by Yamamouchi purchased over 50 per cent of its raw materials in Ireland. Garrett, although occupying a strategically important place in the value chain, made few local purchases. In the case of Lotus's software and disk duplication facility there was significant local purchasing – software manuals from the Irish printing and packaging industry. Indeed, there is evidence that the existence of a printing industry which meets international quality standards (together with graduate software skills) is emerging as a key location factor in Ireland. The IDA operates some local linkage development initiatives which have led to modest improvements in the level of Irish purchases by overseas companies. The IDA conducts a regular 'Survey of Irish Economy Expenditures' which indicates some improvement in local purchasing.

In Scotland it was found that local content and local purchasing were limited in the electronics sector. Despite heavy promotional focus on this sector and a significant concentration of investment in Silicon Glen, research evidence suggests a low level of integration (Turok 1993). The firms investigated in our study had very few forward or backward linkages. By contrast, a pulp and paper plant owned by Caledonian Paper had a high level of local content (e.g. through purchases of local forestry products and local energy).

Across the regions, the extent of local purchasing was surprisingly disappointing overall. Equally surprising was the degree to which regional development agencies typically fail to monitor such activity – a notable exception being Ireland.

Summary

Four general observations regarding the quality of recent 'flagship' investment in the less favoured regions can be drawn from the preceding discussion. First, there exist significant variations in the quality of investment between the less favoured regions. These differences cut across the EC policy distinction between laggard regions (Objective 1) and old industrial regions (Objective 2). Ireland (Objective 1) and Scotland (Objective 2) are both characterized by a higher quality of inward investment than Portugal (Objective 1).

In Ireland and Scotland examples were found of plants occupying a relatively strategic position in the corporate division of labour and drawing upon local human resources. Though such plants generally continued to lack control over investment and procurement strategy as well as product development capability, they did contain process development capability, scientific, technical and engineering personnel and staff with higher degrees, a continental or global mandate over given products and local autonomy over non-strategic decisions. They were noted for their recruitment of senior personnel form the local labour market, as well as for the commitment of local managers to the region, especially in terms of winning intra-corporate bids for new investment. They were not noted, however, for their local content ratios, their business with indigenous firms or the local purchase of high value-added inputs and services, although there were some exceptions, notably in Ireland.

In contrast, in Portugal the definition 'flagship' project did not readily extend to capture the qualitative aspects of investments. The establishments were production or assembly-orientated, specializing in tasks often duplicated elsewhere, with limited local R&D capability, skill variability and management autonomy. Closely integrated into the governance structures and global value chain of their parent organizations, they were found to provide little stimulus to the local supplier, skills or knowledge base. In many respects the investments were like traditional branch plants, remote from the textbook 'performance' plant.

A second observation is that the improvement in quality in Scotland and especially Ireland has taken place over time and appears to be related to the provision of 'after-care' services and finance to upgrade investment. Third, important variations in the local embeddedness of the investments can be related to sectoral differences. The least embedded investments were in the so-called 'hi-tech' sectors, notably electronics. Such investments tended to lack strategic functions and made few local purchases. This was true even in Scotland, where some plants were characterized by better labour profiles and product mandates. Finally, the most embedded plants tended to be those which were linked with a genuine (i.e. non-financial) locational advantage of the region. This could be the knowledge base, a skilled work force, a supply industry or even a raw material source.

CONCLUSIONS AND POLICY ISSUES

Conclusions

For the present, reality escapes the new fashions in academe. The textbook 'performance' plant has yet to feature in the context of Europe's less favoured regions in any significant way (see also Chapter 9 below on the Mezzogiorno). Examples of success can, of course, be found, but they are not representative of a major upgrading in the quality of inward investment in less favoured regions. The term 'flagship', in many respects, continues to remain better a description of the international reputation of the investing company than of the plants themselves. One explanation of this gap could be the endurance of hierarchical forms of organization and governance within multilocational firms, resulting in the allocation of particular tasks to individual sites. Another reason could be that companies continue to perceive less favoured regions as locations which lack the infrastructure to support plants which make complex demands on the host economy (CEC 1990). It is likely that both explanations are valid, and mutually reinforcing: corporate organizational choices are influenced by locational characteristics, and vice versa.

To recognize this gap, however, is not to suggest that nothing has changed or that nothing can be done to ameliorate the quality of mobile investment in less favoured regions. The stark difference in quality between Portugal, on the one hand, and Scotland and Ireland, on the other, should not be underestimated. The least industrialized regions of the EU such as Portugal generally have a less developed skills base, fewer advanced training opportunities, poor supplier networks and limited institutional capacity. They are thus less able to support the needs of knowledge-intensive and supply-rich investment. These regions continue to offer a series of cost advantages, most notably low industrial wage levels and lucrative financial incentives (Camagni 1992; Nam et al. 1991). Clearly, their competitive advantage lies in attracting inward investments that are typically cost-driven, and unless major improvements are made to the quality of the supply-side infrastructure these regions will continue to attract such investment. The longer-term risk they run, however, is that of remaining trapped within a field of specialization in low-grade branch-plant activities; a specialization which ultimately will fail to act as a stimulus to endogenous development.

In the case of regions such as Ireland and Scotland, which have pursued a more co-ordinated and strategic approach towards inward investment, there are clear signs of upgrading in the quality of investment. Evidence can be found of plants which possess a product mandate, some product and process development capacity, functional heterogeneity, and middle management and scientific ability. On the other hand, and despite the efforts of agencies established explicitly for the purpose, the record of even the best-quality projects has been modest in terms, first, of their stimulus to local linkage formation (notably the purchase of high value-added products and services from indigenous companies) and, second, the transfer of technology via links with local firms and research establishments (Turok 1993; Culliton 1992; O'Malley *et al.* 1992). It is in the areas of skill formation and entrepreneurial ability that benefits can be said to have accrued to the host region, rather than in the areas of innovation and local linkage formation.

With such regions the question that has to be asked is, what are the factors which have contributed to the upgrading of inward investment? In our analysis three factors in particular stand out in importance. The first is an emphasis by development agencies on generic upgrading of the physical, human and communications infrastructure. The emphasis includes a commitment to industry training initiatives, investment in higher education, the upgrading of transport and communications networks and the offer of high-quality amenities. In attempting to offer a rich supply-side milieu, these regions display a long-term commitment to 'performance'-based entrepreneurship and, in so doing, offer investors a good reason for procuring their higher value-added inputs from within the region.

The second factor is the presence of institutions such as Scottish Enterprise and the IDA which are committed to a proactive, selective, quality-conscious and co-ordinated approach to inward investment. These are agencies which have developed long-term strategies to encourage particular industrial clusters, by seeking out and satisfying selected international firms in targeted sectors. Where sector strategies have been based upon building upon existing local industrial strengths, the offer of 'one-stop' packages to investors by institutions which have both detailed knowledge of a region's assets and the power to mobilize other regional agencies, appears to have helped to attract new investors to Europe who are more open to suggestion concerning the quality and availability of diverse local factor inputs. In addition, the commitment to a targeted strategy has built into it the principle of selectivity, although, in practice, quality expectations have often been relaxed when investors have threatened to take the investment elsewhere. Thus it is not institutional capacity in its own right but the pursuit of a particular regional strategy that is of significance, and this is of relevance to regions which stop at simply creating narrowly focused institutions of economic development (Dicken and Tickell 1992; Amin and Thrift 1994).

The third, and perhaps more significant, factor has been *in situ* upgrading of plants over a period of time. Achievements such as the broadening of a product range, the attainment of a product mandate, investment in new research facilities or expansion of functions are the result of annual improvements in plant performance and the efforts of local managers (usually of indigenous origin) to win new resources and new responsibilities from central management. While the initiative for *in situ* upgrading comes from local managers, the offer of 'after-care' support from local development agencies appears to play a significant role in securing success (see also Chapter 11 below, by Young and Hood). 'After-care' support may include a number of 'soft' incentives such as the offer of help with new recruitment and training targets; the provision and preparation of new premises and communications infrastructure; a link-up with potential suppliers, who in turn are assisted to upgrade product quality and delivery; and assistance with reducing red tape in dealing with government and other public-sector bodies. Thus such support serves not only to improve plant competitiveness but also to strengthen the hand of local managers in negotiations with the parent firm.

The elements of 'good' institutional practice leading up to and after an

Table 8.2 Elements of 'good' institutional practice towards mobile investment

1 Identification of a small number of strategic sectors in order to promote clustering and the build-up of related agglomeration economies, building where possible on existing industrial strengths

2 One-stop provision of incentives and other forms of assistance in order to facilitate the speed of transactions

3 Understanding the needs of firms establishing a relationship of trust with them and support for local managers in their attempts to upgrade the status of the plant (financial and technical)

4 Sector-specific research to identify strengths and weaknesses in the region's resource base of relevance to mobile investors

5 'After-care' support to match investor needs to regional strengths

6 Provision of financial and other incentives to potential suppliers to upgrade product quality and delivery practices

7 Provision of indirect support in the form of infrastructural improvements that can help secure a firm within a region, and also improve the wider supply side characteristics of the region (infrastructure, telecoms supply, generic skills training, etc.)

8 Regular monitoring of the purchasing, R&D and training performance of investors

Source: Amin *et al.* (1994).

216

investment which appear to have had an impact on quality are summarized in Table 8.2. These, together with consistent investment across the supply-side infrastructure, appear to be key factors in influencing the regional development potential of inward investment.

Policy implications

The immediate policy implication of the preceding discussion is that despite the absence of any noticeable transition towards the location of new 'performance' plants in less favoured regions, the pursuit of maximizing 'quality' from investors is a worthwhile policy objective within less favoured regions. Especially in light of intensified trade-off and competition between less favoured regions in the trail of European corporate restructuring post-1992 (see Chapter 7 by Ramsay), regions will have to look for ways which help in rooting investments within the locality. It is an objective, however, which implies forms of intervention and practices which go well beyond simple adjustments to the financial incentives on offer under European and national regional policy.

That said, there does remain some scope for calibrating regional incentives to the quality of mobile investment. It could be argued that the poor quality of 'flagship' projects in countries such as Portugal is, in part, the result of the ability of investors to obtain disproportionately high levels of funding as a result of minimum leverage by regional institutions to ensure compliance with various quality expectations stipulated on paper. Thus a case can be made for cutting back, across Europe, current levels of regional subsidy (automatic and discretionary) in order to reduce the pursuit of short-term, cost-based, investment projects by regions. The level at which ceilings should be set for different less favoured regions is clearly a matter of sensitivity, because of the need to tread a fine line between ensuring that investors are not kept away and minimizing interregional competition for investment via the offer of bigger incentive packages (Allen *et al.* 1989). To reduce incentives to the point of discouraging investment from low-cost less favoured regions would be as undesirable as doing nothing to prevent regions from competing with each other on the basis of the size of the incentive package.

Equally, there is case for regions taking steps to secure 'good'-quality investments in the first instance. A step in the right direction would be to tie the offer of discretionary awards to agreed quality targets. It is important, however, that realistic targets are established for different types of less favoured region. In more 'advanced' less favoured regions like Scotland and Ireland awards might be weighted in favour of rewarding promising spin-offs in the research and supplies linkage potential of inward investment, while in less 'advanced' less favoured regions like Portugal the weighting might be biased towards criteria such as task multiplicity, local decision-making autonomy and skill formation. Without such a division of policy expectations across different less favoured regions no change can realistically be expected in the common practice among investors and development agencies of ignoring the unachievable quality targets set down on paper.

The limits of this approach, however, also need to be acknowledged. Our study has made it abundantly clear that the most common route to plant upgrading in less favoured regions has been incremental change among existing investments. This suggests the need for policy reforms in the direction of 'after-care' support, covering at least three areas. First, discretionary awards should be made available also in the course of the life of an investment, when plans to upgrade the status of a plant are being considered by a company. The offer of incentives could play a decisive role in tipping the balance in favour of the assisted plant within the wider corporate network. Second, and for the same reason, the significance of 'softer' forms of support such as assistance for training courses, linkage programmes, access to local research institutes, and so on, should not be underestimated. What is important, however, is to ensure that such support is sought for genuine upgrading ventures rather than as a means of helping investors reduce operating costs. Third, such direct support should be accompanied by investment aimed at upgrading the general infrastructure of a region (notably communications, education and training, research capacity and industrial premises). But here, too, it is important that regional·agencies should seek to match local strengths to the profile of inward investors. Just as inward investment strategies might focus on particular industrial clusters, wider regional 'infrastructure' programmes should focus on improving particular sectoral, labour market or educational strengths within a region. Otherwise the task of constructing a functional link between inward investment and indigenous needs will remain a distant prospect.

In conclusion, whatever the scope for maximizing the local impact of inward investment within less favoured regions, success rests on building local institutional capability. Such capability requires both a proactive and a strategic approach to inward investment as well as its integration with a broader, longer-term, regional development strategy that focuses on existing industrial strengths. It is a capability which simultaneously has a sense of the desirability of regional specialization in an increasingly competitive 'open' Europe, and a sense of the advantages of having an integrated local economy 'thick' with local interconnections. This is a goal which requires long-term vision, persistence, proactive and innovative development agencies, and co-ordinated inter-institutional behaviour. These are characteristics which certainly cannot be created overnight in regions of absent, inefficient, corrupt or rivalistic institutional traditions. It may turn out that the difference between the less favoured regions of Europe which can and those which cannot embark upon a development path based on attracting and retaining good-quality inward investment will lie in their ability to develop such institutional capacity.

REFERENCES

Allen, K., Yuill, D., and Bachtler, J. (1989) 'Requirements for an effective regional policy', in L. Albrechts, F. Moulaert, P. Roberts, and E. Swyngedouw (eds) *Regional Policy at a Crossroads*, London: Jessica Kingsley.

Amin, A., and Thrift, N. (1994) 'Living in the global' in A. Amin, and N. Thrift (eds) *Globalization, Institutions and Regional Development in Europe*, Oxford: Oxford University Press.

Amin, A., Bradley, D., Howells, J., Tomaney, J., and Gentle, C. (1994) 'Regional incentives and the quality of mobile investment in the less favoured regions of the EC', *Progress in Planning* 41 (1): 1–112.

Best, M. (1990) *The New Competition*, Cambridge: Polity Press.

Camagni, R. (1992) 'Development scenarios and policy guidelines for the lagging regions in the 1990s', *Regional Studies* 26 (4): 361–74.

Commission of the European Communities (1990) *An Empirical Assessment of Factors shaping Regional Competitiveness in Problem Regions*, Brussels: Commission of the European Communities.

Clarke, T., and Monkhouse, E. (1994) *Rethinking the Company*, London: Pitman.

Culliton, J. (1992) *A Time for Change: Industrial Policy for the 1990s*, Report of the Industrial Policy Review Group, Dublin: Stationery Office.

Curran, J., and Blackburn, R. (1994) *Small Firms and Local Economic Networks*, London: Paul Chapman.

Cusumano, M., and Elenkov, D. (1994) 'Linking international technology transfer with strategy and management: a literature commentary', *Research Policy* 23: 195–215.

Dicken, P., and Tickell, A. (1992) 'Competitors or collaborators? The structure of inward investment promotion in northern England', *Regional Studies* 26: 99–106.

Dicken, P., Forsgren, M., and Malmberg, A. (1994) 'The local embeddedness of transnational corporations', In A. Amin and N. Thrift (eds) *Globalization, Institutions and Regional Development in Europe*, Oxford: Oxford University Press.

Drucker, P. E. (1990) 'The emerging theory of manufacturing', *Harvard Business Review*, May–June, 94–102.

Dunning, J. H. (1993) *The Globalisation of Business*, London: Routledge.

Firn, J. (1975) 'External control and regional development', *Environment and Planning A*, 7: 393–414.

Hakansson, H. (1990) 'International decentralization of R&D – the organizational challenges', in C. A. Bartlett, Y. Doz and G. Hedlund (eds) *Managing the Global Firm*, London: Routledge.

Hedlund, G. (1986) 'The hypermodern MNC – a heterarchy', *Human Resource Management*, 25, 9–35.

Howells, J., and Wood, M. (1993) *The Globalisation of Production and Technology*, London: Belhaven.

Mason, C. (1991) 'Spatial variations in enterprise: the geography of new firm formation', in R. Burrows (ed.) *Deciphering the Enterprise Culture*, London: Routledge.

Massey, D. (1984) *Spatial Divisions of Labour*, London: Macmillan.

Mytelka, L. (1991) *Strategic Partnerships and the World Economy*, London: Pinter.

Nam, C., Russ, H., and Herb, G. (1991) *The Effect of 1992 and Associated Legislation on the Less Favoured Regions of the Community,* Report to the European Parliament, Frankfurt: Institut für Wirtschaftsforschung.

Ohmae, K. (1989) 'Managing in a borderless world', *Harvard Business Review,* May–June, 152–61.

O'Malley, E., Kennedy, K., and O'Donnell, R. (1992) *The Impact of the Industrial Development Agencies,* Report of the Economic and Social Research Institute to the Industrial Policy Review Group, Dublin: ESRI.

Porter, M. (1990) *The Competitive Advantage of Nations,* New York: Free Press.

Regional Studies (1994) Special issue: Regional Variations in New Firm Formation, *Regional Studies* 28 (4).

Schoenberger, E. (1991) *U.S. Investments in the United Kingdom: Tendencies, Prospects and Strategies,* Report for the County Durham Development Company, Durham.

Stanworth, J., and Gray, C. (eds) (1992) *Bolton Twenty Years on,* London: Paul Chapman.

Storey, D. J. (1994) *Understanding the Small Business Sector,* London: Routledge.

Turok, I. (1993) 'Inward investment and local linkages: how deeply embedded is "Silicon Glen"?' *Regional Studies* 27 (5): 401–17.

United Nations (1993) *World Investment Report: Transnational Corporations and Integrated International Production,* New York: United Nations.

Young, S., Hood, N., and Peters, E. (1993) 'Multinational enterprises and regional economic development', *Regional Studies* 28 (7): 657–77.

ACKNOWLEDGEMENTS

This chapter summarizes a longer publication (Amin *et al.* 1994), written with other colleagues, Jeremy Howells, David Bradley and Chris Gentle. We wish to acknowledge their contribution to work that informs this chapter.

9

THE IMPACT OF POST-FORDIST CORPORATE RESTRUCTURING IN A PERIPHERAL REGION

The Mezzogiorno of Italy

Anna Giunta and Flavia Martinelli

Since the late 1970s Western economies have undergone profound industrial restructuring. This term indicates the plurality of changes that have occurred in the organization of contemporary industrial activity, related to both the domain of production (technology, products) and the larger organizational dimension (the structure of firms). It is now widely accepted that this restructuring is of major significance, touching the very foundations of the Western socio-economic system, and involving radical changes in some of its previously dominant features. According to many scholars, a whole 'model of accumulation' – 'Fordism' has come to an end and a new one – labelled 'post-Fordist' for lack of a better characterization is emerging, although its main features are not yet defined. The structural character of this transition is said to be reinforced by the concurrent establishment of a new technological 'paradigm' centred on new information technology.

In this general context, particularly relevant is the evolution of a specific organizational embodiment of the Fordist regime of accumulation: the large multilocational corporation. Such firms and their organizational patterns were severely affected by the crisis and, given their dominance, their restructuring patterns have consequences relevant to the entire industrial structure as well as its spatial division of labour.

The aim of this chapter is to assess the impact of large, Fordist firm restructuring on the economy of a peripheral region such as the Mezzogiorno of Italy. As in other less favoured regions, the industrialization of the Mezzogiorno in the 1960s and 1970s was heavily influenced by the growth strategies of such firms in the last wave of Fordist expansion, i.e. by the location in the region of exogenous 'branch plants'. It is therefore crucial to discuss the regional implications of branch plant restructuring. This chapter is an attempt to evaluate the extent to which the post-Fordist restructuring of large firms in a peripheral region such as the Mezzogiorno represents a rupture with the previous model of industrialization also in terms of consequences for the further development of the regional economy. The findings of the chapter are of direct relevance to questions concerning regional cohesion in the New Europe, since it is our assumption that the regional outcomes of contemporary corporate restructring follow from a mixture of company attempts to reposition in the New Europe as well as respond to new structural imperatives.

The chapter is in four sections. In the first we briefly outline the theoretical foundations of our approach. In the second we review the characteristics of 'late Fordist' industrialization of the Mezzogiorno and provide some aggregate evidence on the 'post-Fordist' crisis and its consequences. In the third section we present the main results of our detailed investigation of corporate responses among a selection of companies in the Mezzogiorno. In the final section we draw conclusions on the regional impact of restructuring and its implications for regional policy.

THEORETICAL FOUNDATIONS

The crisis of Fordism

At a macro-economic level we rely on the French 'regulation' school (see, among others, Aglietta 1976; Boyer 1986; Boyer and Durand 1993; de Bernis 1983; Jessop 1991; Lipietz 1979, 1989). From this approach we derive two major concepts underlying our work: the concept of Fordism as a particular 'regime of accumulation' with its specific 'regulation system', and the concept of structural crisis.

With regard to the first concept, we focus on Fordist firms, that is, large, multi-plant, often multinational corporations, which grew and asserted themselves as the dominant technological/organizational model of production during the Fordist regime of accumulation. They were generally characterized by the large scale of their operations, by monopolistic or oligopolistic dominance of markets in their respective sectors, by the predominance of Taylorist organization of production, by the manufacture of large volumes of fairly standardized output for mass consumer or large industrial markets, by a strong degree of vertical as well as horizontal integration and by a hierarchical organizational structure.

With regard to the second concept, we assume that the 1974–5 global recession was not a conjunctural crisis of adjustment but marked a major historical turning point, i.e. the structural crisis of the Fordist development model and the beginning of the search for a new order, at both operational and regulatory level.

The restructuring of large firms

In addressing the behaviour of Fordist firms we have adopted a dynamic and interactive analytical framework (adapted from Scherer and Ross 1991; cf. also Balloni and Bianchi 1990) as illustrated in Figure 9.1. From the micro-economic point of view, the behaviour of large firms in the 1980s is considered a response to the crisis in the established conditions of accumulation and regulation. Among these, we attach particular importance to two aspects: the demand side of the crisis, i.e. the stagnation and uncertainty characterizing outlet markets; and the rupture in the established rules of international competition due to the emergence of new – Japanese and European – industrial leaders to challenge US dominance. With regard to the latter aspect, the completion of the single European market is of particular relevance to an understanding of large firm restructuring in Europe.

A first major consequence of the breakdown of the Fordist order was the resurgence of oligopolistic rivalry. While, during the Fordist period of expansion, the growth of markets had favoured collusive behaviour within the oligopolistic sector dominated by US multinationals, the crisis provoked the rise of aggressive strategies as well as new types of alliances, to control

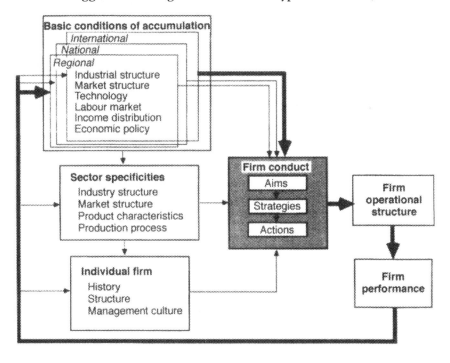

Figure 9.1 Behaviour of large firms: an analytical model

223

market shares. A second and related consequence was the crisis of the Fordist organizational model, i.e. of the rather static, rigid and hierarchical structure of large firms. In order to cope with the increased competition and volatility of markets, Fordist firms were forced to revise their organizational structure and search for more flexible techno-organizational solutions.

Another important assumption in our approach to the behaviour of large firms concerns their oligopolistic nature. In line with one tradition within the theory of multinational corporations (Hymer 1976; Lall 1976, 1980; Jacquemin 1989; Sembenelli 1990; Acocella 1989, 1992), we assume that Fordist firms not only seek to minimize costs but act strategically, i.e. they actively seek to affect the behaviour of other economic agents. More precisely, their behaviour is strongly orientated towards increasing their market power – i.e. their monopolistic position – even on a temporary basis, through the establishment and exploitation of various barriers to entry and competition. That said, the conduct of firms (cf. Figure 9.1) is defined by objectives, strategies and actions (Roth *et al.* 1989). In analysing restructuring during the 1980s we have identified three main corporate objectives: efficiency; market power; flexibility.

The objective of greater *efficiency* – where firms attempt to reduce their costs and/or increase their productivity – is typical of the traditional pattern of competition based on prices, pursued through several strategies: new technology (increased automation and informatization); reorganization of production and management; changes in the transaction structure (degree of vertical integration); further exploitation of economies of scale; search for cheaper inputs; and rationalization of corporate structure (acquisition or disposal of given product lines).

The objective of achieving greater *market power* – whereby firms seek to establish monopoly advantages and other barriers to competition, even on a temporary basis – features a non-price form of competition and includes strategies such as accelerated innovation and/or diversification of products in order to gain monopoly advantages in particular market segments; enlargement of market share through the acquisition of, or merger with, rival firms; and the establishment or exploitation of other deterrents to entry in particular markets.

The objective of *flexibility* is largely coincident with, and partly a consequence of, the preceding two objectives but is worth treating separately, since it represents a major rupture with the previous Fordist organizational model. Heightened competition within uncertain and volatile markets, as well as the accelerated rate of innovation and diversification of products, requires a greater capacity to both induce and respond to changes in demand. Strategies and actions in pursuit of this objective include: changes in the rigid and hierarchical organizational structure towards a more interactive operational system; the introduction of 'flexible' automation; the reorganization of production in terms of 'just in time'; the externalization of particular production phases to independent subcontractors; the introduction of new labour–management relations. All are attempts to increase flexibility in the use of machinery, in the use of labour and in the organization of the production process.

The above picture portrays a wide spectrum of actions. Oligopolistic firms have been, and still are, attempting to pursue multiple strategies, in search of a new organizational and regulatory model. Although some elements that are genuinely constitutive of a new regime have been introduced, several aspects of continuity with Fordism still remain. We shall argue that no definite post-Fordist order has yet emerged from the 1980s restructuring.

The regional impact of large firm investment

Having clarified our conceptualization of large firm conduct during the post-Fordist transition, we turn to the central theme of this chapter, namely what corporate restructuring may mean for branch plants located in peripheral or less favoured regions[1] and the impact of restructuring on host regions. The main question is whether the restructuring process represents a rupture with the Fordist model of peripheral industrialization and whether it is likely to introduce new regional developmental effects.

We have structured our assessment of the regional impact of inward investment under three main headings: *direct employment creation*; the generation and diffusion of know-how and entrepreneurship through the establishment of *local linkages*; changes in the *competitive position* of regions.

In evaluating the Fordist model of investment in peripheral regions we rely on several strands of theory – the 'regulation' approach to 'late' and 'peripheral' Fordism (Lipietz 1986a, b); the theory of the multinational firm and foreign direct investment[2] (Buckley and Casson 1976; Caves 1982; Rugman 1981; Williamson 1985; Hymer 1976; Lall 1976, 1980; Jacquemin 1987; Balloni and Bianchi 1990; Mariotti 1990; Dunning 1981; Schoenberger 1990); the New International Division of Labour theory (cf. Schoenberger 1988 for a critical review); and the rich body of studies on branch plant industrialization in peripheral regions (cf., among others, Hymer 1972; Firn 1975; Townroe 1975; Dicken 1976; McDermott, 1976; Lall 1978; Hoare 1978; Thwaites 1978; McAleese and McDonald 1978; Marshall 1979; Britton 1980; O'Farrell 1980; Martinelli 1985, 1989). All these approaches analyse the increase in investment activity by large firms during the last Fordist expansion of the 1960s and early 1970s in regions quite distant from the home base, both in advanced countries and in less developed ones.

During these years many less developed regions received investment as the outcome of either the multi-regional expansion or the relocation of large firm operations. In explaining such investment the literature stresses the significance of a search for cheaper inputs (especially labour), the penetration of new markets and the establishment of monopoly advantages as the main objectives of firms, within a strategy of strong vertical as well as horizontal integration. There is also wide agreement that the developmental impact of these operations in host regions was poor, precisely because of their Fordist characteristics.

As regards direct employment creation, although levels clearly depended on the capital intensity of processes, this was the only straightforward positive effect of branch plants investment in peripheral regions, at least in quantitative terms. On the other hand, it is also widely aknowledged that the jobs created were generally low-skilled and limited to direct production tasks because of the production-only mission of plants, the pre-set Taylorist nature of processes and the mature and standardized types of products manufactured, all of which required limited managerial and technical personnel at the plant level.

As regards the generation of local linkages, this is perhaps the most important expected regional effect of industrial investment, but one, at the same time, least fulfilled by branch plants. The classic theory of 'growth poles' postulates that the establishment of large manufacturing operations, especially in sectors with high inter-industrial and inter-firm linkage potential, should, in time, generate supply relationships within the regional economy, thereby helping the birth and/or consolidation of local firms as well as the diffusion of know-how and entrepreneurship ('trickle-down' and 'spill-over' effects).

The theory, however, was based on a purely 'technological' view of linkages, and was in need of a more institutional approach if it was to understand the failure of the model (Hirschman 1987). Because of the strong horizontal and vertical integration of Fordist operations (both at establishment and at corporate levels), the multiplier effects of such branch plants within the host regions were, in fact, inherently low. Most such operations worked as pure enclaves, with strong ties with the parent company for intermediate goods and services. Even when linkages were established with local suppliers, owing to the mature nature of products and processes they were generally confined to low-tech production phases. Overall, thus, very little know-how, entrepreneurship and innovation was diffused through local linkages.

As regards the third effect, our concept of competitive position draws upon Porter's (1990) approach to international competitiveness, i.e. the sustained capacity of a region to participate in the dominant markets, in an independent and creative way. A region is lastingly successful when it controls the most strategic, specialized and/or innovative segments of a global value chain.[3] We will argue that although Fordist industrialization did significantly improve the position of peripheral regions by integrating them into the dominant manufacturing system and by raising their level of industrial employment and productivity, such regions were confined to operating in the least advanced segments of the value chain. Most important, their integration had strong HQ-dependence features, in terms of material, services and decision-making inputs. The absence of strategic functions and of advanced, innovative activities in particular severely undermined the ability of branch plants to keep ahead of changes and sustain competitive advantage in the long run.

The extent to which post-Fordist restructuring has broken with the above model is not clear-cut. A number of the strategies and actions outlined earlier – e.g. the introduction of the 'just-in-time' organizational philosophy, the greater innovation and differentiation of products, rigid corporate organization, allowing greater autonomy and complexity at the plant level – would seem to imply greater 'embeddedness' of firms in host regions and hence better developmental effects. Other strategies and actions, however – e.g. the rationalization and reallocation of capacity among corporate units, the search for scale and scope economies – appear more ambiguous in their effects, since they can penalize peripheral regions in favour of more central locations. As we shall see in greater detail below, large firm restructuring has severely affected the Mezzogiorno in terms of plant closures while, among plants which have been kept open and restructured, the developmental role has not significantly improved by comparison with the Fordist model.

EMPIRICAL BACKGROUND: THE INDUSTRIALIZATION OF THE MEZZOGIORNO

Branch plant industrialization in the 1960s and 1970s

Like many other European rural regions, during the period of 'Fordist' expansion[4] and active regional policy support for inward investment in the 1960s and early 1970s, the Mezzogiorno witnessed a significant increase in industrial investment, led by large national and foreign firms. Several studies of the economic transformation of the region after World War II (Graziani 1977; Amendola and Baratta 1978; Del Monte and Giannola 1978; Graziani and Pugliese 1979; Dunford 1986), together with more detailed analyses of its industrial structure based on the CRS data bank[5] (Mercurio 1974; Mele 1975; Testa 1976; Cercola 1977; De Vita, 1978; Cercola 1984; Martinelli 1985; Testa 1981), have shown that 'exogenous' investments in this period constituted the cornerstone of the Mezzogiorno's industrial development, and modernization. On the other hand, many of the studies also stressed that such an exogenous model of industrialization had typically failed to generate a process of self-sustained development, replacing it with a strongly 'dependent' form of integration into the national and international market, in line with observations in other peripheral regions.

Direct employment creation was indeed significant in quantitative terms: by the end of the 1970s exogenous firms – including foreign multinationals, large northern private industrial groups and state-controlled companies – accounted for as much as 60 per cent of regional manufacturing employment in firms with ten employees or more[6] (Martinelli 1985). On the other hand, the jobs created were mostly in low-skilled manual occupations, owing to the 'mature' manufacturing mission of branch plants and the absence of strategic corporate functions.

With regard to the creation of local linkages and know-how diffusion the role of Fordist branch plants in the Mezzogiorno also proved to be poor. Although some local linkages did develop over time (Giannola 1987a, 1987b; Del Monte and Vittoria 1989; Del Monte and De Lutzenberger 1989), they displayed little intrinsic propensity for regional growth and innovation (Varaldo 1979; Del Monte and Martinelli 1988; Martinelli 1989). Linkages established at the local level were in the most elementary, low-skilled, and labour-intensive phases of the production process, whereas for more sophisticated inputs exogenous plants relied upon either suppliers in other regions or associate plants. In fact, linkages among branch plants themselves (often branches of the same company) were strong, further preventing the establishment of relationships with local subcontractors. Moreover, most local firms remained 'captive' suppliers, i.e. strongly dependent on the demand of a few large client firms, showing little capacity to develop their own products, diversify their market and export to non-southern markets (Martinelli 1989).

As regards the competitive position of the Mezzogiorno in the national and international division of labour, Fordist investment significantly contributed to the growth, diversification and modernization of the regional industrial base.[7] However, the accelerated industrial growth experienced in these years was not sufficient to close the gap between the south and the rest of the country, and the integration of the Mezzogiorno into the national and international economy remained dependent in character, both at the macro- and at the micro-economic level (Giannola 1987; Martinelli 1989), thereby undermining the possibility of sustaining an independent competitive position.

No doubt, in assessing the developmental effects of Fordist investment, time must be taken into consideration. Over the fifteen years of 'late Fordist' industrializaton of the Mezzogiorno, branch plants did initiate a process of local growth and integration, however limited and biased. It remains a matter of speculation whether the process would have continued and allowed firms to strengthen their position in the industrial system, since the crisis of the mid-1970s brought this pattern of industrialization to an abrupt halt.

Aggregate change in the 1980s

The 1974–5 economic downturn had a dramatic impact on the Mezzo-giorno. In the second half of the decade investment fell abruptly and a period of stagnation and uncertainty began, both at the institutional and at the economic level. Trends in the 1980s must be analysed in the light of two related processes: the crisis and change in regional development policy; and the crisis and restructuring of large Fordist groups.

As to the first aspect, the whole regulatory framework and the role of the state itself were severely affected by the economic crisis. In a context of strong recession and institutional uncertainty, the active policy of encouraging industrialization was gradually replaced by scattered income-support expenditure. The share of 'supply-side' expenditures, geared to the creation of a regional industrial base (such as direct investment by state-controlled corporations and capital subsidies to private investment) fell in favour of 'demand-side' transfers, i.e. resources geared to sustain the income of households and firms (such as wage subsidies, unemployment benefit, pensions).[8] Nationwide, but particularly in the south, the maintenance of employment was ensured by state subsidies (the Cassa Integrazione Guadagni).

At the same time, the entire policy framework for the development of the Mezzogiorno was progressively dismantled (ending with the closure of the Cassa per il Mezzogiorno in 1984), with a view to establishing a new comprehensive and more articulated programme. The new legislation, however, was enacted only in 1986 (law 64/86) and, although it grasped the changed nature of industrialization processes, it only belatedly contributed to support restructuring programmes.

Finally, state-owned companies, which had been the major leaders of southern industrialization, especially in the heavy industries, under the political pressures of the moment, changed their role from that of active investors to that of employment protectors and 'rescuers' of private-sector ventures in difficulty.[9]

The crisis of the Fordist model of industrialization and its aggregate effects on the process of accumulation in the Mezzogiorno are documented elsewhere (cf. Giunta 1994). The average annual growth rate of total industrial investment in the region was negative from 1974 to 1984, with a slight recovery only in the latter 1980s (+ 1.6 per cent), while in the rest of the country it remained negative only during the 1981–3 recession and subsequently rose to 4.5 per cent beween 1984 and 1989. In fact the contribution of the Mezzogiorno to total national industrial investment fell from a historic maximum of 37 per cent in the 1970–3 period to an average of 23 per cent in the 1980s. The result of this decline in investment was a significant slow-down in the process of capital accumulation: the ratio of investment to gross regional product in the Mezzogiorno progressively decreased from 33 per cent in 1973 to 24 per cent in 1989.[10]

As regards employment, official statistics from the 1991 census are still not available by size of unit and sector. Provisional data show that in aggregate terms the industrial sector of the Mezzogiorno (including construction and mining) lost as many as 24,300 plants and 110,500 employees (13 per cent and 9 per cent respectively of the regional population) between 1981 and 1991. Negative trends in industrial employment were recorded also in north central regions (− 10 per cent), but here the decrease was coupled with a significant increase in productivity and a shift from manufacturing to service activities.

A more precise assessment of the role of large exogenous firms in the deindustrialization of the south during the 1980s can be derived from the CRS data bank (cf. Giunta 1994). According to this source, the manufacturing sector in the Mezzogiorno (excluding firms with fewer than ten employees) recorded an aggregate employment decrease of 18 per cent (Table 9.1). The highest portion of this loss was among exogenous establishments: they lost 98,400 jobs, i.e. 25 per cent of their 1981 workforce and as much as 78 per cent of the total regional loss. Firms of local origin instead lost 28,000 employees, i.e. 10 per cent of their own 1981 workforce and 22 per cent of the total regional loss.[11] Also relevant is the fact that the highest decrease is found in the largest establishment size class (500 or more employees). Here exogenous firms lost 87,700 jobs, i.e. 35 per cent of the 1981 work force in the same class and as much as 69 per cent of total manufacturing employment loss in the Mezzogiorno.

The crisis of Fordist branch plants is also reflected in the sectoral composition of employment loss. The highest decreases were recorded by the heavy industries (steel, petroleum refining and chemicals), which lost 33 per cent of their 1981 jobs. The toll was also high in the electromechanical industries − electronics, electromechanical equipment, machinery (− 20 per cent), while the motor industry showed a marginally better performance (− 4 per cent). Also dramatic was the crisis of the traditional sectors: industries such as textiles, clothing, leather and· footwear and furniture and fixtures recorded an average decrease of 20 per cent.

The above figures clearly support the hypothesis that a substantial change in the role of exogenous 'Fordist' plants in the Mezzogiorno has taken place. While in the 1960s and early 1970s their expansion had accounted for the majority of manufacturing employment and value-added growth[12] as well as for the sectoral diversification and modernization of the regional industrial base, during the 1980s their restructuring represented a disproportionately high share of total employment loss.

Part of these losses is explained by closures and part by the restructuring process, which yielded significant reductions in employment. It is not possible to separate precisely the 'closure effect' from the 'restructuring

Table 9.1. Employment change in plants of firms with ten or more employees operating in the Mezzogiorno, by size and ownership, 1981–91 (%)

size classes by No. of employees	Ownership Southern	Extra-regional North Italy	State-owned	Foreign	Total	Grand total
Under 20	6·74	17·36	1·51	68·30	20·10	*7·24*
20–49	− 2·44	3·60	30·52	41·60	11·29	− *0·78*
50–99	− 21·94	− 10·46	− 10·80	14·48	− 7·07	− *17·73*
Total	− 4·93	− 3·31	1·58	25·22	1·06	− 4·03
100–199	− 19·13	− 16·08	− 10·75	8·40	− 10·81	− *14·75*
200–299	− 21·72	3·43	− 20·59	57·27	4·84	− *3·58*
300–499	− 23·33	− 34·52	− 31·27	27·69	− 18·80	− *19·71*
Total	− 20·41	− 17·49	− 23·10	27·30	− 10·18	− 13·79
500–999	− 60·32	− 57·20	− 11·57	− 18·24	− 32·57	− *34·63*
1,000–4,999	− 31·78	− 43·48	− 11·12	− 35·99	− 28·42	− *28·60*
Over 5,000	–	49·64	− 72·73	–	− 48·54	− *48·54*
Total	− 46·14	− 36·10	− 36·00	− 27·26	− 36·20	− 35·24
Total	− 10·21	− 25·10	− 32·17	− 5·61	− 24·75	− 18·80

Source: CRS Data Bank.

Note: It must be stressed that changes in the number of employees within each ownership group are also due to changes in ownership through acquisitions. In particular, the remarkable growth of northern firm employment in the over 500 size class is due to the acquisition by Fiat of the Alfa Sud plant rather than to absolute employment growth. In the same way, the better employment performance of the Foreign group is due to several acquisitions of both public and northern Italian firms.

effect', but a few indications can be derived from data on the evolution of large plants (500 employees or more) in the south as of 1981 (Giunta 1994).[13] Of these 194 plants, as many as seventy-five (39 per cent of the total) closed down altogether in the course of the 1980s, and five (3 per cent) moved into a smaller size class. Of those which were still operating in the Mezzogiorno in 1991, sixty-three (33 per cent) had not changed either size class or ownership, whereas forty-nine (25 per cent) had changed ownership or merged. Eight plants (4 per cent) had entered the 500 or more employees size class from a lower one, and three entirely new plants in this size class had appeared.

In conclusion, throughout the 1980s the southern manufacturing base and its capacity to generate income were severely affected, while the dependent features of the regional economy assumed pathological dimensions. The accompanying industrial restructuring radically reversed trends observed in previous decades. Both the modern and heavy industries reduced the workforce and were unable to offset the employment crisis of local traditional industries. While in the 1970s, and especially in the first half of the decade, investments by exogenous firms had directly and indirectly spurred some growth of small and medium-size local firms, the negative performance of large branch plants in the 1980s affected smaller ventures in a similar direction.

THE RESTRUCTURING OF BRANCH PLANTS: A CASE STUDY

In order to assess the regional implications of branch plant restructuring in the Mezzogiorno, especially in terms of competitiveness and local linkage effects, more qualitative insights are needed. In this section we present some findings gathered in the course of an in-depth survey of selected branch plants carried out in 1991.

The sample consists of ten large establishments, randomly selected among the population of non-southern manufacturing plants operating in the Mezzogiorno since 1977 with more than 500 employees. Ownership and sectoral characteristics are described in Table 9.2. The sample is certainly not representative of the whole branch plant structure of the Mezzogiorno. But in the specific industries and size class we have chosen, our sample covers 40 per cent to 100 per cent of the population, so the findings can be considered representative of actual sectoral trends in the region.

In line with the aim of the research, the industries selected were characterized by the presence of typically 'Fordist' firms and operations. In addition to household appliances (washing machines), food processing (canned and frozen food) and clothing, which perfectly fitted this requirement, we also included two more innovative sectors, electronics and telecommunications equipment, which, none the less, produce large volumes of fairly standardized output, both for mass consumer markets (telephones, office equipment) and for the industrial market (switchgear).

The methodology adopted was that of a case study based on qualitative, rather than quantitative information. Information was gathered through lengthy interviews with managers of the plant (and in some cases of the parent company) as well as union representatives. The focus of the interviews was on the patterns of restructuring undertaken by firms between 1977 and 1991, with particular regard to their southern facilities.[14]

Before discussing the detailed results, it is worth stressing that our survey provides mixed evidence. Although a number of strong common restructuring patterns do emerge – e.g. innovation of products, flexible automation, adoption of 'just-in-time' organization – a marked differentiation of behaviour and strategies remains, explained by sector specificities as well as the individual history, structure and culture of firms.[15] Moreover, and in line with the hypothesis advanced earlier, most firms implemented several

Table 9.2 Manufacturing plants in the Mezzogiorno: structure of the sample and relative population

Industry	No. of plants with over 500 employees in		No. of plants interviewed in 1991	% of relevant population	Ownership			
	1977	1991			Northern private	State-owned	Foreign multinational	
Household appliance	2	2	2	100	1	–	1	
(Code name)					(HP)		(HM)	
Electronics	8	5	2	40	1	–	1	
(Code name)					(EP)		(EM)	
Telecommunications	5	4	3	75	–	1	2	
(Code name)						(TS)	(TM1; TM2)	
Food processing	5	4	2	50	–	1	1	
(Code name)						(FS)	(FM)	
Clothing	5	2	1	50	–	–	1	
(Code name)							(CM)	

Source: CRS Data Bank.

concurrent restructuring strategies, which confirms the 'structural' nature of the process as well as the need to face the crisis on a number of fronts.[16]

The analysis of the survey results below is grouped under five areas of restructuring: corporate reorganization; products; processes; employment; and vertical integration.

Corporate reorganization

With regard to strategies concerning the reorganization of the corporate structure, there is widespread evidence of a major 'reshuffling' of the oligopolistic sector throughout the 1980s. We shall deal here with two major aspects: ownership changes linked with corporate-wide industrial concentration and rationalization strategies; and changes in the operational structure of the firm – i.e. the reallocation of production capacity, product 'missions', and corporate functions between the different territorial units.

Ownership changes

As is well known, throughout the 1980s markets in Europe experienced a new wave of concentration, characterized by an intensification of acquisitions and mergers (see Chapter 7 by Ramsay). To these trends must be added the less documented, but significant, growth of inter-firm agreements in particular areas. Both trends were relevant in all the sectors we examined. On one hand, such strategies are related to the crisis of output markets and the heightened rivalry in the oligopolistic sector; on the other, they also respond to the challenges posed by the unification of the European market and the need for European firms to strengthen their position *vis-à-vis* foreign multinationals. As confirmed by our survey, they pursued two objectives simultaneously: increasing the market power of firms, through the enlargement of market shares, and increasing efficiency, through the dismissal of 'peripheral' or less productive ventures and the exploitation of economies of scale and scope in the 'core' business.

In our sample, eight out of ten firms experienced corporate-wide 'reshuffling', involving either acquisitions/sell-offs, mergers, joint ventures or alliances.[17] In seven cases 'reshuffling' affected in a direct way establishments operating in the Mezzogiorno: four plants changed ownership altogether, i.e. were acquired by another firm, two were involved in joint ventures or strategic alliances with a foreign multinational, and one was involved in the merger of two national firms.

Rationalization of operations

Largely but not exclusively linked with ownership 'reshuffling', was reorganization of the corporate operational structure, i.e. reallocation of pro-

234

duction capacity and/or product 'missions' among the different territorial units of the firm. This process implied 'disinvestment' in some plants (closure, lay-offs) and the concentration/expansion of production capacity in others.

Our survey confirms that the main objective of such rationalization was to increase efficiency by achieving 'technical' economies of scale at the plant level. In this regard it is important to stress that in seven out of the ten establishments (mostly foreign ones) the reorganization of the corporate structure involved a significant increase in the production capacity of the southern facilities. In five of the cases the expansion of southern capacity was even at the expense of 'northern' plants,[18] where the parent firm closed and/or transferred particular product lines or the whole establishment altogether. In all cases, among the reasons given for privileging the Mezzogiorno were the lower cost of labour and/or the higher cost of lay-offs in the region, compared with elsewhere.[19]

Another important aspect of the rationalization process was greater production specialization within plants: although product lines are now more 'diversified' (i.e. more 'models' or versions of the same product are manufactured), the mission of establishments has been 'refocused' on fewer product lines or phases. In six out of ten cases the reorganization of corporate operations has meant a change in the previous production mission of the plant and/or greater specialization, although only in five cases did this imply a significant 'upgrading' of the plant's productive role within the corporate division of labour. The main reason given for this greater product specialization was the need fully to exploit investment in new technology.

Reallocation of corporate functions

Within the 'reshuffling' process, we also paid attention to the territorial allocation/reallocation of corporate functions. 1980s restructuring does not seem to have changed in any significant way the 'operational' mission firms gave their southern plants. Advanced R&D laboratories, marketing and all strategic management and planning functions remain safely at the central firm's headquarters or northern plants. Such a typically Fordist corporate division of labour has actually been sustained by the development of new information technology and the creation of intra-corporate telecommunications networks.[20]

A slight change for the better can, none the less, be observed for a limited number of functions closely related to the production process, such as design, engineering, production planning. In fact changes in the organization and technology of production have increased the need for a direct relationship between some of these functions and production itself. In five cases this has involved the upgrading/establishment of some research and product development activities in the south, either in the plant or in its surroundings. It is worth stressing that such moves are partly related to the enactment of the new legislation (in 1986) on the development of the Mezzogiorno, which provided subsidies for investment in R&D.

Overall, the reorganization of corporate structures has had mixed effects. Among the positive ones we can recall that in more than half our cases, once the firm had decided to maintain its southern facility the decision involved an increase in production capacity, i.e. a strenghtening of its role in the corporate division of labour. Also positive is the upgrading/reinforcement of some product development and engineering functions in the region. On the other hand, no major change appears in the production-only role assigned to peripheral branch plants, i.e. the absence of the most strategic R&D, management, planning and marketing functions, which remain located in the more central regions.

Product innovation and differentiation

All ten firms in our sample have implemented an active strategy of product innovation, upgrading and/or differentiation. This is the only thoroughly consistent strategy observed sample-wide. As already mentioned, such a strategy was made imperative by the crisis of demand and by renewed rivalry within the oligopolistic sector over shrinking market shares. Through accelerated innovation of products, upgrading of quality and increased differentiation of product models, firms attempted to restore or increase their market power at the expense of rivals, seeking to establish even temporary monopoly advantages in particular market segments. Such a need to be 'ahead' of the market, through constant changes in products, seems to have become a permanent feature of large oligopolistic firms.[21] As such it represents a major rupture with the Fordist organizational model, which was based on the mass production of a few highly standardized products.

Product strategies vary considerably between sectors. In the most mature industries (household appliances, food processing, clothing) product innovation has been more superficial: the basic structure of the product has not changed, while the quality and/or design content, as well as differentiation of models, has been significantly increased.

An interesting example is the case of the foreign multinational clothing plant. While other large firms in this sector have closed their facilities down (shifting production to less developed countries or decentralizing it to small subcontractors in the north), this firm has radically changed its product/market philosophy. In contrast to its previous Fordist approach (few, highly standardized models for an undifferentiated international market), it has now adopted a highly differentiated product portfolio, with a high design content that is continually reviewed. To achieve this outcome, it signed an agreement with a famous French fashion house, which provides the design and the label under which its products are marketed. Such a strategy has allowed the firm not only to survive the sectoral crisis but even to expand its market share. The most interesting aspect is that this product/market strategy is the only major change implemented by the firm. In other areas, including production processes, the firm exhibits an amazing degree of continuity with its pre-1980s organizational, operational and technological model.

In the two more innovative sectors – electronics and telecommunications – product strategies are, as expected, more radical in character. The accelerated pace of innovation in basic electronic technology necessarily involves a fast rate of product development. Throughout the 1980s both our electronics firms displayed continued evolution of products. But the most dramatic effects concern the telecommunications sector. All three firms in our sample had to engineer in this decade the transition from electromechanical to electronic product technology. As a consequence, in all plants whole product lines were closed down, while entirely new phases and products were introduced: assembly of electronic boards, electronic calculators, fax terminals, digital telephones, electronic switching equipment. In some of these phases (particularly the assembly of electronic boards) and products (fax machines, telephones, desk calculators orientated to the consumer market) innovation in products was also coupled with a significant increase in the differentiation of models. In the assembly of electronic components on printed circuit boards product differentiation is high, since plants also produce on a 'customized' basis for associate plants or large independent customers.

In terms of product strategies, it would seem that southern plants have been party to the general trends in their sectors, moving away from their former Fordist specialization in mature, standardized products. It remains to be seen, however, whether such changes have brought southern branch plants to the same level as their northern counterparts. In five out of our ten cases products manufactured in the south exhibit the same level of innovation, the same technology, quality and/or design content, as well as the same degree of product differentiation, as their northern counterparts. In the other half of the sample, however, although the standard of some products is now similar to that of more central plants, a significant proportion of output consists of the less advanced product lines/phases within the parent firm's portfolio.

Production and management processes

With regard to management and production processes, there is ample evidence that 1980s restructuring was characterized by heavy investment in new fixed capital, i.e. the replacement of old production equipment, and a significant increase in the level of automation. It is also widely known that such investments were coupled with the adoption of new information technology, Japanese just in time supply and, in more general terms, a more flexible organizational philosophy.

In restructuring along the above lines, large firms have pursued multiple objectives. In the first place they have sought to reduce costs through a general increase in productivity. Automation, for example, has permitted an increase in labour productivity, as well as a reduction in the percentage of defective products, while the adoption of 'just in time' has helped to reduce the cost of stocks. Second, firms have sought to become more flexible. It has been argued (Sembenelli 1990) that flexible automation has allowed large firms to bypass the traditional trade-off between automation and flexibility within the Fordist organizational model, thereby permitting a further exploitation of economies of scale and scope. Finally, the increased flexibility of processes has improved the capacity of firms to exert market power through the continued innovation and diversification of their product portfolio.

Below we examine three major and interrelated aspects of the recent restructuring of processes: automation; the introduction of flexible organizational principles; the role of scale economies.

Automation

Restructuring has involved a significant substitution of existing capital equipment and a further increase in the capital intensity of processes, with, among other things, a remarkable displacement of direct labour. But this new wave of industrial automation has been radically different from that in previous rounds.

Up to the 1970s automation was synonymous with 'mechanization', i.e. with the dominant technological trajectory set by the Fordist model. Automation meant the segmentation of the production process into elementary phases, repetitively performed with the help of highly dedicated machinery, and organized in a rigid sequence (Taylorism). In contrast, the automation of the 1980s, in addition to the traditional aim of increasing the productivity of labour, was also geared to acquire flexibility. This implied, among other things, the necessity to have more 'versatile' machinery (i.e. able to handle several operations or perform the same operation with varying components) as well as more flexible processes (permitting the various phases of production to be integrated in different ways). The association of mechanization technology with the fast developing new information technology 'paradigm' enabled these two objectives to be combined in what is generally called 'flexible automation'.[22]

As regards the rapid diffusion of flexible automation throughout the 1980s – ranging from the individual computer-controlled work station to fully integrated 'flexible manufacturing systems' – there is ample evidence of this diffusion and, in this respect, our sample confirms the general trend. With one notable exception (the clothing firm), all the firms have in the last decade significantly invested in new machinery (in some cases achieving the complete replacement of previous production equipment). In all nine plants such restructuring involved a remarkable increase in capital intensity and the displacement of a large proportion of the production work force. More important, all the plants consistently introduced important elements of 'flexible automation'. Allowing for slight differences related to sectoral and corporate specificities, in all the plants the old Fordist assembly line has been partially or totally superseded by programmable work stations, which though still in sequence, can be organized in more flexible ways.

This change was most striking in the household appliance example, where the previous long and rigid sequence of operations has been replaced by much shorter lines of flexible work stations. Equally radical has been the reorganization of processes in the electronics and telecommunication firms. Here whole component fabrication phases have been eliminated (in favour of bought-integrated components) and entire assembly lines have been replaced by completely automated work stations. In all three sectors quality control and testing procedures have also been almost completely automated. The introduction of automation has been less relevant in the food-processing sector, which was already highly mechanized. Here technological change in the 1980s mostly concerned the computer integration of phases and food conservation techniques. Within the sectors, six out of nine plants also introduced (or were about to introduce) elements of computer integration within production itself and/or between production and management (design, inventories).

In contrast with the above general trend, however, a number of assembly phases have remained manual. This is the case with the final assembly of telephones, fax terminals and desktop calculators, as well as quality control in the food-processing sector. The explicit reason given for this choice was that human involvement in many instances allows greater flexibility than any sophisticated work station.

The case of the clothing firm represents the one exception which confirms the rule. In contrast with all other cases, no investment was made by this firm in production technology. Manufacturing is carried on with the same equipment as twenty years ago. The versatility of both machines and labour allowed 'flexibilization' of the old assembly line, without actually necessitating a change in the material technology.[23]

Finally, it is worth stressing that all nine firms that invested in new equipment did use regional financial incentives.

Flexibility

We have defined flexibility as the capacity of firms to adjust rapidly to (or engineer) changes in demand, without significantly raising their costs. There is a larger dimension to flexibility, however, which exceeds the technological level and involves changes at the very heart of corporate organization, i.e. in the whole information and transaction structure.

The flexible organizational paradigm seemed incompatible with the large hierarchical structures of Fordist firms, and at the end of the 1980s a lively debate developed over this issue. Some scholars supported the view that the new imperatives of post-Fordist accumulation would favour more agile industrial structures such as small-firm 'industrial districts' or, in general, 'networks of firms', while the rigid, hierarchical structure of Fordist firms was bound to end its dominance (Sabel and Piore 1984; Scott 1988; Scott and Storper 1989). More recently, however, other scholars have stressed that large firms not only can and do introduce significant elements of flexibility in their organizational structure but also utilize their size and level of organization as a source of the capital and human resources required by such a transformation (Amin and Robins 1990; Martinelli and Schoenberger 1991; Harrison 1994; Sembenelli 1990). Large firms are thus able to couple the advantages of flexibility with those of size. Our survey broadly confirms the latter hypothesis: a radical transformation in the rigid organization of Fordist firms is under way, although with some limitations and problems at plants in the Mezzogiorno.

A good part of the new organizational philosophy can be summarized by the label 'just-in-time'. In contrast with the Fordist 'just in case' approach, 'just in time' implies a need for close interaction between product development, production and sales. In a context of market uncertainty and rapid changes, production must keep up with demand, with firms reducing stocks of both intermediate and finished products to a minimum. In the 'pure' version (the Japanese model) this type of organization has an important corollary: a significant proportion of sub-assembly and component fabrication is delegated to reliable suppliers which are territorially contiguous in order to minimize transaction time and costs.

In our sample all the firms stressed that the introduction of 'just-in-time' has been a lead strategy in the restructuring process. However, from the evidence provided, the adoption of such a model in the Mezzogiorno remains, in our view, a statement of purpose rather than an achievement. In all plants production planning is now more sensitive to adjustments, stocks have been significantly reduced, and there is much closer integration between the product development, production and marketing functions. However, plants still operate on the basis of medium- to long-term production programmes,[24] and there remain significant limits to the reduction of inventories, especially in areas involving intermediate products. This is probably the greatest weakness of 'peripheral' 'just-in-time', at least in the Mezzogiorno. As will be stressed later, the majority of southern branch plant suppliers are located outside the region, and this implies the maintenance of stock 'buffers' (from two-week to two-month inventories). The occasional crisis of some of these long-distance transactions[25] has already proved to undermine the full application of 'just-in-time' philosophy.

Economies of scale

We have already mentioned that in applying the new technological-organizational paradigm economies of scale can play a significant role. Indeed, several studies (Camagni 1986; United Nations 1986; Cainarca *et al.* 1989; Gros-Pietro and Rolfo 1989) have shown that the adoption of flexible automation has remained largely confined to big firms. In addition to financial constraints there are also know-how barriers, which limit the introduction and full exploitation of flexible and integrated manufacturing technology smaller firms.[26]

In our survey several actions confirmed the cumulative impact of 'technical' economies of scale. The investment required to introduce flexible automation involves very large aggregate volumes of production and, indeed, the majority of plants significantly increased their output in those product lines or phases in which automation was introduced. The specialization of many plants in fewer product lines or phases, their absorption of production capacity previously located in the north, the introduction in a few instances of two and even three shifts, the increase in 'customized' production (e.g. in the assembly of electronic boards) for associate firms or other large clients, are all moves which point to the need to maximize production volumes and fully exploit capital investment.

In conclusion, at the level of the production process, patterns of restructuring seem to represent a substantial rupture with the Fordist model of branch plants. In the first place the rigid assembly line has been almost completely superseded by more flexible lines composed often of computer integrated work stations. Such changes have, among other things, significantly raised the level of productivity: according to managers, productivity levels within southern plants are no different from those within equivalent northern plants.[27] Second, elements of flexibility have been introduced in the organization of plants, in accordance with 'just-in-time' principles, with a closer relationship between the various phases of production and marketing. Southern plants are no longer just production outposts, but participate in a more active way in the information and planning system of the firm.

On the other hand, the application of 'just-in-time' in the south encounters limits related to the distance of the majority of suppliers. It is also debatable whether the 'new' assembly lines represent a true discontinuity with the Fordist ones, in terms of skills and job satisfaction. As will be stressed in the next section, manual skills have been traded for control ones: workers monitor the correct set-up of machines and components and then push buttons. In this respect we can speak of 'flexible Taylorism', rather than of a radical change in work practices.

Employment

The impact of restructuring on direct employment has been enormously important, both quantitatively and qualitatively. It is important to recall that seven out of ten firms in the sample maintained and even increased production capacity within their southern facilities (i.e. their ouput volumes). In addition, in all the plants there has been a significant increase in labour productivity.

Quantitative changes

In terms of employment levels, however, the plants have experienced severe cut-backs. Total employment in the ten cases examined amounted to 20,059 in 1977, dropping to only 11,331 in 1990, with a net aggregate loss of almost 9,000 jobs (− 43.5 per cent) (cf. Table 9.3). The highest losses were recorded by two plants involved in corporate-wide rationalization processes. The first case (− 78.5 per cent) belongs to a very mature sector – household appliances – and has suffered heavily from the collapse of the former parent company, acquisition by a rival national company and the ensuing rationalization.[28] The second case (− 54 per cent) is also in a mature sector – food processing – and owes its heavy employment reduction to the corporate-wide strategy of industrial concentration and rationalization of operations.[29] The only example of employment increase (+ 3.2 per cent) in the sample is an electronics multinational plant, which operates in a more innovative niche and has implemented a strategy of constant product upgrading and diversification.

The bulk of employment losses occurred, as expected, in direct production labour (cf. Table 9.3). About 8,000 of the total jobs lost involved production workers (− 52.3 per cent), with the level of decrease fairly consistent across the sample. With the exception of the two household appliance plants, the reduction in direct production workers in our sample ranged from 30 per cent to 50 per cent.

The reductions in the manual work force have been chiefly the result of automation, rather than disinvestment. Another cause of the decrease has been the intensification of work, where greater labour productivity has been achieved through the reorganization of the production process and the introduction of productivity incentives. Although its effects were more modest than those following from automation, this restructuring strategy

Table 9.3 Employment change and composition in ten large manufacturing establishments operating in the Mezzogiorno, 1977–90 (%)

Industries and plants	Household appliances		Telecommunications			Electronics		Food-processing		Clothing
	HP	HM	TS	TM1	TM2	EP	EM	FS	FM	CM
% change, 1977–90	(1982–89)		(1984–90)		(1981–91)					
Managerial, technical and clerical workers	−86·0	−20·0	17·3	3·8	−2·8	22·8	104·3	n.a.	24·6	22·3
Direct production workers	−77·6	−19·4	−49·7	−41·1	−31·2	−49·5	−37·4	n.a.	−33·4	−41·6
Total	−78·5	−19·5	−39·6	−19·7	−24·6	−38·2	3·2	−54·9	−23·7	−25·7
% composition in 1977	(1982)		(1984)		(1981)					
Managerial, technical and clerical workers	10·2	16·4	15·1	47·6	23·1	15·6	27·8	ca. 10·0	16·7	25·0
Direct production workers	89·8	83·6	84·9	52·4	76·9	84·4	72·8	ca. 90·0	83·3	75·0
Total	100·0	100·0	100·0	100·0	100·0	100·0	100·0	100·0	100·0	100·0
% composition in 1990	(1989)				(1991)					
Managerial, technical and clerical workers	6·6	16·3	29·3	61·5	29·9	31·1	55·0	ca. 30·0	27·2	41·1
Direct production workers	93·4	83·7	70·7	38·5	70·1	68·9	44·2	ca. 70·0	72·8	58·9
Total	100·0	100·0	100·0	100·0	100·0	100·0	100·0	100·0	100·0	100·0

Source: Survey conducted by the authors in 1991.

Note: The reference years are slightly different in the case of three plants, for lack of consistent information. This does not, however, invalidate our evaluation of trends, since if the appropriate years were available the decrease in employment would actually be higher.

also involved redundancies. Only one case of no automation in our sample (which was in the clothing sector) owes its decrease in direct production workers exclusively to intensification.

Finally, in the electronics and telecommunications industries, the transition from electro-mechanical to electronic product technology must also be mentioned. This has generally implied the replacement of in-house electro-mechanical fabrication processes by external purchases of electronic components, leading to a decrease in labour requirements.

It is difficult to make meaningful comparisons with plants in north central Italy, for lack of comparable data. However, the decreases in employment in southern plants appear to have been better than could be expected. In seven cases, in fact, the reduction of employment in the southern facility was less than in their northern counterparts. Three reasons account for this trend. In the first place, as already mentioned, most of the firms interviewed have maintained or increased their volume of output in the south,[30] and this has certainly compensated for losses resulting from automation. Second, a few firms have actually maintained or transferred to their southern plants more labour-intensive and technology-poor production phases, which, in the north, were either externalized or closed down. Finally, in five cases the corporate decision to maintain and restructure southern facilities implied the closure of some production capacity in the north.

The reasons articulated by firms for such a strategy lie in the allegedly greater rigidities of the southern labour market and the lower cost of southern labour. In the Mezzogiorno there are several economic and institutional disincentives to laying workers off (because of the high unemployment rate), whereas there still exist government employment subsidies (e.g. social security contributions). These institutional features certainly affected firms behaviour in the south. Firms could not freely reduce the labour force: they had the choice of either closing the plant down altogether or maintaining as much previous employment as possible. All our firms have, in fact, used 'soft' dismissal practices, such as incentives to early retirement or self-dismissal.

In summary, and with due caution, it can be argued that within firms which have decided to stay in the south the quantitative impact of restructuring in terms of total jobs displaced, although high, has been somewhat lower than in the north, because of the existence of a number of institutional peculiarities.

The structure of employment

In aggregate terms, a noticeable change in the structure of employment concerns the ratio of non-manual to manual employees, i.e. the weight of managerial, technical and clerical employees within the total work force of our sample. From constituting 17 per cent of the sample's total employment in 1977, this component has almost doubled, reaching 32 per cent in 1990. The increase is due mostly to the absolute decline in the number of manual workers. In fact the average growth in numbers of managerial, technical and clerical employees over the period was only 5 per cent. But this aggregate figure hides quite diverse patterns of behaviour (cf. Table 9.3). While reductions in direct labour proved fairly consistent across the sample, trends in indirect labour show a much greater variance: two firms recorded net losses, two firms maintained about the same level, one more than doubled it, while others recorded increases around 20 per cent.

These differences are explained by three main factors: the differentiated impact of the introduction of new information technology in the management structure of the plant; the different strategies implemented by parent firms concerning the presence of management and other strategic functions at the plant level; the impact of product and process innovations.

In three cases (the two household appliance plants and one telecommunications plant) the main reason for the decrease in indirect labour is explained by cuts in clerical employment which followed the introduction of new information technology in the management system of the plant and the rationalization of a redundant administrative apparatus. In half the sample, by contrast, there has been an absolute increase in the number of managerial and technical employees, as a consequence of the upgrading of some plant research and development functions and the introduction of more sophisticated product and process technology. These cases are, in fact, found in the telecommunications and electronic sectors, as well as in one of the household appliance plants. Here the imperatives of product diversification and innovation have implied greater need at the plant level for design and engineering functions as well as production programming functions. In four of these plants the establishment or the upgrading of in-house applied R&D laboratories involved a significant increase in the recruitment of graduate personnel. In the clothing example, instead, the product-centred strategy has meant an increase in the sales force. The three plants experiencing the least change belong to the mature sectors: household appliances and food processing.

In terms of the skill profile, thus, there definitely appears to have been an upward shift. In seven out of ten plants the majority of the new personnel hired in the 1980s were younger, better trained and educated people, with a large proportion of managerial and technical graduates. It is also worth noting that most of the new skilled personnel were hired in the local labour market.

With regard to direct labour, here too there seems to have been some upgrading. The majority of firms declared they had actively sought to increase the qualifications of production workers, through internal training programmes. In the opinion of most managers, the introduction of new automated machinery, often electronically controlled, has required a broader and more interactive understanding of the production process as a whole than was the case with traditional assembly lines.

Thus the negative quantitative impact of branch plant restructuring appears to be compensated by a shift in the type and quality of jobs, with greater demand for trained technical and managerial personnel as well as production workers. But, despite such improvements, southern branch plants remain heavily orientated to manual tasks. In the large majority of plants, over three-quarters of the total work force are still engaged in such tasks. And, indeed, all plants in the sample remain dependent on the parent firm for most of the higher managerial and strategic functions, marketing in particular.

It can be argued also that the innovations introduced in the production process do not necessarily imply any significant upgrading of manual skills. New technologies may require a better understanding of a larger part of the production process and a measure of information technology 'literacy', but their application still involves the performance of repetitive elementary tasks, namely ensuring that machine parameters are correct and pushing buttons.[31] *De facto*, the labour force is giving up manual skills for control skills and we can thus speak of 'computer-aided Taylorism', rather than of a major transition to a new work model.

In conclusion, the impact of branch plant restructuring on southern employment has been mixed. On one hand, as elsewhere, there has been a general reduction in the work force, mostly due to the automation of processes and the displacement of direct production labour. On the other hand, there has been a partial shift in job composition towards more trained managerial and technical personnel. None the less, this shift remains constrained by the continuing dependence of branch operations upon corporate headquarters for strategic functions.

Procurement strategies[32]

A crucial aspect of industrial restructuring in the 1980s concerns changes in the transactional structure of firms, i.e. in the degree of vertical integration – both at plant and at corporate level – and in the spatial structure of linkages. These issues are at the heart of the current debate on the 'winning' model of post-Fordist industrial organization. As already mentioned, several scholars believe that the flexibility imperatives of post-Fordism, especially the introduction of 'just-in-time', imply a trend towards vertical disintegration and the creation of territorially bound linkages. Examples ranging from 'Toyota City' to the 'industrial district' are recurrently mentioned as proof of this trend. According to this perspective, post-Fordist restructuring would imply an increase in the regional embeddedness of firms and, hence, benefits even for peripheral regions (see Chapter 8 by Amin and Tomaney).

This is not the place to develop a critique of the above proposition (cf. Amin and Robins 1990; Martinelli and Schoenberger 1991; Harrison 1994). It is enough to stress that no clear organizational model has yet emerged from contemporary restructuring patterns, and that sectoral specificities as well as individual firm structures and cultures further complicate the picture. In the case of the Mezzogiorno the results of our survey point in fact to quite the opposite trend: although plants and firms have externalized a number of transactions, there has also been a counter-trend to re-internalize others. More important, external transactions do not involve local suppliers to any significant extent. Furthermore, the quality of local linkages has not been upgraded, in terms of either technology or skill content.

Although in all ten firms in our sample the ratio of purchased goods and services relative to value added has consistently increased (especially in the electronics and telecommunications sectors), the large majority of purchases are made outside the region (cf. Table 9.4). With the exception of one firm (in food processing[33]) the scale of local linkages has not significantly increased. In five plants some phases previously contracted out to local firms have actually been re-internalized. More important, local linkages have remained overwhelmingly confined to low-tech, low-skilled components and tasks, in sharp contrast with linkages established with north central suppliers. Only three plants turn to local subcontractors for some medium-level transactions.

In order to explain these phenomena we examined the influence of four major reorganization patterns: the introduction of 'just-in-time'; the enrichment of corporate functions at the plant level; the intra-corporate division of labour; and changes in the labour market. The first two trends should lead to greater vertical disintegration, while the latter two should work in favour of vertical integration.

'Just in time'

This organizational model aims at reducing costs and increasing flexibility by reducing stocks of both inputs and finished products and by contracting out 'non-specific' and 'non-strategic' phases to reliable external suppliers. In its orthodox version 'just-in-time' also entails a territorially bound system of subcontracting, in order to ensure fast and reliable delivery.

In our survey, however, no significant increase in the volume and/or range of local purchases occurred. Most managers stated that no preference was given to local subcontractors in the reorganization of transactions. This anomaly of 'peripheral just-in-time' can be explained partly by the relatively small distances involved; as shown in Table 9.4, the large majority of inputs

Table 9.4 Procurement in ten large manufacturing plants operating in the Mezzogiorno, by type of inputs and geographical origin, 1991

Industries and plants	Origin			Level of local linkages
	Mezzogiorno	North central Italy	Abroad	
Household appliances				
HP	Small metal parts Small plastic parts Wiring and cabling Timers	Timers (also from affiliates) Electrical components Plastic and metal parts	Engines Electrical components Electronic components	Low
HM	Small metal parts Small plastic parts Wiring and cabling Timers	Electrical components	Engines Electronic components	Low
Telecommunications				
TS	Mechanical parts Metal parts Electronic sub-assemblies (from affiliate plant) Consulting services	Electro-mechanical components Electronic components (also from affiliate plants)	Electronic components	Medium
TM1	Packaging materials Mechanical parts (from affiliate plants)	Electro-mechanical components Electronic components (also from affiliate plants)	Electronic components (also from affiliate plants)	Low
TM2	Electronic sub-assemblies (from exogenous plant) Wiring and cabling	Metallic parts (from affiliate plant)	Electronic components	Low

Electronics			
EP	Mechanical parts Small plastic parts Small metal parts Metalworking phases Electro-mechanical sub-assemblies Wiring	Printed circuit boards (also from affiliate plants) Large plastic parts Electronic sub-assemblies Electronic components	Electronic components (also from affiliates) Printed circuit boards (also from affiliates)	Medium
EM	Plastic components Packaging material Low-tech sub-assemblies	Printed circuit boards Electronic components Plastic and metal parts	Electronic components (also from affiliates)	Low
Food processing			
FS	Raw materials Metal and glass containers Labelling Finished products	Raw materials		Medium
FM	Raw materials Cleaning services	Plastic/paper wrapping Finished products	Raw materials	Low
Clothing			
CM	None	Wrapping and boxes Fabrics Textile components	Fabrics Finished products	None

Source: Survey conducted by the authors in 1991.

are purchased in north central Italy. But for more distant suppliers the Mezzogiorno's anomaly represents a major constraint on the full exploitation of the model's advantages. In a few cases firms have experienced severe production problems arising from bottlenecks in long-distance delivery. Indeed, a number of managers admitted that the strategy of 'global sourcing' they are implementing at the corporate level (see below) may be structurally at odds, in the Mezzogiorno, with the strategy of 'just-in-time'.

Functional articulation

One major shortcoming of the Fordist branch plant model was its lack of managerial autonomy and task specialization. The allocation of manual only functions and the absence of autonomous decision-making functions (such as product development or procurement) were thought to be a major obstacle to plant integration with the surrounding economic structure. Post-Fordist restructuring, with its emphasis on 'time to market' products and hence greater integration between conception, production and marketing functions (Florio 1991), could thus bring with it a stronger propensity to establish local linkages.

The results of our survey do not endorse such expectations. By and large the role of our branch plants has remained merely operational. Only in half the cases has restructuring brought about some upgrading of the product development and engineering functions, while all other major strategic functions have remained in the north. And, among these, only in one case (cf. Table 9.4) have such changes led to the establishment of higher-level linkages with local consultants in the area of design and engineering.

Intra-corporate division of labour

As shown earlier, a major feature of large firm restructuring in the 1980s has been the reorganization and rationalization of the corporate operational structure, through the reallocation of 'missions' between the different territorial units of the firm and greater specialization of individual plants in fewer product lines or phases.

These practices, in the south, have produced two outcomes, equally negative in terms of local linkages. First there has been an increase in intra-corporate transactions in sectors and firms in which plants have become 'vertically' specialized (electronics and telecommunications). In many sub-processing phases – e.g. the highly automated sub-assembly of electronic boards – southern plants carry out customized work for several other branch plants, either of the same parent company or of other large companies. This deepening of the intra-corporate division of labour has further undermined the local linkage potential of branch plants in the region.

Second, in all the plants, including those specializing in terms of product line (especially household appliances), the increased degree of 'shared' basic technology and/or purchases is supporting a strategy of standardization of components and rationalization of suppliers. In order to exploit technical/contractual economies of scale as well as enhance the quality of components, firms are standardizing components across their diversified product portfolio, and are selecting fewer and larger 'global' suppliers to serve the whole corporate structure rather than the individual plant. Since few local firms in the Mezzogiorno can boast a technological level comparable to that of more central suppliers, this trend to 'global sourcing' is working against local linkages.

Labour market

A fourth aspect to consider in explaining the re-internalization and/or non-externalization of phases in our sample concerns changes in the productivity and cost of labour. On one hand, there has been throughout the 1980s a significant decrease in labour conflicts and collective bargaining. On the other hand, as mentioned earlier, labour in the Mezzogiorno still costs less than in the north, because of government incentives.

According to the transaction cost approach (Williamson 1985), less conflictual industrial relations at the plant level can decrease internal co-ordination costs, thus favouring greater vertical integration. The need for job reassignment owing to labour redundancy resulting from automation would further strengthen this trend: processing phases which, because of their intrinsic characteristics, could be contracted out would be performed in-house. However, according to our survey, although industrial relations have significantly improved, such improvements are similar to those registered in north central Italy, and cannot be considered an explanatory factor.

More decisive in whether to bring back or maintain in-house production, according to most managers, is the sheer lower cost of labour, as well as the higher costs and the political difficulties involved in laying off workers in this region. In at least five cases these factors have played a major role in southern plants being assigned production capacity formerly located in the north. In four cases southern plants have been assigned more labour-intensive and low-tech production phases than their northern counterparts.

In summary, despite differences related to sectoral and firm specificities, branch plant procurement strategies in the Mezzogiorno have not come to reverse the pattern set in the Fordist period. Plants remain vertically integrated and have not increased the degree of local involvement. Their greater specialization within the corporate structure, together with the intensification of intra-corporate linkages, the limited enrichment of corporate functions and decision-making autonomy, and factors related to the regional labour market, to a large extent explain this pattern. The introduction of 'just-in-time', supposed to bring about increased linkages with local suppliers, is not fulfilling its promise: transactions remain internal to the firm and/or with suppliers outside the south. The trend to 'global sourcing' and the absence in the Mezzogiorno of suppliers able to compete with north central suppliers have served to reinforce this vicious circle.

CONCLUSIONS AND POLICY IMPLICATIONS

The empirical evidence presented in the last two sections confirms most of the hypotheses raised earlier about the behaviour of large firms in the 1980s and also provides new insights as to the impact of such restructuring on the economy of the Mezzogiorno.

Above all, the corporate-wide reorganization of Fordist firms has taken a heavy toll of the Mezzogiorno in terms of plant closures. About 40 per cent of all large branch plants operating in the region at the beginning of the decade closed down in the course of the 1980s, and this has entailed a dramatic and irreversible loss of both manufacturing capacity and employment. On the other hand, for branch plants that were kept open, the restructuring process has yielded quite ambiguous results. Although there are significant ruptures with the previous Fordist industrial model, there are also substantial elements of continuity and, on balance, the developmental role of such establishments in the regional economy of the Mezzogiorno shows very little improvement.

Rupture and continuity with Fordism

Among the main ruptures with the Fordist model we can confirm:

1 The general shift from standardized to more innovative and differentiated products.
2 The introduction of flexibility in the form of both technology (flexible automation) and organizational principles (flexible processes, 'just-in-time').
3 Greater integration between production and strategic functions (although mostly at the corporate level, rather than at the plant level).
4 Significant 'convergence' of southern branch plants with other more central ones in terms of product/task specialization and process technology.
5 In a few instances a greater presence at the plant level of R&D functions, but strictly confined to product development and engineering.

However, if we borrow Schoenberger's (1990) distinction between traditional 'price-sensitive' branch plants and new 'performance-orientated' plants, the establishments we investigated remain closer to the former traditional model. In line with the observations of Amin and Tomaney in Chapter 8 of this volume on Portugal, Ireland and Scotland, the Mezzogiorno's branch plants still exhibit strong 'Fordist' characteristics. Among these we may mention:

1 The absence of more strategic functions at the plant level.
2 The subordinate status of plants within the corporate division of labour as regards decision-making autonomy.
3 The low propensity to stimulate local linkages.

The regional impact

In terms of employment creation the impact of restructuring has been severe. The further automation of processes and the intensification of work have severely reduced the need for direct labour, slightly compensated by an improvement in the occupational profile, linked with the introduction of new products and processes. In a few instances, the establishment or the upgrading of product development and engineering functions has involved significant increases in the number of graduate personnel. On the other hand, the increase in the skill requirements of manual labour is questionable, and we have suggested the term 'computer-aided Taylorism' to capture this ambiguity. Finally, the fact that most high-level functions are left at headquarters level, i.e. outside the Mezzogiorno, remains a major constraint on managerial skill formation and the transmission of entrepreneurial know-how into the region.

As regards the creation of local linkages, restructuring in the 1980s has straightforwardly negative implications. The introduction of 'just-in-time' practices and the need to reduce fixed costs, which would seem to imply greater recourse to external, local suppliers, did not improve the low propensity of branch plants to establish linkages in the Mezzogiorno. Although external procurement has increased, both at plant and at corporate level, the increase has not involved regional suppliers. In fact the rationalization and 'globalization' of procurement have led to a deepening of the intra-corporate division of labour, as well as favouring the selection of larger suppliers outside the Mezzogiorno. From this point of view, the application of 'just-in-time' techniques in the Mezzogiorno remains anomalous. The few linkages with local suppliers that have been kept remain overwhelmingly confined to low-technology, traditional work phases. In terms of innovation diffusion and enhancement of entrepreneurship via local linkages the role of branch plants in the Mezzogiorno has declined rather than improved.

As regards the competitive position of the Mezzogiorno, the dramatic number of plant closures in the 1980s has weakened the modern productive base of the south and the region's contribution to national manufacturing output. In addition, the crisis of the branch plant sector does not seem to have been compensated by any substantial growth of local small firms or service activities. On the whole, thus, the competitive position of the Mezzogiorno in the national and international division of labour has worsened.

Despite significant changes, the traditional lack of local embeddedness of Fordist branch plants in peripheral regions has not decreased with post-Fordist restructuring. The globalization of competition, trade liberalization and the completion of the single European market have actually increased the footlooseness of multilocational firms. Large firms are attempting to recover monopoly advantages and competitiveness through an increase in industrial concentration and the segmentation of markets by products rather than regions. Regions do not matter any more as specific markets, only in the traditional sense of providing local comparative advantage.

In this context, although many peripheral regions in Europe now offer improved locational opportunities in terms of labour markets (more educated labour force) and infrastructure (telecommunications, transport), they cannot compete with more central regions, which remain more attractive for investment because of the innovation and supply-supporting nature of their economic base. The comparative locational advantage of peripheral regions still lies in the cheaper cost of factors (capital and labour), often linked with state incentives.

Regional policy implications

What are the implications of the above findings in terms of regional policy? The post-Fordist reorganization of branch plants does not seem to be working in favour of peripheral regions. Policies in support of exogenous investment are increasingly being questioned as costly without giving any assurance of embeddedness and developmental contribution. The recent neo-liberal focus of national and supranational regulatory bodies (e.g. the EC) on competitiveness and free trade is a further constraint on regional convergence (see earlier chapters in this volume). This new climate is clearly witnessed in the Italian case through the termination in 1993 of the forty-three-year-old regional policy of assistance to the Mezzogiorno. The disbursement of incentives to investment is now a general task of the Ministry of Industry, with no explicit mandate (or financial coverage) for the south.

In this rather bleak institutional context, for three main reasons we strongly support the view that an active industrial policy must be resumed in the Mezzogiorno and that it must continue to focus on exogenous investments.

First, large exogenous firms are the only barrier to the complete deindustrialization of the Mezzogiorno. Although the closure of many branch plants has diminished the aggregate contribution of the region to national manufacturing value added, investment in those which have remained open has significantly improved southern levels of industrial productivity and performance (Ditta and Padovani 1992). Local small and medium-size firms, because of internal weakness and external constraints, have proved unable to ensure the industrial development of the Mezzogiorno. Large, exogenous industrial firms continue to remain the only possible engine of any process of regional economic conversion.

Second, time must be taken into account. The restructuring process is not yet complete. A new round of investment has been undertaken and a new industrial model is being established, which both need further adjustment. The still ambiguous features of the post-Fordist model, if appropriately guided and supported, could be made to secure greater regional embeddedness. For example, the cost of long-distance 'just-in-time' supply could induce firms, if the appropriate policy measures were taken, to transfer some sourcing to the south and, in time, to develop local linkages. After all, even in the Fordist period, branch plants did over time start a process of local integration. Another example relates to the development of strategic functions. We have seen that in a few instances the need of a closer relationship between product development and production has involved the establishment or upgrading of certain R&D activities in the Mezzogiorno. This still limited trend could be further encouraged with the apropriate incentives.

Finally, and closely related, there is the question of locational comparative advantage. Our field work clearly shows that the existence of financial incentives on the factor side (labour and capital) was one of the main reasons given by firms for reinvesting in the Mezzogiorno. We believe that there is no viable alternative for peripheral regions, at least in the medium run, to offering traditional cost advantages. This is in contrast with the prevailing policy orientation of the EU. However, there is still room for national action, which should not be passively abandoned, but could be changed to take into account the changed strategies of large firms. Restoring traditional locational advantages might involve improved and innovative measures. Financial aid could be targeted to specific activities and objectives and, more important, coupled with closer interaction with, and monitoring of, large firm investment strategies. The 'after-care services' initiative established in Scotland (cf. Young and Hood, Chapter 11 in this volume) is one very interesting example of such an approach.

NOTES

1 By this term we mean regions such as the Mezzogiorno of Italy, but also other rural regions in industrialized countries, such as Ireland and parts of Canada,

which all experienced a process of industrialization led by branch plants during the last wave of Fordist expansion in the 1960s and early 1970s. In the course of the chapter we shall contrast these regions with more 'central' or 'northern' ones, meaning areas of older and more articulated industrialization.

2 Some of these authors, particularly those of the 'transactional' school explain the growth of multilocational investment as an efficiency objective, i.e. gains deriving from internalizing transactions; others focus instead on the search for new markets and the reinforcement of market power as main motives (cf. Balcet 1989 for a thorough review).

3 To empirically assess the effects of branch plant investment in such terms is quite difficult and our considerations are thus rather speculative.

4 In Italy such a phase corresponds to the concept of 'late Fordism' as identified by Lipietz (1986b).

5 The CRS data bank, based in Naples and in existence since 1975, covers all manufacturing establishments of firms with at least ten employees operating in the Mezzogiorno. Information covers the year of establishment, ownership, employment size and the products of all plants.

6 Foreign multinationals accounted for 10 per cent, whereas large north Italian firms and state-controlled companies contributed 16 per cent and 24 per cent respectively. Small and medium northern firms contributed the remaining 10 per cent.

7 In fact the regional contribution to natural manufacturing value added increased from 11 per cent in 1960 to 16 per cent in 1975 and, within the region itself, the contribution of the modern sectors (electro-mechanical equipment, machinery, transport equipment, steel, chemicals) to regional manufacturing value added increased from an average of 26 per cent in the 1950s to an average of 33 per cent in the first half of the 1970s. Moreover, the share of employees vis-á-vis self-employed workers in the manufactoring sector rose from 59 per cent in 1951 to 75 per cent in 1973, and labour productivity improved dramatically, increasing from 67 per cent of the national average in 1960 to 88 per cent in 1973 (Del Monte and Giannola 1978).

8 As argued, rather than strengthening or spurring the growth in local manufacturing supply, the demand ended up sustaining the market for extra-regional products (Giannola and Lopes 1992). According to Wolleb and Wolleb (1990), the change in policy for the Mezzogiorno can be explained by the need to channel national sources into the restructuring of the northern productive base. But, despite the recovery of the Italian economy from 1983 to 1989, the composition of transfers to the south in these last years did not change significantly.

9 All new investment projects were stopped, whereas throughout the 1970s public companies acquired several establishments and firms from private groups, especially in food processing, textiles, chemicals and electrical machinery, with the aim of preventing closure and revitalizing operations. In fact they only postponed closures.

10 The rate of industrialization (manufacturing employees per thousand inhabitants) fell from forty-eight in 1981 to thirty-nine in 1989, ie. three times lower than in the rest of the country (Ditta and Padovani 1992).

11 It must be stressed that the better performance of local small firms may be overestimated, given the greater difficulties involved in the statistical coverage of such an elusive and fast evolving population, compared with the more 'conspicuous' exogenous ones.

12 According to census data, between 1971 and 1981 large establishments (over

500 employees) accounted for as much as 42 per cent of the total increase in manufacturing employment in the region. Between 1970 and 1974 the average annual rate of increase of industrial value added in the Mezzogiorno was 27 per cent higher than in the rest of the country (Del Monte and Giannola 1978).

13 The analysis was based on a comparison of the 1981 and 1991 CRS files.

14 It is worth stressing that our unit of observation is the plant, but in many aspects information necessarily concerns firm strategies and actions.

15 The type of ownership (foreign multinational *v.* domestic company, state-owned corporation *v.* private company) as well as the specific history and structure of the parent company (e.g. fast-growing *v.* static firm, specialized company *v.* diversified holding, etc.), explains a large proportion of observed differences in corporate behaviour and impact, even within the same sector. For further details on this point see the full report on the survey (Martinelli and Giunta 1992).

16 It is also worth mentioning that all the changes concerning our southern plants occurred in the latter half of the 1980s (i.e. 1986–9).

17 The only two firms that did not experience any ownership change were the multinationals, which, in general, exhibited the more stable behaviour in our sample.

18 It is important to bear in mind that we use the terms 'northern' and 'central' to denote more industrialized regions, whether in the north of Italy or in other countries.

19 In a few cases (foreign firms with one major Italian facility, based in the Mezzogiorno) another reason mentioned to explain the decision to maintain and restructure the southern facility was the need to keep in close touch with the Italian market.

20 We should also stress that such a clear-cut division of labour between production and strategic functions appears to involve several plants within the corporate structure of our firms. Also a number of the northern plants are now more dependent on central management and service functions, with the exception of those located in very central regions (and close to headquarters). We can thus reasonably propose the hypothesis that a process of status 'convergence' may be occurring across corporate operational units, regardless of location.

21 We believe, indeed, reversing the commonly accepted view, that the segmentation and differentiation of consumer markets are in large part a consequence, rather than the cause, of revived oligopolistic competition.

22 In this regard we wish to stress that we are strongly opposed to current technological determinism. We believe that technological innovation is an endogenous variable, influenced by firm behaviour. In a neo-Schumpeterian perspective, innovations are the result of strategies geared to overcome a change in the external conditions of accumulation and/or to gain competitive advantage. It is evident that when a particular 'technological paradigm' becomes dominant it then also becomes an exogenous variable, which conditions the behaviour of firms.

23 This case, as well as the assembly of fax machines, telephones and desk-top calculators in the electronics and telecommunications sectors, confirms among other things, how flexibility is not synonymous with programmable automation: flexible processes can be organized regardless of technology (cf. Martinelli and Schoenberger 1991).

24 Although all firms stressed the possibility of rapidly adjusting or changing production runs, in response to market demands, many also underlined that

there still are cost constraints on changing the set-up of machines. Therefore good planning geared to maximize production batches still counts.

25 E.g. the Yugoslavian war, strikes by air cargo handlers, etc.

26 Given the highly 'systemic' character of the new technology, the introduction of flexible automation at the production level only partially exploits opportunities. The full advantages of the new paradigm can be reaped only when it is integrated at the level of the whole corporate organizational structure (Rolfo 1990; Sembenelli 1990). From this point of view, large hierarchical firms are more likely to have the know-how necessary to adopt and integrate the new technological paradigm efficiently than less structured industrial systems such as 'networks of firms'.

27 Although, as already stressed, in the telecommunications and electronics sectors a number of product lines and phases are still technologically mature and labour-intensive, partly in order to absorb redundant employment from automated lines.

28 It is interesting to note that the multinational rival of the national household appliance plant recorded one of the lowest employment decreases, owing to its strategy of internalizing the amount of production it used to contract out.

29 This is indeed the only case of actual 'relocation' of operations: three older facilities were closed down and production capacity was concentrated in a new plant in the same region.

30 This was often coupled with the introduction of a second and even a third shift, partly to increase the utilization of costly equipment, partly to absorb redundant labour.

31 Two managers explicitly stated this view (one in the household appliance sector and one in the electronics sector).

32 For a more detailed analysis of the following findings see Giunta (1992).

33 This is the case of a firm which externalized the manufacture of tin and glass containers. It should also be mentioned that the food-processing sector is the only one where a significant amount of local purchases are raw materials, i.e. fresh vegetables and fruit, and where some technology and know-how has spilled over into the local agricultural system.

REFERENCES

Acocella, N. (1989) 'Efficienza e strategia nel processo di multinazionalizzazione: verso una teoria più generale', in N. Acocella and R. Schiattarella (eds) *Teorie della internazionalizzazione e realtà italiana*, Naples: Liguori, pp. 75–96.

Acocella, N. (1992) 'The multinational firm and the theory of industrial organization', in A. Del Monte (ed.) *Recent Developments in the Theory of Industrial Organization*, London: Macmillan, pp. 232–51.

Aglietta, M. (1976) *Régulation et crises du capitalisme*, Paris: Calmann-Lévy.

Amendola, M., and Baratta, P. (1978) *Investimenti industriali e sviluppo dualistico*, Milan: Giuffrè.

Amin, A., and Robins, K. (1990) 'The re-emergence of regional economies? The mythical geography of flexible accumulation', *Environment and Planning D, Society and Space* 8: 7–34.

Balcet, G. (ed.) (1989) *Economia dell'impresa multinazionale*, Turin: Giappichelli.

Balloni, V., and Bianchi, P. (1990) 'Alcune considerazioni di metodo nell' analisi dei processi di aggiustamento industriale', in V. Balloni (ed.) *Processi di aggiustamento delle industrie negli anni '80*, Bologna: Il Mulino, pp. 13–42.

Boyer, R. (1986) *La Théorie de la régulation: une analyse critique*, Paris: La Découverte.

Boyer, R., and Durand, J.-P. (1993) *L'après-Fordisme*, Paris: Syros.

Britton, J. N. H. (1980) 'Industrial dependence and technological underdevelopment: Canadian consequences of foreign direct investment', *Regional Studies* 14: 181–200.

Buckley, P. J., and Casson, M. (1976) *The Future of the Multinational Enterprise*, London: Macmillan.

Buckley, P. J., and Casson, M. C. (1985) *The Economic Theory of the Multinational Enterprise*, London: Macmillan.

Cainarca, G. C., Colombo, M. G. and Mariotti, S. (1989) '*Sentieri di automazione ed evoluzione della struttura industriale*', in G. P. Barbetta and F. Silva (eds) *Trasformazioni strutturali delle imprese italiane*, Bologna: Il Mulino, pp. 251–302.

Camagni, R. (1986) 'La diffusione dei processi di automazione flessibile: il caso dell' industria lombarda', *Economia e Politica Industriale* 52: 153–285.

Caves, R. (1982) *Multinational Enterprise and Economic Analysis*, Cambridge: Cambridge University Press.

Cercola, R. (1977) *L'industria manifatturiera del basso Lazio*, Naples: Cesan.

Cercola, R. (1984) *L' intervento esterno nello sviluppo industriale del Mezzogiorno*, Naples: Guida.

De Bernis, G. (1983) 'De quelques questions concernant la théorie des crises', *Cahiers de l' ISMEA* 25: 1277–330.

Del Monte, A., and De Lutzenberger, R. (1989) 'The effects of regional policy on new firms formation in southern Italy', *Regional Studies* 23, 219–230.

Del Monte, A., and Giannola, A. (1978) *Il Mezzogiorno nell' economia italiana*, Bologna: Il Mulino.

Del Monte, A., and Martinelli, F. (1988) 'Gli ostacoli alla divisione tecnica e sociale del lavoro nelle aree depresse: il caso delle piccole imprese elettroniche in Italia', *L' Industria* 3: 471–509.

Del Monte, A., and Vittoria, M. P. (1989) "Natalità delle imprese e processo di job-creation nella provincia di Caserta, 1970–86', *Mezzogiorno d' Europa* 45–81.

De Vita, P. (1978) *L' industria manifatturiera della Sardegna*, Naples: Cesan.

Dicken, P. (1976) 'The multiplant business enterprise and geographical space: some issues in the study of external control and regional development', *Regional Studies*, 10: 401–12.

Ditta, L., and Padovani, R. (1992) 'Regioni meridionali e sviluppo industriale negli anni '80', *Rivista Economica del Mezzogiorno* 1.

Dunford, M. (1986) 'Integration and unequal development: the case of southern Italy, 1951–73', in A. J. Scott and M. Storper (eds) *Work, Production, Territory*, London: Allen & Unwin, 225–45.

Dunning, J. H. (1981) *International Production and the Multinational Enterprise*, London: Allen & Unwin.

Firn, J. R. (1975) 'External control and regional development: the case of Scotland', *Environment and Planning A* 7: 393–414.

Florio, M. (1991) *Grande impresa e sviluppo locale*, Ancona: Edizioni Clua.

Giannola, A. (1987a) 'Politica industriale attiva e sviluppo dell' impresa locale nel Mezzogiorno', *Nord e Sud* 1: 35–57.

Giannola, A. (1987b) 'Problemi e prospettive dello sviluppo economico nel Mezzogiorno d' Italia', in Ente Einaudi (ed.) *Oltre la crisi*, Bologna: Il Mulino, pp. 204–44.

Giannola, A., and Lopes, A. (1992) 'Politiche di intervento, sviluppo economico del Mezzogiorno e debito pubblico', in Ente Einaudi (ed.) *Il disavanzo pubblico in Italia: natura strutturale e politiche di rientro*, Bologna: Il Mulino, pp. 549–600.

Giunta, A. (1992) 'Sui legami tra grande e piccola impresa nel Mezzogiorno, una verifica empirica', *Economia Marche* 3: 253–77

Giunta, A. (1994) 'Il ruolo della grande impresa nel Mezzogiorno degli anni '80', *Rivista Economica del Mezzogiorno*' (forthcoming).

Graziani, A. (1977) 'Il Mezzogiorno nell' economia italiana', *Inchiesta* 29.

Graziani, A., and Pugliese, E. (eds) (1979) *Investimenti e disoccupazione nel Mezzogiorno*, Bologna: Il Mulino.

Gros-Pietro, G. (1990) 'Ruolo della subfornitura in un sistema industriale avanzato', paper presented at the conference '*Tendenze e prospettive della subfornitura*', Milan, November.

Gros-Pietro, G. M., and Rolfo, S. (1989) 'Flexible automation and firm size: some empirical evidence on the Italian case', *Technovation* 5.

Harrison, B. (1994) *Lean and Mean*, New York: Basic Books.

Hirschman, A. O. (1987) 'Linkages', in J. Eatwell, M. Milgate and P. Newman (eds) *The New Palgrave: Dictionary of Economics*, London: Macmillan, pp. 206–11.

Hoare, A. G. (1978) 'Industrial linkages and the dual economy: the case of Northern Ireland', *Regional Studies* 12: 167–80.

Hymer, S. (1972) 'The multinational corporation and the law of uneven development', in J. N. Bhagwati (ed.) *Economics and World Order*, London: Macmillan, pp. 113–40.

Hymer, S. (1976) *The International Operations of National Firms: a Study of Foreign Direct Investment*, Cambridge, Mass.: MIT Press.

Jacquemin, A. (1987) *The new Industrial Organization: Market Forces and Strategic Behavior*, Cambridge, Mass.: MIT Press.

Jacquemin, A. (1989) 'Comportamenti strategici internazionali e multinazionali', in N. Acocella and R. Schiattarella (eds) *Teorie della internazionalizzazione e realtà italiana*, Naples: Liguori, pp. 105–26.

Jessop, B. (1991) 'The welfare state in the transition from Fordism to post-Fordism', in B. Jessop, H. Kastendiek, K. Nielson and O. Pedersen (eds) *The Politics of Flexibility: Restructuring State and Industry in Britain, Germany, and Scandinavia*, Aldershot: Edward Elgar.

Lall, S. (1976) 'Theories of direct foreign private investment and multinational behavior', *Economic and Political Weekly* 11.

Lall, S. (1978) 'Transnationals, domestic enterprises, and industrial structure in host LDCs: a survey', *Oxford Economic Papers* 30 (2): 217–48.

Lall, S. (1980) 'Monopolistic advantages and foreign involvement by U.S. manufacturing industry', *Oxford Economic Papers* 32 (1): 102–22.

Lipietz, A. (1979) *Crise et inflation, pourquoi?* Paris: Maspéro.

Lipietz, A. (1986a) *Mirages et miracles: Problèmes de l'industrialisation dans le Tiers-Monde*, Paris: La Découverte.

Lipietz, A. (1986b) 'New tendencies in the international division of labor: regimes of accumulation and modes of regulation', in A. Scott and M. Storper (eds) *Work, Production, Territory: the Geographical Anatomy of Industrial Capitalism*, London: Allen & Unwin, pp. 16–40.

Lipietz, A. (1989) *Choisir l' audace: une alternative pour le XXIème siècle*, Paris: La Découverte.

Mariotti, S. (1990) 'Il riordino della funzione tecnica di produzione dell' industria', in V. Balloni (ed.) *Processi di aggiustamento delle industrie negli anni '80*, Bologna: Il Mulino, pp. 233–66.

Marshall, J. N. (1979) 'Ownership, organization, and industrial linkages: a case study in the northern region of England', *Regional Studies*, 13: 531–57.

Martinelli, F. (1985) 'Public policy and industrial development in southern Italy:

anatomy of a dependent industry', *International Journal of Urban and Regional Research* 9 (1): 47–81.

Martinelli, F. (1989) 'Struttura industriale e servizi alla produzione nel Mezzogiorno', *Politica Economica* 5 (1): 129–87.

Martinelli, F., and Giunta, A. (1992) 'La ristrutturazione dei grandi impianti manifatturieri del Mezzogiorno negli anni '80, Naples: Università Federico II (mimeo).

Martinelli, F., and Schoenberger, E. (1991) 'Oligopoly is alive and well: notes for a broader discussion of flexible accumulation', in G. Benko and M. Dunford (eds) *Industrial Change and Regional Development*, London: Belhaven, pp. 117–33.

McAleese, D., and McDonald, D. (1978) 'Employment growth and the development of linkages in foreign-owned and domestic manufacturing enterprises', *Oxford Bulletin of Economics and Statistics* 40: 321–39.

McDermott, P. G. (1976) 'Ownership, organization and regional development', *Regional Studies* 10: 319–36.

Mele, R. (1975) *L' industria manifatturiera della Puglia*, Naples: Cesan.

Mercurio, R. (1974) *L' industria manifatturiera della Campania*, Naples: Cesan.

O'Farrell, P. N. (1980) 'Multinational enterprises and regional development: Irish evidence', *Regional Studies* 14: 141–50.

Porter, M. E. (1990) *The Competitive Advantage of Nations*, London: Macmillan.

Rolfo, S. (1990) 'Gli effetti dell' automazione flessibile su un gruppo di imprese italiane', in G. M. Gros-Pietro (ed.) *Automazione flessibile e industria*, Milan: Angeli, pp. 143–61.

Roth, A., De Meyer, A. and Amano, A. (1989) 'International manufacturing strategies: a comparative analysis', in K. Ferdows (ed) *Managing International Manufacturing*, North Holland: Elsevier, pp. 187–211.

Rugman, A. M. (1981) *Inside the Multinationals: the Economics of Internal Markets*, London: Croom Helm.

Sabel, C., and Piore, M. (1984) *The Second Industrial Divide*, New York: Basic Books.

Scherer, F. M., and Ross, D. (1991) *Industrial Market Structure and Economic Performance*, Boston, Mass.: Houghton Mifflin.

Schoenberger, E. (1988) 'Multinational corporations and the new international division of labor: a critical appraisal', *International Regional Science Review*, 11 (2): 105–19.

Schoenberger, E. (1990) 'U.S. manufacturing investment in Western Europe: markets, corporate strategy, and the competitive environment', *Annals of the Association of American Geographers* 80 (3): 379–93.

Scott, A. (1988) *New Industrial Spaces: Flexible Production Organization and Regional Development*, London: Pion.

Scott, A. J., and Storper, M. (eds) (1986) *Work, Production, Territory*, London: Allen & Unwin

Sembenelli, A. (1990) 'Automazione flessibile e rapporti tra imprese: considerazioni teoriche ed elementi empirici', in G. M. Gros-Pietro (ed.) *Automazione flessibile e industria*, Milan: Angeli, pp. 245–69.

Senn, L. (1990) 'L' impatto territoriale dei processi di aggiustamento', in V. Balloni (ed.) *Processi di aggiustamento delle industrie negli anni '80*, Bologna: Il Mulino, pp. 65–114.

Storper, M., and Scott, A. (1989) 'The geographical foundations and social regulation of flexible production complexes', in J. Wolch and M. Dear (eds) *The Power of Geography: how Territory shapes Social Life*, London: Unwin Hyman, pp. 21–40.

Testa, F. (1976) *L'industria manifatturiera della Sicilia*, Naples: Cesan.

Testa, F. (1981) *Tipologie aziendali e settori industriali nel Mezzogiorno*, Milan: Angeli.

Thwaites, A. T. (1978) 'Technological change, mobile plants and regional development', *Regional Studies* 12: 445–62.

Townroe, P. M. (1975) 'Branch plants and regional development', *Town Planning Review* 46: 47–62.

United Nations/Economic Commission for Europe (1986) Recent Trends in Flexible Manufacturing, Geneva: United Nations.

Varaldo, R. (ed.) (1979) *Ristrutturazioni industriali e rapporti tra imprese*, Milan: Angeli.

Williamson, O. (1985) *The Economic Institutions of Capitalism*, New York: Free Press.

Wolleb, E., and Wolleb, G. (1990) *Divari regionali e dualismo economico*, Bologna: Il Mulino.

10

RESTRUCTURING OF SCOTLAND'S INFORMATION TECHNOLOGY INDUSTRIES

Strategic issues and responses

Ewen Peters

This chapter considers the strategic issues and responses to the fundamental restructuring under way in Scotland's information technology (IT) industries. The present structure of Scotland's IT industry is described and assessed in relation to key global/industry trends in technology, products and markets. The case for re-engineering the basis of Scotland's long-term competitive advantage from one of cost to one of added value is then made. The related strategic response of local IT firms and development agencies is described and the implications which it holds for wider public policy are considered, especially the 'match' with EC regional and trade policy.

SCOTLAND'S IT INDUSTRIES AND THE CHALLENGE OF CHANGE

Performance and structure

For the last three decades the IT industries have been a major source of investment and the single most important source of growth in Scottish manufacturing output, exports and productivity. Today it is estimated that the sector employs nearly 50,000 people, representing more than one in seven employees in Scottish manufacturing. Scotland's IT industries have also been a key source of added value and international competitiveness (Young *et al.* 1993).

As Figures 10.1 and 10.2 help illustrate, the contribution of the IT industries to the development of Scotland's manufacturing base has largely been built on the world-class manufacturing capability developed in areas of hardware such as computers (i.e. PCs, laptops, workstations, LANs and WANs, etc.) and components, especially integrated circuits, where Scotland

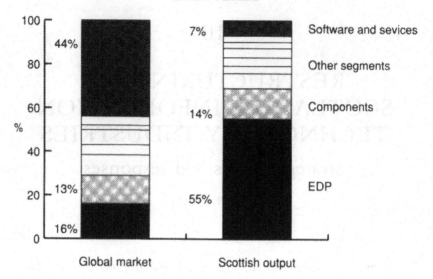

Figure 10.1 Global market *v.* Scottish output in electronics: percentage share by main product segments, 1991

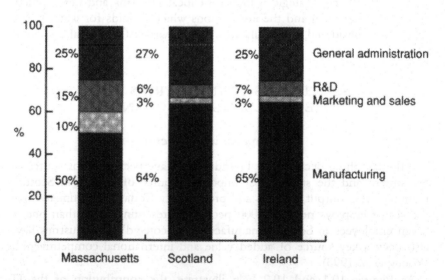

Figure 10.2 Employees in electronics, Massachusetts, Scotland and Irish Republic: percentage split by main functions, 1992

Source: Elsevier 1991, Scottish Enterprise National, Scottish Office, Associated Industries of Massachusetts, Industrial Development Authority estimates, Monitor analysis

264

accounts for 35 per cent and 20 per cent respectively of European output. Furthermore, in a few important instances (e.g. Hewlett Packard at South Queensferry and AT&T at Dundee), manufacturing excellence has been successfully integrated with excellence in marketing and product design and development to create strategic business units capable of global leadership. However, functions which add higher value such as product-related design and development, marketing and the monitoring of product and technology markets generally remain underrepresented within the total industry mix, and this constrains the industry's ability to achieve better alignment with markets, such as software, which offer the greatest opportunity for long-term growth.

Scotland also has a world-class university research base in a number of advanced technologies, notably artificial intelligence, massive parallel processing and opto-electronics. However, beyond the supply of high-calibre graduates, technology links with the IT industries, especially multinational enterprises, remain generally underdeveloped.

To date, foreign direct investment has been the single most important driver of growth. Though the added value which it has created is consistently twice the level of that achieved by indigenous firms (in terms of gross GVA per employee), it has resulted in a concentrated pattern of development: 14 per cent of firms account for 47 per cent of employment and 65 per cent of output.

Historically, the location decisions of the larger multinationals have been influenced by two main sets of factors, namely operating costs and market proximity. On this basis, Scotland has developed a strategic role as a least-cost manufacturing and logistics hub for volume assemblers seeking to exploit UK, European and other wider market opportunities. The specific advantages which Scotland has traditionally offered include:

1 Attractive financial incentives
2 Low labour costs
3 Good logistics and communications
4 Good quality of labour
5 The English language.

Drivers of change

Rapid technical progress, fast-reducing product life cycles and intense international competition are well understood features which accelerate the pace of change within the IT industry. Table 10.1 describes these and other key change drivers in more detail. Furthermore, market orientation and reliance on high-volume assembly of standard product inevitably expose the Scottish economy to the cyclical conditions which characterize this sector (see Figure 10.3).

265

Table 10.1 Industry change drivers

Key consumer trends	*Key product trends*	*Key technology trends*
• The growth of distributed processing on a networked basis • The desire for increased portability and user-friendliness • The anticipated growth in multimedia through the further extension of IT and communications technologies to applications outside work and to leisure and entertainment	• The market for PCs and workstations is expected to remain significant despite growing commodity status, based on: increased performance per unit cost which advances in processor technology will bring, increased user-friendliness, which graphical interfaces and object-orientated programming will facilitate, and the advantages over portables of larger colour screens, and lower cost of manufacture • Over time, however, portable computers are expected to become the preferred machine for many business users: explosive growth in PDAs is expected over the next five years (a PDA is a hand-held electronic notebook with sophisticated telecommunications abilities) • Greater local access and control of computing power will be facilitated by the wider adoption of digital networks based on fibre optics: broad-band optical connections will form the main wired national and international links; local access will be via radio-based links the GSM standard (and its variants) will bring a global standard to mobile digital communications	• Advances in chip design and wafer fabrication technology are expected to continue to (a) increase the processing speed and functionality of processors and (b) increase the storage capacity of memory devices, at lower cost • Advances predicted in flat panel display technology may greatly increase functional integration and make higher levels of miniaturization and greater portability possible (this has profound implications for the configuration of hardware activity within the IT value system, for example injection moulding requirements would change, as would power supplies, and the number of sub-assemblies might greatly reduce – that is, only one mother board would be required) • The move to 'open systems' will ensure greater portability of applications between different hardware systems • The central issue of achieving ever higher levels of user-friendliness is software-critical.

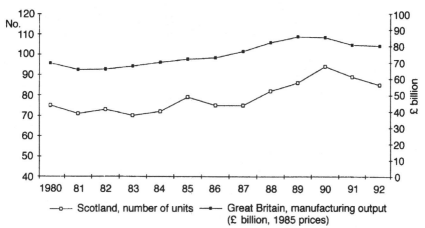

Figure 10.3 Foreign-owned units and output, in electronic and electrical engineering, 1980–92

Thus the IT-related plant closures and contraction experienced recently by areas like Scotland and Ireland reflect a combination of both cyclical and structural factors (see Table 10.2). These forces are expected to strengthen, and will continue to reshape Europe's IT industries in fundamental ways.

Future implications

As the efforts of the IT industries as a whole focus on providing greater value to the customer, long-run profitability and value will flow increasingly from software and services; according to some industry forecasters this balance could shift as far as 80 : 20 in favour of software/services by the turn of the century. Thus, areas whose IT assets are relatively highly concentrated in hardware may need to consider new ways of securing better alignment with this important opportunity for long-term growth.

Taken in conjunction with the growing intensity of time-based competition, this market trend implies that outward-bound logistics (i.e. marketing, sales, distribution, etc.) will attract higher levels of investment than hitherto. The spatial configuration of this investment is likely to reflect, *inter alia*, the continuing need to rationalize distribution echelons and the need to establish/relocate marketing, sales and customer after-care activity to lower-cost areas in Europe which offer good telecommunications and a pool of appropriate technical and multilingual skills.

Furthermore, according to industry analysts (Moschella 1993), the vertically integrated business model that dominated the first three decades of the IT industry is now fast becoming obsolete. Hardware, software and services are each developing a unique set of economies (see Figures 10.4 and 10.5). Unlike the vertically integrated companies of the past such as

Table 10.2 Corporate restructuring

Some Scottish examples

Fifteen major closures/contractions in electrical and instrument engineering over last two to three years, including:

Bull Hn	350 jobs lost – part of general restructuring – all UK manufacturing ended
Unisys	700 jobs lost (including 150 in R&D); part of global restructuring, repair and recover business worth £10 million per annum – hived off to Dutch telecoms company
Segate	Disk drives – 200 jobs lost
Rodime	Disk drives – former Burroughs spin-off – Scottish manufacturing moved to Singapore – seventy jobs lost
Avex	PC subcontract assembly, 180 jobs lost
Conner	Disk drives – Scottish manufacturing ended after only three years to cut costs – 200 jobs lost – massive expansion in Malaysia – 1500 jobs planned initially
AST	Acquired Tandy plant in July 1993, closed in November

Some Irish examples

6,195 jobs lost in the overseas manufacturing sector in 1992; the IT sector accouted for 42%

• DEC employed 1,500 people on three sites, manufacturing at Galway transferred to Ayr; 300 people retained in software

• Amdahl, Wang, Nixdorf, Prime and Concurrent have all closed or greatly scaled back Irish operations because of product obsolescence

• Mostec and Storage Technology are component suppliers which also failed

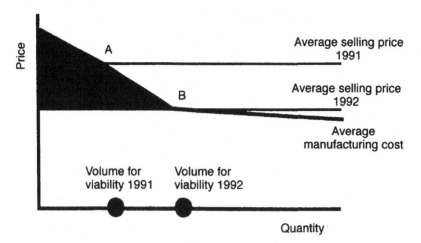

Figure 10.4 Personal computer hardware: approaches equilibrium, 1993 (By courtesy of International Data Corporation)

IBM and DEC, today's industry leaders (Intel, Microsoft and Novell) are unlikely to undertake significant customer service/solution activities. These opportunities are being exploited by a growing array of world-wide partners – dealers, value-added resellers, systems integrators and systems companies – who are better placed to meet the needs of different vertical and geographical markets. Furthermore, the manufacturing excellence of, and scale economies available to, established firms such as IBM remain significant sources of competitive advantage, as evidenced recently in the

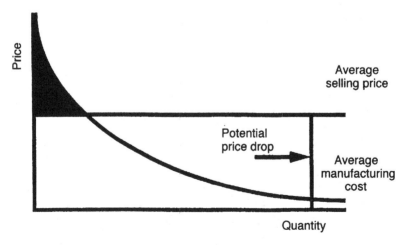

Figure 10.5 Packaged software: look out, below! (By courtesy of International Data Corporation)

269

greater price stability that followed IBM's decision to lower its PC prices substantially. On the basis of the above, conjecture in the US about the outright industry dominance of the 'computerless company' (Rapport and Halvei 1991) may perhaps be premature.

The breakdown of the product hierarchy by which the IT market has traditionally defined and segmented itself (i.e. mainframes, mini-computers and PCs) is opening up new opportunities for rapid product innovation, accompanied by rising rates of planned obsolescence. If customers are to be provided with the benefits they seek, many of these product opportunities will require to be exploited through the fuller integration of hardware, software and service features. Taken in conjunction with the demise of the vertically integrated business model, this helps to explain the proliferation of strategic alliances, not only to share the high and rising cost of research and development but to compete for leadership in important emerging markets.

The commodity-like nature of hardware, intense competition and demanding market conditions suggest that leading original equipment manufacturers will continue to reappraise manufacturing strategies to ensure optimal plant configuration in relation to servicing European and global markets. Future investment (and divestment), therefore, may be expected to remain a function of the individual corporation's need to minimize manufacturing costs and maximize regional sales leverage.

Diversification, rationalization and contraction are also likely among subcontractors and some component suppliers as the products of original equipment hardware manufacturers alter radically both in size and in their material and component make-up.

STRATEGIC ISSUES AND RESPONSES FOR SCOTLAND

The Scottish position

Scotland's position may be summarized as follows. The major long-term growth opportunities in software and services lie in a sector where Scotland has yet to demonstrate significant international competitive advantage. Furthermore, the traditional basis of Scotland's manufacturing advantage is under growing threat from lower-cost locations on the Pacific rim and in Eastern Europe. At the same time, the gap appears to be widening between Scotland and other international locations with local factor conditions which add higher value to the operations of IT firms. As Figure 10.6 illustrates, this includes not only the more advanced economies of the US and Japan, but also economies such as Taiwan and Singapore which only a decade or so ago were regarded as dynamic but perhaps less well developed. The process by which these locations have been able to upgrade their IT activity so rapidly has been documented by researchers from

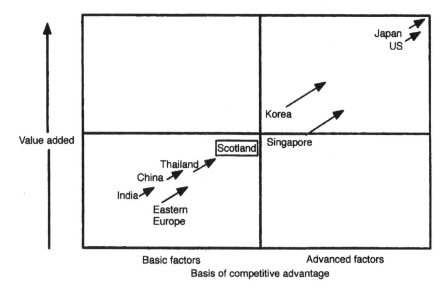

Figure 10.6 Scotland's IT industry: the narrowing cost gap and the widening value-added lag. The length of the arrows represents the relative speed of upgrading (By courtesy of the Monitor Company)

Loughborough University (Tilley *et al.* forthcoming). In the case of Singapore the interventions of government appear to have been especially instrumental (see Table 10.3).

Developing vision and strategy

In danger of remaining strategically 'stuck in the middle', as Porter might choose to describe it (Porter 1985), Scotland requires to re-engineer the basis of its long-term competitive advantage: costs alone are an insufficient basis on which to build, and new sources of added value must be found and/or created. Thus, over the mid-run, the Monitor Company envisages Scotland developing its role in IT as a value-added (rather than least-cost) manufacturing and logistics hub. Beyond this, it is argued, Scotland should aspire to become a knowledge and information hub which adds high worth to the European and global IT value system.

An international benchmarking study informed the development of strategies to achieve this mid-run goal. Through this study the Monitor Company established that robust, internationally competitive IT clusters (e.g. Massachusetts, Silicon Valley, Austin (Texas), Bavaria and Japan) have a number of key characteristics in common, notably a dynamic cycle of innovation and upgrade comprising six key activities which operate in a well integrated fashion and a core set of cluster capabilities which underpin

271

Table 10.3 Process of plant upgrading in Singapore, Taiwan and Hong Kong

---

(a) Interviews by Loughborough University with sister IT plants in Singapore, Taiwan and Hong Kong identified the following upgrade process in operation:

- Parent multinationals initially located product design of mature and/or non-core products with successful manufacturing subsidiaries.
- However, product design extended well beyond modification for local/regional markets, as most IT products were found to be serving global markets.
- Given the global and unpredictable nature of market growth, large design teams of around 150 people on average have emerged with responsibility for complex product design of products generating volume sales.
- The average time over which this type of design activity built up at plant levels was half as long in Singapore and Taiwan as in the UK.
- The design work identified, especially in respect of PCs, monitors and consumer products, was directly comparable with the type of design work carried out at the most capable UK sites of multinationals.
- The reason most cited by local plant managers for success in winning design responsibility was that the parent had moved on to next-generation products – the simpler tasks of turning out updates or variants of products, or redesigning for lower cost, were devolved to plants which already manufactured the relevant product and which offered relatively cheap but capable engineering skills.
- The second most important reason was the aspirations of senior site management and the host country.

(b) The Loughborough researchers identified two basic models of how design can grow at offshore sites:

Model 1 'Environmentally driven growth' typified the multinational experience in Taiwan, where government policies fine-tuned the supply side of the economy via support for local engineering industries, tariff-free components for export-orientated production, and promotion of a strong engineering emphasis in local universities to create a pool of relatively low-cost, high-quality engineering graduates, etc.

Model 2 'Government-encouraged growth' typified the multinational experience in Singapore. While government policy also feeds through on the supply side via infrastructure and skills, companies are encouraged more directly to upgrade. Significant tax breaks are offered under the 'Pioneer Status' programme for progressive plant upgradings and grants are also available under the Research Development Assistance Scheme and the Research Incentives Scheme for Companies. Technology transfer to 'supply companies' is encouraged via the Local Industry Upgrade Programme. Longer-term government-funded research centres will provide an additional support mechanism for company R&D.

---

the cycle of innovation, making faster and more flexible responses to changes in technology, products and markets possible over time (see Figures 10.7 and 10.8). Core cluster capabilities included:

1 A healthy number of internationally competitive firms which were well embedded in the local economy.
2 Demanding local buyers.

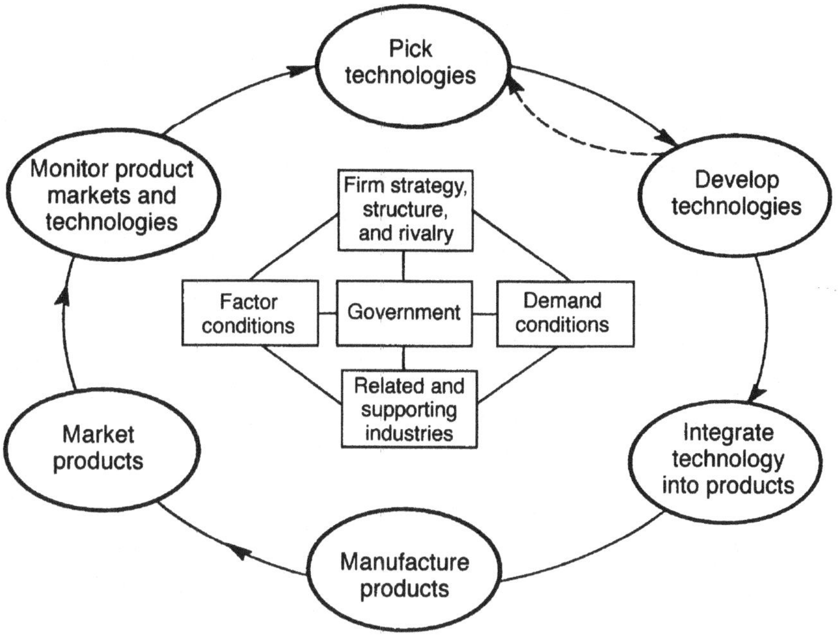

Figure 10.7 Cycle of innovation and its supporting diamond (By courtesy of the Monitor Company)

3 Strong supporting industries.
4 Rich, industry-specific advanced factor conditions.

In all instances, advanced factor conditions were found to be the most important driver of long-term competitiveness. These included:

1 A strong, dynamic IT community tightly networked across firms, institutions and capital providers.
2 A strong education foundation supporting the development of technical and marketing skills.
3 A strong applied research base integrating both firms and institutions.
4 An advanced communications and logistics infrastructure.

An integral part of the Monitor approach is to run an 'action' process in parallel with the 'Analytical' process to achieve maximum alignment of key local interests around an agreed set of strategic priorities for cluster upgrade. Potentially, this process has been greatly strengthened by the establishment of the Scottish Electronics Forum at the end of 1993. Supported by Scottish Enterprise, this industry-led initiative has, for the first time, brought together the leading electronics companies in Scotland, both overseas and indigenous. The objective of the new body is to address

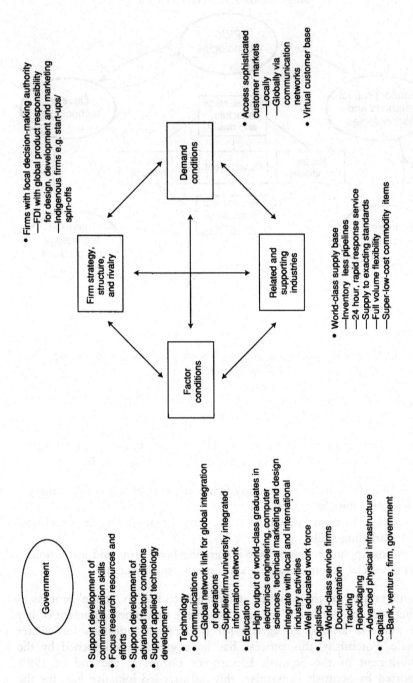

Government

- Support development of commercialization skills
- Focus research resources and efforts
- Support development of advanced factor conditions
- Support applied technology development

- Technology
- Communications
  —Global network link for global integration of operations
  —Supplier/firm/university integrated information network
- Education
  —High output of world-class graduates in electronics engineering, computer sciences, technical marketing and design
  —Integrate with local and international industry activities
  —Well educated work force
- Logistics
  —World-class service firms
  Documentation
  Tracking
  Repackaging
  —Advanced physical infrastructure
- Capital
  —Bank, venture, firm, government

Factor conditions

Firm strategy, structure, and rivalry

Demand conditions

Related and supporting industries

- Firms with local decision-making authority
  —FDI with global product responsibility for design, development and marketing
  —Indigenous firms e.g. start-ups/ spin-offs

- Access sophisticated customer markets
  —Locally
  —Globally via communication networks
- Virtual customer base

- World-class supply base
  —Inventory less pipelines
  —24 hour, rapid response service
  —Supply to exacting standards
  —Full volume flexibility
  —Super-low-cost commodity items

Figure 10.8 Key characteristics of a robust electronics diamond (By courtesy of the Monitor Company)

the immediate needs of the industry whilst building the foundations for a more robust, sustainable, competitive industry.

The work of the Monitor Company served to further catalyse the thinking of the wider 'action' process by enabling a 'road map' to be devised to guide planned action over the short, medium and longer run. This set out six strategic directions for Scotland which may be summarized as follows:

1 *Building world-class advanced factors in critical aspects of infrastructure (logistics, supply and communications) and skills.* In the short run Scotland's infrastructure must continue to be upgraded, both to defend and to build Scotland's position as a value-added and logistics gateway. A skills programme is also required to prepare Scotland for the future competitive needs of the IT industry.

2 *Building world-class commercialization capabilities.* To bridge the gap that exists between its assembly capabilities and its knowledge base, Scotland must seek to develop its indigenous market-driven commercialization skills over the short to medium run. Such mechanisms, when created, would lend further support to the commercialization activities of original equipment manufacturers and Scotland's major defence electronics companies, whilst nurturing more start-ups and entrepreneurial behaviour.

3 *Strengthening key sub-clusters.* In the medium run the portfolio of existing and embryonic sub-clusters (i.e. client-server computing, semiconductors, communications, consumer electronics, defence electronics, optoelectronics, artificial intelligence and parallel processing) will each need to be strengthened through infrastructural and commercialization support which addresses their individual requirements for long-term sustainable competitive advantage.

4 *Developing new market-focused sub-clusters.* Likewise, in the medium term, major opportunities to lever the broader Scottish electronics skills set will need to be identified through, for example, local buyers whose competitiveness could be significantly impacted by IT products, especially where local solutions to their needs provide the basis of global products (e.g. financial and business services, oil-related activity, health care, education, the media, etc.).

5 *Building advanced technology platforms.* A crucial long-term objective is to ensure that the key enabling technologies within Scotland's current technical expertise are successfully commercialized. This would involve identifying enabling technologies that are future-critical in which Scotland has world-class ability, such as opto-electronics. A local environment must then be created to allow these technologies to flourish and provide the basis of future Scottish products and industries.

6 *Developing Scotland as a centre for multimedia.* According to the Monitor

Company, the real opportunity in multimedia lies in the integration of traditional content and technology to create products to serve new, unique market needs. These products will constitute an entirely new arena, that of 'infotainment'. Scotland possesses some of the key sources of advantage required for success in this new market, such as content (via its relatively rich artistic and cultural heritage), world-class capability in both hardware and software, media suppliers and local markets to stimulate new product development. However, levering these assets would first require the successful implementation of the above programmes. In particular, a super-broadband data highway will need to become an integral part of the local communications infrastructure. Thus the exploitation of this opportunity is a long-term goal.

THE WIDER POLICY CONTEXT

The strategic directions outlined above have helped to shape the current agendas of both Scottish Enterprise and the Scottish Electronics Forum as they seek to design and implement programmes and initiatives to help reposition Scotland. However, 'goodness of fit' with the wider economic, business and policy environment must also be considered carefully in any determination of how far and fast local partners can roll-out such a strategy. Environmental scanning and monitoring are a prerequisite if major points of reinforcement and constraint are to be identified at an early stage. In the area of public policy, regional and trade policy present themselves as especially important issues in this industry/area context, and will now be considered more fully.

REGIONAL POLICY

In the internal market of the corporation, parent companies continue to attach high importance to government financial support in determining the outcome of adjusted present value calculations on high-risk/high-value investment proposals and adopt wide coercive spheres of comparison.

A particular concern has grown up among the local subsidiaries of leading IT firms regarding the ability of regional policy to encourage more rapid and substantial upgrading of plant activity which would embed this more firmly in the local economy. For different reasons, this concern is shared by regional economists in academia. For example, research undertaken for the European Commission by Newcastle University (Amin et al. 1994) promotes the case for better calibration of regional incentives to the quality of mobile investment, in pursuit of maximizing regional value added in the EC. The case-study evidence presented also suggests that the current level of deadweight expenditure associated with short-term, cost-based investment projects (drawn to peripheral areas solely by high capital sub-

276

sidies) is unnecessarily high as a result of inter-EC bidding. Moreover, with regard to investment in appropriate local infrastructure and factor conditions, the rules governing the allocation of EC Structural Funds tend to lag behind developments at the regional level, where dynamic structural adjustment may be under way.

The UK's relative position with regard to the general level and focus of direct financial support is highlighted in the European Commission's *Third Survey of State Aids to Manufacturing* (1992). During the time period under consideration, the amount of government aid received by manufacturers in the UK declined significantly. When expressed as a percentage of value added, or ECU per person employed, the level of support provided by the UK was the lowest in the EC. In pursuit of specific horizontal objectives (i.e. innovation, small and medium-sized firms, exports, energy conservation, etc.), the UK directed most of its support to exporters and small and medium-sized businesses. Accordingly, a smaller percentage of UK provision was directed towards innovation and R&D compared with near competitiors like Germany, France, the Netherlands and Belgium. Furthermore, where such support has been provided, it has tended to focus on small and medium-sized firms and/or emphasized the need for collaboration in pre-competitive research.

Some preliminary observations, relevant to the UK/Scottish case, can also be made about the focus of the main policy instruments employed at present. Regional Selective Assistance, the main form of financial support available in Scotland, is subject to EC cash ceilings and directed towards job creation and safeguard. (This tends to favour investment with relatively large job numbers attached, which is perhaps atypical of much higher value-added activity, especially R&D.) The Regional Enterprise Grant is designed to meet the investment and innovation needs of small firms and start-ups. The tax and planning advantages of Enterprise Zones are more attractive to manufacturing and service activities than to the higher value-adding functions of multinational enterprises. The delivery of national training programmes, environmental improvements and property initiatives still account for the bulk of the expenditure of Scottish Enterprise, Scotland's leading economic development body. (With the introduction of a new network strategy, however, SE spend priorities have the opportunity of becoming more targeted on higher value-adding development goals.)

Trade policy

The following illustrates the range of trade issues which bear directly on the local configuration of the value-adding operations of IT firms seeking to access and serve the markets of the EC. These examples highlight how trade measures may be used to stimulate and support the amount of worth which the EC adds to the global IT value system:

1 At the time of writing the Uruguay Round of the General Agreement on Trade and Tariffs (GATT) had not concluded. However, the EC has adopted a liberal bargaining position, proposing an average cut in the external tariff of around one-third. If fully implemented this would reduce the differential between integrated circuits and fully populated printed circuit boards, but would still leave a relatively high tariff on integrated circuits. This reflects the EC's view that upstream components which account for a substantial share of total value added should bear a higher level of duty, and its continued desire to protect the European semiconductor industry.

2 Rules of origin determine the territorial origin of goods from outside the EC where tariffs, quotas and anti-dumping regulations apply. They are especially relevant to overseas-owned multinational enterprises with screwdriver plants in the EC. The basic rule of origin is the country where 'the last substantial process or operation that is economically justified was performed' (EC 1968). The application of this concept varies in practice. Value-added criterion have been applied to television sets and radio receivers, while technical process requirements, such as diffusion, have been applied to integrated circuits. (With the exception of Mitsubishi, all the major Japanese manufacturers have established wafer fabrication facilities in the EC.)

3 Populated PCBs can account for well over 50 per cent of the final equipment cost of some computers, and often include significant Japanese input. A difficulty has arisen over this product category because overseas exporters have established assembly plants in the EC to avoid anti-dumping regulations, but the EC does not regard assembly as a sufficient indicator of origin. The Commission has considered introducing a new rule of origin based on the processes of 'stuffing and engraving'. This would have the effect of significantly raising the amount of value added within the EC. Pressure from trading partners has so far prevented the introduction of such a measure.

4 Under the Generalized System of Preferences (GSP) the EC unilaterally relaxes import restrictions on certain developing countries within agreed ceilings. For newly industrialized economies which have significantly improved their global competitiveness during the 1980s (e.g. Singapore and Taiwan), the ceilings set for sensitive products such as integrated circuits and populated PCBs are expected to become more restrictive. The rule of origin under GSP is that at least 60 per cent of the ex-works price must be accounted for by product procured within the beneficiary country. As such, computer sub-assemblies finally assembled and tested in Singapore are unlikely to qualify for relief. The EC has informally been exerting pressure to encourage higher levels of EC value in such sub-assemblies.

278

SUMMARY AND CONCLUSIONS

This chapter has sought to consider the strategic issues and responses for firms and policy-makers arising from the fundamental restructuring under way in Scotland's IT industries.

Given global/industry technological, product, market and regulatory trends, intensifying place competition globally, and the present structure of the IT industry, the strategic imperative for Scotland, according to the Monitor Company, is to accelerate the process by which the basis of its competitive advantage is re-engineered from cost to value added. This is needed if more rapid upgrading and diversification of IT activity is to be achieved. A wider 'action process' with key interest groups in Scotland's IT industry was also catalysed by Monitor. This enabled six strategic directions to be identified which will guide planned action. These were:

1 Building world-class advanced factors in critical aspects of infrastructure (logistics, supply and communications) and skills.
2 Building world-class commercialization capabilities to bridge the gap that exists between Scotland's assembly capabilities and its knowledge base.
3 Strengthening key sub-clusters, both existing and embryonic (i.e. client-server computing, semiconductors, communications, consumer electronics, defence electronics, opto-electronics, artificial intelligence and parallel processing).
4 Developing new market-focused sub-clusters, especially where local solutions to IT needs provide a basis for global products (e.g. financial and business services, oil-related activity, health care, education, the media, etc.).
5 Building advanced technology platforms to ensure that the key enabling technologies within Scotland's current technical expertise (e.g. opto-electronics) are successfully commercialized.
6 Developing Scotland as a centre for multimedia by integrating traditional content (via its relatively rich artistic and cultural heritage) and technology to create products to serve new unique market needs.

The establishment of the Scottish Electronics Forum, a new industry-led partnership supported by Scottish Enterprise, represents a potentially significant institutional innovation which may enhance the development and implementation of appropriate support programmes and projects. However, in rolling out this local strategy, the 'fit' with wider public policy must also be considered so that points of reinforcement and constraint may be identified. In this industry/area context, regional policy and trade policy are especially important issues.

This preliminary review suggests that the strategic coherence, co-ordination, flexibility and focus of present regional policy could be further enhanced (perhaps significantly so in certain instances), to strengthen and promote local development strategies which aim to maximize regional value added.

At the Scottish/UK level, the Monitor analysis and action guide would encourage the more rapid embedding of the new network priorities for Scottish Enterprise so that its funding and action continue to focus increasingly on support for higher value-added activity. There may also be a case for reviewing the ability of Regional Selective Assistance to promote/support more high quality investment/reinvestment effectively. In reality, the case for seeking out new alternative forms of incentive may be even stronger. More generally, the question is posed as to how well the present tools of UK regional policy interrelate to produce strong synergies and reinforcements to maximize regional value added.

At EC level, more regular review of Structural Fund allocation criteria may be appropriate to ensure that a firm focus on maximizing regional value added is achieved. It has also been suggested that EC rules could be used to encourage better calibration of financial incentives to secure more high-quality investment/reinvestment, especially from multinationals. Furthermore, were the deadweight attributable to inter-EC bidding associated with schemes of capital assistance available in certain member states to be reduced, more resources might be available to devote to this end.

However, the global nature of the competition which the regions of Europe face for direct investment could limit progress towards such an objective. This compounds the difficulty of achieving 'a level playing field within the EC', as significant differences in the level and type of subsidy/incentive available from competing locations (both within and outwith the EC) are likely to persist. It is hard, therefore, to disagree with the conclusion that, beyond the further dismantling of tariff and non-tariff barriers, the need for a new GATT on subsidies and incentives to attract/retain direct investment is the next pressing challenge facing the global economy (UN 1993).

The EC's stance on trade policy, especially with regard to the maintenance of differential tariffs on populated PCBs and ICs, rules of origin on anti-dumping and rules of origin under the Generalized System of Preferences may provide a stronger set of reinforcements for the maximization of regional value added in those areas of the EC with significant dependence on the IT industries.

However, with progressive moves to greater liberalization under GATT, such artificial support can be expected to continue to diminish in importance. The main virtue of EC trade policy in this respect appears to be to 'buy time' for development bodies such as Scottish Enterprise – as they seek to implement, through partnership, local development strategies which focus more firmly on the maximization of the regional value added to be derived from the expanding activities of the IT and other high-technology global industries.

REFERENCES

Amin, A., Bradley, D., Howells, J., Tomaney, J. and Gentle, C. (1994) 'Regional incentives and the quality of mobile investment in the less favoured regions of the EC', *Progress in Planning* 14(1): 1–112.

Commission of the European Communities (1992), *Third Survey on State Aids in the European Community in the Manufacturing and certain other Sectors*, Brussels: CEC.

Council of the European Communities (1968), *Common Definition of the Concept of Origin of Goods, Regulation 802/68. Ref. OJL148*, Brussels: CEC.

Monitor Company (1993), 'A Strategy for the Scottish Software and Electronics Clusters', unpublished report for Scottish Enterprise, Glasgow: Monitor Company.

Moschella, D. C. (1993) *IT Industry Disintegration Revisited – Implications for 1993 and Beyond*, Special Executive Briefing, International Data Corporation.

Porter, M. E. (1985) *Competitive Advantage*, New York: Free Press.

Rappaport, A. S., and Halvei, S. (1991) 'The computerless company', *Harvard Business Review*, July/August: 69–80.

Sacerdote, G. (1993) *Multimedia – Hype or Reality? A European Perspective*, New York: Arthur D. Little.

Tilley, J., Williams, D. J., and Conway, P. P. (forthcoming) *Globalisation of Electronics Manufacture: the Growth of an Electronics Manufacturing Industry*, Loughborough: Loughborough University of Technology.

United Nations (1993) *World Investment Report: Transnational Corporations and Integrated International Production*, New York: United Nations.

Young, S., Peters, E., and Hood, N. (1993) 'Performance and employment change in overseas-owned manufacturing industry in Scotland', *Scottish Economic Bulletin* 47, Edinburgh: HMSO.

ACKNOWLEDGEMENTS

Among other sources, the chapter draws on the unpublished findings of a major review of Scotland's IT industries, undertaken on behalf of Scottish Enterprise by the Monitor Company, the Boston-based consultancy chaired by Professor Michael Porter. The views expressed in this chapter are those of the author.

11

ATTRACTING, MANAGING AND DEVELOPING INWARD INVESTMENT IN THE SINGLE MARKET

Stephen Young and Neil Hood

This chapter addresses the theme of *cohesion and conflict* from the policy perspective of inward investment agencies seeking to attract, retain and develop foreign direct investment from multinational enterprises. The chapter begins with a brief overview of the environment for inward investment in the EC in the late 1990s and the problems and potential for regional economic development. Thereafter the existing activities of inward investment agencies are evaluated, with the main emphasis of the chapter – following the policy thrust of Chapter 8 by Amin and Tomaney – concerning possible policy changes in the areas of promotional targeting, after-care, and merger, acquisition and alliance policy and their contribution to economic development.

THE INWARD INVESTMENT ENVIRONMENT IN THE EC

The changing characteristics of inward investment have been well documented (UN-TCMD 1992) and include:

1 A reducing share of projects in the category of greenfield manufacturing investments, traditionally the main emphasis of the promotional and targeting activities of inward investment agencies.
2 Growth of investment in service sectors such as banking and finance, reflecting long-term structural changes, and increased 'services investment' (e.g. marketing and distribution) in manufacturing industries.
3 A widening of entry modes, with a growth of international mergers, acquisitions and alliances at the expense of wholly-owned greenfield projects. The incidence of international mergers and acquisitions is to some extent a cyclical phenomenon, but alliance activity, whether in the

form of equity or contractual joint ventures and involving different elements of the value chain, is certainly growing rapidly.

These trends are apparent throughout the world, but in the EC the pattern was disguised in the years leading up to the formation of the single market as non-EC companies sought a foothold by any means to pre-empt possible protectionism. In the EC of the 1990s, however, the major additional element to the above concerns multinational enterprise restructuring, entailing expansions, contractions and greater centralization of activity, in response to the single market, enlargement (including countries within the European Economic Area and potentially some of the Central and Eastern European nations) and hesitant progress towards economic and monetary union. Studies of the effects of regional integration on the organization of multinational enterprises in the EC conclude that both centralization of production and/or decentralization of products/processes according to comparative advantage will be in evidence within the single market, with large-scale rationalization potentially occurring, especially among multinational affiliates that previously served markets on a national basis (UNCTC 1990; Young *et al.* 1991; UN-TCMD 1993; Dunning 1993). For host countries and regions in Europe, therefore, the possible positive and negative consequences of corporate restructuring represent a major challenge to be tackled.

Aside from the policy issues which emerge from changing corporate dynamics, inward investment agencies and other government agencies are (or should be) concerned to maximize the regional economic development contribution of multinational investment. Empirical evidence at least for peripheral economies indicates that there have been significant static gains from (mainly) production plants but few dynamic benefits (Young, Hood and Peters 1994). The former relate to structural upgrading resulting from the inflow of investment into industries like electronics, while the performance of foreign companies on indicators such as net output, capital expenditure and wages and salaries has been better than that of indigenous firms; inward investment has also improved the export orientation of regional economies. However the 'embeddedness' of multinational enterprises within the less favoured regions of the EC (Amin *et al.* 1994, and Chapter 8 in this volume, by Amin and Tomaney) and their contribution to long-term economic development have been limited: spin-off and demonstration effects have been low, and there are few illustrations of integrated, entrepreneurial multinational activity or of complete value-added chains of multinational operations that might begin to produce dynamic comparative advantage. The need to address these problems has been argued by academics and others for many years. With the present uncertainties concerning the level and stability of the stock of inward investment in EC countries and regions, the climate is perhaps now more favourable with regard to policy action to try to improve the economic contribution of new and existing multinational firms.

INWARD INVESTMENT AGENCIES IN THE EC AND THEIR OPERATIONS

No complete information is available on the number, size or expenditure of inward investment agencies in the EC. The Industrial Development Authority of the Republic of Ireland was probably the first European country organization to promote inward investment actively as a matter of national policy from 1969–70 (Watzke 1982; Wells and Wint 1990), and it is still one of the most professional. The UK Invest in Britain Bureau was granted a mandate to promote international investment in 1980. It has since been joined by five English Regional Development Organizations, co-ordinated through the English Unit, and three Territorial Agencies in Scotland, Wales and Northern Ireland. In France, the Invest in France Agency is the investment attraction arm of DATAR (Délégation à l'Amén-agement du Territoire et à l'Action Régionale) which has a much wider regional development role for the country as a whole, but there are many regional agencies below the IFA, with co-ordination problems in the past (a difficulty in other countries such as the UK too). With Germany's federal structure, inward investment promotion in western Germany is the respon-sibility of the sixteen individual *Länder*. Following reunification, a Federal Investor Information Centre was established, principally to handle inward investment activities on behalf of the former eastern Germany. To give one final illustration, Spain has two national agencies involved in overseas promotion, ICEX (Institute of Foreign Trade) and ENISA (Empresa Nacional de Innovación SA), plus agencies in each of the seventeen autonomous regions of the country.

As is apparent from the above, the inward investment agencies in Europe are either part of government departments or publicly funded and quasi-governmental. In some cases they are part of organizations whose remit extends beyond inward investment attraction to include wider regional and industrial development and export promotion roles. Considering the inward investment role alone, a number of functions may be performed by inward investment agencies in the EC, as shown in Table 11.1. This table highlights the full range of potential activities, but not all agencies will be involved in every one. For example, the policy formulation role may be restricted to marketing planning or there may be efforts to integrate inward investment with wider industrial policy; in the EC the tendency is definitely towards the former role. Within the EC, there are usually not the formal prohibitions or regulations on foreign direct investment in particular industries which exist in some developing countries. However, because incentives are generally offered to inward investors, approval procedures involving government

Table 11.1 Functions of inward investment agencies

1 Policy formulation	Guidelines for inward investment policy; assessment of the effectiveness of policy; integration with national and regional industrial policies
2 Investment promotion and attraction	Marketing information and intelligence; marketing planning, including targeting; marketing operations outside and inside the country
3 Investment approvals	Screening/evaluation of potential projects
4 Granting of incentives	Consideration of incentive offers; incentive negotiations; incentive approvals. Includes direct financial incentives plus training grants, innovation grants, land and buildings, etc.
5 Providing pre-start-up assistance (after-care)	Includes assistance with public utilities (roads, water, electricity, sewerage, telecommunications), factories and training; links with universities and research institutes; identification of potential suppliers
6 Providing post-start-up assistance (after-care)	Continuation of assistance post-launch. Liaison re possible expansion projects, developing local suppliers, etc.

Source: Young, Hood and Wilson (1994).

departments will normally operate: incentives have to comply with EC rules on regional aid (Young and Hood 1993) and some form of bene-fit–cost analysis, including estimates of the displacement cost of new investments, would be undertaken. The after-care functions are generally underdeveloped, if undertaken at all.

From the perspective of this chapter the main weaknesses in inward investment agency operations in the context of the environment in the second half of the 1990s appear to be the following:

1 Marketing planning, and especially the component of targeting, is in-sufficiently directed towards the real issues in economic development, with crude performance measures such as numbers of projects attracted and jobs created being applied.
2 With the paucity of new greenfield investment, it is becoming increas-ingly important to try to generate expansionary investment from within the existing stock of investors in any given location and forestall

rationalizations. This means that much greater attention needs to be paid to the after-care function.

3 Inward investment agency operations are generally insufficiently integrated within themselves and within wider economic development policies and programmes. These linkages are highlighted in Figure 11.1, focusing upon the significance of targeting and after-care.

4 Both Table 11.1 and Figure 11.1 implicitly assume that the functions of inward investment agencies relate to new greenfield or expansionary projects in manufacturing industry. However, the earlier discussion

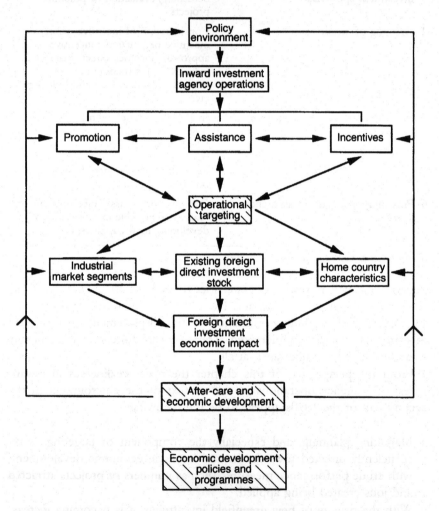

Figure 11.1 Inward investment activity and interrelationships and economic development
Source: Young, Hood and Wilson (1994)

stressed the importance of inward investment in service industries and the growth of mergers, acquisitions and alliances. Some core regions in the EC are actively seeking to attract investments in distribution or R&D, as well as headquarter functions, while peripheral areas such as the Republic of Ireland have a large programme of investment attraction in financial services. Such programmes could well emerge from refined targeting policies. On the other hand, except for notional interest and involvement in joint ventures, inward investment agencies have not been active in acquisitions and strategic alliances. While there is a debate as to whether or not they ever should, the issues certainly need to be aired.

The purpose of this chapter is to suggest some modest new ideas for policy change to begin to address these weaknesses.

DESIGNING PROMOTIONAL AND ATTRACTION POLICIES

In undertaking activities designed to attract greenfield projects to countries and regions in the EC, inward investment agencies operate almost as conventional marketing companies. According to Wells and Wint (1990), agencies may engage in three different types of activity, the first of which is *image-building* designed to improve the image of a country as a place to invest; the second is *investment-generating* activity, with promotional techniques being used to identify and contact decision-makers and encourage investment in the host country concerned; and the third is *investment service* techniques, including investment counselling, assisting with the processing of applications and permits, and the provision of post-investment services. All have the ultimate object of attracting more investment, but their immediate goals are different and their relative appropriateness depends upon particular country circumstances.

Regarding promotional techniques employed, a range of activities would be observed for most countries such as advertising in general financial media; participating in investment exhibitions; advertising in industry- or sector-specific media; investment missions from source country to host country or vice versa, both general missions and industry/sector-specific; conducting investment seminars, both general and industry/sector-specific; undertaking direct mail or tele-marketing campaigns; engaging in firm-specific research and targeting through databases, followed by sales presentations; providing investment counselling services; expediting the processing of applications and permits; and providing post-investment services (Wells and Wint 1990). The foreign investment decision process has many of the same characteristics as the industrial buying decision, representing a discrete, relatively infrequent but important 'purchase' on the part of many of the companies concerned. The time scale for evaluating countries and sites, and then for getting the project up and running, may be extremely lengthy for investment decisions (Hood and Truijens, 1993), and the tipping factor could be something as subjective as the welcoming attitude of local bodies or particular individuals (Welsh Affairs Committee 1988). Because of this, a variety of approaches to target investors through a range of promotional techniques may be desirable. At the same time, inward investment agencies adapt their programmes according to their relative success and some of the activities noted above, especially participation in investment exhibitions and seminars, are regarded as wasteful of resources. By comparison tele-marketing has become much more important. Promotions are co-ordinated from their European base, but many organizations have a spread of overseas offices in the US, in Asian centres like Tokyo, Osaka, Seoul, Taipei, Singapore and Hong Kong, as well as in Europe itself for intra-European investment.

Promotional and attraction policies are simply tools to implement marketing strategy, the main components of which concern the home countries, regions or cities to be targeted in promotions, the sectors or sub-sectors or indeed the characteristics of the class of investor (e.g. R&D intensity, advertising intensity, skilled manpower intensity, etc.) to be targeted. The question of targeting is thus a key one, and one where arguably there is significant scope for refinement of effort in order to generate investment which has the potential to assist long-term economic development.

There is no complete information available on the targeting activities of different investment agencies in Europe, but inspection of the promotional material of a range of agencies indicates that except for Sweden and Denmark virtually all countries target their promotions. Sweden and Denmark follow a general image-building approach, regarding it as sufficient to have both a favourable macro regulatory environment and to promote its existence. Among the remaining countries, the following can be observed:

1 Virtually all agencies have an interest in micro-electronics and information technology.
2 Biotechnology, health care and medical technologies are also common sectors of interest, drawing on medical sector strengths and potential market growth.
3 Other sectors targeted by particular agencies include chemicals, food, advanced materials and material technology, and many more.
4 In respect of individual countries, the Netherlands and Belgium have focused on distribution and headquarters/co-ordination projects, with telecoms-based facilities representing an additional area of project interest in the Netherlands. In Germany the emphasis is on high-tech, high-skill and R&D projects as well as headquarter operations, while in France there is growing interest in service sector projects.

To a large extent the sectors targeted are growth (micro-electronics, health care) or potential growth (biotechnology) industries and would fit many of the other criteria relating to foreign direct investment potential, including research intensity, export orientation and so on. Thus any project aimed at identifying target sectors would have these close to the top of any list. The increasing interest in service sector projects is also a reflection of the changed balance of investment, in favour of services as opposed to manufacturing, which is expected to continue through the 1990s. So the list above is unsurprising, and because of the criteria applied to derive targets inward investment agencies will frequently find themselves competing head-on for particular inward investment projects, despite the fact that such projects may not be best suited to the economic needs of the region or country.

The argument to be presented here is that a new approach to targeting is necessary, but first it is important to weigh up some of the pros and cons of targeting, since what is implied in the proposals to follow is a very significant shift in attitudes and activity.

Considering the cautionary remarks initially, policy studies on investment attraction, while arguing in favour of targeting, have also counselled against taking it too far, especially if it leads to a narrowing of the industrial base. For example, the valid point has been made that over-reliance on any one sector could lead to restructuring problems in the future (Netherlands Economic Institute 1992). In a UK context, moreover, the fact that the country has the widest sectoral representation of US inward investment of any EC member state means that a very focused approach to marketing would inevitably exclude a number of sectors with significant inward investment potential. Both these issues must be recognized when devising any targeting policies.

At an operational level there is another concern which relates to the internal marketing of targeting policies and programmes. It is important that the success or failure of targeting should not simply be assessed by the extent to which inward investment flows coincide with the targets or some broader measures. Targeting sectors can and does have the effect of promoting 'flagships' where existing success in the sectors leads to investors in other sectors choosing the same location. These implications have also to be communicated clearly to the large number of public and private-sector organizations involved with inward investment, since otherwise the publication of strategic targets may be interpreted in a rather literal manner, with major implications for decisions about land, factory space and infrastructure.

A further argument against targeting is that it is not possible in the context of the 1990s when increasing competition among agencies and the turbulence associated with the single market demands greater flexibility in inward investment agency operations. The counter-argument is that even clearer goals and targets have to be set in such an environment if the inward investment agency is not to lose its focus and the potential for generating long-term economic development.

In favour of targeting, then, is the fundamental fact that investment attraction should be seen as part of an integrated programme for a region or country, designed with 'development' rather than simply 'employment' in mind. There is plenty of evidence, as noted earlier, that, while the static benefits associated with inward investment have been favourable, the long-term, dynamic gains have been limited. Targeting *per se* is not a panacea but it is certainly an integral component of any programme seeking economic development benefits. At an operational level, there is a need to recognize that inward investment attraction is a specialized and competitive business, and hence planning and targeting are necessary for effective resource utilization and in response to calls for accountability.

The argument presented here is that the variables utilized in defining target markets to date have been insufficiently directed to the real issues in economic development. Although there has been a good deal of creativity from inward investment agencies, targeting has generally emphasized countries, sectors and firms as inputs rather than outputs of the ensuing investment. 'Developmental targeting' may thus be defined as

> a process which identifies inward investment market segments which match the desired outputs from inward investment (in terms of employment, technology transfer, trade and balance of payments and linkage and spillover effects) to the competitive advantages of countries and regions.
>
> (Young, Hood and Wilson 1994).

The implementation of 'developmental targeting' is not easy, requiring a three-stage approach: first, identifying attractive segments from an economic development perspective; second, assessing the competitive advantage of a country or region; third, matching the two elements to establish the attractive segments for the particular region. The details of how this might operate have been discussed elsewhere (Young, Hood and Wilson 1994). The end result would be a 'matrix of appropriateness', as shown in Figure 11.2. Segment attractiveness would take into consideration the range of outputs from inward investment, and, equally important, these would have to be weighted according to their relative importance to the inward investment agency. Thus if most importance from an economic development perspective was attached to linkage and spill-over effects, indicators associated with local sourcing would be weighted most highly; alternatively, if technology development issues were perceived as most important, indicators linked to the multinationals' record in terms of subsidiary R&D or their track record of working with universities and research institutes would receive the highest ranking. Obtaining the information

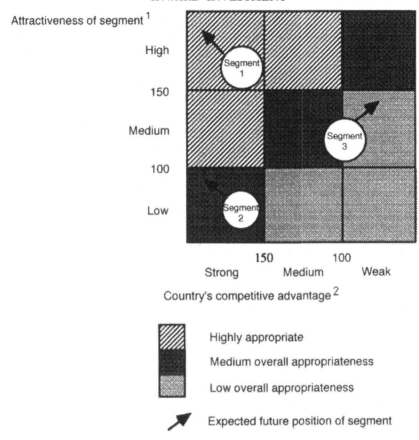

Attractiveness of segment [1]

High

150

Medium

100

Low

150　　　　100

Strong　　Medium　　Weak

Country's competitive advantage [2]

Highly appropriate

Medium overall appropriateness

Low overall appropriateness

Expected future position of segment

Figure 11.2 Matrix of appropriateness
Notes: 1 The values on the attractiveness axis are based on the total attractiveness
values calculated from employment indicators, trade and balance of payments
indicators and technology transfer indicators. 2 The values on the competitive
advantage axis read from left to right and are based on the total competitive
advantage values for each segment.
Source: Young, Hood and Wilson (1994).

would not be easy (and this is probably the major objection to this
approach) and, while published sources should provide clues to the potential in each of the economic impact classifications, some survey work would
probably be necessary.

Turning to the assessment of the competitive advantages of a country or
region, this may be regarded as 'place auditing' (Kotler *et al.* 1993),
establishing the strengths and weaknesses of the area in relation to the
attractive segments identified. Some of the strengths may be potential
strengths if the country intends to build these via, for example, substantial
infrastructure investment in transport, telecommunications or training.

291

The final step is to plot segments on a matrix as in Figure 11.2, which shows a hypothetical rating for a number of manufacturing segments. The three cells in the upper left indicate highly appropriate segments which should be aggressively targeted by the inward investment agency. The diagonal cells stretching from the lower left to the upper right indicate segments that are medium in overall appropriateness: the inward investment agency should pursue them selectively. The three cells at the lower right indicate segments that are low in overall appropriateness and therefore should not be targeted on the basis of this type of analysis.

In order that the matrix is more than simply a snapshot in time, the inward investment agencies should also forecast the expected position of each segment in the next three to five years, given the likely developments in both the segment and the host country. For example, segment 1 could be a sector like telecommunications for the UK. Early deregulation and privatization have begun to open up the UK market to equity investment in both equipment and operations. The country competitive advantage has thus been strengthened and now offers new segment opportunities for the deregulating European market in consequence of changed structures and deregulation in the US and Japan (see Little 1991). The net effect is the potential enhancement of the existing high level of attractiveness of telecommunications in the UK.

The implication of the above is that the inward investment agency and those associated with it in allied activity require to have a clearly determined strategy as to what economic benefits are being sought from inward investment, a theme which runs throughout this chapter. The application of targeting as proposed requires a more integrated approach to economic development, business development and infrastructure. Included within this would be integration of the inward investment agency's and related agencies' activities themselves (as highlighted in Figure 11.1), with the function of after-care being a major component.

DESIGNING AFTER-CARE POLICIES

As the earlier discussion has shown, after-care represents a critical area of activity in the management of inward investment in the single market. However, while after-care is conventionally included as one of the standard functions of inward investment agencies (Table 11.1), the evidence seems to indicate that the activities undertaken have been more symbolic than substantive, and there is in any event a question mark over which is the appropriate organization to undertake after-care. As in the previous remarks on targeting policy, therefore, the aim of this section is to present some ideas for after-care programmes for EC countries and regions.

One of the few writers on the subject defines after-care as 'a category of services that might be viewed as analagous to the marketing concept of "after-sales services"' (Wint 1993: 72) or one which could be considered as 'post-approval services'. To Dunning (1993: 27) after-care activity represents a means of reducing 'the hassle costs of doing business'. The definition developed by the present authors is as follows:

> After-care comprises all potential services offered at the company level by government and its agencies designed to facilitate both the successful start-up and the continuing development of a multinational affiliate in a host country or region, with a view to maximising the local economic development contribution of that affiliate. Related activity would be planned at the regional or national level to ensure a supportive environment for the realisation of the company-specific aims.
>
> (Young and Hood 1994)

By this definition, after-care commences once the investment decision has been made and therefore excludes company search processes, although many of the same organizational challenges and the same organizations are involved at the time of search.

The potential benefits from committing significant resources to after-care fall into a number of categories. In the first place, it is an essential component of customer orientation and customer care. The multinational affiliate, having been attracted to a particular location, has a legitimate expectation of a level of follow-up ('after-sales') service. From the government agency perspective this customer care activity reflects recognition of the local identity of the project and a desire to project that local identity, and concern for its problems and performance. The fact that multinational subsidiaries are larger, faster-growing, more productive and more export-oriented than indigenous enterprises is of major importance. If the concept of 'local identity' can be transmitted to and accepted by the investor, there are likely to be benefits from greater community involvement by the multinational affiliate. In such circumstances, moreover, the multinational affiliate may have an important long-term role in marketing the area to new potential investors, who may visit the plant as part of their site search activities.

Second, the growth of multinational affiliates within a world-wide corporate framework is chiefly related to their comparative performance, and, therefore, any assistance public-sector agencies can provide to help in the improvement of performance is clearly desirable. Third, and specifically related to regionalization and globalization, many multinational corporate networks are being reorganized and rationalized with major divestment programmes being planned and implemented. The potential for public-sector agencies to influence corporate strategic change in favour of local affiliates is clearly limited. On the other hand, it has been shown that multinational global strategies can be identified by an increased level of involvement with the corporations, information which may then be employed to support or defend the local affiliate.

Against this, of course, there are major problems and challenges to be tackled in developing an after-care programme. First and most obvious is the issue of cost: as will be shown later, it is possible to devise certain after-care projects which operate across a sub-sector or at least appeal to a number of firms, e.g. training programmes, but in the main after-care is firm-specific and human resource-intensive.

A second issue concerns the credibility and capability of after-care providers. There is no question that management in many multinational affiliates will view approaches from public-sector officials with scepticism, sometimes even hostility. Building a relationship of trust and openness means that after-care personnel must be credible and capable. This is not so much a problem on issues such as property, since experienced estate management teams exist throughout public-sector organizations. However, having sufficient understanding of issues such as multinational corporate strategy, advanced manufacturing techniques and high-tech supply capacity to be able to engage in constructive dialogue with multinational management (possibly at corporate as well as affiliate level) will never be easy.

A third set of problems and challenges concern the continuity and customer responsiveness of after-care services. Affiliate management in multinational enterprises change positions frequently, with two to three-year assignments being normal, especially for expatriate personnel; even indigenous managers may be moved internationally within the group to gain experience or as a result of promotion. Within the after-care organizations, too, the same difficulty may apply: staff with high-level skills in multinational corporate strategy, manufacturing or finance will be targets for recruitment 'head-hunters'. Neither building nor retaining credibility will, therefore, be easy. In a customer responsiveness context, response time scales are another problem to be tackled by after-care providers: inward investment agencies involved at the cutting edge of selling and negotiation recognize this, local authorities and others perhaps less so.

A fourth problem area concerns which government and public (or indeed private) sector organizations will undertake after-care services and the co-ordination of their activities. In research undertaken in a number of cities and territories in France, Texier and Valla (1992) identified more than twenty public and private organizations in contact with potential investors – and this same range of organizations would be involved post-investment, albeit with different intensity.

The final set of issues relate to the very different circumstances and requirements of the inward investing companies. For example, investor experience in internationalization differs widely, with the first-time international investor being in a totally different situation from a globally networked multinational enterprise. Investor size and technology raise distinct issues concerning expectations. In high-tech (especially large) companies the multinational enterprise affiliate is aware of its significance and bargaining power in a region or country and hence will expect a high level of service, at least on issues of its choosing. The development stage of the investment projects places different demands and a different intensity of demands for after-care. During start-up and the first two years of operation there is likely to be constant interaction between after-care providers and the company, mainly on operational issues. Typically, in the period after this, there is less requirement for after-care and less contact from the after-care providers as the company is integrated into the area and other priorities take over. Yet in fact this is the stage when the longer-term strategic links should be nurtured, to ensure an understanding of corporate policies at group and subsidiary level and to enable the after-care provider to interact sensibly and constructively on issues relating to the strategic development of the facility. Investor requirements may differ, again, by nationality. There is a belief that for cultural reasons (but perhaps it is chiefly inexperience in operating abroad) Japanese investors appreciate a close 'key account'-type relationship with inward investment agencies at the time of search and investment decision-making. If so, it is important to extend this to the after-care stage.

With this background, Table 11.2 lists the series of services which might conceivably be included in a comprehensive after-care programme. A distinction is drawn between strategic, operational and informational services which are specific to the inward investing company and general supply-side services which are crucial but support the development of all companies, indigenous and foreign, within a region. Thereafter, Table 11.3 outlines a number of possible models of after-care which might be implemented by regional or national agencies, indicating the type of investor likely to be targeted for after-care services, the time period to be covered, the nature of the service, and the advantages and disadvantages of the different approaches. The integrated model I is the most ambitious and costly, and envisages after-care as a part of a comprehensive regional economic development plan. It requires co-ordinated commitment from the wide range of public-sector agencies necessarily involved in economic development, as well as co-operation from the multinational stock. The after-care team model II reflects an attempt to replicate at an after-care level the type of promotional service undertaken by inward investment agencies. To match the latter, the team might be organized to cover nationality groupings of investors, or involve sectoral specializations. The size of team necessary needs further investigation: because the span of responsibility is very wide, the group of companies to be handled by any individual could not be large. The after-care team would act as a 'single-door' for after-care services: to be effective, this would extend beyond

Table 11.2 Potential after-care services

1 *Strategic*	
Strategy and planning	Presenting case for new investment to corporate HQ; assisting in intra-group bids for new projects; preventing adverse effects of rationalization. Presenting case for new activities at plant level, e.g. R&D, marketing. Identifying joint-venture/strategic alliance partners
Sites and property	Sites and locational infrastructure. Property: advance factories, bespoke factories, adaptations and extensions
Financial assistance	Presenting case for and/or packaging available financial incentives
Human resources	Development of human skills
Research and development	Innovation and new product development: R&D, marketing research Joint research with universities, etc.; research funding
Manufacturing	Upgrading
Procurement	Identifying and/or developing supply sources and supplier capabilities
Marketing and sales	Market and technological forecasting
2 *Operational*	
Sites and property	Site maintenance, bus services, etc.
Financial assistance	Implementation of grant provisions
Human resources	Recruitment, housing, schooling and education, arranging training/identifying appropriate training courses, legislation
Research and development	Funding applications, staffing
Manufacturing	Quality issues, computerization
Procurement	Standards, movement and sources of inputs
Marketing and sales	Customs issues, foreign exchange matters
Finance/accounting/legal	Taxation, banking
3 *Informational*	Wide range of requirements
4 *General supply side* (to upgrade region as a whole)	Investment in scientific, managerial, technical and manual skills. Investment in health, education, training and leisure facilities. Investment in transport and communications infrastructure. Assistance to develop supplier capabilities.

Source: Young and Hood (1994).
Note: [a] The support to be provided is likely to be one of four types, namely finance, expertise, contacts, or influence.

Table 11.3 Models of after-care

Category of after-care			
I Integrated	*II After-care team*	*III Project-based*	*IV Company friend*
Types of inward investor			
Detailed knowledge of entire stock (foreign and domestic) regularly updated. Priority ranking according to economic development potential	Detailed knowledge of entire stock. Investors ranked according to priority and after-care provided accordingly	Related to target segments, focusing on supplier development, human resource development, manufacturing services, research and development, etc.	Priority to large, high-tech, high profile and/or Japanese investors
Time period for after-care service			
Long-term, against clear, quantifiable objectives	Long-term, but priority in early years of project and when potential reinvestment/restructuring identified	Dependent on time period of project	Mainly first two years after start-up. Annual visit to priority companies, otherwise as requested
Nature of after-care			
Informational and *Operational* to all investors; plus *Strategic* and *General supply side* to 'developmental' facilities. After-care integrated with all regional economic development initiatives	*Strategic, Operational* and *Informational*, depending on priority of investor	*Strategic* and *Operational* linked to project, plus *General supply side* (e.g. assistance to develop supplier capabilities)	*Informational* plus limited *Operational* (local trouble-shooting). May be linked with visits relating to grant award compliance
Evaluation of approach			
Pro: Balanced and integrated approach to economic development. Can avoid excessive emphasis on multinationals	Pro: Single-door for multinational after-care. Committed and systematic after-care service. After-care skills developed by government agencies and recognized by multinationals	Pro: Highly focused. Links company and general regional economic development efforts	Pro: Inexpensive. May identify some areas of opportunity to aid affiliate. Assist companies to develop their own networks
Con: Very costly and long-term. Major commitment needed from wide range of public-sector agencies. Co-ordination problems may lead to excessive bureaucracy. Assumes multinational co-operation	Con: Costly and may lack some focus, depending on method of organizing service. Success dependent on integrating effort with other resources	Con: Costly and returns mainly long-term. Difficulty of obtaining company co-operation (especially among competitors)	Con: Cause resentment among some multinational affiliates. *Laissez-faire* approach may compare badly with that offered to sister affiliates in other host countries. Regional economic development largely left to market mechanisms

Source: Young and Hood (1994).

redirecting enquiries to the appropriate department or agency, to perhaps initial visits in association with the latter and certainly continuous monitoring of relationships and feedback. Reflecting an earlier observation, managing co-ordination would be a major task.

The project-based model III represents an attempt to direct resources to key, specific issues in after-care rather than covering the entire span of after-care activities. Obvious areas for initiatives are supplier development, where the aim is to build up the supplier base as a means of increasing the multiplier effects of inward investment; human resource development, where, for example, training programmes might be initiated to assist the manpower requirements of a number of inward investors in a particular industry sector; research and development, where the intention might be to help develop a research cluster through financial pump priming or to facilitate university–company research linkages. If this model was followed, it would probably also have to include the 'company friend' to deal with other after-care issues.

The company friend model IV *per se* is the minimalist approach to after-care. Even this would seem to represent an advance on what exists at present in that it would at least be systematic. The major problem is that, because of lack of regular contact, it would be difficult to build relationships with the multinationals. To be sure, the company friend concept could help multinational subsidiaries to build their own network of contacts in the period up to and after start-up, but little else might be achieved. If agencies do commit themselves to more active after-care policies, it is accepted that model IV is the most likely option initially, given that the benefits have still to be fully proved. Alternatively there might be some experimentation on a project basis (model III).

There are at least two dimensions on which an after-care service would need to be 'customized' to the circumstances of particular regions or countries. The first relates to the lead organization in after-care, where it is difficult to be specific because circumstances differ so much between countries. It is arguable that an inward investment agency *per se* is not best suited to after-care because the required skills and the nature of the activites are mostly quite different. There does, however, have to be a clear feedback loop into inward investment agency operations, as Figure 11.1 shows. The second area of uncertainty concerns the geographical area covered by an after-care agency. It may be contested that the territorial span of operations should be more limited in the case of after-care because of the personal nature of the service, where the advantages lie in being close to the customer. Co-ordination across a range of bodies would also be easier in a smaller geographical area.

DESIGNING MERGER AND ACQUISITION POLICIES

With the changing forms of international business, the question must inevitably be asked whether or not inward investment agencies and other public-sector bodies should attempt to get more involved in alternative cross-border modes. These include mergers, acquisitions and alliances, or, if wholly-owned subsidiaries are regarded (as in the Asian high-performing economies) as mechanisms for inward technology transfer, in modes such as inward licensing. The argument for doing so is the very obvious one that with new inward investment players from Scandinavia and Central and East Europe, and generally greater professionalism, competition is intensifying. At the same time wholly-owned greenfield projects, the projects for which inward investment agencies compete, represent a small and probably shrinking share of the market.

Turning from this general view to the specifics, however, the arguments against inward investment agencies involvement at least in mergers and acquisitions are quite strong. In the first place the highly developed private-sector mechanisms have proved eminently capable of handling mergers and acquisitions. Second, international mergers and acquisitions are not locationally mobile in the same way that, say, a new greenfield electronics facility is. Mergers and acquisitions are dependent upon identifying suitable merger partners or acquirees, and the desirability and suitability of the latter, not the location, would be the prime motivating factor. Third, while there is little empirical evidence on the economic impact of inward acquisitions, such work as has been undertaken indicates that the long-term effects may be negative. For example, Ashcroft and Love (1993; see also Ashcroft *et al.* 1987) investigated inward take-overs and mergers in Scotland and concluded that the internal effects (improved availability of investment funds, improved financial techniques and the supply of management, technical help and marketing skills) were on balance favourable to the acquired companies. Conversely the external effects seemed to be unfavourable to the Scottish economy, with especial importance attaching to some reduction in local linkages and organizational functions as the firms' demands shifted away from Scotland. Even without such evidence a fourth very telling argument concerns the political unacceptability of being seen to promote inward take-overs. The political furore in Sweden surrounding the proposed merger between Volvo and Renault of France in 1993 illustrates the point clearly. The fact remains, of course, that over time indigenous control of enterprises has probably drifted away from many regional economies in Europe in any event. Finally, inward investment agencies do not have the skills in-house to become involved in mergers and acquisitions. It would be entirely possible to hire or second personnel from the consultancy companies and merchant banks engaged in take-over and merger activity, but the most likely role for any such individual(s) would be to provide a 'regional input' into private-sector services. This regional input would involve identifying indigenous medium-sized companies which lacked the resources to internationalize or required a wider product range and were willing to enter into discussions concerning possible mergers. However, the joint venture or licensing route might be more acceptable in such circumstances.

Given that any merger and acquisition role for inward investment agencies could be only small-scale and low-key at best, the issue is whether more could or should be done to encourage other forms of international business arrangements, including strategic alliances, as vehicles for economic development. The range of international market entry and development options is wide (Young *et al.* 1989) but most obviously (and to simplify discussion) would include international joint ventures, licensing agreements and management contracts. As regards strategic alliances, in many ways these are little different from the more conventional forms of international activity, at least in terms of mechanisms used, but the motivations are different. A number of major types of strategic alliance conditions have been identified, including technology development coalitions, operations and logistics coalitions, marketing, sales and service coalitions and multiple activity coalitions, but from the perspective of this brief discussion comment will be restricted to joint technology development (e.g. pre-competitive, R&D project-specific R&D, cross-licensing to share independently developed technologies; for further details see Dunning 1993).

Table 11.4 compares the possible contribution of these alternative modes to host regions and countries, using inward investment by multinational enterprises and their potential contribution as the baseline. It should be noted that there has been virtually no study of such arrangements from the viewpoint of host economy impact. With this caution, the table indicates a very different range of potential contributions associated with the various modes. There is, however, one important aspect in which the non-wholly-owned subsidiary mode differs from all others and this concerns the participation of local firms. At the extreme, closure of a multinational subsidiary would effectively end the host economy's involvement in the product area, except for the expertise built up by suppliers, who, in any event, might have great difficulty in finding alternative markets. With the other modes, the specific association with a local enterprise should mean some direct transfer of management and/or technology and hence greater embeddedness, even if the arrangements do not generate a large number of jobs. From the viewpoint of selling the value of such contractual agreements to government and the media, the latter does create some difficulties, although it allows a better understanding to emerge of the non-job constituents of economic development.

Is there a role for inward investment agencies and the public sector in

300

Table 11.4: Hypothetical impacts of alternative international business arrangements on host economies

	Impacts on host economies[a]			
	Employment, labour markets and productivity	*Technology tranfer and innovation*	*Trade and balance of payments*	*Linkages and spill-overs*
Inward investment (new, greenfield, wholly-owned manufacturing subsidiaries)	●	Usually limited	●	Usually limited in high-tech industry
Inward investment (joint equity ventures)[b]	More limited than with wholly-owned manufacturing subsidiaries	● Potentially significant	More limited than with wholly-owned manufacturing subsidiaries	● Possibly greater than with wholly-owned manufacturing subsidiaries
Inward licensing[c]		● Associated with transfer of patented technology, etc.		
Inward management[d] contracts	● Management know-how			
Joint technology[e] development		●		● If agreement involves university research or contract R&D for multiple clients

Notes:

(a) Only first-order effects are shown. ● indicates main likely positive impact.

(b) Joint equity ventures involve equity sharing between at least two partners in a particular enterprise or investment project.

(c) Contracts in which a foreign licensor provides a local licensee with access to technology or know-how, plus production rights within a certain geographical area.

(d) Contracts in which the management of an indigenous enterprise is undertaken by a foreign company for a specified period; training of local management would usually be included.

(e) Contracts for co-operative R&D and joint technology development; may involve contractual joint ventures or licensing.

promoting alternative international business arrangements? It is arguable that the private-sector mechanisms for partnering or marriage broking of whatever type are geared primarily to large companies where substantial fee income can be generated. It is less certain that the private market is efficient where small and medium-sized enterprises are involved, as is reflected, for example, in EC initiatives such as SPRINT (the Strategic Programme for Information and Technology Transfer) and BC-Net (the Business Co-operation Network), which were designed specifically to help generate cross-border networks of small and medium-size businesses. There are in addition a plethora of company/product/technology data-bases operated usually by public-sector bodies.

If new initiatives were to be considered by public-sector agencies, two approaches would seem to be possible. The first might take the form of *product/technology search*, where the objective is to identify products or technologies in use in advanced overseas markets such as the US or Japan, with the aim of persuading foreign companies to transfer them into domestic economies through the medium of the arrangements described above. The second approach, *company gap filling*, would actually start with a group of companies in the indigenous sector (in the same industry or with common technologies, for example), and on the same basis of corporate audits establish the management/product/technology require-ments to facilitate growth and, indeed, outward internationalization. The inward investment agencies or some related organization would then be concerned with identifying potential partners overseas which could fill the gaps.

Limited initiatives of such types have been attempted and further experimentation is undoubtedly needed. The crucial point is that regional or national competitive advantage might lie outwith the sectors/segments in which new greenfield investments predominate. The food industry is a case in point: the sector is characterized by international merger, acquisition and alliance activity, not new wholly-owned manufacturing subsidiaries. Here there may well be scope for public-sector involvement in interna-tional product/technology search or company gap-filling initiatives to enhance corporate and national competitiveness.

CONCLUSION

The argument in this chapter is that environmental changes in the inter-national business field (in part, but only in part, related to EC-specific factors) have taken place much more rapidly than public-sector responses. Hence the remaining years of the 1990s may well see significant policy and organizational creativity to reflect these international business dynamics. Attracting new greenfield wholly-owned subsidiaries in manufacturing will undoubtedly remain a specialist inward investment agency function, with hopefully more attention paid to the long-term economic contribution of inward investment through more refined targeting policies. At the same time the after-care function, traditionally associated with inward investment agencies, should become a real as opposed to a notional activity. In addition efforts will undoubtedly be made to capitalize upon the wider range of forms of international business and to integrate inward investment agency and associated activity with industrial policy as a whole. This chapter has presented some preliminary ideas for policy initiatives to progress these operational activities.

REFERENCES

Amin, A., Bradley, D., Howells, J., Tomaney, J. and Gentle, C. (1994) 'Regional incentives and the quality of mobile investment in the less favoured regions of the EC', *Progress in Planning* 41 (1): 1–112.

Ashcroft, B., and Love, J. H. (1993) *Takeovers, Mergers and the Regional Economy*, Edinburgh: Edinburgh University Press.

Ashcroft, B., Love, J. H., and Scouller, J. (1987) *The Economic Effects of the Inward Acquisition of Scottish Manufacturing Companies, 1965 to 1980*. ESU Research Paper 11, Edinburgh: Industry Department for Scotland.

Dunning, J. H. (1993) *Multinational Enterprises and the Global Economy* Wokingham: Addison-Wesley.

Hood, N. and Truijens, T. (1993) 'European locational decisions of Japanese manufacturers: survey evidence on the case of the UK', *International Business Review* (2): 39–63.

Kotler, P., Haider, D. H., and Rein, I. (1993) *Marketing Places*, New York: Free Press.

Little, A. D. (1991) 'Telecommunications: Issues and Options 1992–2010', report to the Commission of the European Communities, October.

Netherlands Economic Institute (in co-operation with Ernst & Young) (1992) *New Location Factors for Mobile Investment in Europe*, Rotterdam/London, April.

Texier, L., and Valla, J.-P. (1992) 'Systems of Actors in Territorial Marketing: an Extension of Interorganizational Marketing Theory', paper presented at the eighth IMP conference, Lyon, France, September.

United Nations Centre on Transnational Corporations (1990) *Regional Economic Integration and Transnational Corporations in the 1990s: Europe 1992, North America, and Developing Countries*, UNCTC Current Studies Series A, No. 15, New York: United Nations.

United Nations – Transnational Corporations and Management Division (1992) *World Investment Report 1992: Transnational Corporations as Engines of Growth*, New York: United Nations.

United Nations – Transnational Corporations and Management Division (1993) *From the Common Market to EC 92*, New York: United Nations.

Watzke, G. E. (1982) 'An Irish Sweepstakes for American corporations', *Journal of General Management* 7 (4): 31–9.

Wells Jr., L. T., and Wint, A. G. (1990) *Marketing a Country: Promotion as a Tool for Attracting Foreign Investment*, Foreign Investment Advisory Service Occasional Paper 1, Washington DC: International Finance Corporation and the Multilateral Guarantee Agency.

Welsh Affairs Committee (1988) *Inward Investment into Wales and its Interaction with Regional and EEC Policies*, HC 86–I, London: HMSO.

Wint, A. G. (1993) 'Promoting transnational investment: organizing to service approved investors', *Transnational Corporations* 2 (1): 71–90.

Young, S., and Hood, N. (1993) 'Inward investment policy in the European Community in the 1990s' *Transnational Corporations* 2 (2): 35–62.

Young, S., and Hood, N. (1994) 'Designing developmental after-care programmes for foreign direct investors in the European Union', *Transnational Corporations* 3 (2) (forthcoming).

Young, S., Hood, N., and Peters, E. (1994), 'Multinational enterprises and regional economic development', *Regional Studies* 28 (7): 657–77.

Young, S., Hood, N., and Wilson, A. (1994) 'Targeting policy as a competitive strategy for European inward investment agencies' *European Urban and Regional Studies* (2): 143–59.

Young, S., McDermott, M., and Dunlop, S. (1991) 'The challenge of the single market' in B. Bürgenmeier and J. L. Muchielli *Multinationals and Europe 1992*, London and New York: Routledge.

Young, S., Hamill, J., Wheeler, C., and Davies, J. R. (1989), *International Market Entry and Development*, Hemel Hempstead: Harvester Wheatsheaf.

ACKNOWLEDGEMENTS

Some of the material in the section on inward investment agencies in the EC and their operations and the following section on designing promotional and attraction policies is extracted from Stephen Young, Neil Hood and Alan Wilson, 'Targeting policy as a competitive strategy for European inward investment agencies', *European Urban and Regional Studies* 1 (2) 1994, pp 143–59. Copyright permission has been granted by the publishers, Longman Group Ltd. Some of the material in the section on designing after-care policies is extracted from Stephen Young and Neil Hood, 'Designing developmental after-care programmes for foreign direct investors in the European Union', *Transnational Corporations* 3 (2) 1994 (copyright United Nations).

Part IV

TOWARDS COHESION

12

A FRAMEWORK FOR COHESION

Ash Amin and John Tomaney

The neo-liberal project of the 1980s has failed. Within Europe it has presided over low levels of growth, high levels of unemployment and growing social and regional disparity. More than ever Europe requires policies committed to active macro-economic management and full employment. Such policies, however, will be insufficient on their own to tackle regional problems or the problems of building a 'Social Europe'. In turn, and paradoxically, tackling these problems will be central to achieving full employment, and ultimately, creating a secure base for cohesion.

It would be too easy, however, to dismiss the latest phase of European integration and its uneven outcomes as simply the manifestation of a neo-liberal policy agenda. In fact, within EU policy itself, there exists a real and unresolved tension between the pursuit of market-led solutions and active intervention in favour of economic expansion and the achievement of social justice and solidarity. For instance, some aspects of EU regional policy are innovative in proposing the development of regional institutions and encouraging regions to submit long-term, integrated development plans in seeking EU funding. Similarly, the Commission's autumn 1993 White Paper on employment issues draws attention to the need to link policies on growth with those aimed at tackling unemployment and social exclusion. But these innovations continue to exist within – indeed, are overshadowed by – a wider market-led policy agenda.

In this final chapter our aim is to propose that the separation of cohesion issues from policies for economic efficiency which pay little regard to the social foundations of growth is an erroneous polarization, and one which will prove to be self-defeating. Pulling together arguments developed by the majority of contributions to this volume, we wish to outline the elements of an alternative framework for cohesion that makes a clear break with the economics of neo-liberalism. It is a framework for growth which combines the principles of managed economic expansion with the principles of decentralized governance and industrial democracy.

Central to the achievement of a socially and regionally balanced form of economic growth is the need for positive policy action on a number of related fronts. In what follows we outline what we consider to be four priority areas of policy reform necessary for cohesion: an expanded regional policy; the decentralization of economic activity; expansionary macro-economic policies; and active employment measures aimed at creating a Social Europe. The aim of the discussion, rather than to provide comprehensive policy recommendations, is to outline the basic principles for achieving a socially and economically cohesive Europe.

AN EXPANDED REGIONAL POLICY

Current EU regional policy reveals both the possibilities and the limitations of tackling regional disparities through structural policies. On the credit side, the Structural Funds have been a stimulus to innovation in the design and implementation of regional policy. The reforms of the Structural Funds in the 1980s represented a major advance in so far as they extended principles of programming. The 1989 reform in particular required regions to move towards a comprehensive system of regional planning in the less favoured regions – a development which has been reinforced since. The new framework regulations for the operation of the Structural Funds enacted in 1993 went further and developed the principle of 'regional partnerships', with a clear consultative role for the social partners, as the basis on which planning should occur. As a consequence, in many European regions where regional institutions are weak (such as the UK) the existence of EU regional policy has been the catalyst to the development of local planning structures which are essential if regional structural problems are to be effectively tackled.

It is clear that the development of strong sub-national political and administrative structures is necessary for the successful development and implementation of structural policies (Amin and Tomaney 1995; Begg, Chapter 4 of this volume). Simple subsidies on capital or labour, while sometimes necessary, are insufficient to ensure the development of longer-term solutions to the problems of the less favoured regions. It is even clearer that market forces alone will not ensure successful adaptation of regional economies. Thus the simple model of structural change and resource allocation based on market signals, as accepted by both the monetarist and Keynesian orthodoxy, is insufficient for the task of upgrading productive structures consistent with the development of an innovation-orientated or 'learning economy' (Storper 1995; Nelson 1993: Lundvall 1992). Such decentralized institutions are a key element of a 'developmental state', concerned with active supply-side upgrading, which can be contrasted with a 'regulatory state' that sees adjustments occurring as a function of the unfettered operations of markets (e.g. Crouch and Marquand 1989; see also Sabel 1994).

The importance of strong and legitimate regional-level institutions is an important lesson of the superior performance of the German economy. The rich institutional structure of the supply side promotes innovation and upgrading in Germany and, in contrast to neo-liberal theory, appears to add to rather than detract from competitiveness (Matzner and Streeck 1991). The lesson of such experience is that successful structural policies are often those adopted by institutions small enough to develop an intimate under-standing of the micro-economics of regional development but large enough – and with the necessary political legitimacy – to act upon them. As Hausner (1995: 22) argues:

> an industrial policy oriented towards structural changes in the economy and the promotion of producers' adaptability to the conditions of domestic and international competition must focus on meso-level structures in the given economy and its social environment. There-fore, the creation of intermediate level structures that would facilitate economic restructuring is the top priority of industrial policy and the goal of economic strategy.

Such regionalization seems particularly important in the context of the regulatory implications of the emerging 'learning economy' as described in Chapter 1. If a Europe-wide shift to the higher-order and knowledge-based activities of the learning economy is to be achieved, the development of fine-targeted active labour market policy or industrial policy will be required. According to Matzner and Streeck (1991: 8):

> For this the structure of public administration must be such that it can reach down into the networks that mediate exchanges in civil society, putting these to effective use. Where the state is not well-equipped for this purpose, the conscious design or reform of appropriate state, or para state, institutions may assume critical significance for employment.

Beyond its institutional merits, however, the substance of EU regional policy remains unconvincing in its own right as a means of improving the development and employment prospects of the less favoured regions. A first area of concern is the still inadequate level of resources assigned to the Structural Funds, as outlined in some detail in Chapter 1. Another area of concern is the priority attached to small firm entrepreneurship, as described in Chapter 1. A large part of the EU's justification for this heavy focus on small firms derives from concern about the effectiveness of previous policies which have focused on attracting foreign direct investment. In its fourth Periodic Report on the state of the regions the European Commission (1991: 70) observed:

> . . . while foreign investment can be an external catalyst for local business to set about upgrading their activities there is also the risk of creating a dependent economy. The Irish experience is very

instructive in this respect where the new activities from outside . . . have not forged links with the domestic sector, resulting in a kind of dual economy where the growth of a competitive sector of national firms has not been stimulated significantly.

The focus on small firm entrepreneurship is a means of promoting endogenous rather than dependent development. While concern about the impact of foreign direct investment is justifiable, the focus on indigenous entrepreneurship is not without its own limitations. Referring to the Irish example, O'Donnell (1993) notes that post-war industrial policy attached priority to the attraction of international mobile investment, in part because indigenous industry was regarded as simply too weak to play the central role in industrialization. He warns that a focus on endogenous paths to development obscures an understanding of the global economic structure in which local economies reside, necessitating a careful articulation of indigenous and exogenous opportunities in order to give regions a foothold in the international economy.

One aspect of such articulation is the need to develop strategies capable of maximizing the local spin-off effects of inward investment, instead of rejecting it out of hand. Ireland, for example, has been characterized by an important debate on the appropriate role of foreign direct investment in economic development – a debate of considerable significance for policy concerns about the creation of effective meso-level industrial policies (for a review of the debate see Tomaney 1995). The most recent review of Irish industrial policy has attempted to resolve the conundrum of whether to support indigenous industry or overseas industry (Culliton 1992). It argues that the grant-aid budget for inward investment should be reduced and focus on the promotion of local strengths to create industrial clusters of related and reinforcing industries. The critical question concerns the degree to which a balance is struck between support for externally owned or indigenous firms.

The emphasis in the Culliton report on the use of policy 'selectivity' to establish industrial clusters around 'sources of national competitive advantage' could represent a way of squaring this circle. O'Donnell (1993) identifies two implications for industrial policy that arise from the proposed focus on industrial clusters. First, all firms and industries are not of equal significance to a country or a region's long-term development and, second, the economy should not be seen as just a random collection of firms and industries: certain aggregations of firms and industries are significant in creating competitive advantage (Porter 1990; Peters, Chapter 10 of this volume). An important theoretical and practical task arising from these propositions is that of judging which industries are more significant than others and which existing or potential aggregates of firms and industries are relevant to regional competitiveness. A key policy task then becomes that of promoting the 'economies of association' and networking that appear to underpin clusters.

The means by which these economies of association are achieved are complex. However, there is now considerable evidence to suggest that if relations between public and private organizations concerning business services, finance, innovation and training are co-operative the overall performance of firms situated in such a regional milieu is better than it would be otherwise (Pyke 1994). Thus micro-regulatory networks of institutions give spatial definition to inter-firm networking or industrial clusters. As far as the role of public policy is concerned, a number of factors seem important (Amin and Thrift 1994), including:

1 A thick layering of public and private industrial support institutions.
2 High-grade, sectorally specific labour market intelligence and associated training.
3 Rapid diffusion of technology transfer.
4 A high degree of inter-firm networking.
5 A disposition towards innovation.

Much work needs to be done to translate these insights into workable policies for less favoured regions. However, what seems certain is that the development of policies aimed at building clusters will depend on building local institutional capability, including competent development agencies. Such agencies should be able to operate a more targeted approach to new inward investment and develop after-care policies and supplier chain initiatives. Their efforts would have a great deal more force if incoming large firms were obliged to sign Regional Planning Agreements as a *quid pro quo* for the receipt of investment incentives. Agreements would need to go far beyond the normal stipulations concerning investment and job levels, to spell out in detail the contribution that assisted large firms would play in supporting the development of local supply chains. For both existing and new development agencies, as Young and Hood note in Chapter 11 of this volume, development agencies will need to take more seriously than hitherto the development of after-care policies aimed at extending and deepening the contribution of inward investment to the host economy. More generally, such an approach would represent a shift away from the process of wasteful and unregulated 'competitive bidding' for inward investment in which most regions now engage.

It is clear that democratically accountable but autonomous and well-resourced regional development agencies are essential to the operation of integrated and long-term strategies for regional development. Such strategies would seek to avoid convenient, if dubious, solutions to regional problems such as the attraction of 'high-tech' firms to replace 'sunset' industries. Instead the emphasis would be on developing industrial strategies aimed at reinforcing existing industrial strengths and upgrading supply-side support for key sectors of the regional economy.

A DECENTRALIZED ROAD TO COHESION

Expanding regional policy in new directions will prove to be ineffective, however, if appropriate action is not taken at the central level to ensure that decentralized industrial policies are allowed to work. We argued in Chapter 1 that the bias of 'non-spatial' EU policies such as Technology Policy, Competition Policy and other policies designed to raise scale efficiencies towards the interests of core regions has served to undermine the efforts of EU Regional Policy. An obvious corrective is the need to add a regional dimension to these policies, consisting, at the very least, of measures designed to limit outcomes with damaging consequences for less favoured regions.

The area of Competition Policy provides an illustrative example. There is compelling evidence that merger and take-over activity is an important mechanism by which regional economies are harmed as a consequence of the post-acquisition run-down of strategic functions, even if employment levels in the acquired firm remain unaltered. External acquisition thus exacerbates existing inequalities within and between member states and adversely affects cohesion (Love 1993). As a consequence, any merger policy, whether operated at the national or at the EU level, should incorporate the assumption that a merger will have a detrimental impact on a regional economy unless the opposite can be proved (Standing Committee on the Scottish Economy 1988). At the national level, for instance, the size thresholds qualifying take-overs for consideration by the merger authorities might be reduced in the case of assisted regions. Defence of regional economies would be best achieved through a direct regional input, via regional governments, into national merger regulation.

As revealed in Chapter 7, by Harvie Ramsay, much merger and acquisition activity, especially as a consequence of the completion of the single market, is occurring across national borders. Such mergers are now regulated under the terms of the EU Merger Regulation. However, the regulation is inspired by neo-liberal conceptions of immediate efficiency gains as measured by market criteria and do not acknowledge that the effects of mergers go far beyond this narrow definition. As such it does not embody a concern with economic cohesion, nor does it allow for non-competition issues to influence the European Commission in its treatment of merger approvals. In addition the majority of mergers remain small-scale and intra-national, emphasizing the importance of embedding a concern with the regional consequences of mergers at every level of the regulatory process.

Such efforts alone will not secure the flow of investment into the less favoured regions. We agree with Williams *et al.* when they argue that 'decentralization through secondary devices will only be effective if primary economic mechanisms are used as the locational big stick' (1991: 342) to indicate the necessity of complementary action at the centre in order to divert activity to the periphery.

This is a controversial suggestion, not only because it challenges the assumption that decentralization may impair the efficiency of firms located in core regions, but also because such a strategy would require a radical shift in the priorities of the EU. As has been argued in this book, the renewed push to economic integration in the 1980s and 1990s was prompted by concern about 'Eurosclerosis' or the EU's poor competitiveness in relation to the US, Japan and the newly industrializing countries. The prevailing orthodoxy has been that efforts to restore European competitiveness require the removal of any locational constraints on Europe's large firms. Sceptics, however, have argued that this position overstates the uncompetitiveness of European industry and underestimates the scope for decentralization (Grahl and Teague 1990; IPPR 1989; Leborgne and Lipietz 1990; Williams et al. 1991).

Some of these commentators base this argument on the enduring strength of the German economy. It is argued that a key feature of German industry is the extent to which in recent times it has relied on home-based trade (most EU countries now run substantial trade deficits with Germany). In other words, German competitiveness has not crucially depended upon European economic integration. It is suggested that one task of policy should be to decentralize activity from the prosperous European core to the European periphery. While relocation may mean added constraints on industry, it is argued that compensating gains are likely to result from the growth of production and markets on the European periphery – at present the continued stagnation of the less favoured regions within and adjacent to the EU deprives the European economy of a growth dynamic. Here, inequality is seen as a cause as well as a consequence of economic crisis.

For some observers, in practical terms such a decentralization of activity from the core (dominated by German industry) would be most effectively achieved by appreciation of the Deutschmark and the currencies of other core countries:

> Given the stickiness of locational decisions, a sustained once and for all appreciation of the DM against other currencies would provide a considerable inducement for the Germans to manufacture outside Germany (Williams et al. 1991: 342; see also Dunford and Perrons 1994; IPPR 1989).

Clearly, the politics of a solution that forces the strongest nation in Europe to make the home base more expensive for its own manufacturing are likely to prove controversial. However, here it is the principle of placing a programme of decentralization at the heart of any concerted effort to achieve cohesion that we wish to articulate. Such a programme, in combination with the kinds of enhanced structural policies we described earlier, would represent a more serious attack on regional disparity.

MACRO-ECONOMIC POLICY

Any policy aimed at decentralizing activity from the European core will have a chance of success only if it is placed in the context of a planned reflation of the European economy. The history of European integration suggests, as is argued by Dunford in Chapter 5, that high sustained levels of growth have generally contributed to the narrowing of regional disparities in income and employment. Periods of high growth have tended to be periods of regional convergence as a result of faster levels of growth on the periphery, while periods of low growth and recession have been periods of divergence.

The neo-liberal orthodoxy rules out growth-orientated macro-economic policies on the grounds that they are inflationary. Neo-liberal policies, therefore, have emphasized the use of monetary rather than budgetary measures as the mainstay of macro-economic policy, but these have proved to be inherently deflationary. However, as Michie observes in Chapter 3, the principal problem facing the European economy now is not the threat of inflation but historically high levels of unemployment and social inequality, both of which are a drain on resources and a block on further economic expansion. This view questions the risk of uncontrolled inflation associated with the adoption of more expansionary policies in the context of Europe's worst recession since the 1930s, with its high levels of unemployment, underutilized resources and excess capacity (Cripps and Ward 1994). A sustained reflation of the European economy under these circumstances would need to go some way before it unleashed destabilizing inflationary tendencies.

Even if a strong case can be made in defence of reflationary policies, the major policy obstacle in Europe, however, is that neo-liberal orthodoxies are now embodied in the constitution of the EU. As Grieve Smith observes: 'The Treaty of Maastricht raises the fundamental question of whether the movement towards economic and monetary union in Europe necessarily, or inevitably, conflicts with the goal of restoring full employment' (1994: 260). The great paradox of the current phase of European integration is that it has achieved a basis for the co-ordination of macro-economic policy, but in ways that have encouraged the adoption of deflationary policies in the face of rising unemployment. As argued in earlier chapters of this volume, the Maastricht ceilings on debt and deficits in relation to GDP could severely limit the growth of aggregate demand, with obvious implications for output and employment, especially in the

EU's less favoured regions. It is essential, therefore, that if a meaningful attack is to be made on the unemployment crisis and growing social and regional disparities Europe must extricate itself from the underlying macro-economic philosophy and convergence requirements of the Maastricht Treaty.

What are the essential pillars of an alternative reflationary programme? One key issue concerns the desirability and feasibility of management of the economy at both the European and the national level. Certainly at the national level it has been fashionable in recent times to reject the possibility of macro-economic management. This is a challengeable position, not least in the light of the experience of the UK economy in the period after sterling's exit from the ERM in 1992. As Will Hutton (1994: 12) has put it:

Two years on, a devaluation and well-judged tax increases have delivered a well-balanced recovery. The macro-economic aggregates that were so disastrously managed in the 1980s have fallen into place – a sharp reminder that if governments can line up the economic skittles correctly, getting the timing of exchange rate shifts, tax increases and budget deficits correct, the rewards can be many times greater and more immediate than supply-side initiatives . . . the current mania to regard macro-economic management as subordinate to micro measures is wildly overdone.

The growing interdependence of the European economies, however, strengthens the case for a co-ordinated policy response to the growth in unemployment and social disparity, not least because this is now a European problem. This does not in any way imply a need to wait for monetary union, nor does it mean that an individual member state may not take the reflationary lead. In a context of integrated production and markets, it is clear that if all countries were to expand demand and output together, it could lead to a mutually reinforcing cycle of growth.

A co-ordinated macro-economic policy should be directed towards the achievement of growth and full employment, with the emphasis on the convergence of income levels and unemployment rates rather than the nominal indicators enshrined in the Maastricht Treaty (levels of public deficits, government debts, inflation rates and interest rates). In particular, a more flexible exchange rate regime than that envisaged in the Maastricht Treaty is essential if the weaker member states and regions are to be allowed the policy latitude necessary to tackle their own structural problems. Whatever the merits of monetary union as a long-term objective for the EU, it seems certain that it can be achieved smoothly only on the basis of real convergence of productive performance rather than convergence around nominal indicators. Rigid adherence to the Maastricht criteria and timetable could spell disaster for the less favoured regions and even for the EU as a whole. This is perhaps the real lesson of the upheavals in the Exchange Rate Mechanism in 1992 and subsequently.

The main stimulus to growth is likely to come from expansionary budgetary policies. Fiscal expansion would fund an investment-led development strategy in which the goal would be to increase the productive potential of weaker economies, which at present contribute little either as producers or consumers. Faster growth in the weaker economies, however, would stimulate increased demand for the goods and services of stronger regions. Dunford and Perrons (1994: 179) note that:

> A strategy of this kind would require a major planned programme of public expenditure financed out of taxes – especially on land, property, speculative incomes and pollution, direct intervention into the financial system to generate extra lending to firms at low interest rates, and legal requirements that financial institutions purchase bonds issued by nationalised industries to finance capital investment programmes. If the state cannot mobilise sufficient resources to reflate publicly it should resort to state action to ensure that the private sector reflates.

Given the still small size of the EU budget, such fiscal stimulus would be mainly national in origin and would lend weight to the kinds of structural policies outlined earlier in this chapter. However, there is a potentially important role for the EU to play. The Delors White Paper (CEC 1993), with its emphasis on environmental infrastructure improvements, illustrates one set of potential actions at the European level. Focusing investment on environmental and socially and economically sustainable forms of development would be an essential element of any investment-led reflation. However, the difficulties in allocating adequate resources to the proposed European Investment Fund illustrate also the problems of orchestrating action at the European level.

In short, the achievement of cohesion will be brought about only by a concerted effort to expand the European economy as a precondition for the pursuit of decentralization and enhanced regional policies.

COMBATING SOCIAL EXCLUSION: CREATING JOBS

Chapter 1 and in particular Chapters 6 and 7 by Teague and Ramsey make it plain that the history of EU intervention in the regulation of labour markets has been disappointing. Indeed, as large European firms have seen their hand strengthened, the position of trade unions in most member states has been weakened. In such a context the outlook for improving the position of labour is not good. Unions have been powerless to resist successive rounds of rationalization, relocation of production and erosion of the conditions of those remaining in employment. Current proposals for

European works councils, while welcome in themselves, are unlikely to have much effect on the strategies of Europe's large corporations.

As Ramsey notes in Chapter 7 the publication of the Delors White Paper on employment, growth and competitiveness represents a belated response to Europe's current employment crisis. But the White Paper, and related discussions, are characterized by ambivalence about whether the European social model represents a burden or an asset to industry in Europe. In these debates Europe's poor employment creation record is typically contrasted with that of the US, which has adopted a labour market policy based on deregulation. The UK government, which has also adopted the deregulation route, presents its route as a model for Europe, pointing to its success in attracting inward investment. In this account the high levels of social protection and welfare payments characteristic of the European social model amount to 'rigidities' which are the main cause of 'Eurosclerosis'.

Numerous commentators have observed, however, that both the UK and the US economies achieved their employment record by creating large numbers of poorly paid and insecure jobs. Moreover, the simple dichotomy of 'rigid' Europe vs. 'flexible' US fails to capture the complexity of the relationship between labour market policy and economic performance. For instance, Nolan (1994) points out that in countries such as Germany and Sweden more flexible working arrangements have been achieved within the context of collective bargaining agreements. Such countries have proved more successful than the UK in maintaining an internationally competitive manufacturing sector, by moving into high value-added market segments. In the German case, Matzner and Streeck (1991) attribute this qualitative shift to the 'institutional constraints' placed on employers. Chief among them are high levels of unionization, co-determination rights and effective employment legislation which compel firms to compete in world markets on factors other than low wage costs. Only in such market areas can Europe hope for economic survival, given the impossibly low wage rates and long working hours available to firms in the developing countries.

In the long run British labour market policy precludes the adoption of supply-side upgrading along the lines of the 'developmental' model outlined earlier. There can be little question that an approach based on the UK model would represent a further threat to the living standards of European workers. As Cripps and Ward (1994: 252) argue:

The low level of the overall burden of taxation in the UK and Spain helps to keep costs of employment down in these countries, and may help attract business for which low labour costs are a major competitive factor. Conversely, high revenue shares in France and the Netherlands may reflect the relatively strong competitive performance of these countries within the single market – and indeed may contribute to strong performance by funding higher expenditure on education and training and on infrastructure.

An added problem is that the deregulation of labour markets – and the accompanying enthusiasm for the regional regulation of industrial relations – may give rise to inflationary tendencies that centralized forms of wage bargaining appear to avoid (Teague, Chapter 6 in this volume).

European employment protection initiatives, as they began to be developed in the 1970s, were partly inspired by recognition of the impossibility of the wage cutting route as a model for European industry Clearly, a rejuvenated European Social Policy could play an important role in providing certain minimum European conditions. As Ramsey argues in Chapter 7 a return to the principles of the Social Charter, which called for harmonization of participation rights, would represent an important step towards the creation of a European co-determination model. More important, as Ramsay states, there is a need to revisit the 'silent clauses' of the Social Charter on the right to join a union, to bargain collectively and to strike. The point to be made is that 'institutional constraints' need to be increasingly conceived at the European level, if we are to avoid the consolidation of a two-tier Europe in terms of labour standards.

Linked with questions of employment rights is the debate concerning the reduction of working hours. Higher levels of growth in the EU are a necessary condition for tackling regional disparities, but it is clear that some regions do not need or desire unexpurgated growth. The experience of core regions of the European economy, such as south-east England during the late 1980s boom, reveals that high growth can rapidly translate into problems of inflation, overheating and serious problems of environmental degradation. In an overall European context of sluggish growth and regionally polarized development, any effort aimed at the decentralization of economic activity with the aim of balanced economic growth will need to address the question of the reform of working time, so that new jobs can be created out of existing and increased levels of employment.

In Chapter 1 it was noted that economic stagnation and high levels of unemployment coexist with increasingly intensified experience of work for those who remain in employment. Leborgne and Lipietz (1990: 199) have highlighted the potential importance of redistributing work through the reductions of working hours as a basis for achieving greater economic and social cohesion and the transfer of faster growth from the prosperous regions to the less favoured regions. They connect the role of a national monetary authority with issues of working time by proposing:

> Firstly, . . . applying a policy that would quickly reduce working hours in the surplus countries. Secondly, . . . giving the deficit countries some latitude in order to speed up their growth and to conclude better agreements and arrangements in industrial relations. This presupposes

greater autonomy of monetary management at the national level and the ability to apply safeguard clauses if an excessively 'liberal' social policy jeopardizes the trade balance too severely. This implies that any progress towards the introduction of a common external currency – the European currency unit, or ECU – must be accompanied by a greater flexibility of the rate of exchange of national currencies *vis-à-vis* the ECU. And this implies a growth of the net transfers towards the deficit regions.

The above proposals are not intended to amount to a comprehensive coverage of measures required to reduce social divisions in Europe. Nothing, for instance has been said of the plight of individuals and social groups currently excluded from employment or socially marginalized; or of the kinds of active labour market and employment policies necessary to help such groups. Similarly, we have not discussed the sort of welfare reforms which are needed to ensure an automatic transfer of minimum welfare rights to all Europe's citizens. Our aim, instead, has been to argue that the question of social cohesion should not be separated from actions aimed at improving and redistributing work, and, through this route, setting the European economy itself on to a quality-seeking path to growth.

CONCLUSION: DEMOCRATIC, NOT MARKET, POLITICS

From the perspective of the mid-1990s, the licentious promotion of the single market and market disciplines as a solution to Europe's growth problem, including the problems of the less favoured regions, seems to have waned. National sovereignty still dominates economic policy, and, as the difficulties surrounding the ratification of the Maastricht Treaty have revealed, national allegiances remain a powerful political force in Europe. Consequently, to make an uncritical case for European solutions as an answer to the problem of growing social and economic inequalities in Europe, is perhaps to demand too much from a Europe lacking the appropriate institutions, and, more important, to fail to recognize the relevant locus for solving many of these problems. We agree with Teague in Chapter 6 of this volume that:

> crucially these matters will most likely be resolved, or at least addressed, within the confines of existing national boundaries. . . . Of course, the links between local municipalities and the EU centre will continue to exist, particularly with regard to the operation of the Structural Funds. But these connections will only complement or augment the key power relation between the regional administrative tier and the national government. A Europe of the member states will be with us for a considerable time to come.

319

A potential guarantor of less favoured regions' interests in the EU could be what Teague calls 'co-operative intergovernmentalism'. Such an approach rests on the idea that economic integration between the member states gives rise to negative externalities which can be addressed only by collaborative action. In such a scenario the EU would act to support rather than override the policies of the nation state. As such nation states will be forced to take seriously the question of building strong regional institutions. Reform, rather than abandonment, of the nation state, as we have argued elsewhere (Amin and Tomaney 1995), seems to us an admirably realistic starting point for tackling the regional problem.

The point, however, is not simply about the spatial scale at which action should be taken. It is about a far more significant issue, namely whether Europe is to be shaped by market forces and Europe's increasingly remote political elites. Cohesion has to be about the political empowerment of diverse communities and the delivery of political agency to those who do not possess it. Otherwise, popular rejection of European referendums of whatever kind will recur, because of the perception of being ruled by unaccountable bureaucracies or by a plutocratic political elite. Equally unavoidable will be growing disenchantment with quick-fix, economistic solutions for what are, in essence, social and political problems.

The political horse needs to be put before the economic cart (Marquand 1994). But it has to be a politics that goes beyond putting blind faith in existing institutions. In this book we have shown that central to cohesion are such actions as enhancing the power of workers and unions, the institutional and economic empowerment of the regions, the pursuit of decentralized economic policies, the inseparability of questions of efficacy and equity. These are aspects of cohesion which necessitate a widening and deepening of the political franchise, active public participation and debate – in essence, a democratic renewal of European politics.

REFERENCES

Amin, A., and Thrift, N. (eds) (1994) *Globalization, Institutions and Regional Development in Europe*, Oxford: Oxford University Press.

Amin, A., and Tomaney, J. (1995) 'The regional dilemma in a neo-liberal Europe', *European Urban and Regional Studies* 2(2), forthcoming.

Commission of the European Communities (1991) *The Regions in the 1990s*, fourth Periodic Report on the social and economic situation in the regions of the EC, Brussels: Commission of the European Communities.

Commission of the European Communities (1993) *Growth, Competitiveness and Employment* (White Paper), Brussels: Commission of the European Communities.

Cripps, F., and Ward, T. (1994) 'Strategies for growth and employment in the European Community', in J. Michie and J. Grieve Smith (eds) *Unemployment in Europe*, London: Academic Press.

Crouch, C., and Marquand, D. (1989) *The New Centralism: Britain out of Step with Europe?* Oxford: Blackwell.

Culliton, J. (1992) *A Time for Change: Industrial Policy for the 1990s*, report of the Industrial Policy Review Group, Dublin: Stationery Office.

Dunford, M., and Perrons, D. (1994) 'Regional inequality, regimes of accumulation and economic integration in contemporary Europe', *Institute of British Geographers, Transactions* 9: 163–82.

Grahl, J., and Teague, P. (1990) *1992 – the Big Market*, London: Lawrence & Wishart.

Grieve Smith, J. (1994) 'Policies to reduce European unemployment', in J. Michie and J. Grieve Smith (eds) *Unemployment in Europe*, London: Academic Press.

Hausner, J. (1995) 'Imperative *v.* interactive strategy of systematic change in Central and Eastern Europe', *Review of International Political Economy*, forthcoming.

Hutton, W. (1994) 'Finding macro path by mistake', *Guardian*, 7 November, p. 12.

Institute of Public Policy Research (1989) *The German Surplus: an Economic Problem in the New Europe*, London: IPPR.

Leborgne, D., and Lipietz, A.(1990) 'How to avoid a two-tier Europe', *Labour and Society* 15(2): 177–99.

Love, J. (1993) 'EC mergers regulation and regional economic cohesion', *Environment and Planning* A 26: 137–52.

Lundvall, B. A. (ed.) (1992) *National Systems of Innovation*, London: Pinter.

Marquand, D. (1994) 'Reinventing federalism: Europe and the left', in D. Miliband (ed.) *Reinventing the Left*, Cambridge: Polity Press.

Matzner, E., and Streeck, W. (1991) 'Towards a socioeconomics of employment in a post-Keynesian society', in *idem* (eds) *Beyond Keynesianism: the Socioeconomics of Production and Full Employment*. Aldershot: Elgar.

Nelson, R. (ed.) (1993) *National Innovation Systems: a Comparative Analysis*, New York: Oxford University Press.

Nolan, P. (1994) 'Labour market institutions, industrial restructuring and unemployment in Europe' in J. Michie and J. Grieve Smith (eds) *Unemployment in Europe*, London: Academic Press.

O'Donnell, R. (1993) *Ireland and Europe: Challenges for a New Century*, Policy Research Series Paper 17, Dublin: Economic and Social Research Institute.

Porter, M. (1990) *The Competitive Advantage of Nations*, London: Macmillan.

Pyke, F. (1994) *Small Firms, Technical Services and Inter-firm Cooperation*, Geneva: International Institute of Labour Studies.

Sabel, C. F. (1994) 'Learning by monitoring: the institutions of economic development', in N. Smelser, and R. Swedberg (eds) *Handbook of Economic Sociology*, Princeton: Princeton University Press.

Standing Commission on the Scottish Economy (1988) *Interim Report*, Glasgow: Fraser of Allander Institute.

Storper, M. (1995) 'Territorial economies in a global economy: what possibilities for middle-income countries and their regions?', *Review of International Political Economy*, forthcoming.

Tomaney John (1995) 'Recent developments in Irish industrial policy', *European Planning Studies* 5(1), forthcoming.

Williams, K., Williams, J., and Haslam, C. (1991) 'What kind of EC regional policy?' *Local Economy* 5: 330–46.

INDEX

Printed in the United States
by Baker & Taylor Publisher Services